Prentice-Hall, Inc.
Englewood Cliffs, N.J.

Elias M. Awad

Graduate School of Business
DePaul University
Chicago, Illinois

SECOND
EDITION

BUSINESS
DATA
PROCESSING

To Ralston D. Scott

Library of Congress Catalog Card No.: 68-22230

Printed in the United States of America

Current printing (last digit):
14   13   12   11   10   9   8   7   6   5

PRENTICE-HALL INTERNATIONAL, INC., *London*
PRENTICE-HALL OF AUSTRALIA, PTY., LTD., *Sydney*
PRENTICE-HALL OF CANADA, LTD., *Toronto*
PRENTICE-HALL OF INDIA PRIVATE LTD., *New Delhi*
PRENTICE-HALL OF JAPAN, INC., *Tokyo*

PREFACE

Continuing technological advances in data processing have contributed significantly to the improvement of operations in business, and in other formal, nonbusiness organizations. Although the principles underlying most computer systems remain essentially the same, there has been rapid change in the design, and in the types and sizes, of computer systems. The need for reflecting these developments has led to the publication of this second edition.

The reader will find that this edition, like the first, offers a comprehensive treatment of the field. The language remains nontechnical. Some of the major features or changes are as follows:

1. Chapters begin with a general outline and end with a glossary of basic terms and with questions for review. Problem and exercise material underscoring key features of each chapter are presented in the workbook, PROBLEMS AND EXERCISES IN DATA PROCESSING, which accompanies this book.

2. Part I consists of a major revision of Chapter One. Brief historical mention of the first, second, and third generation computers is included in Chapter Two. Two new chapters, *The Systems Concept and Sources of Data in Business Organizations* (Chapter 3) and *The Data Processing Cycle—A Manual Approach* (Chapter 4), have been added.

3. Part II, "Punched Card Data Processing," now contains a brief

review of the UNIVAC 1700 series, the UNIVAC 1001 card controller, and the UNIVAC 1004 card processor.

4. Part III, "Electronic Data Processing," features a complete revision of Chapter 17, *Input and Output Devices* (with a comprehensive treatment of the various types of the IBM 360, Model 20 computer system), introduction to the octal system in Chapter 19, *Coding Systems,* and reorganization of Chapter 16, *Secondary Storage* (with an illustration on sorting data on magnetic tape and a section on real time, on-line systems), plus a summary of the principles of FORTRAN and COBOL in Chapter 22, *The Control Unit and the Stored Program.*

Two additional chapters have been added in this part as well. Chapter 18, *Man-Machine Interface—The Computer System Revolution,* explains and illustrates the role and the uses of real-time processing, display devices, and on-line communication, and gives a brief account of voice communication, as well as a broader coverage of terminal equipment. Chapter 24, *Systems Analysis and Design,* presents key principles of that subject and a detailed treatment of decision tables.

This text is designed for a basic course in data processing for first or second-year students in Business Administration, in Departments of Economics, in Liberal Arts colleges, and in Technological Institutions. It can be used for either a quarter or semester course of three sessions per week. The objective is to provide the student with a basic understanding of data-processing principles, to acquaint him with the equipment, and to help him analyze and describe the impact of these principles on the business organization. Included are principles related to both punched-card and electronic data-processing equipment. Stress is laid upon the "what" and the "why" and the capabilities of the various components used and not upon the "how" of these components. In other words, descriptions of "how to do it" are used only when such descriptions are valuable in explaining *what* is done and *why* it is done.

Prior background in machine operation, or in mathematics—beyond the usual competence in basic algebra attained in high school—is not required. Nor is the purchase or rental of special equipment necessary in teaching from this book. However, a live demonstration on a desk machine, such as the MINIVAC, or a film showing the components as a system in operation, is always helpful.

I am indebted to many people who directly and indirectly contributed to the preparation of the manuscript. I especially thank Ralston D. Scott, Professor of Economics, Southern Illinois University, Edwardsville campus, for his sustained interest, helpful suggestions, and critical review of various sections of the manuscript. Professor Scott's decision to add the first data processing course to the business program of the Rochester Institute of Technology in 1961 made the testing and the development of the materials in the first edition possible.

I also thank the International Business Machines Corporation, the UNIVAC Division of the Sperry Rand Corporation, the Burroughs Corporation, and Electronic Associates for permission to use and adapt the copyrighted photographs of the machines and schematics presented in the text. Special thanks go to Mr. Jim DuBois, manager, Mid-America Exhibit Center, Burroughs Corporation, for his cooperation in acquiring various photographs against a tight publication schedule, and to Rita Putko for general assistance. The Burroughs Corporation, UNIVAC, American Telephone and Telegraph, and Prentice-Hall, Inc., have been very cooperative in granting permission to reprint sections included in Chapters 18 and 22.

Of those who deserve special mention, I am especially indebted to: Jim Bacci, College Book Editorial Production, Prentice-Hall, Inc., for his helpful suggestions and full-time dedication to the production of the book; to Frederic K. Easter, Jr., Editor of Business Books, Prentice-Hall, Inc., for his encouraging remarks and enthusiastic support throughout the revision of the manuscript; to Mary Dedinsky for typing various sections of the first fifteen chapters; and to Sandy Tremaine, without whose help in typing, proofreading, and indexing, the manuscript could not have been completed on schedule.

ELIAS M. AWAD

CONTENTS

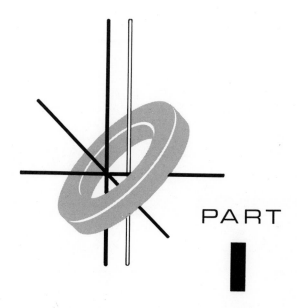

PART

Data Processing–
An
Overview

WHAT IS
DATA PROCESSING?

SINCE THE BEGINNING OF TIME, man has manipulated data and, using the communication methods and devices available to him, has passed useful information to other men. Ancient caves, showing the carving of word-pictures, hieroglyphics on stone tables, and maps of battles illustrate the result of his early efforts to process and transmit information. Man recognized early the value of developing tools to help in his physical and mental work. Thus, the axe became an extension of the hand as it increased its force in breaking a log; the telescope, an extension of the eye in identifying faraway objects; the bicycle, an extension of the leg; and the telephone an extension of the ear.

As civilization progressed, man's genius for devising ways of harnessing the forces of nature, replacing animal power by engine power, has resulted in our use of jet transportation, space exploration, and, last but not least, the *electronic computer—an extension of the human brain.* Being one of the "marvels of the age," modern computers work so rapidly that most people are blinded with such admiration for their performance that they really believe the machines think for themselves and will, thus, revolutionize in some unexplained way the whole structure of business. Just how a "hunk" of steel encasing electronic circuits can accomplish this is not considered by the uninitiated. One should realize from the beginning that these machines are to be regarded as tools which aid in mental work of a repetitive nature. They can do nothing that a human being does not instruct them to do in the first instance.

Why Process Data?

Data processing, whether business or scientific, consists of recording and reporting meaningful information manually, electromechanically, through the use of punched-card equipment, or by a computer. Everybody must process data, whether performing a decision-making function as an individual, a head of a family, a student, a leader of a social or political organization, or an owner of a business—large or small. In most cases, pencil and paper as manual aids have been and still are used in solving problems and processing data. In the distant past, under a barter system, the environment in which a businessman operated did not require any evidence of his work or any elaboration on his mental calculation. Calculations were so few that he could mentally perform them as quickly as a sophisticated computer performs electronically the greater volume of such calculations today. As communities expanded, and the barter system was replaced with monetary systems, the basis of business relationships changed also from an intimate, personal one to that of an impersonal relationship. This change required businessmen to record their activities in writing and to produce records for analysis and for future reference.

Understanding of the past often is basic to planning future endeavors and guiding men in their present actions. For example, today's trend in credit buying, with its attendant need for keeping records on accounts receivable and accounts payable, illustrates one reason why data processing has become so important in economies where business life is conducted primarily on the basis of "man's faith in man."

The Problem

As business life became more complex, human effort of a specialized nature was called for. Information related to business required all the presently known steps of recording, classifying, calculating, and summarizing. Much of the routine work necessitated specific processing methods which started with the manual method (for example, a bookkeeper using pencil and paper) and evolved into the mechanical (for example, the use of a cash register) and presently the electronic state (for example, the use of computers).

Executives continually face the problem of finding time for creative thinking in the decision-making process. Too frequently they must spend most of their working hours developing systems for, or doing the work incident to the manual or mechanical processing of, routine data. Full consideration of this problem of freeing executives from the burdens of extensive handling of routine data involves a study of: (1) the physical factors that create large masses of data, (2) the costs involved, (3) the number of people available, (4) the necessity to reduce errors, and (5) the need for speed in preparing reports.

The physical factor

Pressures exerted from without and from within business firms make the job of data processing a "must." External factors include, among others, the following: Some customers purchase merchandise for cash; most purchase on account. For the latter, billing is required at the end of a specific period after factors such as adjustments, returned items, and discounts are taken into consideration. This creates assets in the form of accounts receivable on the seller's books. Suppliers, too, ship merchandise to the seller on account, creating a liability in the form of accounts payable on the books of the seller. Once received, items have to be counted and recorded. They have to be listed and checked (that is, inventoried). The supplier has to be paid, after allowance for returned or defective merchandise (if any) and cash or quantity discounts are taken into consideration. Owners (stockholders, single proprietors, or partners), on the other hand, require periodic reports of the current status and business activities of their firms. Such information is needed to determine whether a profit is being made, which in turn guides the decision of whether to continue to operate the business, whether to invest more money in it, or whether to sell out.

In addition to these types of records, the government requires a multitude of reports from business firms. Taxes have to be paid and supporting statements produced concerning realized net income, the specific tax-deductible expenses incurred, and the periodic report of Social Security payments withheld. Many other statements are also required for various reasons.

Internal factors, too, create the need for a host of records. Pressures within the firm necessitate the processing of all types of expenses and revenues in a predetermined order. For example, payroll and payroll taxes, revenue from sales, the updating of inventory, and the handling of receivables and payables all need processing. These and many other activities require building a data-processing system efficient enough to present all necessary reports accurately and economically with as little waste of time as possible.

The cost factor

The time element and timing are important, for many of our present firms no longer practice the technique of price competition as much as they do cost competition. A business firm may be able to compete more successfully by practicing efficiency through reducing its operating costs than through reducing the retail price. In other words, firms that are "low-cost" firms producing a quality product are those that are likely to command the markets for particular products. Furthermore, factors such as technological change, innovation, and growth in size and complexity justify the need for and the importance of cost control in business. Business data processing can play a major role in this respect by reducing the amount of time taken to produce necessary records and reports accurately and quickly in situations where volume is the rule rather than the exception.

The labor factor

The number of clerical workers in business in the United States has increased tremendously in the past forty-five years. This increase has been more than four times the increase in factory help, and has been caused by the fact that, as data have increased, more clerical workers have been required to analyze these data. The widespread use of manual methods of handling data has increased this need for clerical workers. At this rate, in fifty to 100 years, securing enough people to do the necessary clerical work by present methods would be a difficult, if not impossible, job. This, as well as the increase in the volume of data and the emphasis upon accuracy and economy, has prompted the search for better methods of processing data.

The error factor

Once learned, most of the basic steps followed in analyzing any transaction become routine and consequently require little creative thinking. However, because it seems to be man's nature to think and make decisions in performing each step, there is a wide margin for error, especially if the steps involve some exceptions. For example, in computing the total pay of full-time salesmen working for a manufacturing concern on the basis of salary and commission, a payroll clerk will have to look up each salesman's base pay and add to it any commission based on a percentage of the value of items which he has sold to date. After a while, this job becomes routine, and the steps seem mechanical and dull. Consequently, errors occur and perhaps multiply with prolonged work on the same application, because of carelessness, boredom, and environmental conditions, such as pressure for deadlines, and so forth. In nonmathematical terms, the mental fatigue resulting from a repetitious clerical job can be likened to the physical fatigue resulting from a repetitious physical exercise such as touching your toes with your hands twenty to fifty times or setting-up exercises repeated 100 times (the number depending on one's age).

The speed factor

The use of modern data-processing systems results in communicating knowledge as it is needed. Without this kind of communication, such knowledge has little practical use in the making of day-to-day, "on the spot" business decisions. The business environment in the United States is one that stresses time and its cost very heavily. People tend to eat fast, walk fast, and work fast and, in this way, to achieve goals within the schedules they assign to themselves. With all other factors being equal, a European takes more time to accomplish the many jobs that Americans do, simply because of the European's tendency to relax more and perhaps enjoy his work at a slower rate of speed. One of the things that makes this country a leading, wealthy nation, is the ability and willingness of its people to find ways and means of using time efficiently. We have become used to getting more done within a given period of time than have the people of any other nation, because we have learned to work fast *with-*

out loss of efficiency or quality. As a result, competition becomes more intense, because the aim of most business firms is to produce more and to produce it more efficiently. Firms have become quite cost-conscious as a result of their interest in mass-producing quality products at the lowest price possible.

Importance of Rapid Decisions

For a business to survive in such a competitive system, executive decisions have to be made fairly rapidly and on as sound a basis as possible. Placed in its proper perspective, students of management recognize that decision-making is the result sought by all the techniques involved in the management process. Many "split-second" decisions are required daily. These decisions require reliable and accurate information, presented in an understandable form at the time it is needed, if it is to be useful to the executive in his decision-making capacity. Because the slower manual approach is no longer considered satisfactory in meeting this demand, machines that can do significant repetitive jobs fast, with a high degree of accuracy, obviously are needed. Once this is understood, the role of high-speed data-processing equipment in business becomes clear.

The Solution

Business data-processing systems are capable of repeating an operation for the hundredth time as accurately and quickly as for the first time, no matter how routine or boring it may be. Speed and accuracy are built into the system when the equipment is designed. Provided the source data are prepared correctly, processing of them by a computer can be performed very fast and with a degree of accuracy close to perfection. If source data are not prepared in an accurate form, however, the result is, of course, inaccurate. The machine comes up with inaccurate results just as easily as it does with correct ones, because *it can be no more accurate than the person who prepares the data for its use.* The advanced preparation of instructions for use by the machine is called *programming.* People who do it, called *programmers,* must be trained especially for the job.

Fig. 1-1 outlines the work done by humans in preparing a problem and feeding relevant information to a machine system for processing. Note that the number of people needed match, approximately, the number of machines used. If this data were to be processed manually, probably about ten or twenty times this number of people would be needed, depending on the type of calculating machines, input and output devices, or other supporting equipment.

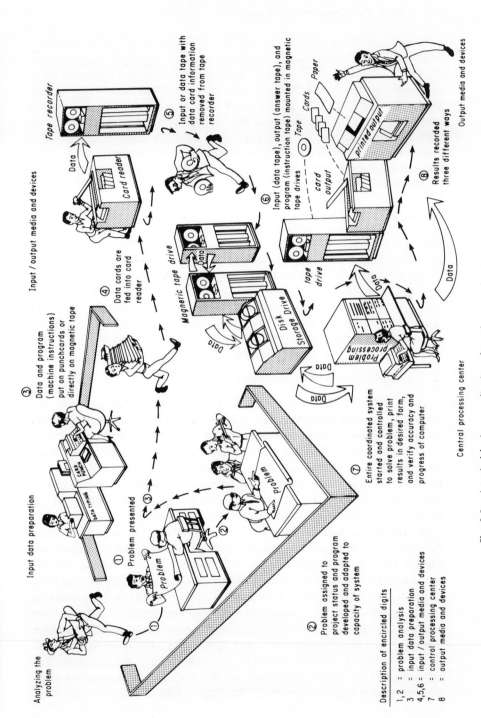

Fig. 1-1. A typical business application of an electronic data-processing system

Analyzing the problem

Input data preparation

Input / output media and devices

① Problem presented

② Problem assigned to project status and program developed and adapted to capacity of system

③ Data and program (machine instructions) put on punchcards or directly on magnetic tape

④ Data cards are fed into card reader

⑤ Input or data tape with data card information removed from tape recorder

⑥ Input (data tape), output (answer tape), and program (instruction tape) mounted in magnetic tape drives

⑦ Entire coordinated system started and controlled to solve problem, print results in desired form, and verify accuracy and progress of computer

⑧ Results recorded three different ways

Central processing center

Output media and devices

Tape recorder

Card reader

Magnetic tape drive

Disk Storage Drive

Problem processing

tape drive

card output

printed output

Tape

Cards

Paper

Data

Problem

CARD PUNCH

DATA TYPING

Description of encircled digits

1, 2 = problem analysis
3 = input data preparation
4, 5, 6 = input / output media and devices
7 = control processing center
8 = output media and devices

9

Fields of Data Processing

The two clearly defined fields of data processing are punched card and electronic. Although the principles of operation used in each field are essentially the same, electronic is not only faster than punched card, but differs in the method of handling data. Although certain equipment is commonly used in both, each uses certain other equipment peculiar to its own needs. Consideration of economy and space usually governs the choice of which to install.

Punched-card Data Processing

Punched-card data processing is the technique of preparing business reports following a routine which begins with the recording of source documents, such as sales reports and other similar types of reports, in a coded form into punched cards. The cards are then fed through equipment capable of detecting and interpreting the holes punched in them. The holes represent information about transactions and are punched in the cards in accordance with a predetermined code. The cards must be of a standard size so that they can be accommodated by the machines.

Necessity for punching information on cards

In its initial stages, information is usually written on paper of *any* size. To use these different-sized reports directly in machines would require the development of a machine flexible enough to adjust automatically to receiving and reading the desired information on the various-sized reports. Such a machine would be too complex in mechanical design to prove satisfactory from the cost standpoint. Also, the likelihood that more than one transaction will be shown on each report would make the job of processing the data in such a machine very difficult if not impossible. For example, on a sales slip, a salesman may record the sales of different items to a certain customer. The items can be anything from furniture and rugs to tweezers and rubber bands. It is an easy task, of course, to figure out the total overall sales made by that particular salesman, because each of his reports is a complete document and his total sales is the grand total of his reports. But, in figuring out his total sales of each different item sold during the week, each sales report would have to be analyzed individually. The situation becomes more complex if several salesmen in different districts, or several branches in each district, are involved. The processing of such data manually, and the preparation of the desired report, are highly expensive, owing to the clerical time involved in completing the job.

Transactions with different prices and quantity, and other related information, are frequently handwritten. This method is the one used by an order department when dealing with customers who order merchandise by mail, by salesmen who take orders on the sales floor, and by the credit department in taking down information about a customer desiring to open a credit account. Handwriting differs from one person to another. To date, no machine has been developed commercially that can deal with all handwritten reports.[1] If a machine is to process data for the purpose of producing meaningful reports, it must be able to *read* and *interpret* accurately what it reads. Because machines cannot "read" handwriting or printed words, another solution had to be found before they could be used to process data. Thus, variations in the sizes of documents, recording of unrelated transactions on those documents, and the fact that they are handwritten or printed present a complex situation for the processor. In order to work out the above problem—or, in fact, any other similar problem in using business records—a standard method of recording facts becomes necessary. This is attained through the use of punched cards, which are then fed into punched-card machines for processing.

Standardization of recording

Punched-card machines can perform work on data and produce reports much faster, more accurately, and more efficiently than can be done manually if the data are standardized in the initial stages. In the case of the salesman's reports, each of the items he sold would be recorded by punching holes in separate cards. Thus, homogeneous, or like, items can be grouped together very easily. The cards become permanent records and can be used indefinitely for future processing.

The unit-record principle

Standardization of recording is achieved through using punched cards based on the *unit-record principle*. This means the punching of a single complete transaction in a standard-size card. If more data flow in for the purpose of updating a specific transaction, the new data must be punched in a second card and an updated result, after processing, would then be punched in a third card. For example, suppose that on January 1 customer *A* purchases a suit from a retailing firm for $100 on account. Terms of payment: two equal installments of $50, the first due within fifteen days, the second at the end of the month. The procedure followed

---

[1] Major progress has been made in developing machines to read handwriting. A few models are available and are very promising in reading and interpreting accurately certain handwritten information.

on January 1 is as follows: General information, such as the customer's number, name and address, and so forth, in addition to the amount of $100, is initially punched in a card to record the necessary data for reference. Next, the card is fed through an accounting machine which is designed to handle punched cards. The machine reads and interprets the holes in the card and, on a statement form, prints the account number, name, and address of the customer, the item purchased, and its amount. This statement is mailed to the customer following his purchase of the item. On January 15, the customer pays his first installment of $50. Upon the receipt of the check by the firm, the name, address, and account number, along with the amount of $50, are punched in a card called the *payment card*. The calculator first reads the initial card containing the $100 debit and next the payment card containing the first installment of $50. On the payment card, it subtracts and punches the remainder (the balance of $50), along with the other necessary information, and the payment card becomes the customer's updated record. On January 31, when the second installment is paid, a new card is punched to record all the necessary information and the final payment of $50. It is then merged with the updated record of January 15 and the $50 payment is subtracted from the $50 balance to show that the account has a zero balance.

From this illustration we can see that this simple transaction, multiplied many times during the week, requires a host of punched cards as well as a number of punched-card machines set up to work as a team in processing the desired data and preparing needed reports.

Electronic Data Processing

In the early 1920s, the word *robot* was introduced by Czech author Karel Čapek in his play R.U.R. (*Rossum's Universal Robots*). The word is still used to describe modern computers, because a computer under human control can perform intelligent routine manual work at high speed.

At present, no routine record-keeping activity involving volume can be immune to the influence of the computer and the revolutionary change it is bringing in performing the clerical work necessary to business. Its blinking lights and whirring reels are modernizing accepted ways of doing things by getting them done faster. In its broader economic implications, the demand for computers is creating jobs in new industries, as well as in old, at the same time as the computers are replacing numbers of people who hold routine jobs. In an expanding economy, such as that presently obtaining in the United States, where labor markets are characterized as "tight," the release of workers from one set of routine jobs results in their obtaining other routine jobs at a different level of operation. This eases the tension in the markets for labor.

Time is needed before a majority of people understand, clearly and meaningfully, the capabilities and impact of the computer. Whether we like it or not, we have already entered the age of the so-called "thinking" machine. These machines, made of metal and glass, properly set up by a human being, perform mechanical, repetitive activities that once required hours of routine manual work. They can be *programmed* to perform involved, as well as routine, numerical calculations. They have a "memory" unit that can store data, that is, pieces of information, for future need. Computers can also be programmed to compare two factors and choose the proper course of action among several alternatives. For these reasons, one is tempted to believe that these electronic "brains" are capable of thought because of the exact way they simulate a man's (the programmer's) thought patterns. Simulation of man's thought patterns, however, does not endow the machine with the ability to think.

To the uninitiated, electronic data-processing machines become more and more awesome as manufacturers narrow the gap between the clerical capabilities of the machines and those of man. The human imagination and creativity used in designing and building the machines go unnoticed while the necessary impersonal numeralization and standardization of information are pointed to as "dehumanizing" the business world. Man, the shallow sophisticate infers, has become a number at the mercy of machines. However, one should realize that it is man who creates the machines, not vice versa. The "dehumanization" has been balanced by a corresponding "humanization" in the construction and design of the "robots." One can reason that the effort and time that were once spent on processing data manually are now spent in devising ways, systems, and machines to process them electronically. From this viewpoint, man spends his time thinking creatively instead of routinely. Over the last century, the substitution of machines for labor has, according to the record, benefited human beings by creating jobs rather than allowing them to be destroyed by starvation.

Nature of the work performed by computers

Generally speaking, there are two types of human thinking: creative and routine. Creative thinking demands imagination and insight. It is the type of thinking done by a composer when he composes a symphony or by a mathematician when he develops a new formula or theory. No definite set of rules exists for attaining such results. Routine thinking, on the other hand, is the habitual, perfunctory approach to performing work based on a definite set of rules. It requires essentially little talent other than that involved in following instructions accurately. Any person can figure out the sum of two one-digit numbers, or translate into English a simple paragraph in Spanish. Most of our daily work involves routine thinking which takes a lot of time because of the repetitive detail making it up. The computer is primarily designed to do the routine "thinking," in order to save human time and energy for more creative thinking, and to give consistently more accurate results. It can be programmed to serve in the capacity of a record-keeper, a clerk, and/or an office worker. One of its most significant applications is in keeping track of inventories in a store and updating them every time new supplies are received or a certain quantity is sold.

Capabilities of computers

Computers have a built-in self-control. Once they are fed the proper instructions, they can process information in such a way that human attendance or supervision is no longer necessary. We should remember that initially, a human being, called a "programmer," makes all the required decisions and converts those decisions into instructions for the computer. The computer, in this respect, is like a person learning to drive an automobile for the first time. The instructor sitting beside the student tells him what to do first, and how, when, and why he needs to operate which controls. He tells the student driver when and how to start up in first gear, how to shift into second, and what to do next. He instructs him further in the proper method of slowing down by applying his brakes and taking his foot off the gas pedal, and in shifting into a lower gear when approaching a red traffic light or a stop sign. Under such conditions, we may say that the instructor is in command of the automobile. He is making all the decisions. The student driver is merely obediently following and executing the instructions like a robot. He does not control the automobile until he drives alone and has to make all the necessary decisions regarding operation and manipulation of the automobile in traffic. A computer works primarily *like the student driver,* receiving instructions and executing them as directed. *It never progresses to the status of driver* as does the human being who is being taught to drive. This points out clearly the difference between *simulating* thought patterns and thinking.

Classification of computers

Computers fall into two classifications: digital and analog. The latter *measures,* whereas the former *counts.* In a digital computer, all arithmetic computations depend eventually on counting, in the same manner as an abacus depends on the counting of beads for similar functions. By contrast, there is no counting of unrelated or discrete quantities in an analog computer.

THE DIGITAL COMPUTER. In the digital computer, for example, addition of 115 and 352 is performed by the use of an adder, which consists of two counters. The first counter stores the 352. The second amount (115) is added through the utilization of a second counter, which now works simultaneously with the first. The sum of 467 is shown in counter one only after counter two holds 115. Mechanically speaking, counter one is increased by one every time counter two is increased by one also. That is, counter two drags with it counter one as 115 is being registered in it, thus causing addition to take place and the correct answer to be shown in counter one. Subtraction is performed by adding the second quantity in reverse. For example, when a twenty-cent item is purchased and a twenty-five-cent coin is offered by the customer, the clerk hands back the difference of five cents as follows: Counting begins at twenty to account for the price of the item, and addition in change begins until twenty-five is reached. That is, *21, 22, 23, 24, 25;* or five cents in change.

Multiplication is performed by repetitive addition. For instance, 4×6 means that four is added to itself six times; that is, $4 + 4 + 4 + 4 + 4 + 4 = 24$, or that six is added to itself four times; that is, $6 + 6 + 6 + 6 = 24$. Division is accomplished by repetitive subtraction. For example, in dividing fifteen by three, the following subtractions are made:

$$
\begin{array}{rl}
15 - 3 = 12 & \quad 1 \\
12 - 3 = 9 & \quad 1 \\
9 - 3 = 6 & \quad 1 \quad \text{Number of} \\
6 - 3 = 3 & \quad 1 \quad \text{Subtractions} \\
3 - 3 = 0 & \quad 1 \\
\end{array}
$$

Total Number of Subtractions   5,   or Quotient.

THE ANALOG COMPUTER. The idea of an analog computer was developed by Dr. Vannevar Bush, of the Massachusetts Institute of Technology, who was the first to build such a machine. It was called the *differential analyzer*. Early analog computers represented occurrences by the length of a rod or the rotation of a shaft. They were not always very accurate, since their mechanical moving parts wore down in time. The present use of vacuum tubes and transistors makes the more recent versions of analog computers more accurate, faster, and more dependable than their predecessors. See Fig. 1-2.

The name *analog* comes from the word *analogous* or *similar*. The thermometer, for instance, records various mercury levels based on changes in the temperature. When the temperature rises, the mercury level rises; when the temperature falls, so does the mercury level. That is, changes in the temperature are shown by analogous or like changes in the level of the mercury in the thermometer.

Fig. 1-2. Analog computer *(Electronic Associates, Inc.)*

The same principle of similarity is used in analog computers in performing arithmetic functions with measurements. Numbers are represented by physical quantities. Measurements are made, and the results are displayed and later used in various arithmetic operations to generate similar new data.

The analog computer, then, is a mathematical instrument, an example of which is the slide rule. In fact, two rulers can act in the same capacity as an analog computer (Fig. 1-3). For instance, in adding 6 + 3, first place ruler *A* on top of ruler *B*. Move ruler *A* to the right until its left edge is on top of number three on ruler *B*. The sum nine is now displayed immediately under number six of ruler *A*. Try different examples and see how simple it is.

In Fig. 1-3, a physical quantity was used to represent a number. In fact, we represented each of the two numbers by a length on a ruler. The sum was obtained simply by adding the length.

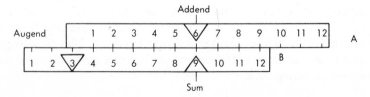

Fig. 1-3. Two rulers used as an analog computer

Best type of computer?

Both digital and analog computers have been used to solve business and scientific problems more quickly and more accurately than man is able to acting alone. However, statistics indicate a greater demand for digital than for analog computers. In terms of accuracy, the results shown by an analog computer contain systematic errors which must be allowed for; that is, its instruments are apt to show a value of a given quantity slightly different from the true value. The true value of 199 V of the voltage in a circuit, for instance, might be shown as 200 V on the dial. Such a "systematic error" will affect the final results by the same amount of deviation.

By contrast, the digital computer does not commit errors as such, unless there is a major flaw owing to faulty current flow. The most expensive analog computer is reported to be accurate to within .0001 of 1 per cent. Results derived from a digital computer are 100 per cent accurate if the data fed into it describe accurately the conditions of the problem required to be solved.

Probably the most important reason for the wide use of the digital computer is its flexibility in handling various types of problems. To solve a problem on an analog computer, a set of electrical components have to be wired and placed in the right position. Solving a different problem means a rewiring process—which is time consuming. On the other hand, loading a new program into its input component is all that is required by the digital computer for solving a different type of problem. Although an average program sometimes takes several days to prepare, it is less time consuming, in that it can be used indefinitely to work out different solutions to the same type of problem.

From the foregoing, we can conclude that each type of computer is designed to handle a particular set of problems. Analog computers are ideal for use when physical measurements are manipulated as data for arithmetic operations, when the solution of the problem involved needs one cycle of operations, and when a high degree of accuracy is not critical. When 100 per cent accuracy is demanded, and repetitive routine mathematical operations are involved, the digital computer is the one to use. Since business demands are of the latter type, this accounts for the greater demand for digital computers.

Computer terminology

Computer designers and users of digital computers borrow terms from the fields of engineering, mathematics, and psychology in order to describe the component parts and the functions of these machines. For instance, they speak of machine "memory," machine "language," machine "logic," and even machine "intelligence." Because the adoption of such terms is meant for the use of trained computer people, they may lead to mental confusion, and hence misunderstanding, on the part of the layman. On the other hand, when properly explained, these terms tend to be much easier to use in describing the components of computers and their functions than serial numbers or more technical names.

Computer Applications

Since the early 1950s when computers became commercially available, hundreds of applications have been developed in virtually all fields. In fact, there are enough present-day computer applications to fill a large volume. Generally, they are classified as applications involving: (1) *simulation,* (2) *real time,* or (3) *delayed time.*

Simulation

Simulation involves generating near-real environmental and other factors to test or to determine the probability of success of an operation. Before the first manned space flight was executed, all data pertaining to elements affecting such a flight were gathered and processed by a computer. Astronauts underwent simulated (or as close to reality as possible) flights in order to condition and adapt themselves to their forthcoming space journey.

Analog computers are more widely used in applications involving simulation of elements under various conditions. Analog computations convert the results of a simulated run into graphs which depict in detail the occurrences that are taking place. Other areas that use simulation include testing of proposed models, or prototypes, in the auto and aircraft industries, testing of new weapons, and sharpening the analytical ability of business executives through participation in "management games."

Real-time Applications

Real-time applications pertain to situations where the computer produces given results almost instantaneously, so as to have immediate control over the project under study. One of the early uses of real-time programs was in monitoring the performance of astronauts at every phase and every stage of their flight. This allows instant decisions to be made to minimize wide deviations from the planned course, or to correct likely errors, a flexibility which is not possible if any other computational technique is used.

Most of the airlines handle reservations on a real-time basis. Passenger specifications (for example, early Friday morning, first class, nonstop jet flight from Chicago to New York) are keyed into a keyboard by the receiving branch. The central computer system receives the messages, checks the status of the closest flight, searches for available seats, verifies, and reserves a space for the customer, in a matter of seconds.

Another interesting real-time application involves a "talking" computer that answers stock data inquiries. Since the spring of 1965, the Quotation Service of the New York Stock Exchange's Market Data System installed an IBM computer system to aid subscribers in receiving instantaneous data on stock prices, quotations, and volume, via telephone. For information regarding a given stock, the broker dials a four-digit number which connects him with the computer system. The computer searches for the data and collects the answer from a *Voice Answer Back* unit which stores a 126-word vocabulary on a recording drum. Additional information can be obtained by adding three to the first four-digit code. For example, if the code of the stock involved is 5427 and the broker desires more information on it, he would dial 8427.

In the summer of 1967, a part of the first meeting of the Congress on Medical Electronics and Biological Engineering produced a first in intercontinental medical communications. Two electrocardiographs were recorded in Tours, France, transmitted (by RCA communication channels, via satellite) to the computer complex at the health service's medical systems development laboratory in Washington, D.C., and, minutes later, the findings were relayed back to Tours.

Delayed-time Applications

Delayed-time applications, such as updating files, pertain to the processing of data some "delayed" time after the data have been received. Other examples include processing of checks, bills, and income tax reports.

The Internal Revenue Service's computer system is built around a master-file concept of tax administration. All transactions pertaining to an individual taxpayer are merged into a single account through the use of an identification number which helps in associating the tax data with the taxpayer. The master-file approach also compares one year's tax return with another year's return for the same taxpayer, balances due (if any), refunds to be made, and information returns with tax returns.

Digital computers are used in real-time and delayed-time applications while analogs are used in those involving simulation.

Government Use of Computers

The potentialities of the use of electronic data processing by agencies and departments of the Federal Government are clearly outlined in a memorandum sent to heads of departments and agencies by President Johnson, and shown as Fig. 1-4 on the pages following.

THE WHITE HOUSE

WASHINGTON

June 28, 1966

MEMORANDUM FOR

HEADS OF DEPARTMENTS AND AGENCIES

I want the head of every Federal agency to explore and apply all possible means to

    -- use the electronic computer to do a better job

    -- manage computer activity at the lowest possible cost.

I want my administration to give priority emphasis to both of these objectives -- nothing less will suffice.

The electronic computer is having a greater impact on what the Government does and how it does it than any other product of modern technology.

The computer is making it possible to

    -- send men and satellites into space

    -- make significant strides in medical research

    -- add several billions of dollars to our revenue through improved tax administration

    -- administer the huge and complex social security and medicare programs

    -- manage a multi-billion dollar defense logistics system

    -- speed the issuance of G.I. insurance dividends, at much less cost

    -- save lives through better search and rescue operations

Fig. 1-4. Press release of President Johnson's memorandum

-- harness atomic energy for peaceful uses

-- design better but less costly highways and structures.

In short, computers are enabling us to achieve progress and benefits which a decade ago were beyond our grasp.

The technology is available. Its potential for good has been amply demonstrated, but it remains to be tapped in fuller measure.

I am determined that we take advantage of this technology by using it imaginatively to accomplish worthwhile purposes.

I, therefore, want every agency head to give thorough study to new ways in which the electronic computer might be used to

-- provide better service to the public

-- improve agency performance

-- reduce costs.

But, as we use computers to achieve these benefits, I want these activities managed at the lowest possible costs.

At the present time, the Federal Government

-- uses 2,600 computers

-- employs 71,000 people in this activity

-- spends over $2 billion annually to acquire and operate this equipment, including special military-type computers.

Clearly, we must devote our best efforts to managing this large investment wisely and with the least cost.

I approved a blueprint for action when I approved the Bureau of the Budget "Report on Management of ADP in the Government."

The Congress recognized this need when it enacted Public Law 89-306 (the Brooks Bill) last October. This legislation provided specific authorities to

-- the General Services Administration, for the procurement, utilization, and disposition of automatic data-processing equipment

-- the Department of Commerce, for the development of data-processing standards and the provision of assistance to agencies in designing computer-based systems

-- the Bureau of the Budget, for exercising policy and fiscal control over the implementation of these authorities.

These agencies are seeking actively to put into effect ways for improving and reducing the cost of this huge and complex operation.

In my Budget Message for 1967 I told the Congress of my intent to make sure that this huge investment is managed efficiently.

The Federal Government must give priority attention to

-- establishing better and more effective procurement methods

-- making fuller use of existing facilities through sharing and joint-use arrangements before acquiring additional equipment

-- re-utilizing excess equipment whenever feasible

-- achieving, with industry cooperation, greater compatibility of equipment.

I expect all agencies to cooperate fully with the Bureau of the Budget, the General Services Administration, and the Department of Commerce in accomplishing these objectives.

I want the Director of the Bureau of the Budget to report to me on December 31, 1966, and every six months thereafter, on the progress that is being made throughout the Federal Government in improving the management of this very important technology.

GLOSSARY OF TERMS

ANALOG COMPUTER: A calculating device that processes data by measuring variations in electrical and/or other properties.

BUSINESS DATA PROCESSING: The routine performed through various necessary operations for generating data relevant to a business application.

DELAYED TIME: Pertains to processing data at some time after they have been received.

DIGITAL COMPUTER: A calculating device which processes data represented by combinations of discrete (versus continuous data in the analog computer) data.

ELECTRONIC DATA PROCESSING: The processing of data by an electronic device such as a computer.

PROGRAMMING: Preparing a logical sequence of events which the computer must follow and execute to solve a problem.

PUNCHED-CARD DATA PROCESSING: The production of records and reports by means of punched-card machines (or systems) which use a punched card as a primary medium.

REAL-TIME: Pertains to the processing of information or transactions as they actually occur. It is actually a concurrent operation for computing and physical processing.

SIMULATION: Representation of a phenomenon by computers or models in order to mirror the effects of certain changes in the original.

STANDARDIZATION: Establishment of specific procedural requirements for the efficient production of a large volume of goods or for processing of data.

"THINKING" MACHINE: A term used colloquially to refer to electronic computers.

UNIT-RECORD PRINCIPLE: (1) A separate record that is similar in form and content to other records; for example, a summary of a particular employee's earnings to date. (2) Sometimes refers to a piece of nontape, auxiliary equipment; for example, card reader, printer, or console typewriter.

REVIEW QUESTIONS

1. List three applications of data which affect your daily life.
2. What factors led to the recognition of the need for developing faster tools such as computers?
3. Expound briefly on the need for processing data. In view of the historical developments regarding man's achievements in developing tools to help realize his goals, what future developments in the area of data processing do you believe are likely to take place? Point out valid reasons to support your answer.

THE DEVELOPMENT OF AUTOMATIC MECHANICAL AIDS TO CALCULATIONS

ORIGIN OF THE DIGITAL COMPUTER—CHARLES P. BABBAGE   The Difference Engine   The Analytical Engine   ORIGIN OF THE ANALOG COMPUTER

MODERN DEVELOPMENT OF THE BABBAGE IDEA—FIRST-GENERATION COMPUTERS

SECOND-GENERATION COMPUTERS

THIRD-GENERATION COMPUTERS

MAN ALWAYS HAS BEEN CHALLENGED by mathematics and the need to solve mathematical problems. To most people, however, the job of solving a formula is both boring and time consuming. For this reason, attempts have been made from the very beginning to make calculating less tedious and much faster.

The history of data processing is a compilation of man's continuing effort to find better and more efficient ways of gathering and processing useful data as his business life increased both in complexity and in size. In the process man had to adapt his needs to the advancing technological levels of his environment. Technological advancements involving better ways of processing data, however, did not always render older methods obsolete. Instead, man, in several cases, continued using some of the older methods of data processing (either in the original or in modified form) while also making use of later developments.

Early Methods of Calculation

Until the nineteenth century, people found business calculations a very complex job, because they had to be done "in the head." This was so primarily because writing materials were very scarce and, therefore, too expensive to use for ordinary purposes. Paper was probably made by the Chinese before the time of Christ, but not until the fourteenth century A.D. did the science of paper-making spread into Europe. We are told that paper manufacturing was originated by the Moors in Spain early in the twelfth century. Large-scale paper manufacturing in Italy occurred in 1276. Later, mills began to spread into countries such as England, France, and Germany. Paper made from pulp, however, was an invention of the nineteenth century. Thus, not until comparatively recent times has paper been available on a mass-production basis.

Finger Counting

The lack of paper caused early man to do most of his calculations mentally, with the aid of his fingers. Probably, each of his fingers represented one of the animals he owned or the measures of grain he stored. Simple additions were carried out by finger tallying. For example, to add five and two, one holds up two fingers, then five more fingers, and counts the total number of upraised fingers to get the result of seven. When more complex

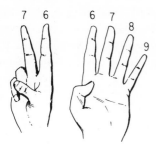

Fig. 2-1.   Finger multiplication

forms of calculation were devised, they were initially performed by the use of fingers. Finger training was so important that it was taught in Roman schools, and various methods were devised to do "advanced" operations such as multiplication and division. For instance, the student was required to learn the multiplication table up to 5×5 only. His fingers took over in figuring out the product of any numbers between five and ten. Suppose we wish to multiply 9×7. In order to do that, we would raise four fingers on one hand, representing six, seven, eight, and nine, and two fingers on the other hand, representing six and seven—that is, the numbers over five. The product is obtained as follows: The sum of the fingers raised (that is, $4 + 2 = 6$) determines the value of the tens position, and the product of the fingers not raised ($1 \times 3 = 3$) determines the value of the units position: thus, sixty-three. Try this method, using different numbers between five and ten, and see how easy it is to multiply. Also, try to visualize how long the average firm of today would take, using this method, to figure out bills to send to its customers at the end of the month.

The Abacus

Man was limited in how far he could go with his finger-counting facilities. His ingenuity later led him to overcome these limitations by using pebbles and other similar small objects for counting.

The verb *calculate* is derived from the Latin *calculus,* which means "pebble" or "a small piece of marble." Experienced calculators of early times performed their calculations by the use of a manual device containing pebbles placed in grooves or beads strung on a string called an *abacus,*

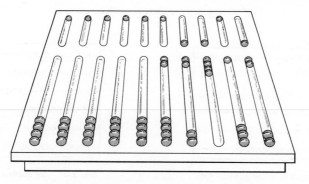

Fig. 2-2.   Roman counting board using pebbles

or a counting board (Fig. 2-2). In the typical abacus (Fig. 2-3) the beads are strung on strings in the form of rows. Each row contains ten beads, representing the ten fingers. The position of the row represents the decimal value of the beads in it. The beads in row *A* have a value of one each, representing the units position; beads in row *B* have a value of ten each, representing the tens position; and beads in row *C* have a value of 100 each, representing the hundreds position; and so forth.

Performing calculations on the abacus is a manual operation. All beads must start in the left part of the device. To get number 436, as shown in Fig. 2-4, first move six beads to the right in row *A* to represent the units position, which is *six*. Second, move three beads in row *B* to the right to denote the tens position, which is *three;* and last, move four beads in row *C* to the right to denote the hundreds position, which is *four*.

Addition, the most common arithmetic function performed, is accomplished by successively adding values represented by beads in the different rows. If we wish to add 255 to the above number (436), we would do the following:

1. Move five beads in row *A* to the right. Because we have only four beads left in that row, addition of 5 + 6 is accomplished by moving five of the six beads in row *A* to the left and moving one bead from row *B* to the right instead, as shown in Fig. 2-5. In regular addition, 5 + 6 = 1 and carry one.

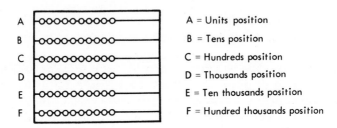

A = Units position

B = Tens position

C = Hundreds position

D = Thousands position

E = Ten thousands position

F = Hundred thousands position

Fig. 2-3. Typical beaded abacus

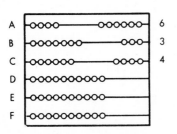

Fig. 2-4. The number 436
on an abacus

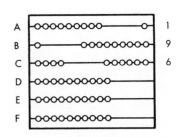

Fig. 2-5. The number 691
on an abacus

2. Next, move five beads from row *B* to the right, giving a total of nine tens, and
3. two beads from row *C* to the right, showing a total of six hundred. The answer, then, is 691. That is, in row *A*, the total is one, the units position; in row *B*, it is nine, the tens position; and in row *C*, six, the hundreds position.

The abacus was used efficiently in addition and subtraction. However, even when it came to multiplication or division, limited historical data show that many people have used the abacus for these purposes, too. Multiplication was done by repeated addition. To multiply 4 × 5, for example, either five is added to itself four times (5 + 5 + 5 + 5), or four is added to itself five times (4 + 4 + 4 + 4 + 4). In either case, the product is twenty.

Division was executed by repeated subtraction: a method which is at present performed by digital computers. For example, if seven Turkish horses cost eighteen liras each, their total value is obtained by the sum of 18 + 18 + 18 + 18 + 18 + 18 + 18. Likewise, if we wanted to know how many Turkish horses could be bought with ninety liras (approximately $15), we would take:

$$
\begin{array}{ll}
\text{18 from 90, leaving 72;} & 1 \\
\text{18 from 72, leaving 54;} & 1 \\
\text{18 from 54, leaving 36;} & 1 \quad \text{Number of} \\
\text{18 from 36, leaving 18;} & 1 \quad \text{Subtractions} \\
\text{18 from 18, leaving } \ 0. & 1 \\
\hline
\text{Answer:} & 5 \quad \text{Quotient.}
\end{array}
$$

The above approach shows that we can buy five Turkish horses with ninety liras. This is an extremely simplified application compared to those worked out by people of earlier times. Their methods were extremely complex, because they had to be practical. The abacus has been used until comparatively recent times, partly because of the scarcity of writing materials and partly owing to the lack of a practical numbers method. Even after written methods of calculations were devised, the influence of the abacus still remained. Today, its influence is seen in the use of the word *calculate,* as well as in the use of the term *buying over the counter.* The latter is derived from the times when merchants in the Middle Ages used boards or counting tables on which they computed their customer's account.

Some question exists concerning the origin of the abacus. Although several nations claim to have originated it, the idea probably developed in many nations and was later carried into other parts of the world by merchants and travelers. Its original home is believed to have been Egypt or Babylon. The ancient Hindus used one type of abacus called the *sand-tray* or *dust-board,* which was also common in both the Roman and Greek civilizations. Some scholars trace the origin of the term *abacus* to the Semitic *Abai,* meaning "dust." However, others are of the belief that the Greek *abax,* which means "tablet," is a more likely origin. Other types of abaci include the Chinese Suan-pan, the Japanese Soroban, the Russian S'choty, the Armenian Choreb, and the Turkish Coulba.

The Development of Manual Aids in Written Calculations

Double-entry Bookkeeping

Sketchy historical data suggest the birth of double-entry bookkeeping to have occurred in Italy in the fourteenth century. In 1340, a double-entry ledger was found in Genoa, showing a merchandise account for pepper. The account was debited with various expenses and credited with receipts. The balance was transferred to a "profit and loss" account.

In 1494, Luca Paciolo of Venice published his book, *Everything About Arithmetic, Geometry, and Proportion.* He summarized the existing routines of bookkeeping, and pointed out that the chief objective of book-keeping was the preparation of key information on assets and liabilities. He emphasized the use of: (1) a memorial (daybook), (2) a journal (formal debits and credits in Italian currency), and (3) a Quaderno (ledger).

Between the early 1400s and the 1800s, record-keeping methods were developed and expanded, but little was done to speed up the process of recording business transactions, calculating various amounts, or producing business reports.

The "Grating" Method

Arab, Hindu, and European calculators were the first to develop techniques of written calculations. The Arabs originated a "grating" method which was used by the Hindus in multiplication. This method involved a tablet consisting of a number of squares with diagonals. The idea was to place the multiplier on the top of the tablet with its high-order position on the top left column. The multiplicand was placed to the left side of the tablet with its high-order position in the top left corner also (Fig. 2-6). The squares hold the product of the two digits opposite it. For example, assume the multiplication of 217 × 14. The number 217 is placed on top of the tablet: the two is on the left corner, one on top of the middle column, and seven on top of the right column. The number fourteen (the multiplicand) is placed on the left side of the tablet with one (highest power) to the side of the top left corner.

The lower halves of the upper three squares show the product of multiplying 217 × 1. The bottom three squares display the product of multiplying 217 × 4. Notice that the carry of two in twenty-eight (product of 7 × 4) is displayed in the upper half of the square which shows twenty-eight. The product of 217 × 14 is attained by adding diagonally, as shown in Fig. 2-6.

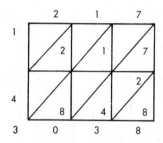

Fig. 2-6. "Grating" method
of multiplication

The "Bones" Method

The above "table" approach was used later in 1617 in Napier's "bones." John Napier, of Merchiston, Scotland, attempted to reduce tedious calculations involving large numbers. His "bones," or rods, made a great impression on the Europeans and Chinese. To explain: each rod is divided into nine squares, each of which is divided diagonally. The top square holds a digit (that is, 1-9). The remaining eight squares in the rod hold the product of multiplying that number by 2, 3, 4, 5, 6, 7, 8, and 9. The rods for multiplying 1, 3, 7, and 4 are shown in Fig. 2-7. Once set up, one can easily obtain the product of 2 × 374 or 5 × 374 or any other numbers from the top squares and the left rod, because the numbers in the middle are used to obtain the product only. For example, in order to get the product of 3 × 374, we add diagonally the values in the third square of each of the rods of the multiplication (from right):

Units position	2 (the contents of the right diagonal column).
Tens position	The sum of the second diagonal column, or 1 + 1 = 2.
Hundreds position	The sum of the third diagonal column, or 2 + 9 = 1 and we carry 1.

The carry is in the thousands position; therefore, the product is 1,122.

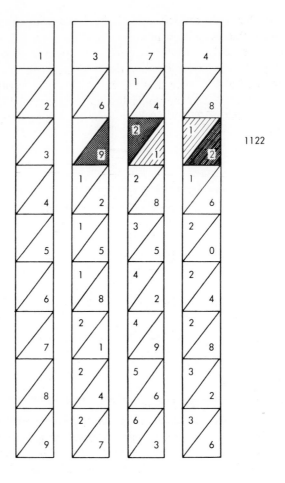

1122

Step 1. Add the contents of the first diagonal column.
Answer is (2) (Units position)

Step 2. Add the contents of the second diagonal column.
Answer is (1+1)=(2) (Tens positions)

Step 3. Add the contents of the third diagonal column.
Answer is (2+9)=(1) and carry (1) (Hundreds position)
Therefore, the product is   1 1 2 2

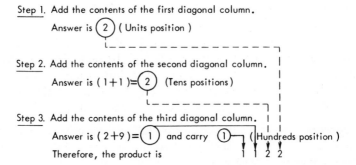

Fig. 2-7. Napier's bones

32

The "Sluggard" Method

The Arabs and the Hindus rarely used any multiplication tables. But when written calculations became more and more common, calculators in the sixteenth century introduced a written method which, when used, would obtain the product of numbers up to 10 × 10, similar to the Roman approach using the fingers. The multiplication table of 5 × 5 had to be learned. The method was called the "sluggard" method. For example, assume the multiplication of 8 × 6. The numbers *six* and *eight* are recorded in the manner shown in Fig. 2-8. Opposite these two digits, their differences from ten are written. The product, then, is obtained as follows:

Fig. 2-8. The "sluggard" method

The tens position of the product is obtained either by subtracting 2 from 6 or 4 from 8 (that is, 4).

The <u>units</u> <u>position</u> of the product is obtained by multiplying the 4 and 2 (that is, 8). So, the product of 6 x 8 is 48.

The "Arabic Numerals" System

The history of our number system is of Hindu origin, based on the use of ten fingers. The system was brought to Spain by the Moors in the ninth century as a result of the expansion of the Moslem Empire at that time. Later it was introduced into Europe. The number system was modified in India into what we now call the "Arabic numerals." Actually, true Arabic numerals are still in use in the Middle and Near East.

Fig. 2-9 is an example of the Arabic numerals and their translation into the currently used English numerical symbols.

Fig. 2-9. Arabic numerals

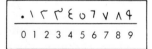

The Development of Mechanical Aids to Written Calculations

Numerical Wheel Calculator

Because of the widespread use and knowledge of the Arabic system of numeration in Christian Europe about the thirteenth century, mathematicians began to develop computing devices to calculate at a much higher level than that of the abacus. The first of such devices was the numerical wheel calculator (the world's first adding machine) made around 1642 at the age of eighteen by Blaise Pascal, one of the seventeenth century's greatest mathematician-philosophers. Pascal built his calculator because he wanted to aid his father, who at that time was the superintendent of taxes in Rouen, France. His calculator (Fig. 2-10) was capable of registering decimal value by the rotation of the cog wheel gear by one to nine steps, with a carry lever to operate the next higher digit wheel as a given cog wheel exceeded ten units of registration. This is considered the first real calculating machine to be developed. The present-day odometer is an example of a machine which applies Pascal's use of a series of cog wheels to calculate data.

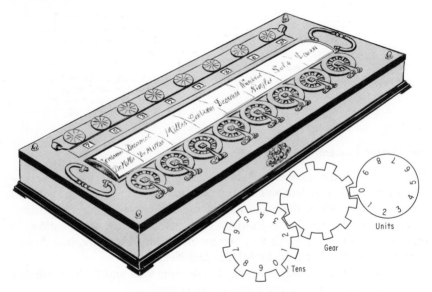

Fig. 2-10. Numerical wheel calculator

"Four-Function" Machines

In 1673, Gottfried Wilhelm von Leibnitz, a philosopher and mathematician, showed how a mechanical multiplier could be made. He felt that multiplication could be treated like addition. For example, multiplying 5 × 4 means five added to itself four times or four added to itself five times. In this case, two counters would be needed: one to perform the addition, and the other to show when addition should stop. Division was looked upon as the reverse of multiplication, and subtraction was adding the second quantity in reverse. Thus, these four basic arithmetic operations were based on counting. Leibnitz built his "stepped-wheel" machine when he was about twenty-five years old. It was later manufactured in 1694. However, this machine, as well as that of Pascal, was not considered dependable in its operation.

One of the more dependable and successful calculating machines was developed in 1820 by Charles Xavier Thomas, of Colmar, France. It performed all the four functions of arithmetic. In 1872, Frank Stephen Baldwin, of the United States, introduced a different principle in his calculating machine from that on which the Thomas machine was based. He began building his machine a year later, thus marking the beginning of the calculating-machine industry in the United States.

Key-driven Calculating Machines

The invention and development of key-driven devices and machines such as the typewriter and the cash register played a major role in the advancement of data processing, particularly in the recording and reporting functions. In 1887, Dorr Eugene Felt patented his comptometer (known then as the "macaroni box"). Improved versions of Felt's machine are still in wide use today. In 1890, W. S. Burroughs, a bank clerk, invented a key-set adding-printing machine geared to minimize the drudgery of bookkeeping. The machine, operated by a crank, was designed to record, summarize, and calculate.

Fig. 2-11. First practical adding-printing machine (*Burroughs Corporation*)

About 1911, Jay R. Monroe and Baldwin introduced the Monroe calculator, the first commercially successful keyboard machine.

The so-called accounting machines were not developed until after World War I. These were machines capable of printing values in a columnar arrangement, in addition to performing the functions of recording, calculating, and summarizing, which are common characteristics of most adding machines. Included in this category are billing machines which automatically extend amounts on invoices, and payroll machines that handle tax and other deductions in arriving at the net pay, while simultaneously providing copies or registers for accounting purposes.

Although electric motors provide greater speed and facility, all devices classified as adding machines, calculators, or accounting machines are considered "nonautomatic" equipment. All of them require a human worker to control and operate each step of processing.

The Development of the Punched Card and the Punched-card Machine

Joseph Marie Jacquard

In 1801, an event occurred which was to have far-reaching effects on the later development of automatic equipment. It was the perfection of the first punched-card machine, built by Joseph Marie Jacquard of France, to weave intricate designs into cloth. The outstanding feature of this machine was its ability to follow a set of instructions punched into cards. Due to the "fear of machines," Jacquard had difficulty gaining public acceptance for his machine. In the city of Lyons, he was physically attacked and his machine was destroyed. Through Napoleon's support, he rebuilt his machine and proved its usefulness in weaving. Lyons' prosperity in the mid-1800s was attributed largely to the success of Jacquard's loom.

Developments in the United States

The history of punched cards and the electromechanical data-processing machines using them dates from the late 1800s. It all started because the pressing demands on the United States Bureau of the Census created a need for developing better and faster methods of processing census data. As required by the Constitution, the United States Government must take a national census once every ten years. In the beginning, computation and compilation of data were performed manually.

During the nineteenth century, population increased greatly in the United States. Information of more complex nature, which was demanded at every census, made the manual method impractical. By the time the desired information was ready for publication, it was already obsolete and useless. To combat this situation, the Census Bureau sought the aid of a noted statistician as a special agent for the 1890 census. His name was Herman Hollerith. At that time, Dr. Hollerith was experimenting with punched-card components in the hope of coming up with a machine that would process census data faster and more efficiently than the manual system. The 1880 census took seven and a half years to finish, a total time considered by Hollerith as a tremendous waste.

By 1890, Dr. Hollerith completed a set of machines ready to process the 1890 census. It was the first large-scale punched-card data-processing machine installation. It included a card punch (a keyboard invented by Hollerith) which punched holes in 3" × 5" cards to record data, manually fed electromagnetic counters, and a sorting box. In operation, a punched card was placed in the pin-press, and a hinged box was lowered to activate a counter and open the lid of a sorting slot. Cards were deposited at a speed of fifty to eighty cards a minute. A test tabulation of 10,000 returns showed that enumeration time was three-fourths and tabulating time was one-eighth of that required for earlier systems. The census job was completed in two and one-half years, despite an increase in population from 50 million in 1880 to 63 million in 1890, a saving of over five years' time.

In 1896, Hollerith formed the Tabulating Machine Company (absorbed in 1911 by IBM), where he developed his machines for commercial sale. His first customers were the railroads, which used his machines for computation of freight statistics. IBM's real name at that time was the Computing-Tabulating-Recording Company. It was changed officially to IBM in 1924.

After Hollerith resigned, S.N.D. North, Director of the U.S. Census Bureau, hired James Powers (a comparatively little-known statistician from New Jersey), in 1905, to develop more equipment in a new mechanical laboratory subsidized by Congress. Powers developed several tabulating and other punched-card machines which were used successfully in the 1910 census. He developed the *simultaneous-punching* principle which involves the keying in of all the information to be punched in a card. Then, by depression of a certain key, the information can be punched simultaneously. This technique has the advantage of allowing the key-punch operator enough time to check and ascertain that the data to be punched are correctly keyed in. This is in contrast with the *serial technique* of punching, which causes a character to be punched in a column each time a key is depressed. The simultaneous principle is at present used in the UNIVAC keypunch.

Powers resigned his job with the Census Bureau in 1911 to form the Powers Accounting Machines Company in order to capitalize on his sorter and punching machines. His company was merged in 1927 with other office supply companies to form Remington Rand Corporation. Presently, data-processing equipment is marketed through the UNIVAC Division of Sperry Rand Corporation.

Developments in England

In 1926, work of mechanizing calculations on navigational tables was initiated by Dr. L. J. Combie, another pioneer in the field of computation, who was the deputy superintendent of the Nautical Almanac Office in England. Astronomical data were often faulty and unreliable because of the many mistakes resulting from the use of manual computation. Combie applied Hollerith's system in preparing the tables for the Nautical Almanac. Pertinent data were punched on cards in order to compute the position of the moon daily at noon and midnight from the year 1935 to 2000 A.D. From the results of the computations, the tables of the Nautical Almanac were prepared by the National Cash Register Company's accounting machines—hooked up in pairs and operated from a single shaft—a modern version of the Babbage difference engine.

The Development of Automatic Mechanical Aids to Calculation

Origin of the Digital Computer—Charles P. Babbage

Automatic computation began in 1812 with Charles P. Babbage, an English mathematician who mastered thoroughly the basic fundamentals of digital computers, to the marvel of those associated with him. His dreams and ideas were not fully appreciated, however, until the last decade of his century.

Born in 1792 in Devonshire, England, Babbage became wealthy when his father (a banker) died leaving him a sizable inheritance. He received a formal education interrupted by many personal factors. He taught himself enough mathematics to find out later at Cambridge University that what he already knew was far beyond the background of his teacher. At that time, he became interested in investigating applications of mathematics to practical projects, such as machine tools, and in a revival of the study of mathematics. Up to that time, universities such as Cambridge were still dominated by the theories of Newton. With two of his friends, George Peacock and John Herschel, whose father discovered the planet Uranus and who himself later became a noted astronomer, he formed the Analytical Society. In 1828, with no scholarly distinction, Babbage was elected to the Lucasian Chair of Mathematics (Newton's Chair) and held it for eleven years, an unprecedented event in view of the fact that he had not delivered even one lecture at the University.

The difference engine

One of the better-known contributions of Babbage was the "difference engine" (Fig. 2-12). In 1812, while in the Analytical Society quarters

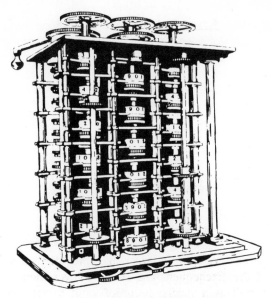

Fig. 2-12. Babbage's difference engine

looking at a table of logarithms full of mistakes, he began to think in terms of the use of a machine capable of computing mathematical tables. The French Government had already used several computers which could add and subtract only. The job performed on the tables was initially divided into simple operations, each of which was assigned to a separate computer. Babbage firmly believed that he could develop a special-purpose machine capable of doing the computations automatically. Fig. 2-13 presents the main idea of computing tables. It is centered around the fact that the level difference between values computed for a formula remains the same. Once achieved, the subsequent values themselves can be produced by addition only. The table in Fig. 2-13 shows the level difference between A^3 in the formula $B = A^3$.

The third-level difference corresponds to the third power of A in $B = A^3$ and is constant. If we wish to compute any other value of A, it can be done by addition alone. For example, in computing the value of $A = 8$, we would add $6 + 36 + 127 + 343$ to give us the sum of 512. Additional numbers in D2 can be found by simple addition, that is, 42, 48, 54, 60, and so forth. From these numbers, the numbers of the second column (D1), and ultimately of the first column, can be found.

The foregoing idea was demonstrated in a model of the difference engine which Babbage made in 1822. It was received with such great interest and enthusiasm that the Royal Society promised to subsidize

When A is		B would be =	1st. diff. D 1	2nd. diff. D 2	3rd. diff. D 3
0	then	0			
			>1		
1		1		>6	
			>7		>6
2		8		>12	
			>19		>6
3		27		>18	
			>37		>6
4		64		>24	
			>61		>6
5		125		>30	
			>91		>6
6		216		>36	
			>127		
7		343			

Fig. 2-13. Computing tables

Babbage's project for developing a larger machine, after an interview with the Chancellor of the Exchequer. The British Government built a workshop for him, as well as a special fireproof vault to safeguard the blueprints of his engine. However, Babbage took more time than anticipated to complete his model. This was because he became interested in a new idea involving a machine of fantastic capabilities which he wanted to build instead. This "defection" led, in 1842, to the official withdrawal of the government from any further support for the project, which forced Babbage to give up its construction. A model of the difference engine built in 1859 for the Registrar General was adopted four years later by life insurance companies and for several years was used to compute life tables.

The analytical engine

In 1833, while the difference-engine project was suspended for a year, Babbage conceived the idea of building an analytical engine which would be capable of performing any calculation. It was to be the first general-purpose digital computer. Babbage worked on it for the remaining years of his life and financed it completely from his own funds. He died in 1871 with the job undone, a disappointed man, although he left thousands of drawings which outlined the details of building the engine. Later his son, Major General H. P. Babbage, took up his father's project and succeeded in completing part of the arithmetic unit.

Babbage's plan to build what seemed to his colleagues to be a fantastically large engine, at a time when such a machine was beyond the grasp and comprehension of the majority of mathematicians, probably hampered the serious development of his ideas for over 100 years. Once he developed the idea of the analytical engine, he virtually abandoned the rather simple and useful difference engine. The analytical engine was to contain a storage capacity for 1,000 members, of fifty digits each. He designed the machine to accept input from cards invented by a Frenchman named Joseph Marie Jacquard for the control of looms. The engine fascinated Babbage during the major part of his life. However, his failure to express himself adequately, because of his impatience with people who were slow thinking as far as mathematics and mechanics were concerned, made him a poor salesman of his ideas. He tried without success to solve his problems independently with his own means—problems which eventually occupied the efforts and talents of two generations of engineers. Because of his lack of success, he became a frustrated and unhappy man, and once told a friend that he could not remember a single completely happy day in his life. He seemed to feel that mankind in general was against him, and especially the English people and the British Government. Despite this failure to "sell" his ideas, we may still think of Babbage as one of the great pioneers in the field of computation. He was a philosopher, a mathematician, a professor, and the writer of over eighty books and papers. This was the product of a "man of vision" who possessed the foresight, courage, and imagination to work on and develop what he believed was possible and would be helpful to mankind.

Origin of the Analog Computer

All of the foregoing counting machines described were digital, in that they operated on separate pieces of data. Many analog devices were known in the early history of Western Europe, and the first analog computation is believed to have been the use of graphs to solve surveying problems.

The first widely and extensively used analog computer was the slide rule, developed in the early 1600s (Fig. 2-14).

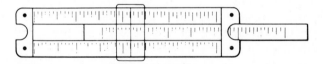

Fig. 2-14. A slide rule

Among other arithmetic functions, multiplication and division are performed simply by subtracting or adding the distance on the frame to that on the slider.

One of the first large-scale analog computers was built by Lord Kelvin in 1872 to predict the height of tides in English harbors. The action of its pulleys and weights acted to simulate the effect of the moon, the sun, and winds on tides. The change of the impact of these factors, combined with complex formulas stored inside the machine, produced graphs which indicated the degree of change of tides. Although this particular machine was bugged with imperfections, it, nevertheless, is considered a significant accomplishment in the development of today's analog computers.

Modern Development of the Babbage Idea—
First-generation Computers

Over 100 years passed before another machine similar to the one visualized by Babbage was developed. In 1937, Professor Howard G. Aiken, a physicist at Harvard University, developed some ideas involving mechanical calculations. Through Dr. Brown, who then was a consultant to IBM and a professor at Harvard, Aiken sold IBM his ideas, which resulted in a research grant to Harvard for developing a sequential computer. Seven years later (May 1944), through the efforts of Aiken, an automatic sequence-controlled calculator (named the Harvard Mark I) was put into service. Its calculating elements consisted of mechanical counters driven through electromagnetic clutches controlled by electro-mechanical relay circuits. The Mark I has often been referred to as a "mechanical brain." It adds, subtracts, multiplies, divides, and compares quantities. Also, it has the ability to refer to any tables stored in it for the solution of specific problems. In addition, it can be adapted to solve various kinds of problems for engineers, physicists, and mathematicians. It was the first machine to do long series of arithmetic and logical functions. After the Mark I, the Mark II, Mark III, and Mark IV were constructed by Professor Aiken.

In the early 1940s, Dr. John W. Mauchly of the University of Pennsylvania became aware of the need for a high-speed electronic device able to do great quantities of statistical calculations for weather data. During World War II, a contract for the project was made between the University of Pennsylvania and the U.S. Government.

In 1945, Professors Mauchly and Prosper Eckert used the facilities of the Moore School of Engineering to build a large general-purpose computer, called the ENIAC (electronic numerical integrator and calculator). It is this machine (the first all-electronic computer) which the press at that time referred to as the "mechanical brain." The ENIAC was considered very fast in working out long calculations. Initially, it was used primarily for solving mathematical problems in the areas of ballistics and aeronautics. Its main drawback was that it was designed for a special set of problems, thus making the change of programming relatively slow. The

ENIAC was moved to Aberdeen Proving Grounds in Maryland in 1947 and continued in operation until late 1955.

Also in the mid-1940s, Dr. J. von Neumann, another pioneer, issued a report to a group connected with the Moore School of Electrical Engineering at the University of Pennsylvania, in which he described the basic philosophy of computer design. This philosophy has been incorporated in today's computers. Von Neumann himself did not believe that all his theories were practical, but with today's advanced technology, almost everything he described in his theoretical paper has become reality. One often hears that computers were designed based on the "von Neumann concept."

As a result of Dr. von Neumann's paper, the Moore School of Electrical Engineering took over the project of developing the EDVAC (electronic discrete variable automatic computer) for the Aberdeen Proving Grounds. The EDVAC used punched paper tape for input, and a program, which controlled the sequential operations, was placed in the memory of the machine. It was the world's first commercial electronic data-processing machine.

Since then, many machines have been developed. The EDSAC (electronic delayed storage automatic computer) was built in 1949 in Cambridge, England, and the ACE (automatic computer engine) in London by the National Physical Laboratory. In 1946, Eckert and Mauchly left the University of Pennsylvania and negotiated a contract with the National Bureau of Standards, forming the Eckert-Mauchly Corporation. They started to develop the UNIVAC. It was delivered to the Bureau of the Census in 1951 and was used continuously twenty-four hours a day for twelve years. The UNIVAC (universal automatic computer) is well known for having predicted the victory of President Dwight D. Eisenhower in the election of 1952. The Eckert-Mauchly Corporation later became a division of Sperry Rand Corporation.

In England, the MADAM (Manchester automatic digital machine) at the University of Manchester was constructed by Ferranti, Ltd. At the University of London, the SEC (simple electronic computer) and the APEC (all-purpose electronic computer) were developed.

Since 1958, hundreds of large and small computers have been made available for commercial purposes. Among the computer manufacturers are The International Business Machines Corporation, General Electric Corporation, Radio Corporation of America, Sperry Rand Corporation, Honeywell, Inc., Burroughs Corporation, National Cash Register, and Control Data Corporation.

Compared with later computers, first-generation computers were bulky in size, somewhat inflexible, and demanded strict observance of air-conditioning requirements. However, they had advantages over the electromechanical data-processing machines. Their increased speed was attributed to the use of vacuum tubes for switching, and they were also the first practical hardware to allow internal-type programming. It was this latter feature which provided comparison and "logical-decisions" ability to be applied during calculations of data, and which, since then, has led to computers being referred to as "thinking machines."

Second-generation Computers

In this second-generation stage, the transistor replaced the vacuum tube, thereby shrinking the physical size of the computer without decreasing its effectiveness. In fact, processing speed was increased, and scores of medium- to large-scale computers with built-in error detection and correction devices were designed to handle data at the millisecond (1/1,000 of a second) and microsecond (1/1,000,000) speed. Air-conditioning requirements became less strict and peripheral equipment also was improved. High-speed printers and readers made on-line data processing possible. More sophisticated software and programming techniques also were significant.

Fig. 2-15.   Burroughs 5500 computer system

Third-generation Computers

Third-generation computers are the latest in computer technology. They are characterized by increased programming and peripheral sophistication and greater miniaturization of hardware. The IBM 360 system is believed to be the first commercially available data-processing system whose design is based on the use of microelectronic circuits. See Fig. 2-16. A product of IBM's solid logic technology, the circuits perform calculations in billionths of a second.

More effective use of input/output devices and random-access devices (for example, disk memory) enables an organization to store virtually all its operating and functional data. Furthermore, data-communication equipment facilitates transmission of data from any area to the computer for storage, connects operating facilities between two or more computers, and allows any recording or inquiries to the computer system from remote sta-

Fig. 2-16.   IBM 360 computer system

tions at high speed. Optical scanning and MICR (magnetic ink character recognition) also are widely used in business organizations such as banks and insurance companies. The nanosecond (one billionth of a second) programming speed is here to stay.

Finally, we are now capable of commercially operating several projects simultaneously (that is, parallel processing) and in real time so as to be able to manipulate incoming factors that are external to the program in the computer.

GLOSSARY OF TERMS

ABACUS: An early calculating device which operates by sliding beads or counters along rods.

ANALYTICAL ENGINE: The first general-purpose computer, developed by Charles P. Babbage around 1833.

DIFFERENCE ENGINE: A special-purpose computer developed by Charles Babbage around 1812 to compute mathematical tables.

EDVAC: Electronic discrete variable automatic computer, developed by the Moore School of Engineering as the first commercial electronic computer.

ENIAC: Electronic numerical integrator and calculator (the first all-electronic general-purpose computer) built in the early 1940s by Professors Eckert and Mauchly while at the University of Pennsylvania.

MARK I: A first-generation American computer (an automatic sequence-controlled calculator) developed by Professor Howard Aiken of Harvard in May 1944.

NUMERICAL WHEEL CALCULATOR: The world's first adding machine, invented by Blaise Pascal about 1642.

SECOND-GENERATION COMPUTER: Refers to transistor-built (versus vacuum tubes) computers, capable of processing data at the millisecond and microsecond speeds with high-speed printers and readers (for example, the IBM 1401 computer system).

SERIAL-PUNCHING PRINCIPLE: A character-at-a-time punching of data in a card.

SIMULTANEOUS-PUNCHING PRINCIPLE: A technique introduced by James Powers, whereby data to be punched are first keyed in and then (by a release key on the keyboard) punched simultaneously into a card.

THIRD-GENERATION COMPUTERS: Computers characterized by greater miniaturization and by more effective input/output and random-access devices (for example, the IBM 360 Model 30 system).

UNIVAC: Universal automatic computer, initially developed by Professors Eckert and Mauchly. It is now a product of the Sperry Rand Corporation.

REVIEW QUESTIONS

1. Why were business calculations once considered complex? Explain.

2. Explain finger counting. Demonstrate the addition of $4 + 3 = 7$.

3. Show how the product of multiplying 8×7 is obtained by the use of the fingers.

4. What is an abacus? In what arithmetic functions is it used primarily? Explain its basic operation.

5. Discuss the origin of the abacus.

6. What is the "grating" method? Who originated it? Explain its operation.

7. Who invented "Napier's bones"? Why?

8. Explain briefly the way Napier's bones perform the multiplication function.

9. Show how multiplying 7×9 is done by the use of the "sluggard" method.

10. Who built the world's first adding machine? What was it called? Why did he build it?

11. State briefly the main ideas of Leibnitz. What were the results of these ideas?

12. Summarize the life of Henry Babbage.

13. What is the main idea around which Babbage's difference engine was centered? Explain and give an example.

14. For what reason(s) was the construction of the difference engine abandoned? Explain.

15. Describe generally the analytical engine. Was it completed during the lifetime of Babbage? Why?

16. What is the main contribution of Professor Howard G. Aiken to the computer world? Describe it.

17. Describe the ENIAC. Who built it? What was its main drawback?

18. What factors were responsible for the initiation and, later, the development of punched-card data-processing machines? Explain fully.

19. Describe the main contributions of Dr. Hollerith to punched-card data processing. What is the name of the company resulting from his works?

20. Explain the main contributions of Dr. Powers to punched-card data processing. What company was eventually formed which to date practices and develops machines based on his ideas?

21. In what respect is a slide rule similar to an analog computer?

22. What is meant by a *second-generation* computer? How is it different from a first-generation computer? A third-generation computer?

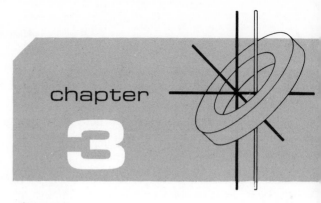

THE
SYSTEMS CONCEPT
AND SOURCES OF DATA
IN BUSINESS ORGANIZATION

THE TERM "SYSTEM" HAS BEEN SUBJECT to a great deal of misunderstanding and indiscriminate use. For some time, most of the developmental work related to this concept has been done by management scientists, who have drawn upon work previously done by others. Biologists refer to a "system" as a complex of elements standing in interaction. A nation is a system composed of its people, government, and various institutions; the human body is a system composed of many interrelated parts. Likewise, a business organization is a system composed of many interrelated activities or components. Each component is called a *subsystem* which interacts with other components (subsystems) to contribute toward the realization of preplanned goals. Like the human body, the failure of one subsystem could conceivably hamper the functioning of others in the system.

The Systems Approach in Business Organizations

From the foregoing, we realize that the systems concept stresses: (1) relationships between subsystems, and (2) the influence these relationships have on the behavior and performance of other subsystems. We must, then, attend to the organization of the required manual and machine-related data-processing operations in order to generate information about a particular project, and to make it available in the desired form and at a minimum cost to those who need it, when they need it.

Using the organization as a system, we then use each of the seven inner circles in Fig. 3-1 to constitute a subsystem, which in turn generates information to help the other six subsystems to function while carrying out its own system as an entity.

For example, while the payroll department is a subsystem (component) in an organization, it consists of a complete information system in terms of the various operations that it must do to produce payroll data (Fig. 3-1). Implied in this activity is the fact that each subsystem would have its own objective, while what it does also contributes to the accomplishment of pronounced organizational objectives.

One major consequence of the systems approach to data processing is to look into the role of each organizational subsystem in a broad sense. One should bear in mind that for the effective operation of a management information system, no subsystem can work separately from, but must rather work in harmony with, the other subsystems, so as to exercise proper interrelationships between the system-producing information and the system-producing decisions. This is referred to as the *total-systems concept*.

To illustrate the systems concept, let us look into the primary information requirements of a business organization.

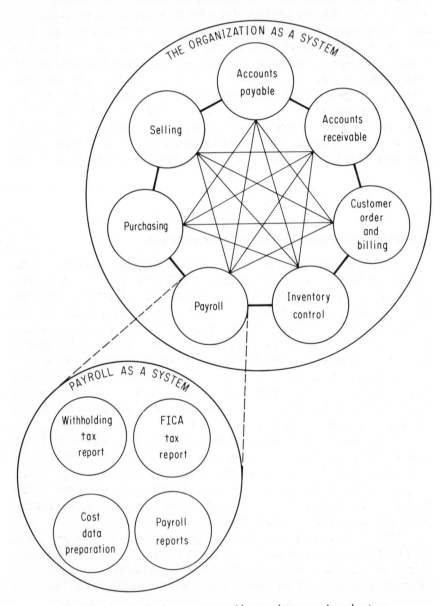

Fig. 3-1. An organization as a system with seven data-processing subsystems

Sources of Data

Most of the information a business organization, especially a manufacturing firm, receives, is generated as a result of the day-by-day operations and the interaction it makes with the environment. No business is designed to survive and grow without active and constant dealings with various external and internal groups.

Fig. 3-2 is a schematic diagram of eight key operations (source and flow of information) of a manufacturing firm. Because these operations are interrelated, they generate masses of data throughout the organization. Information derived from various operations results in records and reports to be used by management in making the decisions necessary for running the organization.

Purchasing

Purchasing consists of procurement of raw materials, equipment, and supplies to meet the needs of the various departments of the organization. In a medium-sized to a large manufacturing firm, the purchasing function is centralized in one department—the purchasing department. After the decision has been made regarding the type and quantity of product to be manufactured, a quota is decided upon, based on past sales volume, quantity on hand, and an estimate for next year's sale. The sales department has data available to furnish production-planning personnel any or all information with regard to actual and predicted sales.

Once a production quota has been approved and authorized, the stockroom is checked for the available amount of supplies. For example, assume that the production-planning department of the American Manufacturing Company has decided to stock 2,000 units of a given item for the year ending December 31, 1968. If the company follows a policy of having a minimum "safety stock" of 400 units to prevent a total shutdown, then the net amount to be purchased is 1,600 (2,000 − 400). Next, the net quantity of items needed is requisitioned by filling out a *purchase-requisition* form, requesting the purchasing department to place an order for the needed supplies. The purchasing department, in turn, locates and determines the supplier(s) from whom the order is to be filled, and follows this action by drawing up a purchase order.

The *purchase order* is made in three copies: the original, which goes to the supplier from whom the goods are to be purchased; first carbon, to be retained by the purchasing department; and second carbon, sent to the receiving department. Figs. 3-3 and 3-4 involve a purchase requisition and a purchase order. In Fig. 3-3 Jim Adams approved the purchase requisition. Mr. Mabbs, the purchasing agent of the company, followed up the requisition by signing a purchase order to procure the 1,600 items from Bennett Electronics (the supplier).

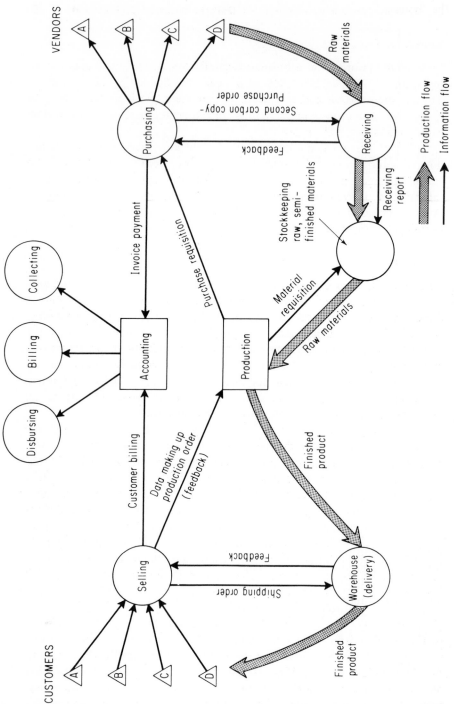

Fig. 3-2. A schematic diagram of information flows in a manufacturing concern

AMERICAN MANUFACTURING COMPANY
4813 Dempster Street,
Skokie, Ill.

Requisition No. _M110_   Date _August 30, 1968_

Please purchase for
delivery . . . .   _Before Sept. 30_

Quantity	Description	
200	Transformers	392K
300	Switches	410A
100	Capacitors	17 Z
400	2 ft.-wires	1 S
600	Reactors	007J

Requisitioned by _E. M. Walters_   Approved by _Jim Adams_

Purchasing Agent Memorandum of Order

Purchase order no. _1704_   Issued to _Bennett Electronics_

Date of Order _Aug 20_   _Evanston_

Fig. 3-3.   Purchase requisition from production department to purchasing

Purchasing is a specialized function and involves an up-to-date knowledge of the quality and various competitive brands available on the market. The purchasing agent not only needs to satisfy the specifications of the department regarding the materials, but is also expected to procure the materials at the best possible price. To do so, means sampling several competitive brands, and sending a *request for quotations* or *bids* for similar quality products. Soon after the source of supply has been determined, a purchase order is prepared.

Receiving

As soon as the shipment is received, it is checked and verified (against a copy of the original purchase order) by the receiving department. The

```
┌──────────────────────────────────────────────────────────────┐
│                                              No. 1704          │
│              PURCHASE  ORDER                                   │
│        AMERICAN MANUFACTURING COMPANY                         │
│               4813 Dempster St.,                              │
│                 Skokie, Ill.                                  │
│                              Date  Aug. 30, 1968             │
│  To:  BENNETT ELECTRONICS     Deliver  Before Sept. 30      │
│         312 Church St.,        Ship via  Best way           │
│         Evanston, Ill.         f.o.b.                        │
│                                Terms  2/10, n/30            │
├──────────────┬──────────────────────────────┬───────────────┤
│   Quantity   │          Description          │    Price      │
├──────────────┼──────────────────────────────┼───────────────┤
│     200      │  Transformers   392K          │     4.00      │
│     300      │  Switches       410A          │     2.00      │
│     100      │  Capacitors     17A           │     4.00      │
│     400      │  2 ft. - wires  1S            │      .50      │
│     600      │  Reactors       007J          │    10.00      │
│              │                               │               │
├──────────────┴───────────────────┬──────────┴───────────────┤
│                                   │       AMER. MFG. CO.     │
│  Req. No.  ___M110___    By       │   Richard Mabbs          │
│                                   │     purchasing agent     │
└───────────────────────────────────┴──────────────────────────┘
```

Fig. 3-4.   Purchase order from purchasing department to vendor

receiving clerk: (1) inspects the merchandise to make sure it is in good condition; (2) counts, weighs, and determines the quantity received and records these quantities on his copy of the purchase order; and (3) initials the copy of the purchase order and forwards it to the purchasing department to be filed in the "receiving" records.

When the sales invoice is received by the purchasing department, a checklist is used to verify the data it contains. The invoice describes the merchandise shipped, shows the amount charged, and provides other important information. In our example (Figs. 3-3—3-7), the purchasing department of the American Manufacturing Company received a sales invoice of the 1,600 units ordered from Bennett Electronics (Fig. 3-5).

BENNETT ELECTRONICS
312 Church St.,
Evanston, Ill.

Invoice No. 2390

	FOR CUSTOMER'S USE ONLY
Register No.	Voucher No.
f.o.b. checked	
Terms approved	Price approved _E.D.M_
Calculations checked _C.E.D._	
Materials received _9/6/68_ _Mon_ _Rec. Clerk_	
date / signature / title	
Satisfactory & approved	
Adjustments	
Accounting Distribution	
Audited _J.E.M._	Final Approval _K.O._

Customer's Order No. and Date _1704_ _8/30/68_

Requisition No. _M110_

Contract No. _____

Sold to: AMERICAN MANUFACTURING CO.
4813 DEMPSTER ST.,
SKOKIE, ILL.

Date Shipped: _Sept. 1, 1968_ from _Evanston_

How shipped & Route _Eastern Trucking_

Terms: _1/10, n/30_

Quantity	Description		Unit Price	Amount
200	Transformers	392K	4.00	800.00
300	Switches	410A	2.00	600.00
100	Capacitors	17Z	4.00	400.00
400	2 ft.- wires	1S	.50	200.00
600	Reactors	007J	10.00	6,000.00
				$8,000.00

Fig. 3-5. Sales invoice from vendor to purchasing department

55

```
┌─────────────────────────────────────────────────────────────────────┐
│                                                                       │
│   Goods Checked to Invoice           _____      │
│                                                                       │
│   Invoice Checked to Purchase Order for:                              │
│                 Merchandise          ___CQ_____      │
│                 Prices               ___CQ_____      │
│                 Discount Terms       ___CQ_____      │
│                 Freight Terms        ___CQ_____      │
│                                                                       │
│   Invoice Footings and Extensions Checked  _____      │
│                                                                       │
│   Approved for Payment          _Frank Esenbach_____     │
│                                                                       │
│   Paid by Check No. __1400___  Date __Sept 16, 1968_____       │
│                                                                       │
└─────────────────────────────────────────────────────────────────────┘
```

Fig. 3-6.   Check sheet

Upon proper inspection of merchandise by the receiving department, a purchasing department clerk initials the check sheet on the "goods checked to invoice" line (Fig. 3-6). Next, the clerk checks the invoice against the first carbon copy of the purchase order for details regarding the merchandise ordered, prices, and discount and freight terms. If they are correct, he places his initials on the "invoice footings and extensions checked" line of the check sheet. Finally, the purchasing department approves payment and sends the invoice to the accounting department for disbursement.

Date	Invoice	Amount		
			SECOND NATIONAL BANK	No. 1400
9/16/68	2390	8,000.00		
			Chicago Sept. 16, 1968	
			Pay to the Order of BENNETT ELECTRONICS S 7,920.00	
			EXACTLY $ 7,920.00 AND 00 CTS. - - - - - - - - - - dollars	
Total		8,000.00	AMER. MFG. CO.	
Discount		80.00	Frank Esenbach	
Net		7,920.00	Treasurer	

Fig. 3-7.   Payment check from accounting department to vendor

Disbursements

The terms of the invoice received from Bennett Electronics were 1/10, n/30; meaning 1 per cent cash discount will be allowed if the purchaser (American Manufacturing Company) pays the invoice within ten days from its date. Otherwise, the purchaser is expected to pay the full amount (in our example, $8,000.00) within thirty days. Cash discounts are designed to encourage prompt payment. This is a common practice used by vendors. When the accounting department receives the invoice, the treasurer approves payment by placing his initials on the check sheet on the "approval for payment" line. The cashier then draws a check and gives it to the treasurer for his signature (Fig. 3-7). The invoice is sent to the bookkeeper who makes an entry, debiting (reducing) the *accounts payable* account by $8,000.00 and crediting (reducing) the *cash* account by the amount of the check ($7,920), and crediting (increasing) the *cash discount* account by $80.00 (1 per cent of $8,000.00) (Fig. 3-8). A summary of the foregoing activities is shown in Fig. 3-9.

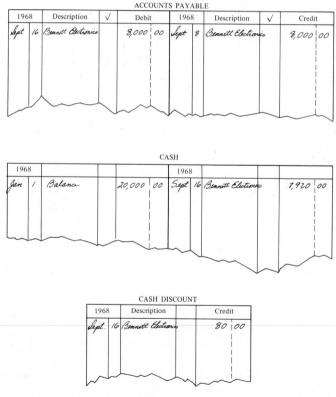

Fig. 3-8. Bookkeeping entries for invoice

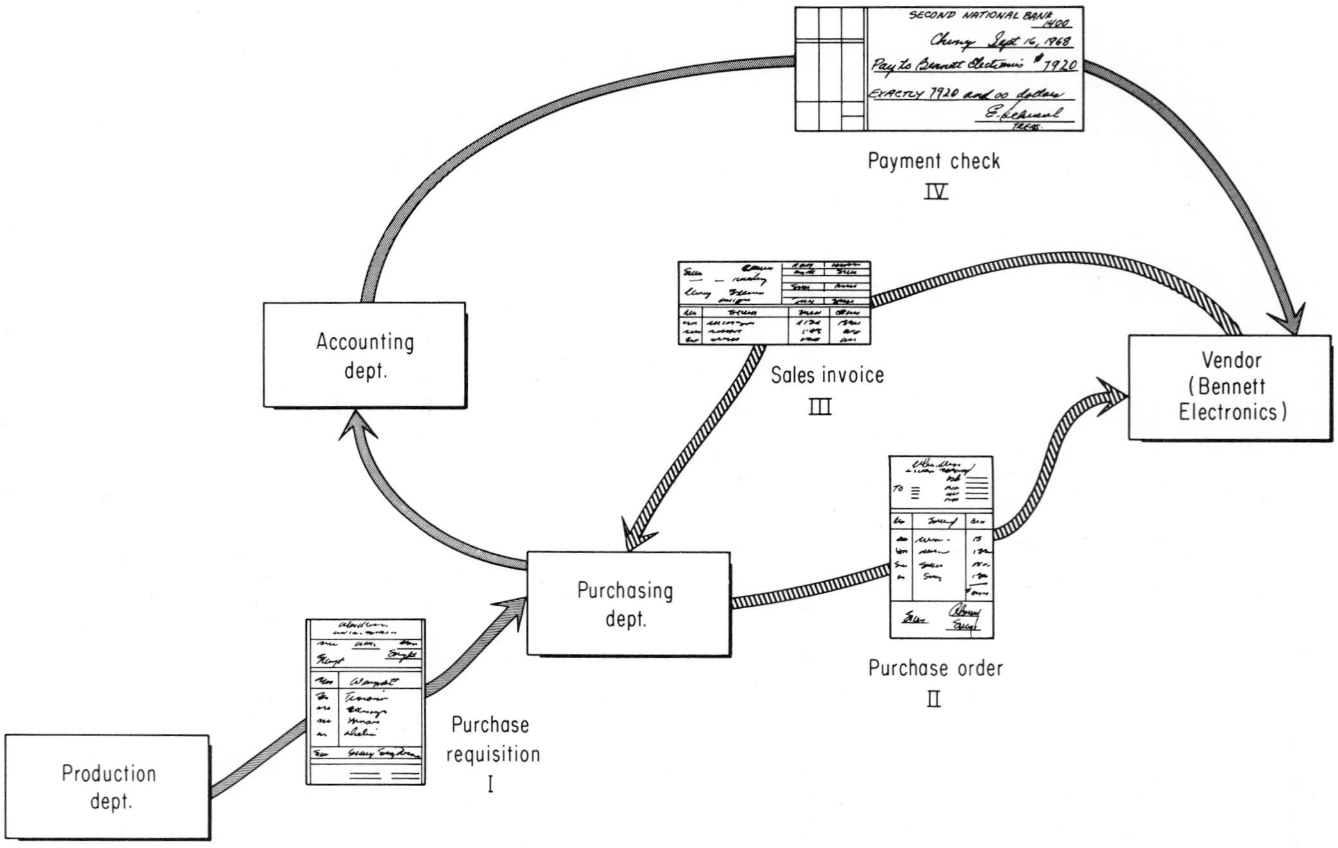

Fig. 3-9. Summary of purchasing operation

Vendor
(Bennett
Electronics)

Payment check
IV

SECOND NATIONAL BANK

Purchase order
II

Sales invoice
III

Purchasing
dept.

Accounting
dept.

Purchase
requisition
I

Production
dept.

Stockkeeping

In addition to the information relayed to the purchasing department, the receiving department sends the stockkeeping department a receiving order, showing the quantity and source of the supplies received. The incoming raw materials and supplies, then, are stored by the stockkeeping department, which, in turn, updates its *stock records* to indicate the net amount of such supplies available. Future *material requisitions* received from the production department effect a credit entry by the amount requisitioned thus showing the amount remaining on hand. The stock clerk sees that the production and other departments get what is needed to prevent any stoppage for lack of materials.

Production

To produce a finished good requires preplanning of several elements:

1. Design and development of the product(s) under consideration.
2. Procurement of machines and tools to manufacture the product.
3. Selection and training of personnel to supervise and handle the machinery and tools.
4. Requisitioning of adequate quantity of raw and other materials and supplies to initiate and continue production.
5. Provision of quality control and maintenance of the production facilities.

The foregoing elements are vital steps, whether the company in question manufactures given products by special order or in advance of anticipated sale. In the former case, a copy of a sales order initiates production. The latter case is the more common type of production. Manufacture of merchandise is initiated by a *production order,* which is usually originated by the production-planning department. The production-planning department, in cooperation with the sales and other involved departments, gathers, evaluates, and forecasts the volume of units to be produced. Once received, the production department requisitions the purchase of needed raw materials which reactivates a series of steps involving the purchasing department, suppliers, receivers, and stockkeeping personnel.

Sales

Finished goods are shipped from the production department to a warehouse where they are stored and from which shipments to customers are carried out. Any goods that are held for sale are packed and shipped upon the receipt of a sales invoice, shipping order, etc.

In manufacturing, a sales transaction is recorded on a form called a *sales invoice.* The sales department, whose primary job is to contact customers and sell merchandise, is made up of a number of salesmen with adequate knowledge about the company products, price discounts, and shipping details. An order is handled by, and involves, the following general steps:

1. The files are checked for the availability of the desired merchandise.
2. A copy of the sales order is handed to the customer for acknowledgment of the order.
3. A copy of the sales order is sent to the warehouse or the shipping department to authorize delivery of the merchandise involved. A shipping order also can be used.
4. The sales department keeps the original copy of the sales order on file for future reference.
5. A copy of the sales invoice is sent to the accounting department for billing.

Billing and Collection

Billing is a manual, punched-card, or electronic operation, involving primarily the preparation of customers' invoices and the charges connected with them. An invoice contains the information which supports the seller's claims for the amount for which the customer is being billed. The general steps in billing, among others, include: (1) recording descriptive details in a coded form and the quantity and unit price of each item; (2) calculating the total price of each item by multiplying unit price times quantity; (3) adding the "total price" column; (4) adding shipping costs and local and state taxes, if any; and (5) adding steps (3) and (4) to the invoice.

Once completed, the invoice is mailed to the customer for collection. Initially, his accounts receivable account shows a debit balance by the amount of the invoice. When the amount is received, the accounts receivable clerk makes an entry on the books crediting the customer's account. Such information later becomes a part of the profit and loss statement under *sales*. Debit balances of *accounts receivable* accounts are shown in the balance sheet under *current assets*.

Delivery

Once authorization to ship a given order has been received, the shipping department packs and transports the goods to the proper destination. The department follows this action by sending a notification of shipment to the sales department or other departments concerned.

The Income Statement

The foregoing sources of data generated a manufacturing and distribution cycle which began with the production of goods and ended in their sale and delivery. This cycle continues as long as the company operates. Since profit is the primary goal, earnings are periodically prepared in the form of a profit and loss or an *income statement*. This statement contains information regarding income from sales, cost of goods sold, general and selling expenses, and Federal income-tax expense. Fig. 3-10 serves as an illustration.

AMERICAN MANUFACTURING COMPANY
Income Statement
For the year ended 12/31/68

Net Sales		$100,000
Cost of Goods Sold:		
Beginning inventory (12/31/67)	$15,000	
Net purchases	8,000	
	$23,000	
Ending inventory (12/31/68)	11,000	
Cost of goods sold		12,000
Gross Profit on Sales		$ 88,000
Selling Expenses	$11,000	
General Expenses	14,000	
Total operating expenses		25,000
Net Income Before Taxes		$ 63,000
Income Tax		21,000
Net Income		$ 42,000

Fig. 3-10. Income statement—an example

The details of the income statement indicate the type and volume of routine and repetitive information which flow through the various departments of a business organization. Integrating these departments (subsystems) and the data they generate, into a data-processing system is a challenge in itself. When done properly, it contributes to minimizing data-processing costs and producing highly effective reports for use in managerial decision-making at all levels.

Organizational Disbursements

In addition to the billing and collecting functions, the accounting department also performs a disbursing role with regard to employee payroll. Payroll involves the determination of employees' earnings. In a practical application, permanent files, containing data such as rate of pay, and number and type of deductions to be made, are used in connection with the data from time cards to compute employees' earnings. The *earnings record,* listing cumulative earnings, deductions, and other relevant data for each employee is used to prepare such statements as Social Security reports, income-tax reports, and the like.

A payroll application is a separate function. Depending on the number of employees, the number of shifts per day, union-company labor agreements, number and type of deductions, and the method used in preparation of the payroll, payroll may constitute a full-time job which justifies its assignment to a subdepartment, called the *payroll department.*

GLOSSARY OF TERMS

DISBURSEMENTS: Payment of financial obligations (for example, invoices).

INCOME STATEMENT: A formal report (summary), showing the net profit or loss of a business during a specific period of time.

MATERIAL REQUISITION: A form sent by the production to the stockkeeping department, requesting needed materials.

PRODUCTION: Operations involving the transforming of raw or semifinished materials into finished products.

PURCHASE ORDER: A form (based on data provided in a purchase requisition) filled out by the purchasing department ordering a specific supplier to ship merchandise.

PURCHASE REQUISITION: A form in which the amount and type of materials needed by a specific department are requested.

PURCHASING: A function consisting of procurement of equipment and supplies for the various departments of an organization.

RECEIVING: A function involving checking and verifying incoming supplies against a purchase order.

SALES INVOICE: A document, indicating the type, quantity, and price of merchandise shipped (sold).

STOCKKEEPING: A function related to the storage of stock and updating the amount of supplies on hand.

SUBSYSTEM: A component of a system (for example, in a punched-card data-processing system, the key punch is a primary component).

SYSTEM: A group of components (procedures or techniques) united by some form of valid interaction to make up an organized whole (entity).

TOTAL-SYSTEMS CONCEPT: Relates management information system by stressing interrelationships between the system-producing information and the system-producing decisions.

REVIEW QUESTIONS

1. What is a system? A subsystem?

2. The institution at which you are a student is looked upon as an open, dynamic, educational system. Illustrate the elements involved and the components which are within the overall framework of its system. What type of interactions does it make with its environment? Explain.

3. Explain briefly the production flow (key operations) that take place in a manufacturing organization. Relate information flow to each of the key operations.

4. Distinguish the difference between the following operations:

   a. purchase requisition vs. material requisition
   b. shipping order   vs. purchase order
   c. stockkeeping   vs. receiving
   d. production order   vs. purchase order
   e. purchase requisition   vs. purchase order
   f. accounts payable   vs. disbursement
   g. billing   vs. invoice payment
   h. production order   vs. shipping order

5. What is an income statement? What type of information does it provide?

chapter

4

THE DATA–
PROCESSING CYCLE
A Manual Approach

DATA ORIGINATION

DATA INPUT

DATA MANIPULATION

SORTING   CALCULATING AND RECORDING   SUMMARIZING
DATA REPORTING AND COMMUNICATING   DATA STORAGE

THE PUNCHED-CARD DATA-PROCESSING CYCLE

EACH ORGANIZATION, LARGE OR SMALL, whether it is a sole proprietorship, partnership, or a corporation, must process data regularly. The processing may be as simple as writing up a credit memorandum or as complex as preparing the payroll of General Motors' employees. Depending on the size of the firm, the volume and frequency of the volume of data involved, the repetition of applications, and the internal and external contacts of the organization, a business firm, generally, has the choice of processing data manually, electromechanically, or electronically by using manual methods, bookkeeping machines, a punched-card system, or a computer.

All factors being equal, a small-size establishment (for example, an ice cream stand or a grocery store) would find immediate need for manual-electromechanical means of data processing, in contrast with large firms (for example, Ford or Eastman Kodak) which find it almost imperative to utilize punched-card systems or computers for handling their large volumes of daily data. Fig. 4-1 serves as a general illustration.

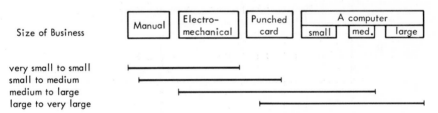

Fig. 4-1. Data-processing needs by size of business

One wonders what it is about data processing (other than volume) that takes so much time? The answer lies in the matter of procedure. Chapter 3 presented the types, make-up, and sources of information flow generated by a business organization. To process the data resulting from this information flow, five separate but related phases, called the data-processing cycle, are usually required. This cycle consists of: (1) data origination, (2) data manipulation, (3) data reporting, (4) data communication, and (5) data storage. Although shortcuts may be used to complete each phase, as well as the work between phases, the overall sequence is, nevertheless, fixed.

Data Origination

Raw data for processing business information are found on original papers (handwritten or typed) called *source documents*. Examples include paychecks, time data, and sales and purchase orders. What types of source documents were generated in the illustration of American Manufacturing Company (Chapter 3)? The production department initiated a purchase requisition, the purchasing department made up a purchase order, the receiving department activated a check sheet, the accounting department received a sales invoice, and the sales department wrote up a sales order and transferred related information to the accounting department for billing and collection; all this information constitutes source data which are later

	Employee No. *4012*					
	Employee Name *Sam Elliott*					
	Dept. *Data Processing*			Week Beginning *Dec. 9, 1968*		
	A.M.		P.M.		EVE.	
M O N	8:00	12:00	1:00	5:00	6:01	7:31
T U E S	8:00	12:01	1:00	5:00		
W E D	8:15	12:01	12:50	5:04	5:30	8:00
T H U R	7:55	12:00	1:00	4:50		
F R I	8:00	12:10	12:55	5:00	6:13	7:43
S A T	8:00	12:30				
S U N						

Fig. 4-2. Data origination—a time card

used for verification of the transactions involved and their manipulation (either manually by a journal entry on the books, or electromechanically by recording them on a punched card or a magnetic tape to be run on a computer) for further action.

Payment for the amount of time worked is based on a fixed hourly rate for the regular working day, plus additional payment (usually one and one-half times the hourly rate) for overtime. As we see in Fig. 4-2, Sam Elliott worked a total of fifty hours during the week beginning December 9, 1968. If the regular workweek is forty hours, his overtime is ten hours.

Data Input

Input data consist of original or source transactions which require processing. Source data are recorded either manually (for example, by use of a pencil) or by a mechanical device (for example, by use of a time clock). Either device is called an input device. In manual data recording, a pencil serves both as an input and as an output device, since it is used both for recording the original data and listing the results obtained from the computations.

Proper recording of data involves: (1) *editing,* that is, deciding on the kind of data that require processing; and (2) *verifying,* checking on the validity and accuracy of such data. In the example regarding Mr. Elliott's time card, the timekeeper would need to compute the total amount of regular time and overtime worked, and verify any related figures, before this information would become a part of the payroll data for further processing.

While editing input data, one should condense (code) as much information as possible. Coding reduces the amount of data to be recorded and processed and is a means of identifying different classes of data. It can be either alphabetic (using letters) or numeric (using numbers), or alphanumeric (using both numbers and alphabetical characters). In Fig. 4-2, Mr. Elliott's employee number is 4012. The first two digits form a code to denote the department of which the employee is a member. The last two digits represent a serial number. Regardless of the type of data-processing equipment used, reading a number is more convenient and more accurate than reading a name, since a given name might, on occasion, belong to two or more employees in the same department.

To illustrate the procedure used in carrying out the data origination and the remaining phases of the cycle, let us assume a manual approach in processing and preparing checks of hourly employees. Most of us must work for a livelihood. Our needs and wants drive us to seek employment by means of which we will be able to acquire the required income to satisfy these needs and wants. These consist of both short-term obligations (for example, buying food and clothes for the family) and long-term commitments (such as installments on a home mortgage or planning for junior's college education). To an employee, then, a salary or a wage represents the amount of time and interest he invests in his employer's business.

Payroll is one of the most important recurrent events in business organizations and is prepared once a week, once every other week, or once a month, depending on the contractual agreement with employees. A business organization faces two types of wage earners: (1) those who receive a salary which does not vary with the amount of time worked; and (2) hourly employees, whose gross incomes are based on the amount of time shown on their time cards.

Basic payroll *data,* thus, *originate* on the time card for a large part of the work force. The time card in Fig. 4-2 serves as a complete record of Sam Elliott's workweek. On Monday, December 9, 1968, he reported to work in the marketing department by punching in at 8:00 A.M. He punched out at 12:00 for lunch, returning at 1:00 P.M., and punched out again at 5:00 P.M. He worked one and one-half hours of overtime in the evening.

From the foregoing discussion, then, we can conclude that the source document represents input to a data-processing system. Under a manual data-processing system, at the end of the last day of the week the payroll department collects employee time cards from all departments. The remaining steps result in processing the data that are used to prepare the employee's paycheck.

Data Manipulation

After data have been recorded, they are grouped into categories or classes. This precedes the sorting step if the need for classifying is anticipated at the time of recording of data. One of the ways in which recorded data are classified is by department. Sam Elliott's time card is one of many time cards handled in the data-processing department. Assume that there are two other departments: production (employee numbers range from 5001-5025) and purchasing (employee numbers range from 6001-6040).[1] To classify the whole set of time cards by department, we rearrange them as shown in Fig. 4-3.

Manipulation is related to the actual work performed on input data and involves the following steps: (1) sorting, (2) calculating, (3) summarizing, (4) reporting, and (5) storage.

---

[1] Bear in mind that the first two digits (high-order digits) of each employee's number denote his department.

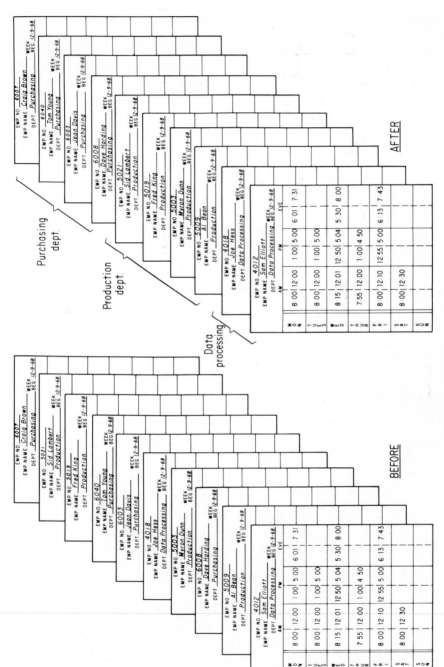

Fig. 4-3. Classifying by department—an example

69

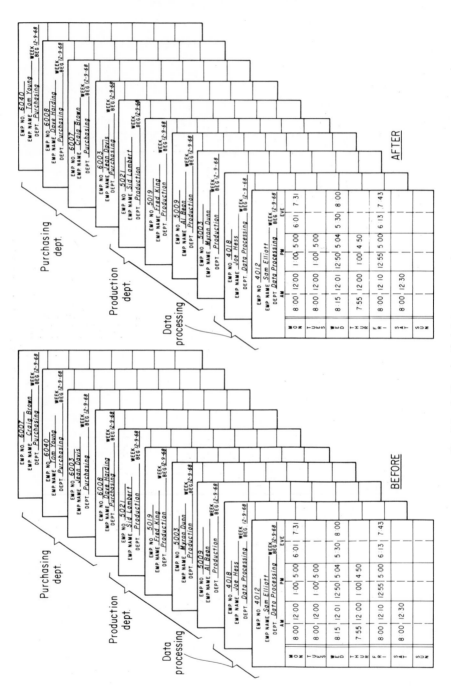

Fig. 4-4. Sorting classified data—an example

Sorting

Sorting involves sequencing information in a predetermined order (alphabetic or numeric). Once the time cards have been classified by department, sorting each of the decks of the three departments would make the completion of the job easier, and would facilitate future filing chores (Fig. 4-4). After the deck has been sorted in sequence, the payroll clerk can handle each group separately, compute the amount of time worked, and calculate the earnings of each employee.

Manual sorting is time consuming and, although practiced by many small business establishments, is not an efficient way of manipulating data for large firms. Motivated by the factors of accuracy, economy, and speed, large firms use the more efficient and sophisticated mechanical, electro-mechanical, or electronic sorting techniques.

Calculating and Recording

The step of *calculating and recording* involves reconstruction of data through the arithmetic processes of addition, subtraction, multiplication, and/or division. It is the most crucial phase of data manipulation since it is at this step that most of the work is done to achieve the solution to the problem; that is, the correct amount of the paycheck after deductions.

In a manual system, the classified and sorted set of time cards next is used to determine the gross pay, the amount of deductions, and the take-home (net) pay of each employee. Gross pay is computed by multiplying the number of hours reported on the time card by the hourly rate. In Fig. 4-2, Sam Elliott worked forty regular and ten overtime hours. So, for a five-day workweek (at the rate of $4.00 per hour), his gross regular pay would be:

$$\text{Regular payment } 40 \times \$4.00 = \$160.00$$
$$\text{Overtime payment } 10 \times \$6.00 = 60.00$$
$$\text{Total gross pay for the week} \quad \underline{\underline{\$220.00}}$$

Net pay is computed by subtracting from the total gross pay the Federal withholding tax, Social Security tax (F.I.C.A.), union dues, health insurance premiums, and other deductions. The amount of the take-home pay is printed on the right section of a two-part form, called the *check*. Details of the deductions are shown on the left part of the form, called the *stub* (Fig. 4-5). The payroll department records detailed payroll data of all employees in a special journal to be used later in preparing income tax and other reports.

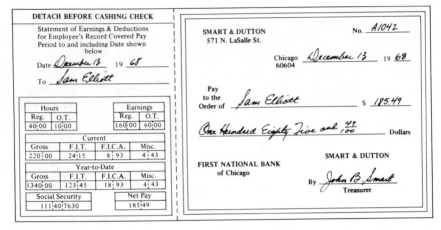

Fig. 4-5. A paycheck—an example

Summarizing

Summarizing is compressing a mass of data into a meaningful and useful form. It involves listing (tabulating) related information and figuring out its total. Management finds summarized lists or reports extremely helpful and time saving and uses them to make decisions more quickly than could be possible if every detail had to be looked over. In a payroll report, for example, an administrator would want specific figures regarding the total amount paid toward wages and salaries for a given week. The recorded payroll details are used to prepare such a report. These payroll reports indicate, by department, who earned which amount, but generally delete mention of deductions, amount of time worked, and the like. Thus, the detailed payroll data could be *summarized* into totals which offer useful information.

Data Reporting and Communicating

Once summaries of data have been prepared, they represent output information and are reported to the user(s). No output is useful unless communicated promptly and effectively to the people involved. Failure to do so is as wasteful and useless as a college student who takes courses for credit but ignores taking the exams.

One major output of a payroll application is the employee paycheck. Fig. 4-5 shows Sam Elliott's net pay of $185.49. He detaches and cashes the check, while retaining the stub for future reference.

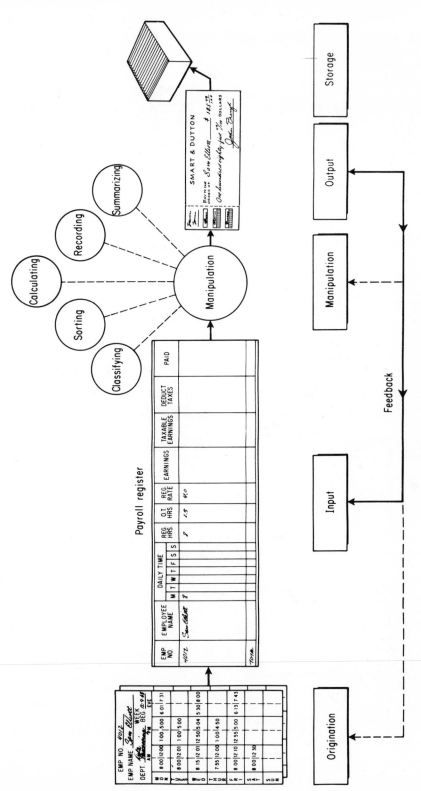

Fig. 4-6. Summary of data-processing cycle

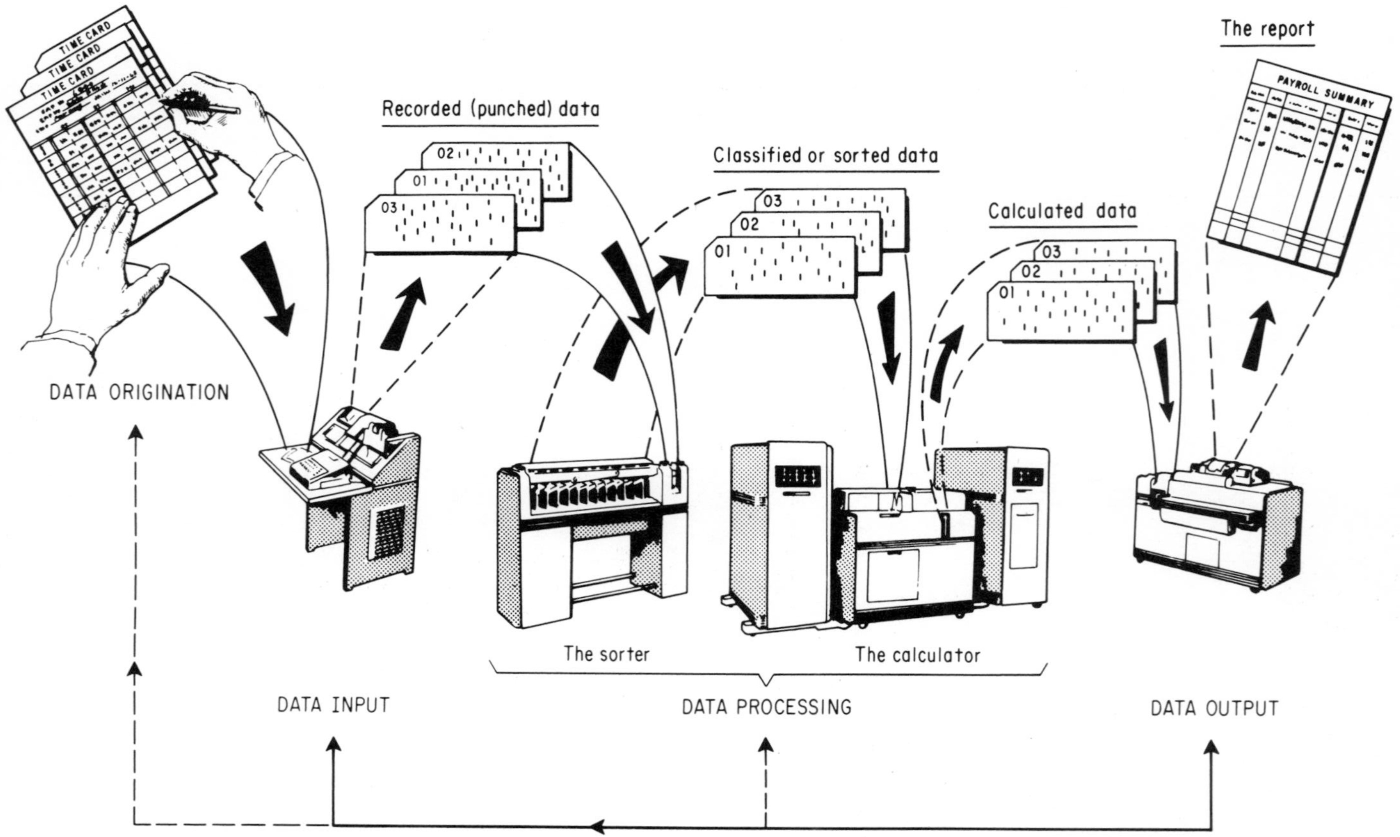

The report

PAYROLL SUMMARY

Calculated data

03
02
01

Classified or sorted data

03
02
01

The calculator

The sorter

Recorded (punched) data

02
01
03

TIME CARD
TIME CARD
TIME CARD

DATA ORIGINATION

DATA INPUT

DATA PROCESSING

DATA OUTPUT

Fig. 4-7. Punched-card data-processing cycle—a summary

Data Storage

The reporting and communicating of output data terminates the data-processing cycle (Fig. 4-6). This step is followed by the storage of existing data for future retrieval. Data storage can be made *manually* (for example, the use of a ledger book), *electromechanically* (in punched cards), or in an *electronic* computer memory.

Before stored data are used again, a comparison is made between the initial objectives and the output. Any detection of discrepancy is analyzed, corrected, and fed back to the proper stage in the operation. This action is referred to as the *feedback concept* of control. It is a vital step in following up on essential information and helps to ascertain consistency and accuracy of the information sought.

In recycling an operation, often the output of the previous machine run becomes the input (raw) data of a new one. This is analogous to unsold (ending) inventory of a retail store at the end of the year becoming the beginning inventory available for sale on the first day of the next year.

The steps making up the data-processing cycle are shown in summary form in Fig. 4-6. They are basic to the use of any system of data processing. Thus, they must be performed no matter whether the approach used is manual, mechanical, electromechanical, or electronic through punched-card machines, or computers.

The Punched-card Data-processing Cycle

The foregoing presentation emphasized the data-processing cycle in a manual system. Like the function of any other system, the manual system simply showed a regular, orderly way of preparing the weekly payroll. Payroll originated on the employee time cards and was classified into arbitrary groups or classes. Next, the amount of hours worked was computed and, using the hourly rate, the gross pay of each employee was calculated. The gross pay was reduced by the total amount of deductions, leaving the net pay. A check, showing all pertinent details, was drawn and handed to the employee(s) concerned. Follow-up reports were finally prepared and communicated to management, and any pertinent data were placed in storage for future reference.

The data-processing cycle employed in a punched-card data-processing system simulates that used in the manual system, with the exception that data are processed by means of punched-card machines which are electromechanical in nature. The punched-card data-processing cycle goes through the following stages:

Stage 1: Data origination and input. Source documents such as time cards or sales invoices are prepared manually (using a pencil and paper or a typewriter) and recorded on punched cards or punched paper tape.

Stage 2: Data processing. Once input cards are prepared, input machines (for example, a card sorter, collator, or punched paper-tape reader) read and manipulate (sort, classify, calculate, and summarize) the data they contain.

Stage 3: Data output. The result of data manipulation is some form of meaningful output in the form of a printed report or a general summary (Fig. 4-7).

GLOSSARY OF TERMS

DATA INPUT: The feeding of source data into an organized data-processing system.

DATA MANIPULATION: The performance of all necessary routines on input data.

DATA ORIGINATION: Determination of the nature (origin) of source data.

DATA PROCESSING: Information handling. Any operation(s) on data designed to achieve pronounced objectives.

DATA-PROCESSING CYCLE: The sequence of required steps in manipulation of valid data.

EDITING: The deciding on of the kind of data to be processed and the checking of its validity and accuracy.

GROSS PAY: The total amount (based on regular and overtime rates) earned by an employee before deductions.

NET PAY: The difference between gross pay and total deductions.

PAYCHECK: A negotiable instrument initiated by an employer ordering a specific bank to pay the amount written on the face of the check.

PAYROLL: A list of employees showing their earnings for a stated period together with other relevant data.

SORTING: Arranging information in alphabetic or numeric sequence.

SOURCE DOCUMENT: An original paper (for example, a sales slip) on which details of a transaction are recorded.

STUB: A detachable portion of a paycheck, on which earnings and deductions are recorded for reference.

SUMMARIZING: Compressing a mass of data into a meaningful and useful form.

TIME CARD: A source document showing the amount of time an employee worked.

REVIEW QUESTIONS

1. What general factors determine the choice of the type of data-processing system? Relate your ideas to a specific organization. Lay out your assumptions and explain the reason(s) for the choice you made.
2. What procedure is involved in carrying out the data-origination phase? What other phases are involved in a data-processing cycle?
3. What is the difference between data origination and data input?
4. What operations are generally included in data manipulation? Explain the role of data manipulation in the preparation of an income statement.
5. What elements constitute a paycheck? Who is involved? What is involved? What type of payroll data is made available with the check?
6. Contrast the steps involved in a manual and a punched-card data-processing cycle. What differences (if any) exist between the two cycles (or systems)? What possible advantages does each cycle provide? What type or size of firm is likely to adopt each system?

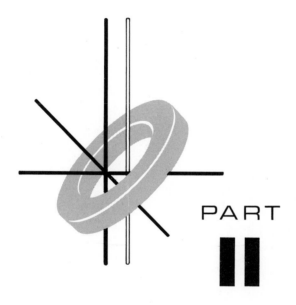

PART

II

Punched-card
Data
Processing

chapter

5

THE
PUNCHED CARD

WHAT IS A PUNCHED CARD?

TYPES OF PUNCHED CARDS   COLUMNS   PUNCHING POSITIONS
EDGES AND FACES

METHOD OF RECORDING DATA ON CARDS

THE HOLLERITH CODE   NUMERIC AND ALPHABETIC RECORDING OF
INFORMATION   Coding Tables   IBM Numeric Coding   IBM
Alphabetic Coding   UNIT-RECORD PRINCIPLE

CARD LAYOUT REQUIREMENTS

FIELD   TYPES OF INFORMATION

CARD DESIGN

IDENTIFYING MARKS   CONTROL FIELDS

USE OF PUNCHED CARDS

DETAIL CARDS   MARK-SENSED CARDS   STUB CARDS   SUMMARY
CARDS

THE NEED FOR THE PUNCHED CARD AND PUNCHED-
CARD EQUIPMENT IN DATA PROCESSING

ADVANTAGES AND LIMITATIONS OF PUNCHED-CARD
DATA PROCESSING

PEOPLE WHO HAVE NOT COME INTO CONTACT with punched cards are rare or nonexistent. Such cards are used extensively as paychecks, time cards, soap coupons, gasoline credit cards, utility bills, *Reader's Digest* or *Time Magazine* bills, and even as tickets for use on turnpikes.

Despite the popularity of, and demand for, computers, punched-card data-processing systems are used extensively. For many users, a punched-card system fulfills their needs both from the standpoint of performance and of economy. Most computer systems rely on punched cards to record the programmer's instructions on tape so that their input devices can convey the instructions to their processing units. At present, although technologically possible, recording instructions to the computer directly on tape is not commercially feasible. Therefore, an understanding of the punched card, and punched-card techniques, is necessary if computer operations are to be understood.

What Is a Punched Card?

Basically, a punched card (also called a tab card) is a rectangular pasteboard of high-quality paper able to resist contraction or expansion owing to temperature or humidity. It measures 7⅜ inches long by 3¼ inches wide by .007 inches thick. Fig. 5-1 is a replica of an IBM card. Notice that the upper right corner is cut. This cut is used primarily as a visual aid to assure the machine operator that all cards in the deck are facing the same direction. Although most unit-record machines do not sense a corner cut, some specially designed machines halt automatically upon detection of a cut in the wrong position. Other visual aids used to increase accurate handling of punched cards include the use of colored cards and striped cards, which are designed to identify better a particular deck of cards or the deck from which a particular card was extracted. To facilitate card handling and processing, cards with round, as well as square, corners are now available.

The punched card is a *unit record* because *only the data related to one transaction* are recorded on a given card. In the illustration given in Chapter 1 involving the customer who bought a $100 suit, three transactions ensued, thus requiring the use of three cards. The first card was prepared at the time of sale. It was merged with a second card—the customer's payment card—on January 15, to determine the unpaid balance. A third card was used on January 31 when the customer paid the balance on the suit. The updated card replaced the other two cards, which were

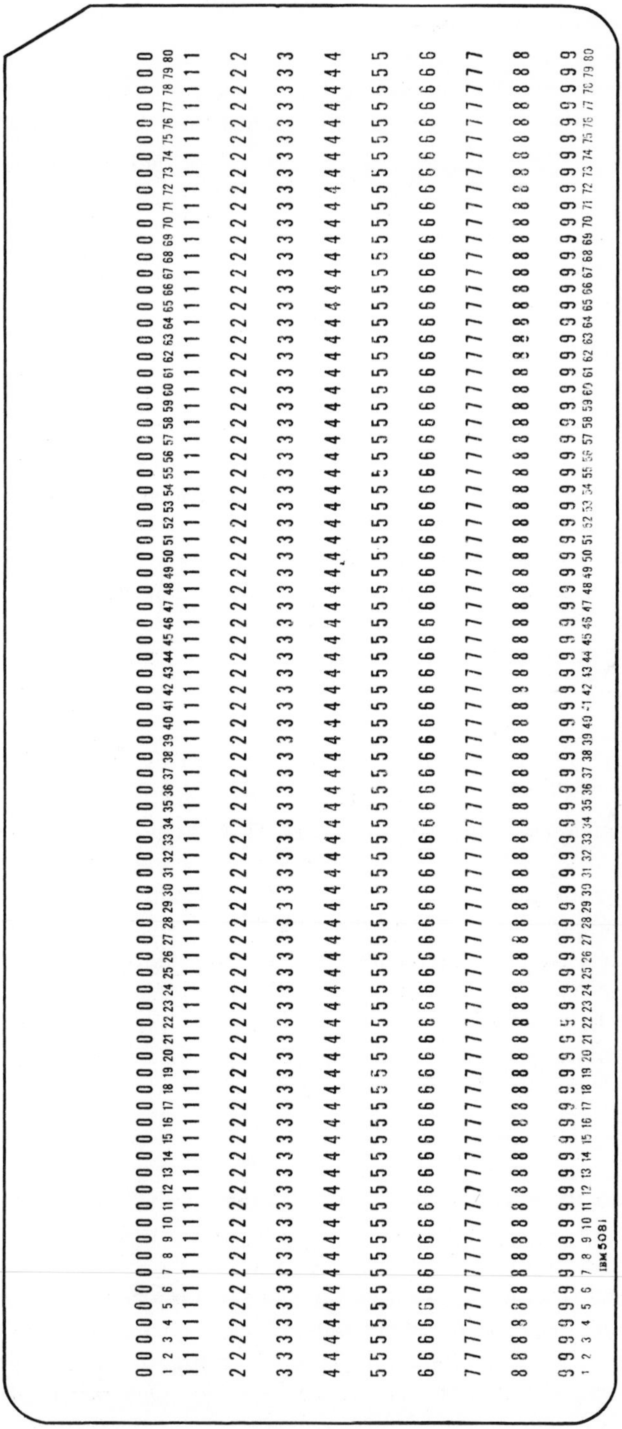

Fig. 5-1. IBM card—actual size

discarded or left in a separate file for future reference. The information on the updated cards in the customers' files is available for several purposes; that is, to determine total sales: (1) for each salesman, (2) for each district, or (3) for all salesmen regardless of district.

Types of Punched Cards

The two major manufacturers of punched cards and punched-card equipment in the United States are: the International Business Machines Corporation, and the UNIVAC Division of Sperry Rand Corporation. The cards of the two differ in that the holes in the IBM cards are rectangular and the ones in the Sperry Rand cards are round. Further, the IBM card is divided into eighty vertical columns, and the Sperry Rand card is divided into an upper row of forty-five columns and a lower row of forty-five columns—a total of ninety columns.

Late in 1966, the UNIVAC Division announced it was dropping the ninety-column round-hole design and discontinuing production of related equipment. The new UNIVAC punched-card line is designed as an eighty-column (rectangular-hole) card—thus making it more adaptive to the IBM card system.

Columns

The IBM card is divided into eighty vertical spaces called *columns*. The columns are numbered horizontally from left to right: one to eighty. In each column one letter, one digit, or a special character can be stored, making a total of eighty characters per card. For example, suppose we wish to punch in a card employee number 40875. Because each column can store only one character, five columns would be required to store 40875. In fact, any five consecutive columns in the card would qualify. If we decided to use the first five columns for that purpose, then digit *4* would be punched in column one, digit *0* in column two, digit *8* in column three, digit *7* in column four, and digit *5* in column five.

Punching Positions

In addition to the card's eighty vertical columns, the IBM card is also divided into *two punching positions:* (1) the zone punching position, and (2) the digit punching position. See Fig. 5-2.

The zone punching position consists of three horizontal rows, two of which are used for zone punching only. They represent the gap on the top of the card. The first row from the top is called *row twelve*. The next one, row eleven, is commonly called the *"X* row." One punch in row *X* (referred to as *X punch*) in a selected column (one to eighty) is often used

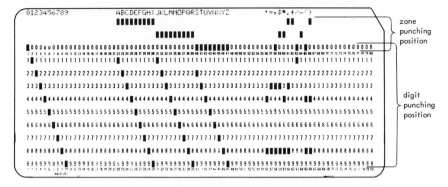

Fig. 5-2. Punching positions of an IBM card

to distinguish a given card(s) from the remaining cards of the deck. The third row is known as the "zero row" and can be used *either* as a zone punching position or a digit punching position.

The digit punching position consists of ten horizontal rows, numbered vertically, to accommodate the digits *0-9* which correspond to the printed numbers on the card. Row zero accommodates digit *0;* row one, digit *1;* row two, digit *2;* and so forth.

Edges and Faces

The top edge of a punched card is called the *twelve-edge;* the bottom edge is called the *nine-edge,* to identify it with row nine. This is used to determine the side of the card which should be fed into the machine. Some machines process data on a card by feeding it in twelve-edge first and others by feeding it in nine-edge first. *Face-up* means that the printed side of the card faces up as it is placed in the feed hopper. *Face-down* means that the printed side of the card faces down as it is placed in the feed hopper. Thus, if a machine processes data on a card "twelve-edge first, face up," the printed side of the card is up and the edge that is closest to row twelve is fed in first.

Method of Recording Data in Cards

As was mentioned in Chapter 1, the main difficulties faced in the processing of data arise from lack of standardization of information in source documents. This is the result of: (1) the need to record several different transactions on a given report, (2) the various methods used to record information, and (3) the use of different sizes of paper forms for recording information. For specific datum to be processed and reported quickly and accurately, the recording of it is standardized by punching holes on a standard-sized card with only one transaction on each card.

The recording of data is accomplished by a key-punch machine in a coded arrangement of punched holes in data-processing cards. Once data are punched, the card becomes a permanently stored reference and can then be taken out of "storage" and duplicated when desired. Such a punched card acts as a medium of communication between the operators and the accounting or other specialized machines. In other words, the punched cards enable men to feed information about certain subjects directly to the proper special-purpose machines for processing so that these machines can *feed back* accurate answers to the problem involved. The former procedure is called *input;* the latter, *output.*

Data must be recorded on a card by using a key-punch machine to punch holes in certain areas in it. Data cannot be written on the card manually, because a machine cannot "read" handwriting. The holes, representing information, are "read" easily and accurately by the machine, because a predetermined machine code enables the key-punch operator to place every alphabetic, numeric, or special character in its proper location so that a special-purpose machine may treat the information mechanically in the way desired.

The Hollerith Code

The machine code used to store information on an IBM card is referred to as the *Hollerith code.* Dr. Herman Hollerith devised the technique of storing certain data in a standard-sized card by following a predetermined code to punch holes in specific locations on it.

Numeric and Alphabetic Recording of Information

Numbers are recorded in a card by punching only *one hole* in a column for each digit. If we need to store, for example, a nine-digit serial number in a card, it would require nine holes in any nine consecutive columns. The punched holes are made in the digit punching position.

If *alphabetic data* are to be recorded, it requires *two holes* in any column for *each letter* of the alphabet. For example, the word *HORSE* punched in a card requires five consecutive columns with *two holes* in each. One must be in the *zone* punching position and the other in the *digit* punching position. In other words, *one hole* is required to *store a digit* in a column, while *two holes* are required to *store a letter* in that column. This technique is standard on all IBM cards and is based on the Hollerith theory of machine coding.

Coding tables

To describe the machine language more clearly, separate tables are presented, one entitled *numeric coding* (Fig. 5-3) and the other *alphabetic coding* (Figs. 5-5—5-7).

IBM Numeric Coding Table

Digit	Digit Punching Position	Zone Pch. Pos.	Row
0	yes	no	0
1	yes	no	1
2	yes	no	2
3	yes	no	3
4	yes	no	4
5	yes	no	5
6	yes	no	6
7	yes	no	7
8	yes	no	8
9	yes	no	9

Fig. 5-3. IBM numeric coding

IBM numeric coding

If we are to punch the number *14036* in columns thirteen to seventeen, for example, we would proceed as follows:

Column 13 would have a hole punched in row 1 for digit *1*.
Column 14 would have a hole punched in row 4 for digit *4*.
Column 15 would have a hole punched in row 0 for digit *0*.
Column 16 would have a hole punched in row 3 for digit *3*.
Column 17 would have a hole punched in row 6 for digit *6*.

Fig. 5-4 is a partial IBM card, showing the results of following the instructions in the above table.

Fig. 5-4. Numeric coding illustration

IBM alphabetic coding

Because there are three zone rows for punching alphabetic characters in the card, that is, row twelve, row eleven, and row zero, the alphabet is divided into three parts, each part containing the number of letters equal to the number of rows in the digit punching position. This is done because *two holes are needed in a given column to represent a letter.* Depending upon the letter in mind, one of the two holes must be in row twelve, eleven, or zero, and the other hole must be in row one, two, three, four, five, six, seven, eight, or nine. Any set of columns may be used for any one of the three alphabetic groupings.

The three parts of the alphabet are:

> *A-I* (first nine letters)
> *J-R* (second nine letters)
> *S-Z* (remaining eight letters)

The letters *A* through *I* are each coded by punching a hole in row twelve and another hole directly below in rows one through nine, respectively. For example, letter *A* would be coded by a hole in row twelve and a hole in row one directly below. Letter *B* would be coded by a hole in row twelve and a hole in row two directly below, and so on for the remaining letters of the alphabet.

Letter	Zone Pch. Pos. in Row	Digit Pch. Pos. in Row
A	12	1
B	12	2
C	12	3
D	12	4
E	12	5
F	12	6
G	12	7
H	12	8
I	12	9

Fig. 5-5. Alphabetic coding—A-I

In Fig. 5-5 the first part of the alphabet, *A* through *I,* is coded by using row twelve for the first, or zone punch, and rows one through nine for the digit punch.

At this point, as is apparent, letter *I* occupies the last usable row on the card. In order to code the second group of letters, *J* through *R,* we

Letter	Zone Pch. Pos. in Row	Digit Pch. Pos. in Row	
J	11	1	
K	11	2	
L	11	3	
M	11	4	
N	11	5	
O	11	6	
P	11	7	
Q	11	8	
R	11	9	

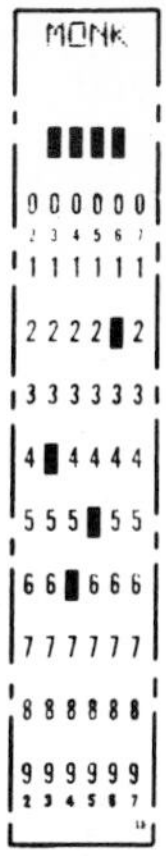

Fig. 5-6. Alphabetic coding—J-R

Letter	Zone Pch. Pos. in Row	Digit Pch. Pos. in Row	
S	0	2	
T	0	3	
U	0	4	
V	0	5	
W	0	6	
X	0	7	
Y	0	8	
Z	0	9	

Fig. 5-7. Alphabetic coding—S-Z

must start with row one again, using row eleven for the zone punch instead of row twelve, and rows one through nine for the digit punch (Fig. 5-6).

Letter *R* now occupies the last row on the card. In order to code the remaining letters, *S* through *Z,* we must, therefore, start over again, using row zero for the zone punch and rows two through nine for the digit punch (Fig. 5-7). Because there are only eight letters left in the third alphabetic group, the IBM Corporation decided to use rows two through nine instead of rows one through eight for the digit punch. This was done, possibly, to avoid punching holes too close to each other, as would be the case if rows zero and one were used, because in the early machines accuracy was sometimes sacrificed if holes were punched too closely together. For this reason, a gap was decided upon and has become a part of the standard procedure, even though modern key-punch machines have been improved to such an extent that the proximity of the holes no longer makes any difference.

We should point out that any set of columns can be used for recording any one word, as the following discussion shows. To illustrate, see how the word *ACID* is stored in columns seventeen through twenty (Fig. 5-5); the word *MONK,* in columns three through six (Fig. 5-6); and the word *STY* (Fig. 5-7), in columns seventy through seventy-two. In *ACID, A* is stored by punching a hole in row twelve (the zone) and one directly below it in column seventeen (the digit). Any other columns could have been used. The above predetermined code is built into present-day key-punch machines so that all an operator must do is press the proper letter of the alphabet on the keyboard and the holes appear in the card as described. Try using the tables to code the word *INVOICE* to see if you get the idea.

Unit-record Principle

As mentioned earlier in this chapter, a punched card is a unit record, because it represents only one transaction. Also, because it is mobile, it can be merged with cards containing different information for the purpose of calculating or summarizing data. The accompanying Fig. 5-8 illustrates an invoice containing six transactions between Do-It-Yourself, Inc., and Mr. Robert Lee Honeywell. The fifty-watt amplifier transaction is used to demonstrate how each transaction is entered in a separate card. For this invoice, six cards would be required to record all the information it contains. For future processing, each of these transactions must first be punched on a card in the same manner as has been done for the one involving the fifty-watt amplifier.

Card Layout Requirements

The cards themselves must be of a predetermined format so that each *unit of information* occupies the same position on all cards representing any given transaction. If the customer's number occupies columns one-five, it must always be punched in that location, and this area should not be used for any other data. Standardizing the location of certain data in a specific location on a card is as important as standardizing the signature location of the bottom right side of a check or placing a postage stamp on the top right corner of a regular mail envelope. This leads us to the important concept of "field."

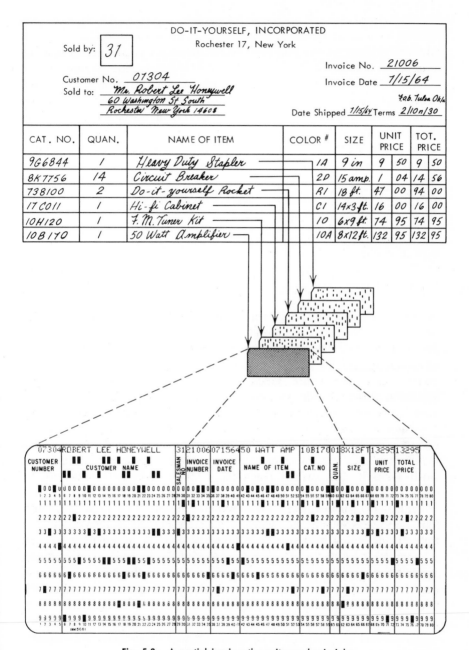

Fig. 5-8. A partial invoice—the unit-record principle

Field

Any one transaction contains a certain number of details called *units of information*. A *field* is a group of consecutive card columns reserved for *a specific unit of information*. Because the punched card in Fig. 5-8 contains eleven *units of information* related to the last transaction in the invoice, eleven fields are used, occupying, in this instance, seventy-seven of the eighty columns available. The length of the field depends on the maximum length of the unit of information. The minimum length of a field is one column and the maximum is the size of the card, or eighty columns.

Types of Information

All information is of two types: fixed and variable. Fixed (or reference) data never change in regard to any one customer. They include, for example, such items as: (1) customer's name and address, (2) mode of transporting merchandise, (3) source of merchandise, (4) catalog number, and (5) description of merchandise ordered. Variable (or classification) data, on the other hand, are information which is subject to change and which permits classifying and summarizing of homogeneous data. For instance, they include: (1) date of the invoice, (2) quantity of each item ordered, (3) quantity sold, (4) transportation charges, (5) terms of payment, and other items of this nature. Fixed information is usually put in the card, beginning at the left side, variable information at the right side, including quantitative information (such as total price) in the extreme right column.

The first field in Fig. 5-8 is the customer-number field. The decision was to make this a five-column field because, in this case, it was assumed that, within the foreseeable future, the number of potential customers of Do-It-Yourself, Inc., would reach the 10,000 mark, but would not be likely to exceed 99,999. Recording a four-digit customer number (for example, 4461) in columns one-five requires the use of columns two, three, four, and five. Column one, which is currently unused, is punched with a zero.[1] In designing fields for the storage of units of information, enough columns must be allotted to each field so that the longest group of digits, or alphabetic characters, can be accommodated. If the current or future need for recording several units exceeds the length of the card, abbreviations of names and other information, where possible, is the normal procedure.

[1] Others use a skip of column one and punch the *4461* in columns two, three, four, and five, the importance being that of an established policy in reference to the above.

Card Design

Because a machine cannot think, it does not make any real difference where a certain fact is punched or in what sequence certain fields are presented. The normal procedure, however, is to lay out the fields in the same sequence as they appear in the source document. This makes it much easier, faster, and more convenient for the key-punch operator to punch the data into the card from the source document. Hence, the expense of key punching is lowered. The process of recording data from source documents is the initial step in the conversion routine and can be very annoying and frustrating to the key-punch operator if the various units of information in the document have to be punched in locations on the card that are out of sequence with the information as presented in the source document.

Identifying Marks

A card may be identified by its format, by different colors, by different corner cuts, by horizontal color stripes, or by a control field. The format shows the way the various fields are arranged on a card and distinguishes it from the other cards which enter the processing routine. For example, in a banking application, a name-and-address card may have basically a customer-number field, name field, a home-address field, and a business-address field; whereas a loan card may have a customer-number field, name field, amount-of-the-loan field, number-of-payments field, and amount-of-each-payment field. In addition to having a different format, the name-and-address card may be visually distinguished by a blue stripe while the loan card may have a yellow stripe. On the other hand, different-colored cards may be used to designate the different kinds of cards.

Control Fields

A control field aids in the location and *reassembling* of a group of cards which has been merged previously with other groups of cards containing all kinds of information for processing. You frequently hear of an X punch in column eighty or an X punch in column twenty-seven. This denotes that only certain cards in a group have an X punched in column eighty or in column twenty-seven. Assume a group of cards containing information on each employee of a firm, including managers, foremen, and the rank-and-file employees. Assume further that, at the end of the year, the board of directors decides to grant a $500 bonus to managers only. In order to enable the machine to select the managers' cards out of all the cards, some distinctive code must be placed on the managers' cards which would not appear in any other group of cards. Usually, this coding is done by punching an X in a column reserved for that purpose. In this example, let us assume the use of column eighty as the X column. Once an X is punched in column eighty of each manager's card in the group, the process of picking these cards out by the machine becomes a simple matter. Every time the machine reads an X in column eighty, it ejects the card containing it into a separate pocket, leaving the other cards to drop undisturbed into another pocket.

Use of Punched Cards

Punched cards have several uses. The type of use depends on the reports and procedures required. The four common types are discussed below.

Detail Cards

Detail cards are commonly used in inventory control where each item in stock is represented by a punched card containing reference and quantitative data. The card at the bottom of Fig. 5-8 is a detail card. It can also be called a transcript card if the key-punch operator punched the data it contains from a source document.

Mark-sensed Cards

Mark-sensed cards are usually used in reproducing small quantities of numeric information and are punched automatically by the reproducer upon sensing the marks made with an electrographic pencil in designated locations on the face of the card.

Stub Cards

Stub cards are adapted to situations requiring stubs which substitute for a receipt. Most of the bills (for example, water and telephone bills) have a perforated stub which when torn off leaves a regular card which is mailed back to the company with a check for the required amount. Banks have made wide use of this type of card. A number of prepunched perforated cards represent the installments a borrower agrees to pay. The set is stapled on the left stub edge in a booklet form.

Summary Cards

Summary cards represent totals or accumulated results of data read from detail cards or a combination of detail and transaction cards. The accounting machine is connected to the reproducer and wired to allow summarized information to be punched.

The Need for the Punched Card and Punched-card Equipment in Data Processing

Key-punch equipment which is used to punch information in cards is needed in both punched-card processing and electronic processing. Recording of data must be standardized in this manner before either punched-card machines or electronic machines can handle it. The key-punch machines are designed in such a way that either numeric or alphabetic coding can be punched by them. Some are designed to punch only. However, the latest models are designed either to punch only or to print and punch simultaneously. If it is desired to print at the same time as the card is punched, the operator need only depress the "A" key in order that the machine punch the proper holes for *A* in the column selected and print the letter *A* simultaneously. Referring to the previous examples, the words *acid, monk,* and *sty* can be printed on the card at the same time as the holes are being punched if this is so desired. If not, the operator need only suppress a switch and the machine will punch but not print. In the event that the information is printed and punched at the same time, no intermediate machine is needed to read the holes in order to print the proper information, as is the case if the card is punched only. After being key punched, the cards can be immediately processed in the proper special-purpose punched-card or electronic machines which read the holes and proceed according to predetermined instructions.

Advantages and Limitations of Punched-card Processing

The use of the punched card in processing business information offers the advantage of standardization of data into a form for more efficient processing. Although the card can store only eighty characters, each character can be a code which actuates a machine to perform a specific function or a series of functions.

The primary limitation of the punched card is the way it is constructed. It may not be folded, spindled, mutilated, or stapled at all. Any change in the overall smoothness of the card could jam the machine used in processing the data it contains. A further limitation is the size of a punched card; maximum storage capacity of eighty characters is actually inefficient since up to 2,000 characters can be "typed" on it.

Finally, requiring data to be punched in specified fields further limits the number of characters that can be stored. For example, assume that the first six columns of a card are a customer's account number, and that in most current accounts, customers' account numbers range from four to five columns in length. In such a case, the sixth column (column one) has had to be left blank, or punched with zero for consistency, and cannot be used for other purposes. Since applications involve thousands of customer accounts, much waste results from rigid standardization of data location in cards.

GLOSSARY OF TERMS

CARD COLUMN: One of eighty vertical areas on a card for storing a character of information.

CONTROL PUNCH: A specific code punched in a card to cause a machine to perform a specific routine.

CORNER CUT: A diagonal cut at the top edge of a card to facilitate visual or a special rail-brush identification.

DETAIL CARD: A card containing detailed information about a specific transaction or account.

DIGIT PUNCHING POSITION: The area on a card reserved to store a decimal digit.

FIELD: A group of consecutive columns reserved for a specific purpose.

HOLLERITH CODE: A punched-card code in which a character is represented by one or more rectangular holes punched in a vertical column.

INPUT: Data entered into a valid system for processing.

MARK SENSING: Cards on which marks made by a special electrographic pencil are shown in designated locations. Mark-sensed spots are then converted by reproducing (punching) the data they represent into the same card.

NINE-EDGE: The bottom edge of a card.

OUTPUT: The result of a processing operation.

PUNCHED CARD: A standard-sized medium, on which input or output data can be stored.

STUB CARD: A card perforated so that a detachable portion can be used as a receipt for reference.

SUMMARY CARD: A card summarizing data read from detail cards.

TWELVE-EDGE: Top edge of a card.

X PUNCH: See *control punch*. Also, a punch in the second card row (one row below the top row) of a Hollerith card.

ZONE PUNCHING POSITIONS: The rows zero, eleven, and twelve punching positions (for coding alphabetic data) on an eighty-column card.

REVIEW QUESTIONS

1. Describe the punched card. Give two examples of its use.
2. Why is a standard punched card necessary? Explain briefly.

3. Explain the role of the punched card in the recording stage.

4. What is the Hollerith code? Why was it called so?

5. How many columns does an IBM card contain? How many data can be punched in each column?

6. Describe the two punching positions of an IBM card. Why are they used? Explain.

7. What is meant by "nine-edge first, face down"? What is meant by twelve-edge first, face up"?

8. How is alphabetic recording of data different from the numeric recording in a card? Explain briefly.

9. What is the unit-record principle?

10. An order form contains seven different types of merchandise ordered by a given customer. How many cards would be required to record them for further processing?

11. What is a field? Explain. Give an example.

12. What are the two main types of information that make up a transaction? Explain, and give an example of each type.

13. Explain the normal procedure used in converting data from source documents into punched cards.

14. By how many different ways may a card be identified? Explain each briefly. For what is a control field used? Give an example.

15. Explain briefly the four primary types of cards.

16. Summarize the advantages and limitations of the punched card.

chapter

6

THE RECORDING OF SOURCE INFORMATION

AS EXPLAINED IN CHAPTER 4, processable business data have to go, in one form or another, through the steps of *recording, classifying, calculating, summarizing,* and *reporting* (or printing). These are the five principal processing steps performed on data when a punched-card system is used. By contrast, in an electronic system, these operations are condensed into three major steps: (1) *input,* which means the recording of data on punched cards, paper tape, or magnetic tape, and the feeding of these data into a computer, which is the main processing unit; (2) *processing,* which means the primary storage in the computer of the data received from step one and the performance of calculations and manipulation on them; and (3) *output,* which is the result of the computations performed on data in the computer, in the form of a printed page, a punched card, a punched tape, or a magnetic tape.

As was mentioned in Chapter 1, a machine has yet to be commercially developed which would be capable of reading and processing any handwritten transactions recorded on various-sized reports. Consequently, the need for a standard-sized report led to the development of the punched card. This necessitated converting the English language into a language which could be handled by punched-card machines. Thus, a "machine language" was developed, examples of which are the numeric and alphabetic coding tables discussed in Chapter 5.

Recording

Before any data can be read and properly processed by machine, they must be recorded in a proper form. This, therefore, constitutes the first step in the punched-card processing cycle. The recording function is performed by utilizing a machine called the *card punch,* commonly called the *key punch,* and another machine, the *verifier,* which checks on the accuracy of the punched data made by the key punch.

The IBM Key Punch

Key punching is the most widely used method of recording data in a card. The key-punch machine bears a striking resemblance to an electric typewriter. The keyboards of the two are similar, as each contains alphabetic, numeric, and special characters.[1] Also, recording is accomplished

---

[1] Some earlier key-punch machines have numerical keyboards only. They are still available and are currently used where the alphabetic requirement does not exist.

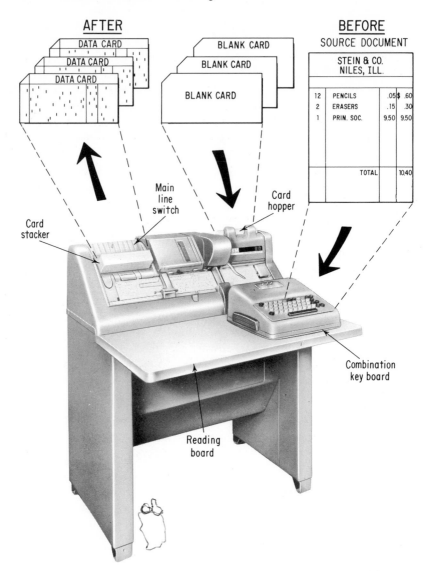

AFTER

DATA CARD

DATA CARD

DATA CARD

BLANK CARD

BLANK CARD

BLANK CARD

BEFORE

SOURCE DOCUMENT

STEIN & CO.
NILES, ILL.

12	PENCILS	.05	$ .60
2	ERASERS	.15	.30
1	PRIN. SOC.	9.50	9.50
		TOTAL	10.40

Card
stacker

Main
line
switch

Card
hopper

Combination
key board

Reading
board

Fig. 6-1. The IBM 26 printing card punch

by stroking the keys. The depression of a key on a typewriter results in printing that particular character on a sheet of paper, whereas the same key depressed on the key punch results in punching a hole or holes in a particular column of a card. However, the idea is the same, that is, to present information on a report for further analysis, evaluation, or control.

In the case of the typewriter, information is *printed* on a standard-sized sheet of paper. In the case of a key punch, the same information is presented in *punched* form in a standard-sized punched card. The key punch punches one column at a time, as the card moves from right to left; the typewriter prints one character at a time as the roller that controls the paper moves from right to left one space at a time. Fig. 6-1 shows the IBM 26 key punch, which prints or interprets directly over the column(s) as it punches holes in the card. Earlier models punch only and do not print.

Keyboard Arrangement

The primary difference between a typewriter and a key punch is in the arrangement and location of the numerical keys. The numerical keys on the typewriter are located in the top row. On the key punch, however, numerical keys are grouped together in such a manner that one hand is capable of manipulating them. This is done for the convenience of the key-punch operator. Because numeric data are punched more frequently than alphabetic data, it is more efficient for the numeric keys to be controlled by one hand rather than two, because this eliminates unnecessary movements. Figs. 6-2 and 6-3 show the arrangement of the keyboard on a key-punch machine.

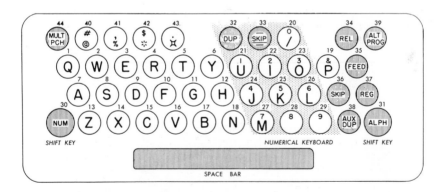

Fig. 6-2. An IBM 26 keyboard chart

The keyboard is normally in alphabetic mode. If numeric data are to be punched, depressing the numeric shift key manually makes the use of the numeric keys possible. If the majority of the operator's work is numeric data, it is better to shift the keyboard into numeric shift automatically by coding a program card for this purpose, as will be explained later.

Fig. 6-3. The IBM keyboard

Other Components of the Key Punch

In addition to the keyboard, the other components of the key punch are:
(1) the *card hopper,* (2) the *punching station,* (3) the *reading station,*
(4) the *card stacker,* and (5) the *program control unit.* (See Fig. 6-4.)

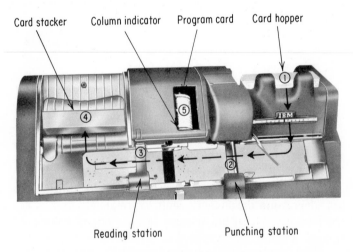

Fig. 6-4. The path of the card through the key punch

Card hopper

A great number of blank cards and a method of "feeding" or dropping them one at a time for punching are essential for the efficient recording of transactions. A device called the *card hopper* takes care of the latter requirement, while the provision of ample numbers of cards takes care of the former. Numerous cards have to be used, because each transaction must be recorded on a separate card. A card hopper holds approximately 500 cards and the cards are placed in it nine-edge first.

Card path

The cards move through the key punch from right to left as columns one through eighty are being punched. Upon the depression of a *feed* key, the first card drops to the card bed. The feed key is depressed a second time to cause the second card to drop to the card bed as the first card then moves to the punching station while the second card waits at the card bed. As soon as column eighty of card one passes the *punching station* and begins to move under the *reading station,* card two moves to the *punching station*. This causes another card to drop automatically from the *card hopper* to the card bed. Thus, the blank cards in the *card hopper* move continuously on their journey from the hopper through the *punching* and *reading stations* for the recording of information and, finally, to their destination in the *card stacker*.

The card hopper is used most advantageously when feeding in numerous cards involving a specific problem or project. When duplicating or punching only one or a few cards, the feeding job can be done faster manually.

Punching station

The punching station is the first of the two stations along the card path, as shown in Fig. 6-4. It contains twelve punch blades aligned or positioned vertically in the same sequence as the vertical layout of the card. The top three punch blades are for the zone punching positions twelve, eleven, and zero. The remaining nine are for the digit punching positions one through nine. Fig. 6-5 shows the alignment of the punch blades against an IBM card which is underneath the punching station housing them. Assume that the blades are on column one, and letter *C* is to be punched. The depression of key *C* on the keyboard causes punch blades twelve and three to penetrate the card, causing two rectangular holes in those locations (Fig. 6-6).

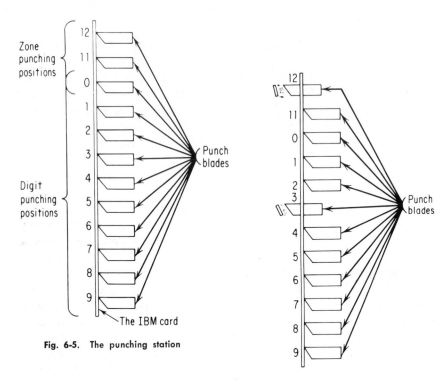

Fig. 6-5. The punching station

Fig. 6-6. Letter C punched in column one

Reading station

The key-punch operator is often faced with the need for punching certain repetitive information in a group of cards. The cards can be punched one at a time, but, because some of the information on a card is the same as that on any other card in the deck, a duplicating technique is desirable so that the job can be done more efficiently.

The reading station aids in the duplication of the data read in the card that moves underneath it and, when the duplicate ("Dup") key is depressed, causes the punching station to duplicate the holes in the card under it in the same location in the card that is under the reading station. The fact that the cards under the reading and punching stations move together one column at a time from right to left makes the duplicating function possible. In a store, for example, assume that on January 1 a television salesman from the hi-fi department sells fifty television sets to customers on account. Terms are net payment within thirty days. The data format on each of the fifty transaction cards is as follows:

Column	Description of the Field
1- 5	Customer-account number
6- 8	Department number
9-10	Salesman number
11-14	Due date
15-18	Date of item
19-23	Item number
24-40	Description of item
41-44	Size
45-48	Color
49-53	Unit Price
54-60	Total Price
61-80	Blank

You will notice, from the data above, that columns six through eighteen contain information that is the same on each of the fifty cards which represent the fifty different accounts. Columns six through eight, the department-number field, will be the same in each of the fifty cards, because all the television sets were purchased from the same department, that is, the hi-fi department. Likewise, in the case of the salesman's-number, due-date, and date-of-item fields, the fifty television sets were sold by the same salesman, on the same day, January 1, and the amount will be due on the same date, January 31. Therefore, duplication of these fields through using the reading station as described is much faster than having the key-punch operator punch the information in each card separately.

Program control unit

The program control unit contains an IBM program card which causes duplicating, skipping, or shifting to take place automatically because of a predetermined series of coded holes, or program, punched in it. It is wrapped around a drum and placed in position before any key punching begins, as is illustrated in Fig. 6-7. In this way, repetitive information in a deck of cards is duplicated in approximately one-sixth of the time taken by the key-punch operator to do the job manually. The degree of accuracy is also increased because of the decrease in the possibility of error owing to the substitution of machine operation for human operation.

Automatic *skipping* through the program card is initiated by an *11* punch (the *one* hole in row eleven) in the far left column of the skip field in the program card. From then on, the number of columns to be skipped is indicated by the sensing of consecutive holes in row twelve of the columns immediately following the *11* punch (Fig. 6-8). Again, using the television salesman example for clarification of this function, we find that columns sixty-one through eighty are blank columns. For the operator to use the space bar once for each blank column would be a waste of time.

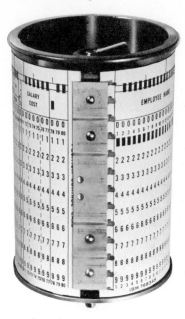

Fig. 6-7. Program control unit (*IBM*)

It is more convenient if skipping can be done automatically. To do this, column sixty-one of the program card is punched with a hole in row eleven to indicate the beginning of the skip operation. When sensed, it will tell the key punch to begin skipping. In order for the machine to skip columns sixty-two through eighty, consecutive holes in row twelve of these columns, referred to as *"12* punches," are made in the program card immediately following the *11* punch in column sixty-one, as shown in Fig. 6-8. Skipping is done at the rate of one card, eighty columns, per second.

Shifting to alphabetic mode from numeric automatically can be controlled through the program card. The keyboard is always in alphabetic mode when the program unit is not activated. The keys are then used like the keys in any typewriter. When numeric punching is desired, the numeric shift key is depressed. However, when the program control unit is activated, the keyboard is *shifted* into *alphabetic* mode automatically when a *1* punch is detected in any column of the program card. In Fig. 6-8 a *1* punch is made in column twenty-four. The zero punch in that column initiates automatic duplication of the field. The size of the shift field is determined by consecutive holes in rows twelve and one in each column. For example, column twenty-four will have a punch in row zero and row one, and columns twenty-five through forty will each have a hole in row twelve and a hole in row one, as shown in Fig. 6-8.

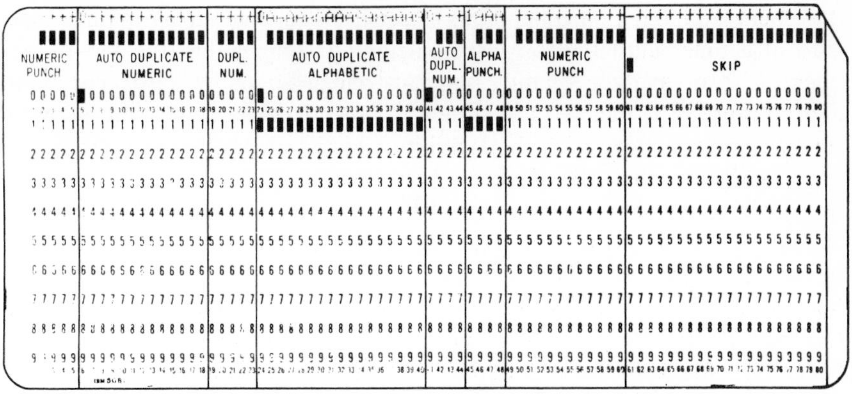

Fig. 6-8. A program card

The program card can also be used to shift from alphabetic into numeric mode. The absence of a *1* punch in the far left column of the numeric field of the program card accomplishes this. For example, columns forty-nine through fifty-three in the television salesman illustration can be punched manually with the unit price if column forty-nine in the program card is left blank. Therefore, columns fifty, fifty-one, fifty-two, and fifty-three should have consecutive *12* punches immediately following the blank forty-nine column. When the operator is ready to punch the unit price into column forty-nine, the keyboard is already in numeric mode. If it were not, the operator would have to shift manually by depressing and holding the "numeric shift" key at the lower left corner for every column to be punched with numeric data.

Card stacker

After the card goes through the steps of punching, reading, duplicating, and skipping, it finally goes out of the reading station to the card stacker. It is fed twelve-edge first. The card stacker is located at the upper left end of the key punch and holds about 500 cards (Fig. 6-4). It contains the cards in which are stored the necessary data for further processing. They are now referred to as *data cards*.

Importance of Accuracy in Recording

The function of recording data manually by key punching them in cards is a comparatively slow and costly one by machine standards. It is slow because, at the initial point of converting source documents into a group of cards for further processing, humans do the reading of the source document and the punching of its contents, one column at a time, one card at a time, until the job is completed. Assuming that the key-punch operator is of average quality, she can punch so many cards per hour and no more. The degree of accuracy is dependent upon the time allowed for the job as well as upon the legibility and accuracy of the source document itself. Because the punched facts can be no more accurate than the source documents from which they were punched, source documents should be clearly written or printed. A key-punch operator can punch in the neighborhood of 160 key strokes per minute. Naturally, her speed fluctuates, based on the type of information she is punching. When either the time allotted for the job is limited, creating pressure on her to punch faster than her normal rate of speed, or the source document is not clear, errors are bound to creep into her work. They must be corrected immediately, because locating and correcting a mistake at this point is less costly than at a later time when processing is being done. Once data have been stored in cards for processing, the cards become a part of other decks of cards, and the values which they contain become a part of the overall results. Errors discovered when processing is under way cause frustrating interruptions, and the time needed to locate them multiplies with the type of error made and the complexity of the system itself. Efficiency is drastically reduced and costs can easily mount beyond a reasonable limit. Therefore, that the facts punched in cards be correct is of utmost importance. In order to verify and check the accuracy of the key-punched data, a machine called the *verifier* is used.

The Verifier

A verifier looks like, and works almost exactly the same as, a key punch. However, the objective is different: The verifier checks or verifies the accuracy of the contents of the data cards. In place of the punching station containing the punch blades, the verifier has a verifying station containing sense pins to feel the holes in the column(s) and compare them with the keys depressed by the operator. The verifier operator uses the information from the source document and keys it in on the keyboard. If there is agreement between the punched card and the keyed-in data, a notch is made on the right edge of the card opposite row one (Fig. 6-9). If there is disagreement, the verifier produces a red signal to indicate that the stored information in the data card may be wrong. This can be the result of error on the part of either the key-punch operator or the verifier operator. To eliminate the possibility of error on her part, the verifier operator rekeys the information and, if it is still in disagreement with the data card, she tries a third time. If disagreement continues to result, the error is assumed by the verifier to be in the data card and to have

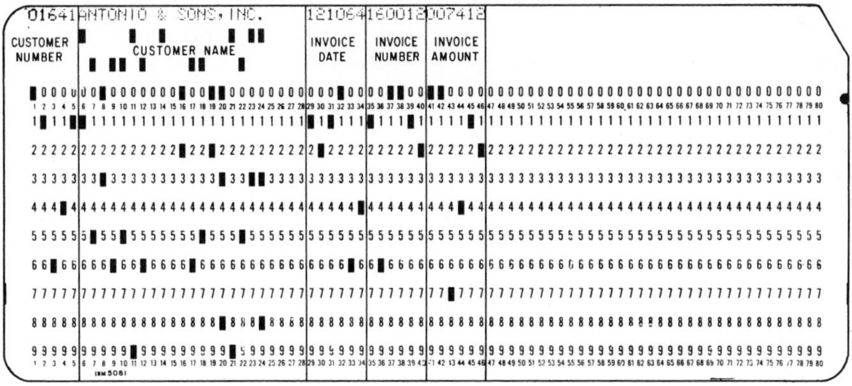

Fig. 6-9.   A verification notch indicating the accuracy of the punched facts

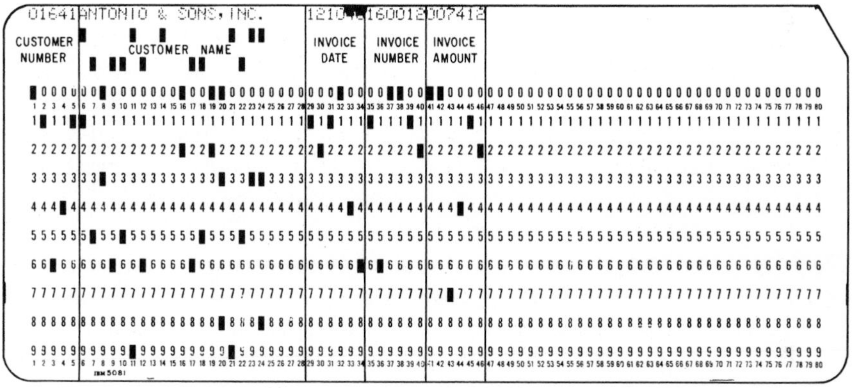

Fig. 6-10.   Error notches—see columns thirty-three and thirty-four

been made by the key-punch operator. Consequently, a notch is made on the top of the column(s) where the error(s) occur (Fig. 6-10).

The error(s) are corrected by punching the correct information in a new card and replacing the incorrect data card with the new card. Fig. 6-10 shows the same card and contents as that shown in Fig. 6-9 except that a punching error was purposely made in columns thirty-three and thirty-four by the key-punch operator to illustrate the role of the verifier in detecting errors. Instead of punching *64* for "year" in columns thirty-three and thirty-four, respectively, as shown in Fig. 6-9, the reverse of the data, *46,* was punched in these two columns (Fig. 6-10). The card was then placed in the verifier and the correct information was keyed-in from the original source document. The verifier compared the two sets of data, and after three tries by the verifier operator, disagreement in the data card was confirmed. Consequently, two notches were made on top of the two incorrect columns thirty-three and thirty-four.

Significance of Verification

Verification of punched cards takes almost as much time as the actual punching of the cards themselves. Despite this fact, it should be patiently done because errors are less costly to locate now than later. It also assures that the stored data are 100 per cent reliable and can be used with confidence for future processing. At times, information that has little future processable value is not verified; alphabetic data are also frequently bypassed.

Other Methods of Data Verification

Batch totals

In addition to verifying information by a verifier, batch totals are often used to ascertain overall accuracy on quantitative data. Source documents are divided into *batches,* each consisting of a reasonable number of transactions which belong to a specific project (for example, sales data for the sales department). The quantities from the source documents are added on an adding machine and the tape total is saved for later cross reference. After the data are key punched and tabulated, the totals derived from the latter machine are compared with the tape totals. Any discrepancies in the totals require detailed checking of the transactions in each batch. Otherwise, one assumes that no key-punching errors have been made and that each individual item is accurately represented on the card.

The decision to use batch totals as a verification method depends on: (1) the amount of data which require key verification—the more data requiring key verification, the less necessary is the use of batch totals; (2) the degree of efficiency of other verification methods, and (3) the feasibility and convenience of preparing batch totals from source documents or from punched cards.

Hash totals

Hash totals represent a predetermined total of accounts, transactions, or values taken from source documents. The total, in itself, has no meaning except as an error detector. Suppose the sales department of a given firm prepared a hash total of the number of items sold. Later, totals derived from a punched-card system regarding the same data are compared for accuracy. Any discrepancies must be accounted for. They are usually the result of: (1) incorrectly punched data, (2) double cards representing one transaction, or (3) a missing transaction. If these steps produce no errors, then, the hash totals must be double-checked.

UNIVAC's Multi-use Concept

Late in 1966, UNIVAC announced it was discontinuing the production of its ninety-column punched-card equipment. Though no details are available at this time, UNIVAC is contemplating the production of a new line called the 1700 series, which is based on the IBM eighty-column card. The primary characteristics of the hardware include: (1) combining key punching and verifying punch; (2) automatic interpreting with punching and verifying in a second machine, and (3) faster sorting with a new 1,000 cards per minute program-controlled sorter.

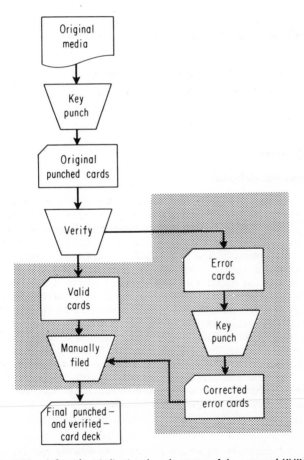

Fig. 6-11.   A flow chart indicating the advantages of the proposed UNIVAC 1700 series

Advantages of the 1700 Series

The punch-card machines of the proposed 1700 series offer time-saving advantages, compared with conventional card preparation. As shown in the flow chart in Fig. 6-11, the error-correction steps (shaded area) can be eliminated. The operator no longer needs to write the correct data on each error card, key punch a complete new card, or refile corrected cards. With the elimination of these time-consuming manual operations, an increase in the quantity and accuracy of card preparation now can be achieved.

Although the new UNIVAC 1700 series is ideally designed to support a basic UNIVAC computer system, it can be used as a complete system and appears to have a distinct advantage over former punch-card systems both in terms of versatility and efficiency.

Occupational Specifications of Key-punch and Verifier Operators

This section presents occupational definitions, education, training, experience, and special characteristics required of a key-punch and a verifier operator.[3]

Key-punch Operator

Occupational definition

Operates alphabetic and numeric key-punch machine, similar in operation to electric typewriter, to transcribe data from source material onto punch cards and to reproduce prepunched data. Attaches skip bar to machine and previously punched program card around machine drum to control duplication and spacing of constant data. Loads machine with decks of punch cards. Moves switches and depresses keys to select automatic or manual duplication and spacing, selects alphabetic or numeric punching, and transfers cards through machine stations. Depresses keys to transcribe new data in prescribed sequence from source material into perforations on card. Inserts previously punched card into card gauge to verify registration of punches. Observes machine to detect faulty feeding, positioning, ejecting, duplicating, skipping, punching, or other mechanical malfunctions and notifies supervisor. Removes jammed cards, using prying knife. May tend machines that automatically sort, merge, or match punch cards into specified groups. May key punch numerical data only and be designated Key-punch Operator, Numeric.

---

[3] Reprinted from *Occupations in Electronic Computing System,* with permission of the Bureau of Employment Security, Manpower Administration, U.S. Department of Labor (Washington, D.C.: U.S. Government Printing Office, 1965).

Education, training, and experience

High school graduate preferred with demonstrated proficiency in typing on standard or electric typewriter. High school or business school training in key-punch operation is desirable. Frequently, one week of training is provided by employer or manufacturer of equipment.

Special characteristics

APTITUDES:

Verbal ability to understand oral and written instructions, such as manufacturers' operating manuals, and to learn operation of machine.

Clerical perception to perceive pertinent detail in tabular material consisting of combinations of letters and numbers, and avoid perceptual error in transferring these data to punch cards.

Motor coordination to read work sheets and simultaneously operate keyboard of approximately forty keys to punch data on cards.

Finger dexterity to move switches on machine.

INTERESTS:

Preference for organized and routine activities to transfer data onto punch cards.

TEMPERAMENTS:

Must be able to perform repetitive duties of operating key-punch machine.

Ability to follow specific instructions and set procedures to transfer data onto punch cards.

PHYSICAL ACTIVITIES AND ENVIRONMENTAL CONDITIONS:

Work is sedentary. Reaches for and handles card decks and source documents.

Near visual acuity to read copy.

Work is performed inside.

Verifier Operator

Occupational definition

Verifies accuracy of data punched on tabulating cards, using keyboard-type machine that rejects incorrectly punched cards. Places punched cards in machine. Depresses keys in same sequence required to punch cards. Removes incorrectly punched cards as indicated by light or by key that will not depress. May punch corrected card, using key-punch machine.

Education, training, and experience

High school graduate with demonstrated proficiency in typing. High school or business school training in key-punch operations is desirable.

Special characteristics

APTITUDES:

Verbal ability to understand oral and written instructions, such as manufacturers' operating manuals to learn operation of machine, and to perform daily assignments.

Clerical perception to perceive pertinent detail in tabular material consisting of letters and numbers.

Motor coordination to read work sheets and simultaneously operate keyboard of verifier.

INTERESTS:

Preference for organized, routine activities to operate verifier machine continuously.

TEMPERAMENTS:

Work situation requires worker to perform repetitive tasks using verifier machine.

Must follow specific instructions to verify punched cards.

Works to precise and established standards of accuracy.

PHYSICAL ACTIVITIES AND ENVIRONMENTAL CONDITIONS:

Work is sedentary with infrequent lifting of decks of cards when loading machine.

Reaches for and handles code sheets, records, and decks of cards.

Near visual acuity to read copy.

Work is performed inside.

GLOSSARY OF TERMS

BATCH TOTALS: The sum of specific quantities (related to batches of source documents) used to verify the accuracy of later operations.

CARD STACKER: A key-punch component, located on the left side of the key punch, designed to hold outgoing (punched) cards.

HASH TOTALS: A sum of numbers located in a specific field or a batch of records, used for checking purposes.

KEY PUNCH: A special-purpose keyboard-operated device used for recording (by punching) data in cards.

PROGRAM CONTROL CARD: A card punched with coded instructions to control automatically certain key-punching operations (for example, skipping, shifting, duplicating).

PUNCHING STATION: The area on the key punch where a card is positioned for data punching.

READING STATION: The area on the keyboard where a card is positioned for the reading device to interpret available holes and cause (on command) the punching station to duplicate the same holes (data) on a blank card.

VERIFIER: A special-purpose keyboard-operated device used to check the correctness of data already punched in cards.

REVIEW QUESTIONS

1. List in the correct sequence and describe the five punched-card data-processing machine functions. Contrast them with the major steps in an electronic installation.
2. Discuss the similarities and differences between a typewriter and a key punch.
3. What is a program card? How is it different from a regular punched card? Why is a program card used?
4. What is the function of the card hopper? The card stacker? Which of the two holds the blank deck of cards?
5. What is the difference (in functions) between the reading station and the punching station? When is the reading station used along with the punching station?
6. What is the difference between batch totals and hash totals?
7. In what ways are data cards duplicated on a key punch?
8. Suppose you have 200 blank cards in which student number 0561 is to be punched in columns one, two, three, and four of each card. You have only a key-punch machine at your disposal. What is the most efficient method of punching the number in the cards?
9. What is the difference between the verifier and the key punch? Explain.
10. Explain why ascertaining the accuracy of data at the key-punching stage is important.
11. Explain UNIVAC's multi-use concept. What are the primary characteristics of the new equipment?
12. Summarize the role and qualifications of the key-punch operator. The verifier operator.

chapter

7

THE REPRODUCTION OF RECORDED INFORMATION

Duplicating Stored Data

STORED DATA ARE DUPLICATED by reproducing, gang punching, or mark sensing. Duplicating is done by a machine called the *reproducer*. It has three purposes: (1) reproducing of data from one card into another card; (2) gang punching of data from a master card into a number of blank cards; (3) end printing. Features can be incorporated in the machine to perform the functions of comparing, summary punching, and mark sensing.

Components of the Reproducer

The IBM 519 reproducer is a document-originating machine, divided into two major parts: (1) the reading unit, and (2) the punching unit.

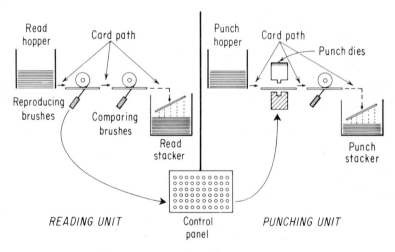

Fig. 7-1. Components of the IBM reproducer

The reading unit

This unit contains a hopper, called the "read" hopper, to hold the cards to be reproduced, and two sets of reading brushes, each set containing eighty brushes to read eighty columns in a card. The first set, called the *reproducing* brushes, read the holes punched in that row, one row at a time. The second set, called the *comparing* brushes, aid in comparing the holes read by the reproducing brushes with those punched in another card by the punching unit to insure accuracy (Fig. 7-1).

The punching unit

The other part of the reproducer is the punching unit. It contains a set of eighty punch dies to punch up to eighty holes, if necessary, in any row of a card, as well as a set of eighty punch brushes to read what is punched and to work with the comparing brushes, through a control device, to insure accuracy of the results.

For example, suppose that we have a card containing number *3333* in columns four, five, six, and seven, and that we desire to put this number into a blank card. The following procedure takes place: The data card with the number *3333* in columns four, five, six, and seven is placed in the "read" hopper twelve-edge first, face down. A blank card is also placed in the "punch" hopper twelve-edge first, face down. If the control panel is properly wired, the depression of the "start" button will cause both cards to move together. Row twelve of the data card moves over the reproducing brushes while row twelve of the blank card moves under the punch dies. No impulse is created, because no holes are present. Only the presence of a hole can cause the brush to make contact with the cylinder above the card to create an electric impulse for action. The cards keep moving in unison, and rows eleven, zero, one, and two pass by with no results. However, when row three with holes in it reaches the reproducing brushes, dies four, five, six, and seven punch holes in the blank card instantly. The cards keep moving through, and rows four, five, six, seven, eight, and nine pass by the brushes with no impulse.

After the data card is read by the reading brushes, it is also read by the comparing brushes and then drops into the "read" stacker. At the same time, the blank card which was just punched by the punch dies is read by the punch brushes and drops into the "punch" stacker. The job is completed.

Uses of Reproducing

Reproducing is common and has many uses, a number of which can be inferred from the following illustrations. A master deck of cards containing basic information, such as the hourly rate of employees, their overtime, their rate of pay, and so forth, becomes worn out and can cause jamming as a result of excessive use. Such jamming may not only result in loss of machine time, but in some cases the master card is twisted and mutilated to the extent that part of the information in it is destroyed. The data-processing employee would have to resort to the source document from which the master card was originally prepared if an alternative were not available to him. This could take a lot of time and run up the cost of processing. In order to avoid any such undesirable incident, the department is wise to make a duplicate of the master cards. The master deck

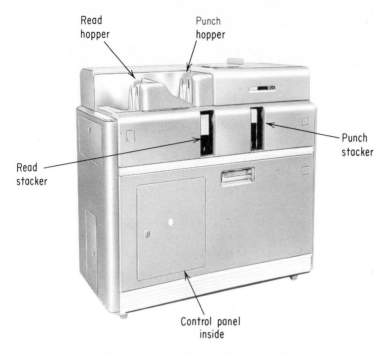

Read hopper

Punch hopper

Punch stacker

Read stacker

Control panel inside

Fig. 7-2. The IBM 519 reproducing punch

can be duplicated simply by placing it in the read hopper and an equal number of blank cards in the punch hopper. (See Fig. 7-2.) The control panel can be wired to read and reproduce columns one through eighty of the master card into columns one through eighty in a blank card in the punch hopper. The reproduced deck drops, one card at a time, into the punch stacker and the original master deck also drops, one card at a time, into the read stacker. This type of reproduction is commonly referred to as the "80-80" method, and 100 cards per minute can be reproduced.

Another use of the reproducing punch is in copying certain data, or fields, from a card(s) in the read hopper into any location in another card in the punch hopper. This process is referred to as "offset punching." For example, assume that Pocket-the-Profit, Inc., a small discount store in Rochester, New York, employs a total of five employees (Nos. 01, 02, 03, 04, and 05). Their hourly rates of pay are set at $1.25, $1.50, $1.75, $2.00, and $2.25, respectively, and they are paid on Friday of each week.

At the time he is employed, a new employee is assigned a number, and a master card is immediately prepared to include the following information:

Column	1- 2	Employee number
	3-30	Employee name
	31-49	Employee's home address
	50-57	Telephone number
	58-64	Employee title
	65-67	Hourly rate
	68-80	Blank

The payroll is prepared on Friday morning. It is computed as follows: The manager of Pocket-the-Profit, Inc. inspects the time cards to get the number of days and the amount of time each of his five employees worked. He reports these to the key-punch operator, who punches the data in five separate cards as follows:

1- 2	Employee number
3-30	Employee name
31-45	Employee title
46-47	Total number of hours for the week

This example assumes that Pocket-the-Profit, Inc. does not work overtime.

The five cards are referred to, from this point on, as the *detail* cards, or *detail file*. After all computations are made and punched in them, the cards will contain details pertinent to the employees and indirectly to their company. From these cards, paychecks can be written and prepared. The management, too, can obtain information from them on the amount of tax withheld for the preparation of periodical tax reports and other related statements in the future.

Based on the data in the detail cards in Fig. 7-3, we see that before any computations for net pay are made, the hourly rate of each employee must be punched in the card, that is, in columns forty-eight, forty-nine, and fifty. The hourly rate is available only in the master card (in columns sixty-five, sixty-six, and sixty-seven). The data-processing department first checks to make sure that the master file and the detail file are arranged in the proper sequence. The first card in the master file, employee number *01,* should correspond to the first card in detail file, employee number *01.* (See Fig. 7-3.) Next, the master deck is placed in the read hopper while the detail deck is placed in the punch hopper. The control panel is wired to read the contents of columns sixty-five through sixty-seven of the master card and to cause the punch dies to punch these data in columns forty-eight through fifty in the detail card. Once this job is done, the detail card contains the employee number, his name, his title, his total hours for the week, and his hourly rate. This card is then placed in the calculator, which multiplies the number of hours times the hourly rate in order to arrive at the gross pay. The gross pay is punched by the calculator in the same card in columns fifty-one through fifty-five. Deductions are later determined and

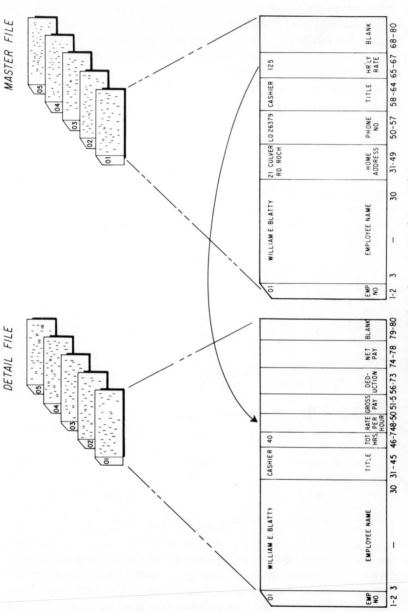

Fig. 7-3. Selected reproduction of data from one card to another—an example

121

subtracted from the gross pay, leaving the net pay for the week. The master deck from which the hourly rate was reproduced should then be taken to the master file until it is needed again.

From the foregoing example, note that, through the control panel, any column(s) from the card(s) placed in the read hopper can be reproduced into any column(s) in the card(s) placed in the punch hopper. The system is flexible and allows the reproduction of one column, or of one or several fields, in entirely different locations in blank cards.

The Comparing Function of the Reproducer

To check on the performance of the reproducer, a unit is built into it which can compare what is reproduced with the original data to insure accuracy. This is similar to the work of the verifier. As is true of the verifier, the comparison made by the reproducer proves agreement between the reproduced cards and the master cards (Fig. 7-4).

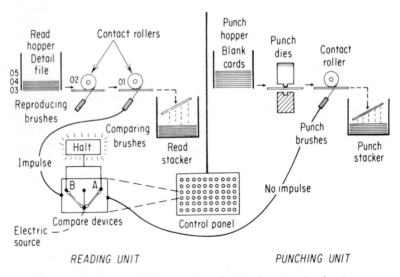

Fig. 7-4. A schematic of the reproducer showing the comparing function

In the diagram, let us assume that another deck of five cards is desired, which will contain only the employee number in columns one and two. Assume, further, that the control panel is wired so that brushes one and two would actuate punch dies one and two upon detecting a hole in columns one and two. The machine is started and the first data card bearing employee number *01* is read by reproducing brushes one and two. Brush one detects hole *0* in row zero of column one—the first available hole, because the card is fed twelve-edge first, causing punch die one to punch in the same location in the blank card. (Refer to Fig. 7-5.) The data card moves further and brush two detects a hole in row one in column two, also causing punch die two to punch a *1* in the same location in the blank card.

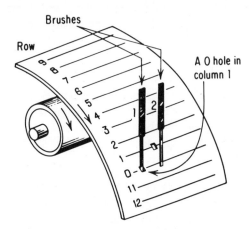

Fig. 7-5. Reproducing brushes one and two sensing holes zero and one in sequence

Suppose that the punch dies do not respond properly to the impulses received from the reproducing brushes and that employee card number *01* was not punched. In this case, when the detail card moves over the comparing brushes in unison with the blank card which moves over the punch brushes, the comparing brushes send an impulse to a compare box. But the punch brushes do not send any impulse, because no holes were punched. This causes an imbalance in the compare device and a contact is made internally, halting the reproducer immediately. An arrow in a box on the outside indicates to the operator the location of the error.

Gang Punching

Gang punching is the automatic copying of punched data from the master card into one or more blank cards. Although the reproducer is used to do it, gang punching differs from reproducing in that the reproducing operation requires use of both the reading unit and the punch unit, whereas gang punching requires use of the punching unit only. A connection is made between the punch brushes and the punch dies through the control panel.

Fig. 7-6 is a diagram of the punch unit of the reproducer and the path of cards in a gang-punching operation. The master card moves to the punch brushes and the first blank card following it moves to the punch

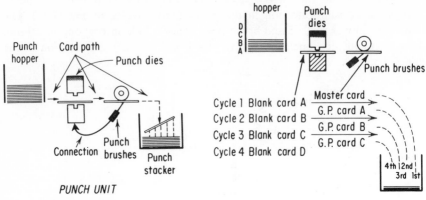

Fig. 7-6. Punch unit of the reproducer used for gang punching

Fig. 7-7. Single master-card gang punching

dies. The punch brushes sense the holes in the master card and, because of direct wiring through the control panel, actuate the punch dies to duplicate the same holes in the same location. Next, the master card drops into the stacker, the reproduced card moves to the punch brushes, and the second blank card moves under the punch dies. At this stage, the reproduced card is considered the same as the master card, because now it has the same information and is positioned at the punching brushes. Its contents are punched in the blank card following it in the same manner as the previous cycle. This cycle is repeated until all cards are completed.

To clarify, assume that a master card is to be gang punched in four blank cards (A, B, C, and D) following it. Fig. 7-7 presents the cycles necessary to complete the operation.

In cycle one, the master card is copied into blank card A. The master card drops into the stacker. In cycle two, gang-punched card A moves to the punching brushes and is copied (by punching) into blank card B. Gang-punched card A drops in the stacker while B moves to the punching brushes and card C to the punching dies. The same procedure applies for cycle three and cycle four. At the end of cycle four, gang-punched cards C and D drop in the stacker, respectively.

The illustration in Fig. 7-7 works well in *single master-card gang punching,* that is, when only one master card is involved and a number of cards are to be duplicated from it. However, when information varies from one group of cards to another, the *interspersed gang-punching method* is used. In this method, a master card heads a group of cards to be gang punched. On the first master card, the procedure is the same as in the single master-card gang-punching method. When the second master card

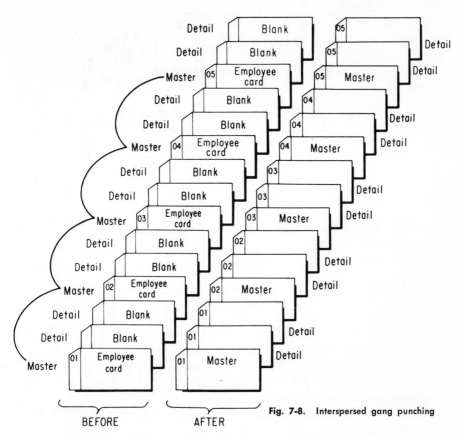

Fig. 7-8. Interspersed gang punching

BEFORE   AFTER

is detected by the machine, the punching pattern then changes to conform to the details in it. (See Fig. 7-8.)

Gang punching can be performed on a key punch. However, using the reproducer is more convenient and efficient because the job can be done faster on it than on the key punch.

End Printing

In addition to reproducing and gang punching, the reproducer is capable of end printing. End printing is converting punched data into printing across the edge of a card, making a quick reference to the data it contains. The information can be read or *interpreted* from the card itself or *transcribed* from a card in the read unit while at the comparing brushes. Eight printing wheels, each containing digits zero through nine and a blank position, effect final printing across the edge of the card as illustrated in Fig. 7-9.

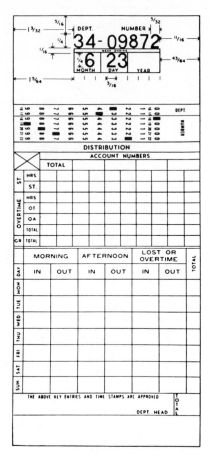

Fig. 7-9. End printing—an example

Mark Sensing

Have you ever observed a representative of the gas and electric company taking a utility meter reading? The meter reader is provided with an IBM card in which are punched basic data, such as the customer's name, his meter number, and other related data. Also, on the right-hand section of the card, short lines are provided to be blackened with a special electrographic pencil to represent numeric data. The reader blackens the proper numbers with the pencil after he reads the meter. This is called *mark sensing*. The cards are later fed into the reproducer, which senses the strokes, or marks, and, through the control-board wiring translates them into punched holes (see Figs. 7-10 and 7-11).

This conversion step is necessary before the data from the mark-sensed cards can be integrated and properly processed for the eventual preparation of customer bills or financial statements.

Mark sensing is usually used for reproducing small quantites of numeric information. Alphabetic information requires double the space (two

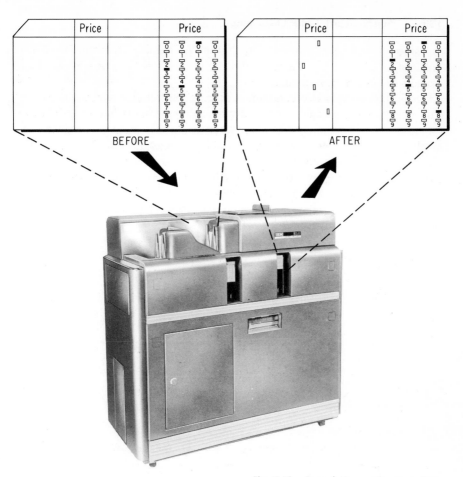

Fig. 7-10. Reproducing mark-sensed data

Fig. 7-11. Eight styles of marks to be sensed

127

holes to each letter) compared with that of numeric information (one hole to each number). Further, alphabetic mark sensing is not so convenient for use by the layman.

Mark sensing is also common in scoring examination sheets where the student answers a specific question by blackening a short line or a column for an answer. Care must be taken when using this method, because the machine does not know when the student changes his mind, even if he blackens a different column for an answer, if he neglects to erase the previous answer thoroughly. Also, the machine will ignore the second answer if the spot is not marked heavily. Many times students also pay heavily in unnecessary loss of points because of their neglect to read carefully the instructions prepared by the manufacturer.

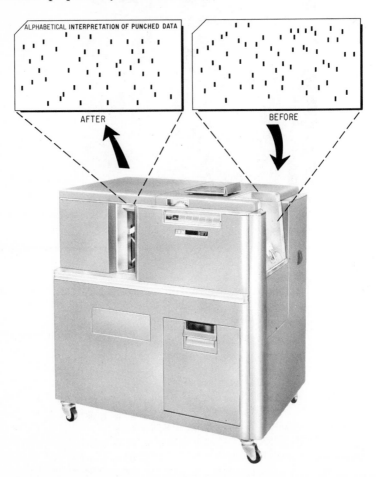

Fig. 7-12. The IBM 557 interpreter

Interpreting

Interpreting is converting machine language into human language. Fig. 7-12 is a photograph of the IBM 557 interpreter, the one most commonly used in data-processing departments. A distinction can be made easily between printing by the interpreter and that done by the key punch. The latter machine prints on the top of the same column that contains the hole(s), whereas the interpreter merely prints across the face of the card.

Interpreting is a helpful supplementary aid in the reproducing function. Because many cards are reproduced or gang punched, a person can read them more easily if the cards are interpreted first than if he has to read the punched holes, a job which is both time-consuming and extremely boring.

GLOSSARY OF TERMS

DETAIL FILE: A reference data file, containing information to be processed later against a master file.

END PRINTING: A function performed by a reproducer where certain data punched in a card are printed across the end of the same card.

GANG PUNCHING: Automatic copying of data punched in a single card into a group of succeeding cards.

INTERPRETING: Related to the interpreter's function of printing on the top of a card the data punched in it.

MARK SENSING: An operation which involves reading characters marked by a special pencil in designated areas on a card and punching them into the same card.

REPRODUCER: A special-purpose machine designed to copy selected data from one set of cards into another set of cards.

SINGLE MASTER-CARD GANG PUNCHING: A gang-punching operation related to a deck of cards consisting of copying data from one master card into a group of succeeding cards.

REVIEW QUESTIONS

1. For what purpose(s) is a reproducer used?
2. Describe the reading unit and the punching units of a reproducer. Draw a schematic of a reproducer.
3. Identify the two sets of reading brushes of the reading unit. What is the function of each set?

4. Describe the procedure in reproducing a data card into a blank card.
5. What is meant by reproducing "80-80"? Explain.
6. Explain how the comparing function of a reproducer is similar to that of a verifier.
7. What is gang punching? How does it differ from reproducing?
8. Assume that a master card is to be punched in seven blank cards. Present and explain the cycles necessary to complete the operation.
9. What is the difference between single master-card gang punching and interspersed gang-punching methods?
10. What is *mark sensing?* When and how is it used?
11. Explain how end printing is done by the reproducer.

chapter

8

CLASSIFYING
INFORMATION BY SORTING

AS STRESSED IN CHAPTER 1, the primary purpose of processing data is to prepare and report business facts vital to management in making informed decisions. After the conversion of source documents into unit records by key punching, the cards are checked and errors corrected by use of the verifier. Once they have been verified and any errors corrected, they are ready to be classified.

Reports to management must be presented in proper and useful form. What is "proper and useful" varies with the type of report required, because reports are needed for various reasons. The sales volume of a company for the fiscal year, for example, can produce many useful and informative facts. The many products sold during the year can be analyzed in order to determine whether they contributed sufficiently to the overall profit margin. Such information helps executives make decisions and future plans about maintaining the present products in stock and about the possible profitability of adding new products. Company sales can be analyzed also in order to see whether the salesmen have met the sales quotas set for them in the product lines which they were responsible for selling. The performance of a particular salesman can be compared with that of other salesmen employed in the same department, based on his sales quota and other pertinent factors, in order to determine whether he qualifies for a raise in salary or in rank within his department or, in some cases, for a transfer to a different branch with a promotion in both rank and salary.

The above example is but one of many situations which can be dealt with intelligently if facts concerning it are *classified* correctly before they are printed and reported. The purpose of classifying, thus, is to facilitate the arrangement of data in proper form for their use in various business reports. For example, if a sales report by salesman is required, it would be useless to present instead a sales report by product or customer number. In other words, the preparation of business transactions in a definite form contributes greatly to their effective use when they are finally printed and reported to management.

What Is Classifying?

Classifying, or sorting, is a process in which like transactions are grouped, or arranged together, in either alphabetic or numeric sequence based on the data punched in them. This is referred to as *sorting in sequence*. It is one of the three primary types of classifications performed on a machine called the *sorter.* The other two types are: *selecting,* or classifying by extraction; and *grouping,* or classifying according to common characteristics.

Sorting in Sequence

Sorting in sequence is a process of preparing like data in either alphabetic or numeric order. Figs. 8-1 and 8-2 show five cards being sequenced in numeric and alphabetic order, respectively.

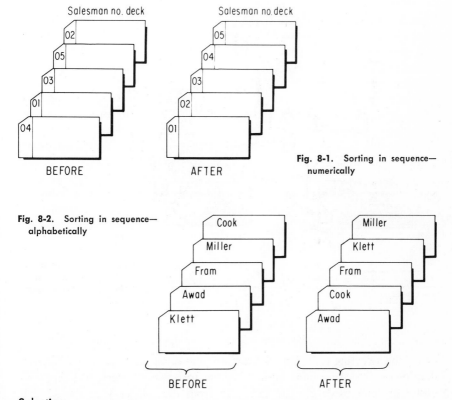

Fig. 8-1. Sorting in sequence—numerically

Fig. 8-2. Sorting in sequence—alphabetically

Selecting

Selecting, or classifying by extraction, is the operation that involves pulling from a certain file a number of cards which require special attention without disturbing the sequence of the remainder of the file. In a public relations department of a business firm, for instance, all employees who have been with the company for twenty years or more would have an *X* punched in a specific column (assume column seventy-five) of their cards in a master file. Suppose that the public relations department is responsible for honoring these employees at an annual banquet. The data-processing manager is instructed to prepare a list of employees eligible for this honor. His department sorts the complete master file and, through the use of the sorter, extracts all cards having an *X* punched in column seventy-five without disturbing the sequence of the remainder of the file. Once the eligible employees' cards are extracted from the master file, they are listed and a copy is mailed to the public relations office. Fig. 8-3 presents a condensed picture of the above example.

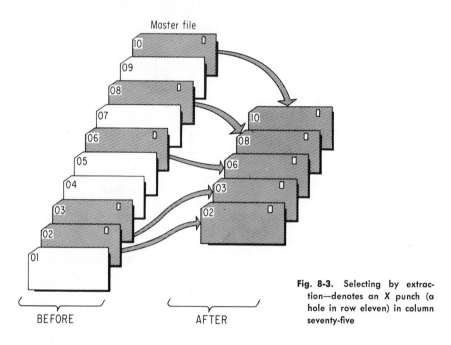

BEFORE AFTER

Fig. 8-3. Selecting by extraction—denotes an X punch (a hole in row eleven) in column seventy-five

The selecting technique is used in many other connections in business data processing. In a banking application, for example, certain delinquent-customer loan cards can be extracted from the master loan file so that listing of these customer accounts can be made and notices mailed to them reminding them of the overdue payment. In an insurance application, there can be extracted from a master policyholders' file all cards pertaining to those policyholders whose insurance policies expire within the current month, for the purpose of preparing a statement of policy renewal. Numerous other examples can be thought of by the student where classifying by extraction would be applicable.

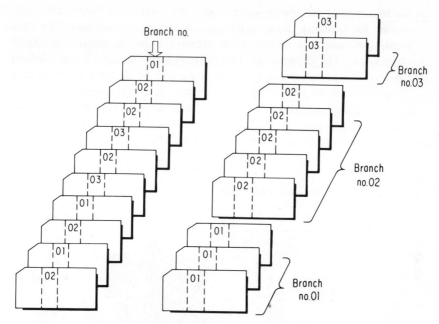

Fig. 8-4. Grouping—classifying by common characteristics

Grouping

Grouping, or classifying by common characteristics, is a process where a mass of data is arranged into related groups, each group having common characteristics. For example, if a sales report is to be presented by branch number instead of by product number, the deck of cards containing the data for a sales report must first be grouped by branches. In this way, all sales cards having branch number one will be listed under branch number one, all cards in branch two will be listed under branch two, and so forth, until the total number of sales cards in the deck would be grouped under their respective branches. This is done by sorting the cards according to the branch-number field, as shown in Fig. 8-4.

The Sorter

Sorting is similar to filing and can be done manually on an economical basis in some small applications. A simple illustration of it is distributing the mail in the proper mail racks or in the "in" and "out" mail baskets. In large volumes of data, however, manual attempts to rearrange them for specific report purposes would be too costly; thus, if a machine can be devised to do the job, it will be used if it cuts down on the cost. The special-purpose machine that can be used for sequence sorting, selecting, or grouping on an economical basis is referred to as the *sorter* (Fig. 8-5).

The IBM 83 sorter is one of the fastest machines in the punched-card data-processing system. Its outstanding feature is the thirteen pockets which hold the cards after they are read. They are numbered from right to left: *reject, 12, 11, 0, 1, 2, 3, 4, 5, 6, 7, 8, 9*. The "reject" pocket receives cards which do not belong in any of the other twelve pockets, an example of which is a blank card. Next to the reject pocket are pockets twelve, eleven, and zero, which are used in combination with the remaining pockets in alphabetic sorting, because a letter is represented by two punches in the IBM card. Pockets zero through nine are used alone for numeric sorting. They are adequate, because one punch in any given column in a card represents a digit.

Fig. 8-5. The IBM 83 sorter

The sorter is constructed differently from other punched-card machines in that it has only *one brush* mounted above a roller. The card passes between brush and roller to be read *one column per pass*. The card is fed into the sorter nine-edge first, face down. This means that row nine of a specific column passes under the reading brush. If a hole is detected, the brush makes contact with the roller underneath the card, causing the card to be ejected into pocket nine. If a hole is detected in row eight, however, the sorter will eject that card into pocket eight instead. This goes on until all the twelve rows of card one are read. When the brush passes row twelve of card one, row nine of card two follows immediately. This process continues until all the rows in a specific column of all the cards in the hopper are read and, consequently, the cards are ejected into their respective pockets.

Sorting in Sequence on the IBM 83 Sorter

For purposes of illustration, let us take the first primary type of classification performed on the sorter, that is, "sorting in sequence." It is divided into numeric sorting and alphabetic sorting.

Numeric sorting

Numeric sorting involves the rearrangement of cards in numeric order by sorting a specific digit field in the cards. The size of the field can be one or more columns, the location of which is immaterial to the sorter, because the reading brush can be moved manually to read any given column regardless of its location in the card.

ONE-COLUMN DIGIT FIELD. Sorting a deck of cards on a one-column digit field is done by moving the "read" brush to the desired column. All cards having a zero in them will eject into pocket zero, those containing *1* will eject into pocket one, and so forth, until the deck is completely sorted. For instance, Fig. 8-6 shows a deck containing ten cards in random order face down.

Assume that the cards are to be rearranged sequentially on column one containing the digits shown at the right in the illustration. The reading brush is moved to the location of column one and the bottom card moves under the brush nine-edge first. The brush detects a hole in row five, which would cause it to drop into pocket five. The next card moves along, and a hole in row one is detected. It drops into pocket one. This process continues until the top card is sensed and consequently dropped into pocket six. The middle of Fig. 8-6 shows the location of the cards in the sorter pockets. The operator reassembles them as follows: The cards in pocket one are placed on top of those in pocket zero. They are followed by pocket two cards, which are placed on top of the combined deck of cards one and zero;

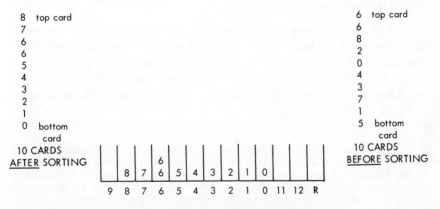

Fig. 8-6. Numeric sorting—one-digit field

those from pocket three are placed on top of those from two; those from four, on top of those from three; those from five on top of those from four; and so forth. After reassembly is completed, card eight should be on the top of the deck and card zero on the bottom, face down. When turned over as a complete deck, zero appears first and behind it, in ascending order, cards one through eight.

Another method of reassembling the cards from the pockets of the sorter is to start with the nine's (cards in pocket nine) and place cards from each succeeding pocket to the right underneath those already removed until cards from pocket zero are placed last.

THE REVERSE-DIGIT METHOD OF SORTING. For fields larger than one column, the reverse-digit sorting method is used. That is, the numeric field is sorted from right to left across the field, one column per pass. All cards have to be sorted on the right-hand column first. When this step is completed, it is referred to as *"pass one."* The cards are reassembled and the stack is placed in the hopper to be sorted on the second column from the right. This is referred to as "pass two." The process continues until the whole field is sorted. Therefore, the number of passes necessary to sort a numeric field is equal to the number of columns in it. Fig. 8-7 illustrates, step by step, numeric sorting by the reverse-digit method, the fastest and most commonly used method of sorting large volumes of data.[1] Pass one involves the sorting of the stack of cards on column nineteen. The cards are reassembled and again placed in the hopper for a second pass. However, this time they are sorted on column eighteen. The cards are reassembled a second time and placed in the hopper to be sorted on column seventeen for a third and final pass. The cards are reassembled by the operator for the final time. The result should show the stack of cards in the proper ascending numeric order.

Alphabetic sorting

Alphabetic sorting is performed in two different ways, depending upon the sorter model used. The two IBM models in use today are the 82 and the 83 (Figs. 8-8 and 8-5). One difference between them lies in their speed. The IBM 82 sorter sorts at the rate of 650 cards per minute, whereas the 83 model sorts at 1,000 cards per minute. Another difference is the methods in which they sort.

---

[1] When several sorters are available, it is often more convenient to divide the work among them. In this technique, the deck is first sorted on the left-most column of the field, thus dividing the cards into ten different groups, each of which can be sorted separately by using the reverse-digit method. When the ten groups of cards have been sorted, they are recombined in a proper sequence. This process is referred to as the *block sorting* technique.

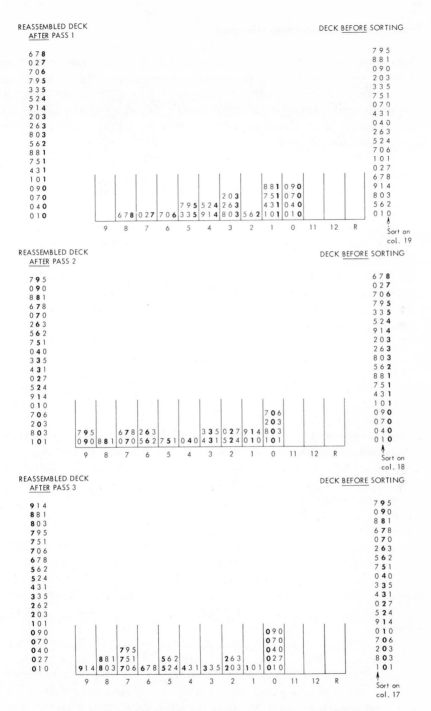

REASSEMBLED DECK
AFTER PASS 1

6 7 8
0 2 7
7 0 6
7 9 5
3 3 5
5 2 4
9 1 4
2 0 3
2 6 3
8 0 3
5 6 2
8 8 1
7 5 1
4 3 1
1 0 1
0 9 0
0 7 0
0 4 0
0 1 0

DECK BEFORE SORTING

7 9 5
8 8 1
0 9 0
2 0 3
3 3 5
7 5 1
0 7 0
4 3 1
0 4 0
2 6 3
5 2 4
7 0 6
1 0 1
0 2 7
6 7 8
9 1 4
8 0 3
5 6 2
0 1 0

Sort on col. 19

REASSEMBLED DECK
AFTER PASS 2

7 9 5
0 9 0
8 8 1
6 7 8
0 7 0
2 6 3
5 6 2
7 5 1
0 4 0
3 3 5
4 3 1
0 2 7
5 2 4
9 1 4
0 1 0
7 0 6
2 0 3
8 0 3
1 0 1

DECK BEFORE SORTING

6 7 8
0 2 7
7 0 6
7 9 5
3 3 5
5 2 4
9 1 4
2 0 3
2 6 3
8 0 3
5 6 2
8 8 1
7 5 1
4 3 1
1 0 1
0 9 0
0 7 0
0 4 0
0 1 0

Sort on col. 18

REASSEMBLED DECK
AFTER PASS 3

9 1 4
8 8 1
8 0 3
7 9 5
7 5 1
7 0 6
6 7 8
5 6 2
5 2 4
4 3 1
3 3 5
2 6 2
2 0 3
1 0 1
0 9 0
0 7 0
0 4 0
0 2 7
0 1 0

DECK BEFORE SORTING

7 9 5
0 9 0
8 8 1
6 7 8
0 7 0
2 6 3
5 6 2
7 5 1
0 4 0
3 3 5
4 3 1
0 2 7
5 2 4
9 1 4
0 1 0
7 0 6
2 0 3
8 0 3
1 0 1

Sort on col. 17

Fig. 8-7. Numeric sorting—the reverse-digit method for multi-digit field

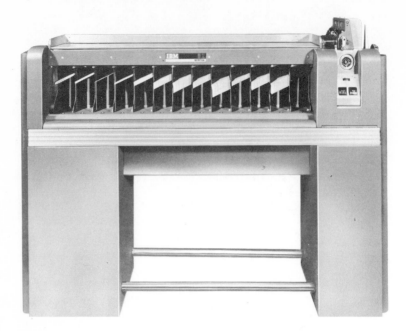

Fig. 8-8. The IBM 82 sorter

ALPHABETIC SORTING USING THE IBM 82. Alphabetic sorting on the IBM 82 takes twice as much time as numeric sorting. Because a letter is represented by two holes in a given column in a card, two passes would be taken to sort on that column. The first pass sorts the digit part of a given column of each card, so that the whole deck is grouped by digits one through nine. Only holes one through nine are sensed in this pass. The second pass sorts the *zone* portion of the same column. In the second pass, the brush will sense holes in the zone punching positions only. The cards fall in one of the zone pockets—twelve, eleven, and zero, in the proper alphabetic sequence. Pocket twelve holds all cards with letters represented by zone twelve, that is, *A-I*. Pocket eleven holds all cards with letters represented by zone eleven, *J-R*. Pocket zero holds all cards with letters represented by zone zero, *S-Z*. As in numeric sorting, cards are fed into the sorter nine-edge first, face down.

Fig. 8-9 shows, step by step, the alphabetic sorting of a deck of twenty-six alphabetically punched cards. For purposes of illustration, only a one-column alphabetic field is applied. However, in the case of a two-letter field, for instance, four passes are required: two passes per column. The right-hand column is sorted first, and the left-hand column is sorted next, as is true in numeric sorting.

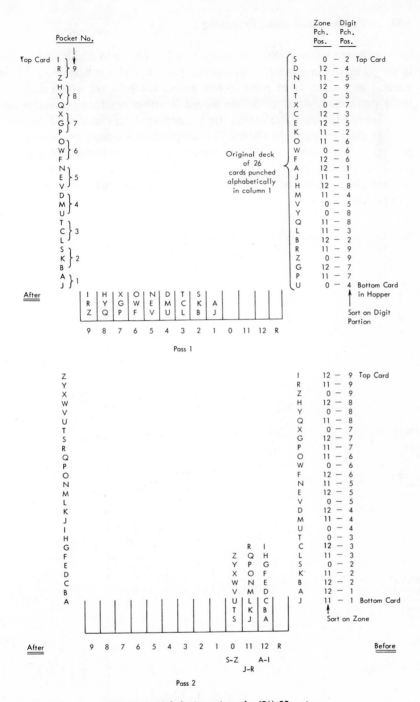

Fig. 8-9. Alphabetic sorting—the IBM 82 sorter

ALPHABETIC SORTING USING THE IBM 83. The IBM 83 sorter is similar to the 82 model in that each has thirteen pockets and one brush to read one column at a time, from right to left across the field on which sorting is to be performed. Also, cards are placed in either machine nine-edge first, face down. However, the alphabetic procedure differs in the 83 model.

In the first pass, the IBM 83 sorter ejects cards bearing letters *A-I* to pockets one through nine, that is, sorting on the digit portion of these letters. The remaining cards are treated as follows: cards containing letters *J-R* are ejected into pocket eleven; cards containing letters *S-Z* are ejected into pocket zero.

Fig. 8-10.   Alphabetic sorting—the IBM 83 sorter

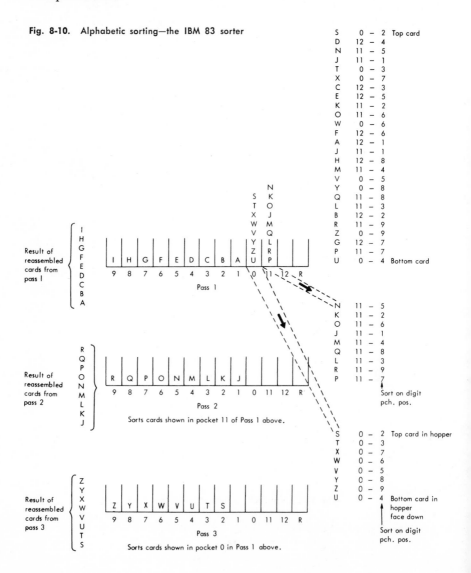

In the second pass, cards *A-I* are excluded because they are already in sequence when reassembled. Cards in pocket eleven are sorted on their digit punching positions and ejected into pockets one through nine, that is, pocket one contains *J*s; pocket two, *K*s; pocket three, *L*s; and so forth. They are reassembled and placed behind cards (*A-I*) sequenced in the first pass.

In the third pass, the cards containing *S-Z* are sorted on their digit punching position and ejected into pockets two through nine. That is, pocket two would contain cards with *S*s; pocket three, *T*s; pocket four, *U*s; and so forth. When reassembled, they are placed behind the partial deck containing cards *A-R* (*A-I* plus *J-R*) from the previous two passes (Fig. 8-9).

Alphabetic sorting on the IBM 83 sorter is, thus, faster than on the earlier model 82, because, after the first pass, the deck of cards to be sorted is progressively decreasing. With fewer remaining cards to be sorted in each of the second and third passes, plus the greater rate of speed of the model itself, the job can be done in a shorter period of time on the 83 than on the 82.

Computation of Sorting Time

The time needed to sort a given deck of cards depends largely upon factors such as the number of cards in the deck, the size of the numeric field to be sorted, the speed of the sorter to be used, and the degree of experience of the operator. The IBM 83 sorter (Fig. 8-5) reads at the rate of 1,000 cards per minute. Assuming that 10,000 cards are to be sorted, it would take a total of ten minutes of machine or running time. The time applies only to sorting the stack of cards once, or on one column. If, for example, the 10,000 cards are to be sorted on a three numeric field, then it would take thirty minutes to sort them properly because the cards have to go through the sorter three times, three passes, before they are finally sorted.

A formula for the computation of total sorting time is:

Total sorting time = Running time + handling time.

$$\text{Running time} = \frac{V \times Nc}{S}$$

V = Number of cards to be sorted
Nc = Number of columns in the numeric field to be sorted
S = Speed of the sorter used

To apply the formula, assume the following data:

> To be sorted: 2,500 cards on a four-digit field, using an IBM 83 sorter, the speed of which is 1,000 cards per minute. Allow 25 per cent of the running time for handling time.

First, we must determine the total running time. Substituting values in the formula, we would get:

$$\frac{2,500 \times 4}{1,000} = 10 \text{ minutes } + \text{ handling time}$$

Total sorting time $= 10$ minutes $+ 2.5$ minutes handling time $= 12.5$ minutes.

If an operator were being paid \$3.00 per hour (or \$.05 per minute) to run the machine, the total labor cost would be: $12.5 \times .05 = \$.625$, or 62½ cents. Compare this with the labor cost involved if sorting this deck were done manually by the same operator.

Occupational Specification of the Card-sorting-machine Operator; Sorter-machine Operator

Occupational Definition

Tends machine that automatically sorts perforated tabulating cards into specified groups. Riffles cards to prevent overfeeding and jamming, and places cards in feedbox. Pushes buttons on sorting control panel to regulate sorting process. Starts machine and sights through holes to verify sorting. Removes sorted cards from bins. Removes jammed cards to clear machine. May reproduce damaged cards on key-punch machine. May operate tabulating machine, verifying machine, or switchboard.

Education, Training, and Experience

High school graduation required. Usually, three months' on-the-job training to learn machine operation and gain proficiency.

Special Characteristics

Aptitudes

Motor coordination to push buttons on sorting-machine control panel to regulate sorting process.
Manual dexterity to riffle and handle cards.

Interests

Preference for activities of a routine, organized nature to perform repetitive tasks of tending machine.

Temperaments

Must be able to perform repetitive tasks of placing and removing cards, pushing control buttons, and starting machine.
Ability to work under specified instructions with little independent action involved.

Physical activities and environmental conditions

Light work. Stands most of work shift.
Reaches for and handles cards.
Near visual acuity to sight through punched holes.
Work is performed inside.

GLOSSARY OF TERMS

BLOCK SORTING: An operation involving a sort of one or more of the most significant characters of a key to serve as a means of making workable-sized groups from a large volume of records to be sorted.

GROUPING: Arranging a mass of data into groups, each having common characteristics.

SELECTING: Extracting cards from a data file for a specific purpose without disturbing the sequence of the rest of the file.

SORTING: Arranging data or documents in a proper alphabetic or numeric sequence.

chapter

9

THE COLLATION
OF SORTED DATA

AFTER DATA CARDS HAVE BEEN CAREFULLY PREPARED from source documents and sequenced, they are placed in a master file for future use. Management may want to use these stored data for a variety of purposes, some examples of which would be the preparation of sales reports, reports on items purchased for resale, classified information on parts ordered for the manufacturing process, information as to the number of employees hired in different departments during the year, and knowledge of the profit made on various lines carried, of the costs involved in certain departments, or of the location of customers. All of this information is stored in cards in the master file in proper sequence. In order to obtain all of the pertinent information for a specific report, the cards containing it must be gathered together from the total number in the master file, or files, involved. The process of picking out cards containing the desired stored data from the mass, or combining information in two different files, is called *collating,* and the machine that has been developed to do this routine job is called the *collator.*

The Collator

The *collator* is actually an auxiliary high-speed filing machine used after classification has been completed. (See Fig. 9-1.) Although a few of its functions are somewhat similar to those of the sorter, it is a flexible, multipurpose, more complicated machine than the sorter. Because it has hoppers to handle two different groups of cards, it can read several columns of two cards at once, whereas the sorter can read only one column of one card at a time—which limits its application in the collating process.

Purpose of the Collator

In an operation where funds are limited for data-processing equipment, functions such as selecting and merging can be done on the sorter instead of the collator. However, the sorter's limitations must be strictly observed if it is to be used in this way. In a merging operation, for example, the sorter can be used *if the merging field is in the same location in each card.* The collator, on the other hand, is designed for merging two different decks of cards much faster than the sorter, and it does *not* require that the merge field in the two decks of cards be located in the same location. The purpose of the collator is to arrange a deck or two of sorted cards into a predetermined sequence for filing or for further processing.

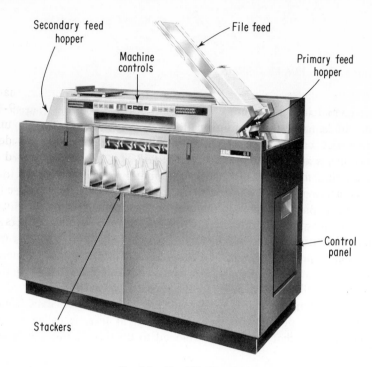

Fig. 9-1. The IBM 88 collator

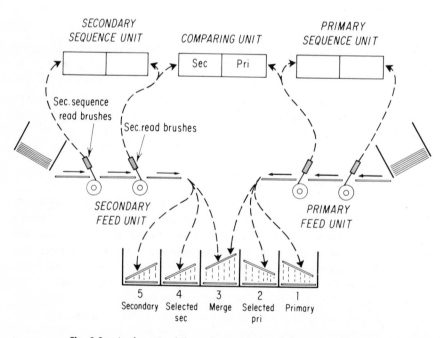

Fig. 9-2. A schematic of the main components of the IBM 88 collator

Description of the IBM 88 Collator

The IBM 88 collator is designed to collate information by merging, matching, merge-matching, sequence checking, selecting, or editing (Fig. 9-1).[1] In order for it to perform these functions, it has two separate feed units, each of which has two sets of eighty reading brushes. The right side of the machine is called the *primary feed unit.* The left side is called the *secondary feed unit* (Fig. 9-2).

Cards moving through from either side eject into one of the five pockets, depending on the type of operation in action. Because the cards move from two opposite directions, they are placed into the hoppers differently. The primary cards are fed nine-edge first, face down, whereas the secondary cards are fed twelve-edge first, face down.

Functions of the Collator

The Merging Function

One of the main capabilities of the collator is the ability to compare two values. Comparing two values manually involves the use of the eyes and the mind. A person looks at one value and then looks at another. Next, he compares and sequences the cards bearing the two values in a predetermined manner. The same basic steps take place in a collator. The brushes are the eyes of the machine, and the control unit (panel) is its mind. The brushes read the values in two cards from separate hoppers. The comparing unit can determine whether they are equal, whether one value is greater than another, or whether one value is less than another.

Merging is taking two separate decks and arranging them into one deck in a given sequence. Before merging, each of the two decks must be in sequence. The card read at the primary reading brushes is compared with that read at the secondary reading brushes. One of three possibilities can exist:

1. The value in a card read by the primary reading brushes is equal to the value in a card read by the secondary reading brushes. This is referred to as *equal sequence.* In this case, the collator is designed to eject first the card from the primary side into pocket three (the merge pocket). Then the card from the secondary side drops into the same

---

[1] The IBM 77 and 89 collators are still available. They perform the same basic functions as the 88 collator above, except that the latter machine includes features such as editing, separate indicators for primary and secondary errors, and an extra stacker for more versatile use. These factors, along with the greater speed, make the 88 collator a superior and a costlier machine.

pocket behind the primary card. In equal sequence, the primary feed always has preference over the secondary feed. This fact is particularly useful, for example, in cases involving the merging of employees' address cards with their master cards for printing purposes. If the address card of an employee is supposed to drop behind his master card, then the address deck should be placed in the secondary feed hopper and the master card in the primary feed hopper.

2. The value in a secondary card is greater than the value in a primary card. This situation is referred to as *low primary*. When it arises, the smaller-value (primary) card drops into pocket three. The secondary card waits at the secondary reading brushes until another primary card contains a value equal to or greater than it.

3. The value in a secondary card is less than the value in a primary card. This is referred to as *low secondary*. In this case, the secondary card (being a smaller value) drops into pocket three and the primary card waits at the primary reading brushes until another secondary card contains a value equal to or greater than it.

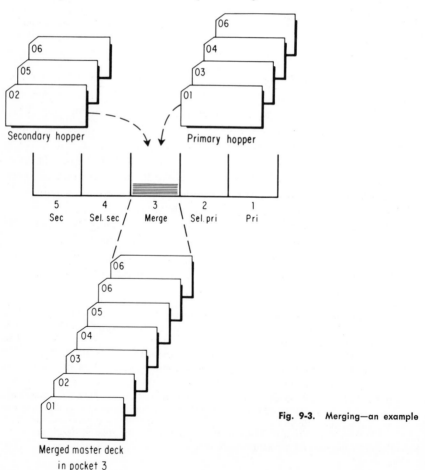

Fig. 9-3. Merging—an example

Merged master deck
in pocket 3

For purposes of illustration, assume that three customer cards were selected out of the master file for temporary use with other information, and merging these cards into the master deck is now desired. In Fig. 9-3, the three customer cards are placed in the secondary hopper and the incomplete master file is placed in the primary hopper. The result is a merged deck in pocket three of the collator, because pocket three is the only pocket that accepts cards from both the primary and the secondary feed units.

During the course of the merge operation in Fig. 9-3, the collator made the following comparisons:

Comparison Number	Secondary Card	Primary Card	Result of Comparison	Action Taken
1	02	—	01	Low primary	Primary card 01 drops into pocket three, while sec. card 02 waits at the sec. read. brushes.
2	02	—	03	Low secondary	Sec. card 02 drops into pocket three, while pri. card 03 waits at the pri. read. station.
3	05	—	03	Low primary	Pri. card 03 drops into pocket three, while sec. card 05 waits at the sec. read. brushes.
4	05	—	04	Low primary	Pri. card 04 drops into pocket three, while sec. card 05 waits again at the sec. read. brushes.
5	05	—	06	Low secondary	Sec. card 05 drops into pocket three, while pri. card 06 waits at the pri. read. brushes.
6	06	—	06	Equal	The primary feed has preference over the sec. Primary card 06 drops into pocket three first, followed by sec. card 06.

Six comparisons were made during the merge operation. The speed at which merging is done varies between 650 and 1,300 cards per minute, depending on results of the comparisons made. The merge operation requires basically the use of secondary and primary reading brushes. However, the sequence reading brushes of both sides can be used simultaneously to check on the proper sequence of the cards coming from both hoppers. If they are activated, and a card is found to be out of sequence, the machine stops automatically and an error light turns on to tell the operator which card (primary or secondary) is out of sequence.

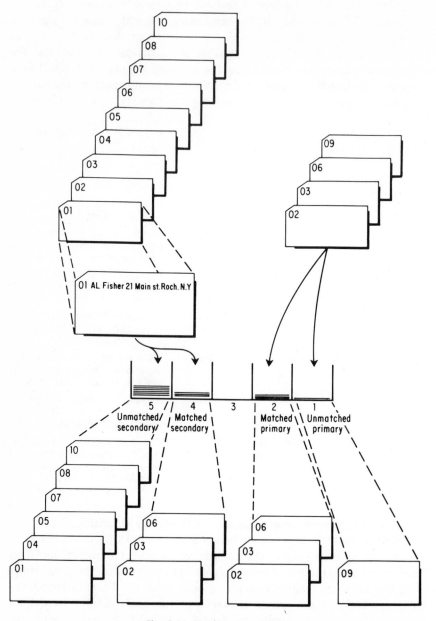

01 AL Fisher 21 Main st. Roch. N.Y

5
Unmatched
secondary

4
Matched
secondary

3

2
Matched
primary

1
Unmatched
primary

Fig. 9-4. Matching—an example

The Matching Function

Matching is a checking function performed by the collator to determine the equality of a specific field in two decks of cards. One deck is fed into the primary feed and the other deck into the secondary feed. In an equal comparison, the equal cards are ejected into pockets two and four. If the comparison is unequal, they are ejected into the extreme pockets (that is, pockets one and five).

To illustrate, suppose that the accounts receivable file of a small business firm contains nine active accounts. At the end of a specific day, four of the accounts are paid up. Assume, further, that the business keeps a separate name-and-address card for each accounts receivable card. In order for the name-and-address file to be updated—that is, to contain only the names and addresses of the unpaid accounts—we must match the paid-up accounts receivable (four cards) against the name-and-address file (09 cards). Fig. 9-4 shows the matched cards in pockets two and four. The cards in pocket five are the name-and-address cards pertaining to the remainder of the accounts receivable file. The card bearing customer number 09 is dropped into pocket one, because it is unmatched, since there is no name-and-address card bearing the same number.

The Match-merging Function

The match-merging function combines the machine's matching and merging capabilities into one operation. *Match-merging* is a routine in which cards in both decks are compared. The cards that match are merged and dropped into one pocket (pocket three) instead of being placed separately into two different pockets. It is one of the most common operations performed on the collator. In a banking application, for example, the consumer credit department keeps a file containing a to-date balance card for each loan made by the bank to a given customer. It is referred to as the *balance file*. Periodically, the bank receives payment of installments made by some customers toward the payment of their loans. After these payments are punched into payment cards, they are compared with the balance file so that each payment card will merge with the balance card bearing the same customer number. This is done for the purpose of calculating the unpaid balance, if any. Fig. 9-5 shows three payment cards placed in the secondary hopper and the balance file placed in the primary hopper. The two decks are compared. Cards 003, 005, and 009 in both decks agree. Under the match-merge operation, they merge together and drop into pocket three. The remaining cards in the balance file drop into pocket two because they find no match in the secondary file.

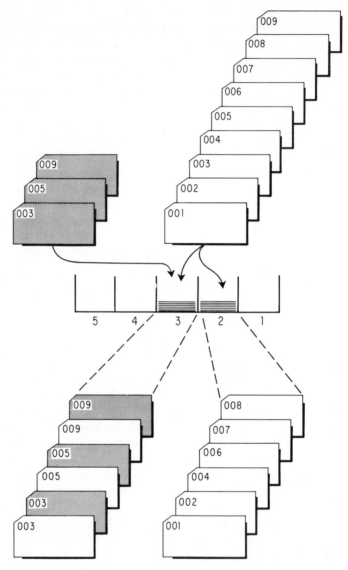

Fig. 9-5. Match-merge—a further example

If, for example, balance card 009 in the primary hopper were missing, the payment card 009 in the secondary hopper will not find a match and will drop into pocket four instead of pocket three. When such a situation occurs, it is investigated and proper corrections made.

The Sequence-checking Function

Sequence checking is the process of determining whether the IBM cards in a given file are in the proper order by comparing each card with the one ahead of it. Depending upon the wiring of the control panel, the primary and secondary files can be sequence checked either separately or simultaneously. Usually sequence checking is done along with merging, matching, or match-merging operations, but it can also be performed as a separate function on the collator if the occasion demands this.

In sequence checking, three possibilities can occur: (1) The value in one card may be greater than the value in another card preceding it. This is referred to as *high sequence*. (2) The value in one card may be equal to the value in another card preceding it. This is referred to as *equal sequence*. (3) The value in one card may be less than the value in another card preceding it. This is called *low sequence*.

In ascending sequence checking, for instance, the file is considered in order if the value of any given card is either equal to or greater than the value of the one preceding it; and vice versa, in a descending sequence-checking operation. Fig. 9-6 shows a deck of ten cards, numbers 001-010. When a sequence check is desired, the following pairs of comparisons are made:

	Cards Compared	Result	Action Taken
1.	001-002	High sequence	Continue to next comparison.
2.	002-003	High sequence	Continue to next comparison.
3.	003-005	High sequence	Continue to next comparison.
4.	005-004	*Low sequence*	Card 004 is out of order. The machine stops immediately. Sequence of the two cards is corrected by the operator, and then the operation resumes.
5.	004-005	High sequence	Continue to next comparison.
6.	005-006	High sequence	Continue to next comparison.
7.	006-007	High sequence	Continue to next comparison.
8.	007-007	Equal sequence	Continue to next comparison.
9.	007-008	High sequence	Continue to next comparison.
10.	008-010	High sequence	Sequence is in order. But because no more cards are left in the hopper, the collator halts automatically. The operator would have to "run-out" cards 008 and 010 from the machine to complete the deck and also to clear the machine for a new operation.

The collator compared ten different pairs of cards, detecting only one card out of order. At that moment, the machine would stop automatically if another operation were being performed. This response is normal when sequence checking is done along with merging.

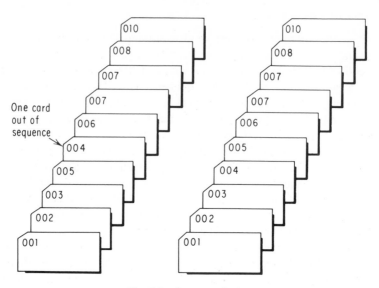

Fig. 9-6. Sequence checking

In sequence checking, two sets of brushes are wired to a sequence unit. They are reading brushes and sequence-checking brushes. Assuming that the procedure in Fig. 9-6 is done through the primary hopper, then the primary reading brushes and the primary-sequence reading brushes would be activated (wired) to the primary-sequence unit (Fig. 9-7).

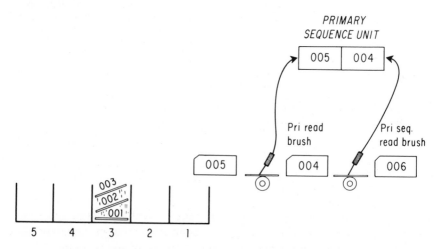

Fig. 9-7. Sequence checking—connections of the two sets of primary brushes to the primary sequence unit

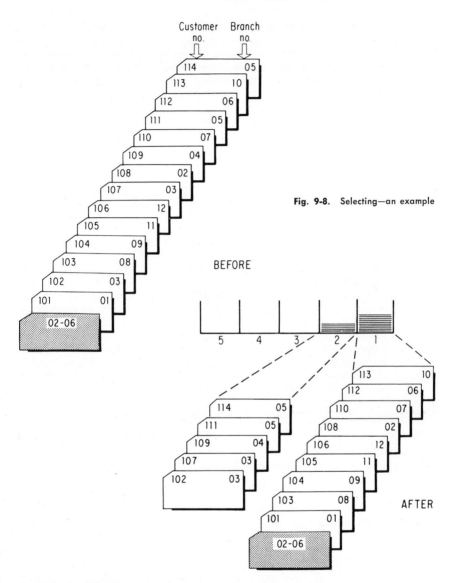

Fig. 9-8. Selecting—an example

The Selecting Function

The selecting function is another basic collating function performed on a collator. It is the pulling out of a file of a card, or a number of cards, having a specific code or value punched in it. A common application involves the selection of cards with an X punched in a specific column out of a file for special processing. Likewise, other types of cards can be selected. Some of these types are:

1. Cards in a file with no code or X in them (NX cards)—for instance, suppose that a master deck of cards contains both male and female employee cards. Assume, further, that all male-employee cards have an X punched in column eighty. Female-employee cards can be selected out of the master deck and dropped into a separate pocket every time the collator fails to detect an X punch in column eighty.

2. A zero-balance card—in an accounts receivable application, all paid-up customer accounts would have zeros punched in the "balance outstanding" field. For the purpose of notifying those customers that they have paid their accounts, the "zero-balance" cards are selected out of the accounts receivable file and dropped into a separate pocket.

3. Cards between minimum and maximum limits—the collator can be wired to select cards that have a value in a specific field which is between two values. For instance, assume that a manufacturing enterprise has twelve branches primarily involved in the sale of given merchandise. Assume, further, that the company desires a sales report involving branches 03, 04, and 05 only. A blank card is punched with a minimum and a maximum of branch numbers 02 and 06, respectively. Then it is placed in front of the master deck containing the sales cards from the twelve branches. The collator would read the first card containing the minimum and maximum values and would select and eject into a separate pocket all cards between these limits. Once they are selected, these cards can be used later in another machine (the accounting machine) for the printing of a report. Fig. 9-8 presents a condensed application of the above example. The coded card is placed in the front of the file. All sales cards from branches 03, 04, and 05 were selected and dropped into pocket two. The remainder of the file was ejected, undisturbed, into pocket one.

Unlike merging, matching, or sequence checking, the selecting function does not require that the deck of cards be in any given sequence or order. The collator selects the cards out of the file independently of their sequential order when compared with the other cards in the deck.

Other IBM Collators

The IBM 77, 85, and 88 collators are numeric collators. They are comparable both in operation and control-panel wiring. They process only numeric data unless a special alphabetic collating device is installed.

The IBM 87 and 188 collators are capable of processing either numeric or alphabetic data and are called alphabetic collators. Both machines are similar in basic functions performed (merging, matching, card selecting, and sequence checking) and speed. The 188 model (Fig. 9-9), however, is a solid-state machine that performs various alphabetic or numeric operations at high speed.

Fig. 9-9. The IBM 188 collator

The UNIVAC 1001 Card Controller

Although the operation of this machine is considered electronic, the card controller (Fig. 9-10) is included in the punched-card data-processing section because its principal function is to arrange decks into groups or sequences for future processing.

The 1001 card controller is a high-speed, multi-purpose machine, the principal collating functions of which include:

1. *Error detection:* some examples are identifying cards that are out of sequence and identifying and selecting duplicate cards within a file or cards with such invalid input as blank columns.
2. *Identifying a specified condition:* such as identifying from a deck of cards those cards which are with or without a particular control punch, zero-balance cards, or cards in which a field is within specified limits.
3. *Matching.*
4. *Merging.*

Being electronic in operation, one unique feature of the 1001 card controller is that it includes 256 addressable locations of core storage (each capable of storing any of sixty-four character codes) and a variable sequence of programming steps. Any, or all, of the information in any given card may be stored selectively for one or more cycles and compared as required by the specific application. All operations are directed through wiring of a removable connection panel.

Fig. 9-10. The UNIVAC 1001 card controller

GLOSSARY OF TERMS

BALANCE FILE: A file containing to-date balance cards for each customer's account or loan.

COLLATING: (1) Combining (interfiling) sets of cards or other documents into a sequence, or (2) selecting specific cards from a file.

HIGH SEQUENCE: A sequence-checking situation which arises when the value in one card is greater than the value in another card preceding it.

LOW PRIMARY: A comparing condition which occurs when the value in a secondary card is greater than the value in a primary card, causing the card under the primary reading brushes to drop in a designated pocket.

LOW SECONDARY: A comparing condition which occurs when the value in a secondary card is less than the value in a primary card, causing the card under the secondary reading brushes to drop in a designated pocket.

MATCH-MERGING: An operation combining the matching and merging functions in one routine. Matched pairs of cards merge in the middle pocket, whereas unmatched cards fall in separately designated pockets.

MATCHING: A checking function to determine the equality of a specific value in two decks of cards.

MERGING: Arranging two separate decks of cards into one deck in a given sequence.

SELECTING: Extracting cards with a specific code or value from a deck of cards.

SEQUENCE CHECKING: An operation designed to determine whether the cards in a given file are in proper order.

REVIEW QUESTIONS

1. What are the advantages of a collator as compared to a sorter?
2. Describe the IBM 88 collator. What are its main functions?
3. Define the following terms:

   (a) matching
   (b) merging
   (c) sequence checking
   (d) match-merging
   (e) selecting
   (f) editing
   (g) low primary
   (h) low secondary
   (i) high sequence
   (j) equal sequence
   (k) low sequence

4. Name the types of cards that can be selected out of a deck of punched cards. Explain each type briefly.
5. Summarize the similarities and dissimilarities of the IBM 88 collator as compared to the 188 collator.
6. List and briefly explain the primary functions of the UNIVAC 1001 card controller.

chapter

10

THE CALCULATING FUNCTION

MODERN BUSINESS FIRMS WOULD BE considerably handicapped without the use of calculations to solve the many problems and applications generated by daily business events. These calculations are the basic arithmetic calculations of addition, subtraction, multiplication, and division. Because most business problems usually involve, at the very least, some simple calculation in arriving at intelligent solutions, a machine called the *calculator* has been developed to handle the routine, repetitive work necessary in this connection.

What Is Calculating?

Essentially, calculating is reconstructing data or creating new data. It is done by the application of simple arithmetic formulas. For instance, the value of four bars of chocolate at a price of five cents each is obtained by multiplying quantity times unit price, or $4 \times 5 = 20$ cents. The product, *20,* is new data, a value obtained as a result of applying the formula: Quantity $\times$ Unit Price = Total Value.

The IBM punched-card calculator performs any, or all, of the four basic arithmetic operations, which are based on program steps or the wiring of a control panel. The calculator takes one step at a time until all the steps are completed. The first step, usually, is to read a field or several fields from a card. Then the machine performs the necessary calculating operations and punches the answer(s) in the same card. Physically, the IBM 604 electronic calculator is composed of two separate units connected by a cable. The first unit has a card hopper and a stacker. This is called the *punch unit.* The other unit is called the *calculating unit.* It is the area where factor storage and calculations are made. (See Fig. 10-1.) Using the example of the four bars of chocolate, a card is first punched with the quantity and the unit price (five cents). It is fed (twelve-edge first, face down) into the punch unit, which reads one row at a time until all the rows in the card are read. The necessary data in the card are transferred from the punch unit to the calculating unit. In the calculating unit, multiplication is performed and, instantly, the product, *20,* is fed to the punching station of the punch unit, which punches the twenty cents in a predetermined field in the original card.

Payroll Calculations

Although the above example is too simple and elementary to justify the purchase or the rental of an electronic calculator, it does illustrate, simply, the basic components and operation of the units themselves. A routine problem which is performed on the calculator is a payroll application. It involves calculation of the net pay of each employee after certain required deductions, such as Federal income-tax withholding and Social Security tax, are made. Although the application may seem too complex to comprehend, it is, in reality, only the result of a series of basic arithmetic operations presented in a definite sequence. Planning the operations in advance is very important, because the machine can perform only those steps which are wired into the control panel. The steps themselves are basic and must be in proper sequence.

For the purpose of illustrating the calculating function, we shall introduce the payroll steps involved in: (1) calculating an employee's gross pay; (2) calculating his Federal income-tax withholding; and (3) determining his Social Security tax. These deductions are mandatory. Calculation of them is, therefore, necessary before net pay can be obtained.

Calculations for Gross Pay

Most business firms, whether manufacturing, retail, or service, must have various men and women capable of performing various duties and functions. At the rank-and-file level, most employees earn their wages on an hourly basis. Assuming that the hourly rate is a standard $3.00 per hour, and no overtime is involved, the formula for gross pay would be:

Total Hours for the Week $\times$ Rate per Hour $= $ *Gross Pay.*

If an employee works thirty-two hours during a given week, at the rate of $3.00 per hour, then his gross pay for that week would be $32 \times \$3.00 =$ $96.00. The product, $96.00, is new data created by the calculator as a result of multiplying two factors: (1) the multiplicand, or the total hours (32), and (2) the multiplier, or the rate per hour ($3.00). These factors can be fed to the calculator either on two separate cards or on one card.

Calculations for Federal Income Tax

An employee's net pay is always less than his gross pay, owing to the required deductions, one of which is the Federal income-tax withholding. According to the Federal income-tax schedule, a single employee pays proportionately more tax than a married employee does, because of the factor of dependents. The more dependents an employee claims, the less the amount of tax he is likely to pay. In fact, some employees are in a bracket where they pay no Federal income tax, because the amount allowed as deduction for their dependents equals and sometimes exceeds their gross pay.

An employee's gross pay per week is reduced by a specific amount called an *exemption*. Assume that an employee is allowed an exemption in the amount of $13.50 for himself and $13.50 for each dependent. The amount of the total exemption is nontaxable. For example, if William Blatty's gross pay for the week is $100.00 and he claims his wife and son as dependents, then the nontaxable amount is: $13.50 × 3 = $40.50. This means that no tax is computed on the first $40.50 of his pay. The taxable amount is computed by subtracting the nontaxable amount ($40.50) from his gross pay. That is, $100.00 − $40.50 = $59.50. The amount of tax to be deducted from his gross pay for Federal income-tax withholding is calculated by multiplying the taxable amount ($59.50) by a certain percentage. Though the actual percentage will vary—rising on a sliding-scale basis as gross pay rises—assume, for purposes of this illustration, that the taxable amount is multiplied by a fixed 20 per cent. That is, $59.50 × 0.20 = $11.90, Federal withholding tax. If Mr. Blatty's gross pay were $40.00 for the week, however, no tax would be deducted, because the nontaxable amount (from three exemptions at $13.50 per exemption) would be greater than his gross pay.

From the foregoing description, we see that three main factors are required before a calculation for Federal income-tax withholding is feasible:

1. Total hours for the week.
2. The rate per hour.
3. Number of exemptions.

As far as the arithmetic operations are concerned, the calculator would perform three multiplication steps and one subtraction step before it arrived at the amount of Federal income-tax to be withheld. Assume the following data:

John Huntley, an employee with Acadia Oil Company, worked thirty-nine hours for the week ending January 10, 1968. The hourly rate is $4.00. He claims four dependents (himself, his wife, and two children). Calculate the Federal income-tax withholding for the week:

Step 1. Multiply: Total Hours for the Week × Rate/Hr. = *Gross Pay,* or 39 × $4 = $156.00.

Step 2. Multiply: Number of Exemptions × $13.50 = *Nontaxable Amount,* or 4 × $13.50 = $54.00.

Step 3. Subtract: Gross Pay less Nontaxable Amount = *Taxable Amount,* or $156.00 − $54.00 = $102.00.

Step 4. Multiply: Taxable Amount × 20 Per Cent = Federal Income-tax Withholding, or $102 × 0.20 = $20.40.

The Federal withholding tax is $20.40, and it can be punched in a reserved field in the card if it is the only result desired. However, because it is, most likely, a part of the over-all payroll deductions, the amount is stored temporarily in a storage unit of the calculator until other related calculations are completed.

Calculations for F.I.C.A. Tax

Under the Federal Insurance Contributions Act (F.I.C.A.), a deduction from gross pay is required by law for Social Security purposes. Under the law applying for the 1968 tax year, a percentage of the first $7,800 of an employee's earnings in a calendar year is withheld every time a calculation for net pay is made. For the sake of illustration, assume that 4.4 per cent of the gross pay is withheld for F.I.C.A. tax. F.I.C.A. deductions terminate as soon as the employee's accumulated earnings reach $7,800 in the calendar year, or as soon as his accumulated F.I.C.A. deductions reach $343.20 (4.4 per cent of $7,800). Therefore, two main points are involved in the calculation: (1) calculating the F.I.C.A. tax; (2) checking on the accumulated F.I.C.A. tax to date.

To apply the example of John Huntley, the amount of F.I.C.A. tax is calculated by multiplying his gross pay by 4.4 per cent, or

$$\frac{\$156.00 \times 4.4}{100} = \$6.86$$

The F.I.C.A. calculation is deducted in full, if the year-to-date F.I.C.A. including this week's F.I.C.A. has not reached the limit of $343.20. When this limit is reached, no further Social Security deduction is made in that year.

Once the Federal withholding tax and the F.I.C.A. tax are determined, the calculation of net pay is comparatively simple. Assuming that no other deductions are mandatory, net pay is obtained by the following formula:

Net Pay = Gross Pay *less* (Federal Withholding Tax + F.I.C.A. Tax).

To calculate the net pay of John Huntley, we substitute:

Net Pay: $156.00 −($20.40 + $6.86)= $128.74.

The electronic calculator is capable of performing all of the arithmetic in connection with gross pay, Federal withholding tax, and F.I.C.A. tax. It stores the amounts individually and punches them in their related fields in the card at the rate of approximately 100 cards per minute. The value of using an electronic calculator can be realized readily if one visualizes a concern employing anywhere from 100 employees to 10,000 and upward.

IBM Punched-card Calculators

Several types of IBM calculating punches are in use today. The most commonly used calculator in a punched-card data-processing system is the IBM 604 electronic calculating punch, referred to as the *electronic calculator* (Fig. 10-1).

CALCULATING UNIT   PUNCH UNIT

Fig. 10-1.   IBM 604 electronic calculating punch

The title *"electronic calculator"* might lead the reader to believe that the machine should be classified under the category of electronic data processing. Although it is similar to an electronic computer, in that it calculates at electronic speed and uses electronic tubes in its arithmetic and storage units, it is used primarily in punched-card data-processing systems rather than in electronic ones. An electronic tube has two states: a *zero* state, when the tube is turned off, and a *one* state (or value) when it is turned on. A number of electronic tubes are combined for the storage and representation of digits *zero* through *nine*. However, the calculator is distinctly different from an electronic computer in the way it is controlled and also in the manner in which it is fed input and presents output. The IBM 604 calculator receives data through a punched card as input and punches the results either in the card or in designated cards that follow. The number of cycles required to complete the calculations depends on the size of the data involved and the type of problem being worked out. The electronic computer, on the other hand, receives input from paper tape, magnetic tape, and so forth, as well as from the punched card. Likewise, output in the electronic computer is made on magnetic tape, paper tape, or other related means.

The IBM 609 calculator (Fig. 10-2) is the latest model and combines the punching and calculating steps in a single unit. Some of its main features include: (1) solid-state components; (2) flexibility (through control-panel wiring) in extending the amount of time needed for complex calculations; (3) operational speed of 200 cards per minute (versus 100 cards per minute of the 604 model); (4) built-in checking feature to ascertain the validity of all input data; and (5) most significantly, its ability to store and remember any data stored in its magnetic core memory. The memory unit consists of thirty-two addressable units of twelve (fixed) digit positions of core storage in each unit. A unit of storage is called a word. A factor (for example, 7243) stored in a specific word can be added to, subtracted from, and multiplied or divided by, another factor, if required.

Fig. 10-2. IBM 609 calculator

Before any calculations are made, the calculator's panel is wired, in order to store the necessary machine instructions. Next, data cards are fed in and (upon the depression of the proper buttons) factors from the first card in sequence are read at the first reading station. While the card is moving to the punching station, calculations are performed and, as the card passes through the punching station, the results are punched in it (Fig. 10-3). Once completed, the "updated" card passes through the second reading station,[1] on the way to one of the stackers.

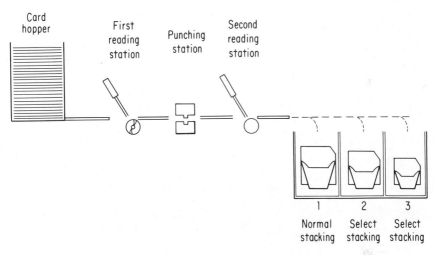

Fig. 10-3. Schematic of IBM 609 calculating punch

Planning and Diagramming a Problem

The Acadia Oil Company regularly processes payroll data of hundreds of its employees simultaneously in the same manner as was illustrated for John Huntley. Prior to the initiation of payroll computations, some planning and diagramming (flow charting) of required steps are necessary. This involves determining in advance what action must be taken and the elements to be taken into consideration in preparation of each employee's check. The preparation of such steps in a logical flow is made (charted) through the use of special symbols constituting a flow chart.

[1] The second reading station is generally used for gang-punching or double-punching purposes.

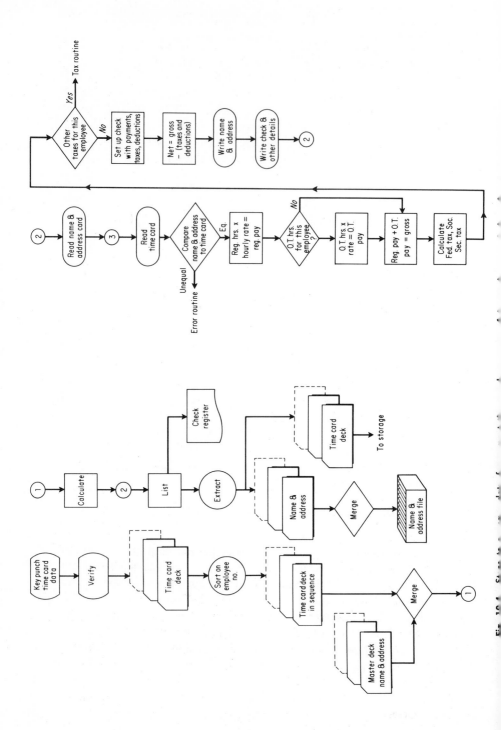

Fig. 10.1 Steps to prepare a list of employees' pay

Fig. 10-4 maps out: (1) the overall steps followed in preparing Acadia Oil employees' data for computations, and (2) the instructions to the calculator regarding the factors to consider and the sequence in which it must compute net pay. They are flow charted for a punched-card system. Once the system is laid out, the personnel involved can easily carry out the details included in the processing cycle.

GLOSSARY OF TERMS

ELECTRONIC CALCULATOR: A calculating machine capable of performing arithmetic functions on punched data, based on programmed steps wired in a control panel.

EXEMPTION: A nontaxable amount withheld from gross pay for each dependent declared.

F.I.C.A. TAX: A tax deducted from gross pay for Social Security purposes.

GROSS PAY: The total amount earned from regular and overtime worked (that is, total hours × rate per hour).

NET PAY: The difference between an employee's gross pay and all related deductions.

OVERTIME: The amount of time worked beyond a standard, full-time load (normally forty hours per week).

REVIEW QUESTIONS

1. What is meant by the term *calculate?* Give an example.
2. What are the main arithmetic functions of the IBM punched-card calculator? Explain.
3. Explain how the punch and the calculating units are used to calculate a given problem.
4. Show (by giving an example) how new data are created in a "gross pay" calculation.
5. What factors are needed in calculating for Federal income-tax withholding? Explain by giving an example.
6. What is meant by F.I.C.A.? For what purpose is F.I.C.A tax withheld?

chapter 11

THE
PREPARATION
OF REPORTS

THE IBM ACCOUNTING MACHINES

CARD READING

PRIMARY CAPABILITIES OF ACCOUNTING MACHINES

THE SUMMARIZING FUNCTION   THE PRINTING FUNCTION   Printing Methods   Types of Printing Operations   *Detail Printing*   *Group Printing*   Form Spacing   The Control Tape   SUMMARY PUNCHING

THE UNIVAC 1004 CARD PROCESSOR

THE END RESULT OF ANY punched-card data-processing application is the production of final reports containing essential facts without which management cannot function well. Printing aids us in the formulation or reconstruction of data to produce those reports by listing or compressing the pertinent facts into a concise and presentable form. Report preparation is, therefore, considered one of the most important functions to be performed.

The IBM Accounting Machines

The machines involved in report preparation are called *tabulators*. The two IBM tabulators most commonly in use are the IBM 402 and 407 accounting machines (Figs. 11-1 and 11-2). Although their basic functions are the same, the latter is a more versatile machine than the former.

The accounting machine processes data through instructions given to it by a control panel. The control panel gives the machine its versatility, in that it tells it what part(s) of the data punched in a card to print, where to print it on the form, what to accumulate, and when as well as where to print the accumulated total or to clear the counters for another operation. Each control panel contains a set of instructions for a specific operation. With the exception of minor adjustments through switches and paper alignment, the accounting machine is made ready to process a new application when the operator simply inserts the proper control panel containing the instructions related to it.

Card Reading

Cards are placed in the hopper nine-edge first, face down. When the machine is started, the first card moves to the first reading station. It is held there until the machine reads all the necessary data punched in it. The reading station contains 960 reading brushes to scan any one of 960 possible holes in a given card; that is, 80 columns × 12 rows of holes = 960 holes. Once a hole is detected, a contact is made, the impulse of which is transmitted to the control panel, which controls the specific functions to be performed by the machine. (See Fig. 11-3.)

After the card is read, it moves over the second reading station and around a drum (clockwise) on its way to the stacker. The speed at which cards are read on the IBM 407 model is 150 cards per minute. The first

Fig. 11-1. IBM 402 accounting machine

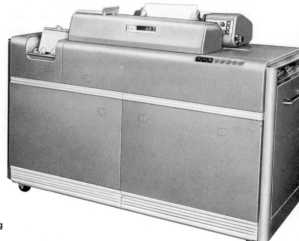

Fig. 11-2. IBM 407 accounting machine

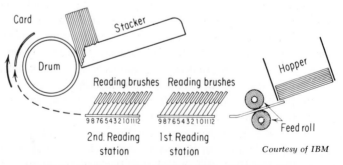

Courtesy of IBM

Fig. 11-3. Card path schematic, IBM 407 accounting machine

reading station is used for comparing certain values in a card with those in another card at the second reading station. Addition and subtraction, as well as printing, normally use the second reading station.

Primary Capabilities of Accounting Machines

The primary capabilities of an accounting machine are: (1) *summarizing,* (2) *printing,* (3) *controlling, spacing,* and *positioning* of the form on which data are being printed, and (4) *summary punching.*

The Summarizing Function

Summarizing aids in the reconstruction of data by compressing them into a more concise and presentable form. It is the end result of calculating and creates data in a new form. The income statement, for instance, is a summary of the operations of a particular business firm through a specific period of time.

In an accounting machine, summarizing takes place in counters capable of accumulating totals after addition or subtraction of numeric values punched in the cards is completed. Counters can total digits, the number of which depends upon their size. A two-position counter totals up to 99, and so forth. In the IBM 407 accounting machine, counters range in size

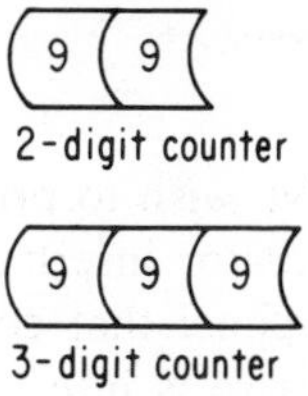

2-digit counter

3-digit counter

Fig. 11-4. Two- and three-digit counters

from three to eight positions. One hundred sixty-eight (168) is the maximum number of possible accumulating positions. This number of positions is achieved by coupling counters together to formulate or total an amount of a size that large. It is accomplished through control-panel wiring.

Fig. 11-5 shows a control panel inserted in a 407 accounting machine (tabulator). With the exception of the sorter, the key punch, and the verifier, all punched data-processing machines are instructed by a control panel (or a plugboard) to read certain columns in a card and process the data they contain. The panel is similar in operation to a telephone switchboard. An electrical circuit is completed when a wire connection is made between the reading brush(es) and the printwheel(s). The connection activates printing.

Fig. 11-5. A control panel inserted in the IBM 407 accounting machine

For example, if we wish to print a character stored in column seventeen of a card, the operator inserts one end of an insulated wire in a hub
(hole) in the control panel that corresponds to reading brush seventeen.
The other end of the wire is inserted in another hub to allow the desired
printwheel to print the character (Fig. 11-6).

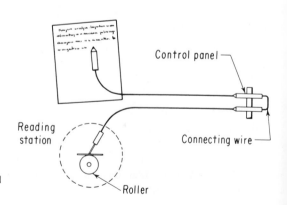

Fig. 11-6. An example of control
panel wiring

Counters can be used to accumulate three main types of totals: (1) major, (2) intermediate, and (3) minor. A *major* total is the total of each of the major sections or divisions making up a business firm, thus representing the largest grouping. An *intermediate* total represents the total of the subdivisions of a business firm. A *minor* total represents the smallest part of a section or a division. It is, in fact, a part of a subdivision or a subsection of a business firm. Assume, for instance, that Company *A* has three districts, each of which supervises two offices of four salesmen in

District	Office	Salesman No.	Total by salesman	Total by office	Total by district
			A B C Company		
			Sales Report		
		For the month ending Dec. 31, 1967			
Eastern	A	11	5.00		
		12	8.00		
		13	7.20		
		14	6.80	27.00	
	B	21	10.00		
		22	8.00		
		23	16.00		
		24	2.10	36.10	63.10 *
Southern	A	31	4.40		
		32	3.65		
		33	5.00		
		34	4.20	17.25	
	B	41	10.00		
		42	8.00		
		43	8.05		
		44	6.00	32.05	49.30 *
Western	A	51	81.00		
		52	62.00		
		53	1.29		
		54	15.04	159.33	
	B	61	7.14		
		62	16.02		
		63	4.06		
		64	9.00	36.22	195.55 *
					307.95 **

* Major Total
** Grand Total

Fig. 11-7. Sales report, showing the three different types of totals

each office. In a formal printed statement of the sales operations of the firm during a specific period of time, the total sales of each salesman is considered a *minor* total occupying usually the far left-hand column. The sum of *each* of the two offices consisting of four salesmen is called an *intermediate* total. It is usually printed in the middle column. The total of the two offices combined represents the *major* total and is printed in the right column. A final or a grand total of the firm can be obtained simply by the addition of the individual major totals of each of the three districts in the right column. The grand total is usually printed with two asterisks to its right (Fig. 11-7).

Fig. 11-7 shows the total sales made by each of the twenty-four salesmen hired by Company *A*. The total for each is called a *minor* total, because it is considered as the smallest grouping as shown in the left-most total column. The middle total column contains six amounts, each of which is the total of the four salesmen reporting to their respective offices. These are called the *intermediate* totals. The right column contains three district amounts, each of which is the total of the two offices. These are called *major* totals, because they are considered the largest grouping. The grand sales total of $307.95 is obtained by the addition of the three major totals in the right column.

The Printing Function

Another function of the tabulator is to print the data accumulated in the counters, in addition to other information which is read from the IBM card. Fig. 11-7 is a printed sales report of Company *A* by salesman, office, and district. It is presented under the summarizing function in order to clarify the three different types of totals which the counters are capable of accumulating.

Printing methods

Printing is done by one of two methods: serial and parallel. A typewriter types one character at a time as the carriage holding the paper in place moves from right to left, until the line is fully printed. This is referred to as *serial* printing. The IBM accounting machine, on the other hand, utilizes the *parallel* method of printing, because it prints one complete line at a time. All the required data are printed simultaneously on it. Speed is the main advantage of the parallel-printing over the serial-printing method.

Printing on the IBM 407 accounting machine is performed by means of printwheels which rotate to the specific digit, letter, or special character. When all of the printwheels are positioned correctly, they are actuated simultaneously, resulting in the printing of a complete line. There

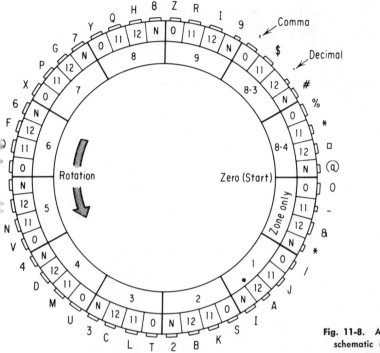

Fig. 11-8. A printwheel schematic (IBM)

are 120 printwheels, each of which can print the ten digits, twenty-six letters, and eleven special characters (Fig. 11-8). They can print within a width of twelve inches, ten characters per inch.

Types of printing operations

The IBM accounting machines perform two types of printing operations: (1) *detail printing,* and (2) *group printing.*

DETAIL PRINTING. Detail printing, or listing, is the printing of part or all of the information punched in a card onto a report form and also includes the added function of addition or subtraction performed by the counters on the amounts in the cards for various types of totals. Detail printing is performed when a detailed report including each transaction is required. There is a line for each card read by the machine (Fig. 11-9).

GROUP PRINTING. Group printing is summarizing a group of cards and printing their totals on a report. Values from the punched cards are entered in specific counters. The counters are "read out" at the end of the group of cards, and their contents are printed on a line. Fig. 11-10 is an example of group printing based on the data indicated in Fig. 11-9.

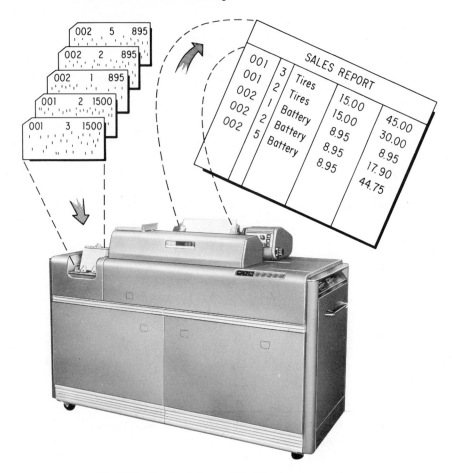

Fig. 11-9. Detail printing on IBM 407 accounting machine

Initially, certain data are read from the first card of a group for identification purposes. These data are printed first on the report. The remaining data in the group of cards are read and their values accumulated in counters. When the last card in the group is sensed, the contents of the counters are printed on the same line with the identifying information.

Group printing can be done because of the ability of the accounting machine to distinguish a card of one group from a card belonging to another group. A specific field in one card is compared with the same field in another card. If they are equal, the machine considers the two cards as a part of the same group. Addition or subtraction is done, and certain values from the second card are accumulated in a counter (or counters) containing values from a previous card (or cards). If, however, the specific field

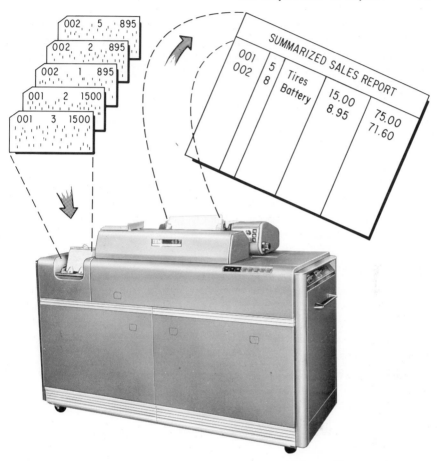

Fig. 11-10. Group printing on IBM 407 accounting machine

in the second card is not the same or equal to the same field in the card previous to it, an unequal compare exists. The second card is considered as a part of a different group. At this time, before reading and starting a new group, the machine goes through a number of steps called *total cycle*. The last card belonging to the present group is added to or subtracted from its respective counter (or counters). The group total is then printed on one line. A space is made, and the machine is ready to handle a new group.

Fig. 11-10 is an example of group printing. Card one bearing part number 001 is compared with card two bearing part number 001. The result is *equal compare*. The machine adds the number of units sold in card one (*3*) in one counter and its value (*45*) in another counter. Next, card two bearing part number 001 is compared with card three bearing salesman-number 002. The result is *unequal compare*. Before card three is read and processed, the accounting machine goes through a total cycle. The units sold in card two are added to the same counter which stores the units sold in card one. Now the amount accumulated in it totals 5 (3 + 2). The value of the units sold in card two also is added to the same counter which stores the value of the units sold in card one. Now the amount accumulated in that counter is 75 (45 + 30).

When this addition is completed, the machine prints on one complete line the contents of the two counters, in addition to the part number and a description of the item which the amounts represent. When this is completed, the machine reverts to the comparing function and compares card three with card four, and so on, until the last card is compared and its group total is printed.

Controlling, Spacing, and Positioning Functions

An accounting machine, like a typewriter, has a carriage into which a sheet of paper is placed and positioned for the preparation of a statement or a report. The carriage of an accounting machine differs from that of a typewriter, however, in that its vertical movement is made automatically through a control tape (Fig. 11-11). Further, because the accounting machine uses the parallel method of printing, the automatic carriage does not move horizontally from right to left as a typewriter normally moves.

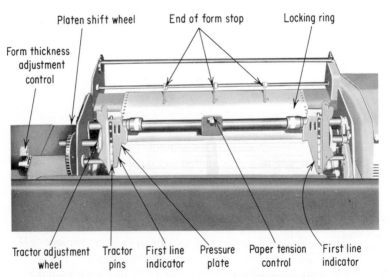

Fig. 11-11. Paper form positioned around the automatic carriage of the IBM 407 accounting machine

Form spacing

Inserting and positioning one form at a time into the carriage is impractical. Because such an effort is time consuming, continuous forms are used which are perforated in such a way that each form can be detached (burst) easily from the other forms. To aid in the automatic vertical spacing of the form itself, its extreme ends are mounted on tractor pins, the movement of which is determined by the location of a punched hole in a control device called the *control tape.*

The control tape

The control tape is a piece of standard-sized paper designed to control the movement of the form by punching holes in specific locations in it. It is divided into twelve vertical spaces, called *channels* (Fig. 11-12). Horizontally, it contains a maximum of 132 lines for the control of the form. In the middle, prepunched round holes are mounted on a sprocket wheel to advance the tape so that its movement is synchronized with that of

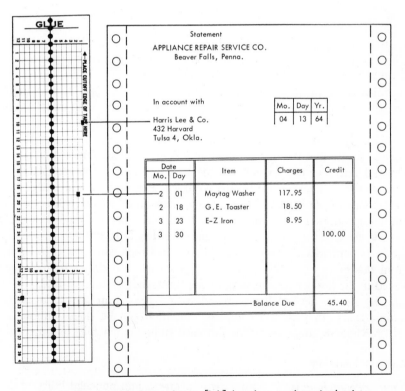

Fig. 11-12. A punched control tape [left] based on predetermined printing locations [right] (*IBM*)

the form. For instance, if the form is on line ten, the control tape is positioned and is synchronized on line ten. Therefore, the length of the control tape is determined by the number of lines the form contains. If a form contains thirty-seven lines, the control tape should be cut to conform to the length of the form (thirty-seven lines) (Fig. 11-12).

A form is divided into two parts: (1) the head, and (2) the body. The *head* of a form includes usually the name and address of the customer, his number (if any), and the date of the statement. The *body* of the statement consists of all the details necessary for the statement being printed. In an invoice, these include the date of the order of the item, the item catalog number, the description of the item, the quantity ordered, the price of each unit, and the total price. Upon determination of the location of all the information to be printed on the form, the top of the control tape is aligned with that of the form and the required holes are punched in it so as (1) to direct the machine to start at the first printing line and to print the address and other related information, (2) to skip to the first body line for printing all the body details, (3) to indicate the first overflow line, and (4) to skip to a predetermined "total" line after the last body line is printed.

The rectangular holes in a control tape indicate to the machine the location of the significant lines. They are punched by an IBM tape punch (Fig. 11-13). A hole punched in *channel one* always indicates the first printing line of a form. *Channel two* usually indicates the first body line of the form to be printed. *Channel twelve* indicates the last printing line or overflow, and *channel four* indicates the location of the predetermined total line.

In Fig. 11-12, a hole is punched in channel one and line ten to indicate the location of the first printing line. A hole is also punched in channel two and line nineteen to indicate the first body line. The intersection of channel twelve and line thirty-two is punched to indicate the last printing line. Another hole is punched in channel four and line thirty-three to indicate the location of the predetermined total line. Once the tape is punched, its ends are glued and then inserted into position (Fig 11-14). A "restore" button is depressed to synchronize the control tape with that of the form. From this point on, after the machine is started and the cards have been placed in the hopper, the spacing of the form, the printing of data, and the skipping to the desired location and to the next form are done entirely automatically. In fact, the complete operation can be done without any need for human attendance. The last card stops the machine automatically.

Summary Punching

Summary punching is the automatic conversion into punched holes of data accumulated in the accounting machine from detail cards. These data rep-

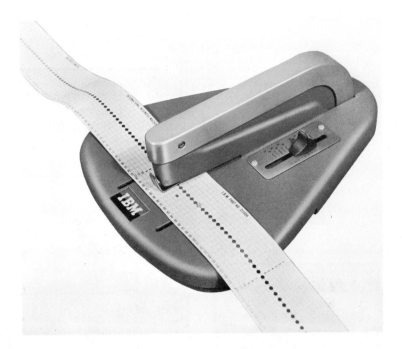

Fig. 11-13. An IBM tape punch

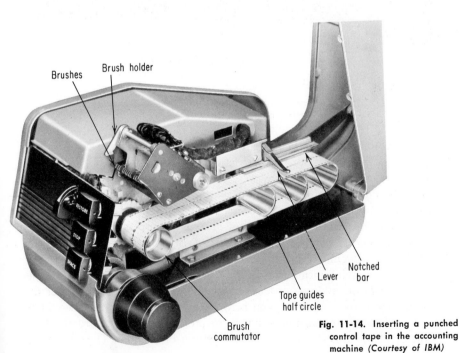

Brushes   Brush holder

RESTORE

STOP

SPACE

Brush
commutator

Tape guides
half circle

Lever

Notched
bar

Fig. 11-14. Inserting a punched
control tape in the accounting
machine (Courtesy of IBM)

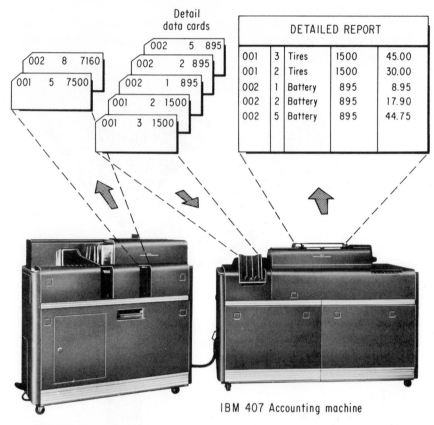

Fig. 11-15. A summary punch connection between the accounting machine and a summary punch machine *(Courtesy of IBM)*

resent the total of a particular group of cards. Summary punching can be, and is, frequently done while detail printing is going on, if the accounting machine is attached by a cable to an IBM 514 reproducing summary punch and if the proper control panels are inserted in both machines. (See Fig. 11-15.) The main value of summary punching is to punch in a new card information which is not shown on any other card. In Fig. 11-15, five cards, bearing numbers *001, 001, 002, 002,* and *002,* are placed in the accounting-machine hopper. The machine detail prints a line for each card. While printing is being performed, the counters in the machine perform the addition of all cards having the same number. After the second card (001) is printed and before card 002 is read, the accounting machine actuates the summary punch to punch in a blank card the total of the first two cards stored in a specific counter or counters. Once punched, the accounting machine prints the contents of the first card 002 and the remaining two cards, the total of which is also punched in another blank card in the summary punch machine.

The UNIVAC 1004 Card Processor

This component (Fig. 11-16) is unique among card-accounting machines. It combines in a single unit the functions of card reading, arithmetic processing, and high-speed printing, and is believed to match the data-processing power of a much larger system. The machine comes in an eighty- and a ninety-column version and input-output speeds are two to three times as fast as conventional tabulating equipment. Data cards are read at 300-400 per minute, and printing is done at 300-400 lines per minute. Each printing line contains 132 alphanumeric print positions, each capable of printing any of the ten numeric, twenty-six alphabetic, and/or twenty-seven symbols.

Fig. 11-16. The UNIVAC card processor

The card processor is a solid-state electronic data-processing machine which features 961 character positions of magnetic core memory,[1] avail-

---

[1] Programming is done through a *plugboard* or a control panel which resembles those of conventional accounting machines.

able at all times for invoice information. Every storage location is, in effect, a net balance accumulator, providing capacity for storing and totaling net amounts, costs, weights, and quantities. Furthermore, its powerful totaling ability is ascribed both to the large core memory and to the use of the "add-to-memory" method of accumulation. The progressive results of computations are stored in the same memory locations occupied by the values which they supersede. Thus, additional storage locations need never be allotted for intermediate totals.

GLOSSARY OF TERMS

CHANNEL: A parallel track in which data are recorded. Also, a means of transmission in data communication.

CONTROL TAPE: A paper tape (control medium) used on tabulators and printers to control the movement of paper forms and the location of data on them.

DETAIL PRINTING: Card-for-line printing. Printing data from each punched card passing through the tabulator.

GROUP PRINTING: A procedure which involves printing one line (group total) for each homogeneous group of cards.

PARALLEL PRINTING: One-line-at-a-time printing, a characteristic of the tabulator.

PRINTING: Preparing data in hard-copy form.

SERIAL PRINTING: One-character-at-a-time printing (for example, typewriting).

SUMMARIZING: The function of compressing data into a more concise and presentable form.

SUMMARY PUNCHING: Automatic conversion into punched holes of data accumulated in the tabulator from detail cards.

TABULATOR: A machine (synonymous with an accounting machine) that reads data from a specific medium (for example, punched cards, or paper or magnetic tape) and prints or produces tables and totals on continuous paper.

REVIEW QUESTIONS

1. List and explain briefly the main functions of the control panel of an accounting machine.
2. How are data cards read in an IBM accounting machine?
3. List the four primary functions of an accounting machine. Explain each function briefly.
4. How is summarizing performed in an accounting machine? Illustrate.
5. What is the function of a counter? What is the maximum value which can be stored in a four-position counter?

6. What types of totals can be represented or stored in a counter? Define each type and present an illustration of your own, showing their significance and their location on a paper form.

7. How is a final or grand total derived?

8. What are the two methods of printing? Explain and give an example of each method.

9. What is detail printing? What is group printing?

10. A deck containing eight cards (account numbers 201, 202, 203, 203, 204, 205, 205, and 206) are placed in the card hopper of an accounting machine. Assuming that detail printing is desired, how many lines would the machine print? How many lines would be group printed? Why?

11. What is meant by total cycle?

12. How does an accounting machine differ from a typewriter with respect to form spacing?

13. What is a control tape? What four main functions does it perform? For what purpose are round holes prepunched in the middle of the tape?

14. Explain the two parts of a form. How are they controlled by a control tape?

15. What is summary punching? On what machine(s) is it used? Why?

16. Explain the unique features and functions of the UNIVAC 1004 card processor.

chapter

12

CASE ILLUSTRATION

BACKGROUND INFORMATION

DATA PREPARATION

RECORDING DATA ON A NEW-LOAN CARD

PREPARATION OF A BALANCE CARD

DATA FIELDS WHY A NINE-DIGIT ACCOUNT-NUMBER FIELD?

THE COUPON BOOK

THE DATA-PROCESSING PROCEDURE

1. RECORDING BY REPRODUCING 2. TABULATING PAYMENT CARDS
3. SORTING PAYMENT CARDS 4. MATCH-MERGING PAYMENTS
WITH BALANCE FILE 5. THE CALCULATING FUNCTION 6. SORT-
ING OLD BALANCE CARDS FROM THE FILE 7. CHECKS AND BAL-
ANCES 8. MERGING NEW-PAYMENT CARDS IN THE BALANCE FILE

THIS CHAPTER INTRODUCES an actual banking application involving the use of the punched-card data-processing machines in the daily-payments section at the Consumer Credit Department, Lincoln Rochester Trust Company, Rochester, New York. The customer's and dealer's names have been changed for obvious reasons. The case study that follows is a step-by-step description of the data as they flow through the various stages and are processed by most of the machines involved in the punched-card data-processing cycle.

Background Information

Dr. Wilhelm Z. Blatty, an associate professor of business administration at a local university, purchased an unfurnished cottage on Lake Ontario, where he intends to spend his future summer vacations. On January 1, 1967, Harry L. Gordon, a furniture dealer in Rochester, New York, advertised in the local newspaper an attractive sale of home furniture, including sofas, tables, lamps, and other similar items.

Even though it was too early in the year for the use of the cottage, Dr. Blatty decided to respond to the advertisement, and he negotiated a sale with Mr. Gordon, the store manager and owner, to furnish the cottage for a total cost of one thousand dollars ($1,000.00). Terms: no service charge if the amount is paid in full within ninety days from the date of purchase, that is, before April 1. The amount of any unpaid balance, however, can be financed after the ninety-day privilege elapses. On January 1, Dr. Blatty agreed to the terms and signed a conditional sales contract for the amount of the purchase ($1,000.00). The furniture was delivered to the cottage the same day.

A business firm such as Harry L. Gordon, Inc., often makes arrangements with a local commercial bank to which it sells the conditional sales contract(s) for immediate cash. At times, a firm is willing to pay a fee or an amount based on a predetermined percentage for the purpose of converting some or all of its notes or, in this case, its sales contracts into cash when cash is needed. However, regardless of the exact reason(s), Harry L. Gordon transferred the contract signed by Dr. Blatty to the bank and received $1,000.00 less a fee which the bank charged for holding it for ninety days. The customer at any point in this process is held liable for $1,000.00 only, regardless of the fee which the bank charged Mr. Gordon, the furniture dealer, himself. The bank fee is merely a cost to the dealer for receiving the amount today rather than waiting ninety days for payment.

In the foregoing discussion, we assume that the bank accepts the sales contract only after investigating and ascertaining the satisfactory credit standing of the customer (in this example, Dr. Blatty's). After Mr. Gordon transferred the contract to the bank, the latter party notified Dr. Blatty that in the future he must deal directly with the bank's main office or any of its branches. Included in the letter, a statement was made to the effect that, if Dr. Blatty did not find it convenient to pay the amount within ninety days, the enclosed coupon book was to be used for payment by installments. It contained coupons each of which represented one monthly payment including interest, to be made by Dr. Blatty (Fig. 12-4). That is, if the loan were extended into twelve monthly payments, the coupon book would contain twelve coupons.

Data Preparation

Upon the receipt of the sales contract, the bank sends it to the consumer loan division for processing. The consumer loan division has a primary function of processing accounts and forwarding them to data processing. Because one form of loan must be distinguished from another form, the loans are recognized by "type." The ten different types of loans are:

0 Home Modernization Loan—for the purpose of remodeling or improving the interior or exterior of a house that is not eligible under FHA. See type six below.

1 American Installment Credit Corporation (AICC) Loan—a conditional sales contract made through automobile dealers for a customer automobile loan.

2 Commercial Contracts Loan—primarily extended to business firms, usually referred to as a *business loan.*

3 Cash Payment Auto Loan—distinguished from type one above in that the customer negotiates with the bank directly and receives a sum of money for the purpose of buying an automobile.

4 Residential Loan—results from conditional sales contracts for the purchase of electric appliances such as refrigerators, toasters, irons, vacuum cleaners, and other similar items.

5 Home Furnishing Loan—any loans resulting from the purchase of home furniture on credit. Dr. Blatty's purchase of furniture from Mr. Gordon is considered a type-five loan.

6 Federal Housing Authority (FHA) Loan—primarily used for home improvement, with conditions set by the authority.

7 Insurance Dealer Auto Loan—extended to a customer for the purchase of an automobile directly through the insurance company which writes the insurance policy.

8 Cash Personal Loan—approved for any reason not properly labeled under any of the other types of loans. For instance, a customer in need of $200.00 for travel expenses.

9 Education Loan—extended to those customers who need financial aid for educational expenses. Students as well as teachers are included.

A clerk types from the original sales contract the required data on a *loan detail* card (Fig. 12-1). Hereafter, all data pertaining to the processing of Dr. Blatty's account will be obtained from this detail card. The loan detail card is not used in the processing of data, but is considered a master card for reference in the future. It is placed in a loan detail file.

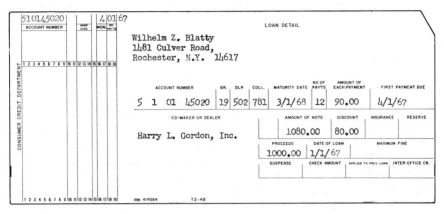

Fig. 12-1.   A loan detail card *(Lincoln Rochester Trust Company)*

On the top of the card, the name and address of the customer are typed. In the middle of the card, the clerk also types an account number and the branch number (*19*) of the bank to which the furniture dealer transferred the sales contract. Next, the dealer number, *502,* is typed, a code assigned solely to Harry L. Gordon, Inc. Each dealer has a different number, a fact which will be useful in later applications in the preparation of sales reports by *dealer* rather than by customer number or by branch.

Next to the "dealer" column is the "collateral" column, bearing number *781.* In the case of Dr. Blatty, his furniture acts as a collateral and can be repossessed in the event that he defaults in his payments. The collateral code for merchandise of this type is 781. The maturity date of the loan is one year from the payment of the first of twelve monthly installments due April 1, 1967. The amount of each payment ($90.00) is computed as follows:

$$\text{Amount of each payment} = \frac{\text{Principal} + \text{interest for year } (8\%)}{\text{Number of payments}}$$

$$\text{To substitute:} \quad \frac{\$1,000.00 + 8\% \text{ of } \$1,000/\text{yr.}}{12} = \frac{\$1,080}{12} = \$90.00$$

The interest rate in this case is 8 per cent per annum.

In the top left corner of the card (Fig. 12-1) is the account number *5 6 28 45020* and the due date of the first payment, April 1, 1967.

Recording Data on a New-Loan Card

Once a nonprocessable *loan detail* card is prepared (Fig. 12-1), the same basic data are punched by a key-punch operator on an IBM card, referred to as a *new-loan card* (Fig. 12-2). The new-loan card will be used later in the preparation of a balance card to represent Dr. Blatty's loan in the balance file and also in producing a coupon book to be mailed to him for monthly payments.

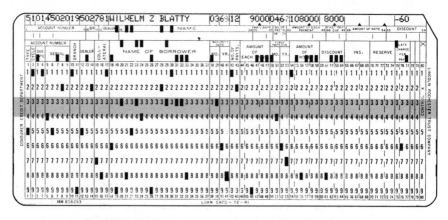

Fig. 12-2. A new-loan card (*Lincoln Rochester Trust Company*)

Preparation of a Balance Card

The next formal step in the data preparation routine is the preparation of a balance card (Fig. 12-3). The balance card is punched with the basic data copied from the new-loan card (Fig. 12-2).

Data Fields

From left to right, the data fields are:

Columns	
1-09	Dr. Blatty's account number.
10-11	The branch number of the bank to which the note was originally transferred.
12-14	Harry L. Gordon's number.
15-17	The collateral number of the furniture purchased by Dr. Blatty.
18-21	The maturity date of the note.
22-23	The number of payments to be received by the bank.
24-29	The exact amount of each installment.

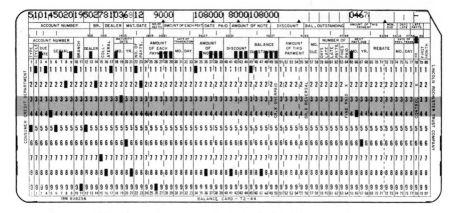

Fig. 12-3. A balance card (*Lincoln Rochester Trust Company*)

30-33   The date of the current payment. Note that no data are punched, because at the time the balance card is prepared, no payment has been made or anticipated.

34-39   The amount of the note.

40-44   The discount or the amount which the bank charged on a $1,000 note, which in effect is an interest expense to the customer (Blatty). He has to pay the discount in addition to the principal amount ($1,000.00), or $1,080.00, which is the total amount of the note.

45-50   Balance outstanding. At this point, the balance outstanding is the same as the amount of the note (cols. 34-39), because no payment by Dr. Blatty has been made yet.

51-56   Amount of this payment field will be punched with the first installment or whatever Dr. Blatty makes on his first payment, due April 1, 1967.

57-58   Is not used in this application.

59-64   Are used to keep track of the number of days Dr. Blatty was late on his payments, the number of late payments, and the number of fines paid.

65-68   The due date of next payment. At this stage, the next payment due date is the first installment on April 1, 1967.

69-73   The rebate field. This is used to compute the amount of rebate due the customer, if and when he pays in advance of the due date or beyond the regular monthly amount. Some customers, for example, make two payments in a month instead of one payment. The second payment, which is paid one month in advance, requires the computation of a rebate to be paid to the customer. This amount is punched in the rebate column.

74-77   The date of the previous transaction, if any.

78   A control field. Note the *X* punch in column seventy-eight. Later, it will be necessary to merge the balance cards with other cards for various applications or to pull it out of a merged deck.

79-80   Is not used in this application. Column eighty, however, will be used (X punched in 80) to aid in separating the balance card from the file after a new balance card is made. This is done by sorting on column eighty.

Why a Nine-digit Account-number Field?

The nine-digit account number assigned to Dr. Blatty's loan reveals related and useful information. It is described as follows:

Column

1   Contains digit 5, which stands for the type of merchandise (furniture) for which a loan was extended to Dr. Blatty.

2   The cycle or the code represents a range within which payment on certain loans is due. Some customers pay toward their loan regularly on the first of the month, others on the fourth, and the remainder at other times during the month. Date of payment on a loan comes under one of the following cycles:

Cycle 1 All regular payments to be paid between the first and the fifth of the month.

2 Regular payments expected between the sixth and the tenth of the month.

3 Payments that fall between the eleventh and the fifteenth of the month.

4 Payments that fall between the sixteenth and the twentieth of the month.

5 Payments due between the twenty-first and the twenty-fifth of the month.

6 Payments that fall due between the twenty-sixth and the end of the month.

Dr. Blatty's payments are due on the beginning of each month, beginning on April 1. Therefore, his payments fall in cycle one, punched in column two. After a grace period is allowed, sorting on column two for a specific cycle will select all the balance cards the payment on which is past due. This function is related to a punched-card data-processing application which selects the delinquent accounts out of the file for the purpose of mailing to the customer(s) "past-due" statements.

3-4   Due-date field; a part of the account number. In Fig. 12-3, 01 is punched in it, denoting the date of payment of each installment. This field can be used also for pulling out the cards with a certain date and then matching them against the payment cards received by the bank during that day. All balance cards that do not match reveal that no payment was made. This will result in the preparation of reports or statements concerning their delinquent status.

5-9   Serial number which is assigned to a customer. For the next customer, it is incremented by one for each additional loan extended.

The Coupon Book

At the same time that a balance card is punched, a coupon book is prepared containing coupons, of the number which is equal to the number of payments set by the bank and agreed upon by the customer (Fig. 12-4). The data punched in each coupon are copied from the new-loan card (Fig. 12-2). Dr. Blatty receives a coupon book containing twelve coupons representing twelve equal monthly payments toward his loan.

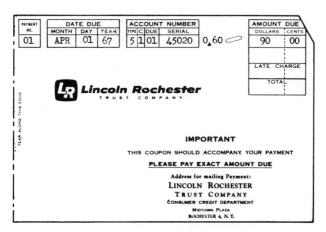

Fig. 12-4. An example of a coupon (*Lincoln Rochester Trust Company*)

Each coupon contains the following information:

Payment Number The serial number of a coupon. For instance, Fig. 12-4 shows the coupon which Dr. Blatty should present to the teller with his first payment of $90.00. The payment number of each of the remaining 11 coupons is incremented by 01.

Date Due Printed on each coupon is the exact date on which payment should be made. For example, coupon No. 01 is due on April 1, 1967. The next coupon (No. 02) is due on May 1, 1967, and so forth, until coupon No. 12, which is due on March 1, 1968.

Account Number Printed, remains constant on each coupon.

Late Charge In Fig. 12-4, a late charge of $.60 will be required in addition to the regular payment of $90.00 if Dr. Blatty fails to pay on the due date.

Amount Due Essentially is the monthly installment. A late charge will be added if payment is made at a later date than April 1.

In addition to the twelve coupons formulating the coupon book, the bank also attaches a copy of the loan detail card (Fig. 12-1) for the customers to keep for income tax purposes. (See Fig. 12-5.)

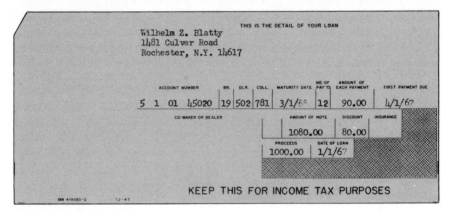

THIS IS THE DETAIL OF YOUR LOAN

Wilhelm Z. Blatty
1481 Culver Road
Rochester, N.Y. 14617

ACCOUNT NUMBER	BR.	DLR.	COLL.	MATURITY DATE	NO. OF PAY'TS	AMOUNT OF EACH PAYMENT	FIRST PAYMENT DUE
5 1 01 45020	19	502	781	3/1/68	12	90.00	4/1/67

CO-MAKER OR DEALER	AMOUNT OF NOTE	DISCOUNT	INSURANCE
	1080.00	80.00	

PROCEEDS	DATE OF LOAN
1000.00	1/1/67

KEEP THIS FOR INCOME TAX PURPOSES

IBM 419583-0   12-47

Fig. 12-5. An example of Dr. Blatty's copy showing the detail of his loan (*Lincoln Rochester Trust Company*)

The Data-processing Procedure

No data processing can be done in the "daily-payments" application until the steps discussed earlier in this chapter are properly taken. From the standpoint of the punched-card data-processing routine, the "daily-payments" application begins only after a customer's loan is approved, a master card (loan detail) prepared, a new-loan card punched with the basic data of the loan, a balance card representing the specific loan prepared and merged in the balance file, and a coupon book mailed to the customer out of which he is able to secure the information with which he can conveniently pay his installments properly.

On April 1, 1967, Dr. Blatty walked to the teller's window of a Lincoln Rochester Trust Company branch. He detached coupon number 01 from the coupon book and handed the teller $90.00 to pay the first installment due in full. At the end of the banking day, all coupons received are sent to the data-processing department, where consumer loans are handled. All coupons go through the same procedure and are processed by the same machines as that received from Dr. Blatty. For purposes of illustration, however, Dr. Blatty's case will be emphasized in detail.

1. Recording by Reproducing

The first logical and required step in the "daily-payments" application is to record the data from the coupon received into a standard-sized IBM punched card, referred to as a *payment card* (Fig. 12-6). The title is self-descriptive, because the payment card represents primarily the amount paid by Dr. Blatty toward his loan. It is punched in the "amount field" or in columns fifty-one through fifty-six. In addition to the amount of the installment payment, the date of the payment, April 1 (cols. 30-33), and the account number (cols. 1-9) are punched so as to relate the payment to the right party and the correct date, thus facilitating proper processing.

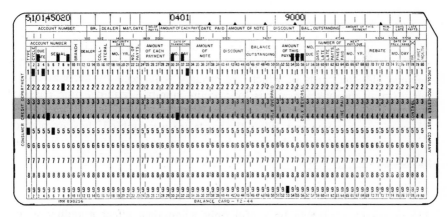

Fig. 12-6. A payment card pertaining to Dr. Blatty's first installment on the loan (*Lincoln Rochester Trust Company*)

A key-punch operator could take Dr. Blatty's coupon and key punch from it his account number, date of payment, and the amount of payment on the payment card. This method offers the same result as otherwise would be the case in punching the same data by the use of the re-producer. However, because a bank such as Lincoln Rochester handles hundreds of payments related to their respective loans daily, the recording of data into a payment card from a coupon can be accomplished more effectively by the use of the reproducer; therefore, recording by reproducing is used.

The coupons are placed in the "read" hopper and a deck of blank payment cards is placed in the "punch" hopper. With the insertion of a wired control panel for this routine, each of the coupons will be reproduced on a payment card.

2. Tabulating Payment Cards

After the coupons are converted into payment cards, the latter deck is placed in an accounting machine and the amount is listed in order to arrive at a total for that day. This move is necessarily performed in order to check on the accuracy of the conversion routine thus far. The total obtained on the accounting machine is compared with the one held at the main office. If both totals agree, it is assumed that the recording stage has been completed successfully. The data-processing department can go on with the application routine. If the total obtained on the accounting machine disagrees with that of the central office, then the error(s) must be located and corrected before any other step(s) is taken.

3. Sorting Payment Cards

The sorting step involves the sequencing of the payment cards by account number. In effect, they are being prepared to be match-merged with the balance file, the cards of which are already sequenced by account number. Sorting the payment cards by account number requires nine passes: one pass for each of the nine columns of the account-number field. Pass one sorts column nine first. When the cards are reassembled, they are placed in the hopper again and the sorter brush is set to read column eight. The operation continues until the nine columns have been sorted.

4. Match-merging Payments with Balance File

The payment cards can be useful only when they effect a reduction in the balance outstanding of the loans pertaining to them. For example, prior to April 1, Dr. Blatty's balance outstanding of his loan was $1,080. As a result of the payment of his first installment of $90.00 on April 1, the balance outstanding of his loan should be reduced to $990 ($1,080.00 − $90.00 = $990.00). The calculating step cannot be performed, however, until both the payment card and the balance card of each loan are merged together. This step is performed on the collator and referred to as the *match-merge* step.

The payment cards are placed in the secondary hopper and the balance cards are placed in the primary hopper. A control panel is wired to match-merge the two decks. A payment card drops behind a balance card in pocket three of the collator *only* if the account number in both is equal. Otherwise, all *payment* cards that have no balance card to match their account numbers are dropped in pocket five (the secondary pocket). All *balance* cards that have no payment cards to match their account numbers are dropped in pocket one (the primary pocket). In the case of Dr. Blatty's balance card and payment card, both were available and, be-

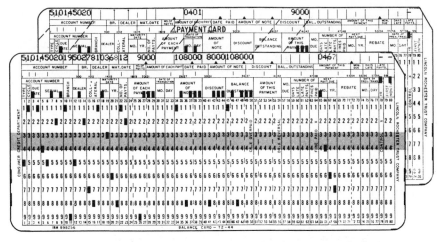

Fig. 12-7. The sequence of the balance card and payment card after a match-merge operation of Dr. Blatty's loan (*Lincoln Rochester Trust Company*)

cause the account number in each card is the same (equal), they were merged in pocket three (Fig. 12-7). Note that the balance card is in front of the payment card. Each of the other payment cards in the stacker should be preceded by a balance card bearing the same account number.

5. The Calculating Function

The merged cards are then placed in the IBM 604 electronic calculating punch. The balance card is read first. The amount of payment ($90.00 in cols. fifty-one through fifty-six) is read from the payment card behind the balance card. The calculator subtracts the amount from the balance outstanding ($1,080 in cols. forty-five through fifty) located in the balance card. The remainder (that is, $1,080 − $90.00 = $990.00) is punched in cols. forty-five through fifty in the payment card. (See Fig. 12-7.) Note that the balance outstanding (cols. forty-five through fifty) is $90.00 less as the result of subtracting Dr. Blatty's payment from the initial amount.

The payment card will be considered a new balance card for the next payment due May 1, 1967. Therefore, when the calculator punches the difference after subtracting the amount of payment ($90.00) from the balance outstanding, it also copies from the balance card into the payment card all the data which were not originally punched in it. See Fig. 12-8 and compare it with the payment card in Fig. 12-7. This transfer of data makes the balance card in Fig. 12-7 useless, because the payment card shows the up-to-date balance outstanding plus the contents of the balance card. From this point on, it is called a new balance card for

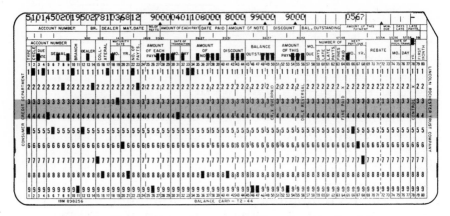

Fig. 12-8. The payment card as an updated record of Dr. Blatty's loan after calculation performed (*Lincoln Rochester Trust Company*)

next month's "daily-payments" application. The calculator has already punched 0567 (May 1967) in columns sixty-five through sixty-eight of the payment card.

6. Sorting Old Balance Cards from the File

Now that a new balance card is available, the old balance card should be pulled out or separated. The file is placed in the hopper of the sorter to eject into a separate pocket all cards with an *X* punch in column eighty. Only the old balance cards have an *X* punched in that column. The collator is, usually, used to extract the desired card from the file, because of the convenience factor. A control panel is wired to cause all cards with *X* in column eighty to eject into a pocket separate from the rest of the cards in the file.

CONSUMER CREDIT DEPARTMENT - PAYMENT JOURNAL -   LINCOLN ROCHESTER TRUST COMPANY

ACCOUNT NUMBER				OUTSTANDING BALANCE	DATE		AMOUNT OF PAYMENT		MO. DUE	PREVIOUS PAYMENT	
T	C	DUE	SERIAL		MO.	DAY				MO.	DAY
5	1	01	45020	990 00	4	01	20	00	5		

Fig. 12-9. A partial payment journal, showing Dr. Blatty's account listed (*Lincoln Rochester Trust Company*)

7. Checks and Balances

Once the old balance cards are extracted, the new payment cards are placed in the accounting machine for a card-for-card listing. In Fig. 12-9, a payment journal is used. Dr. Blatty's account number, new outstanding balance brought forward on April 1, the amount paid, and the next due date are printed. This step is considered necessary because a final check is made by comparing the total "amount-of-payment" column in the journal with the original amount received by the teller of the bank. If the two amounts agree, then the new payment cards can be merged in the main file. If the two totals disagree, the error or errors must be located and corrected before final merging.

8. Merging New-payment Cards in the Balance File

Assuming that the total payments amount is correct, the final step in the application is to merge the new-payment cards in the balance file. The primary hopper of the collator is fed with the balance cards. The secondary hopper is fed with the new-payment cards. The merging process causes both feeds to drop into the proper sequential order in pocket three of the collator.

After the merge operation is completed, the balance file is ready for another cycle when other customers pay their installments the next day. In the case of Dr. Blatty, the same cycle presented in this chapter will recur on May 1, when he makes his second payment.

The eight steps in the daily-payments application which were discussed above are summarized in Table 12-1 and illustrated in the flow chart in Fig. 12-10.

TABLE 12-1

Daily Payments—Summary

Step Number	Key Word	Explanation
1	reproduce	regular payments (from coupon) into payment cards
2	tabulate	all payment cards on payment proof 407 and balance to tickets for the day
3	sort	on columns one through nineteen and card count all payments on account number (serial and day)
4	match-merge	payment cards with balance file (balance cards in primary hopper)
5	calculate	balance outstanding and punch results and other data into payment card (a new balance card)
6	sort	merged deck on X in column eighty
7	list	"new" balance-card deck (previously, payment cards) on tabulator
8	merge	new balance cards in the balance file

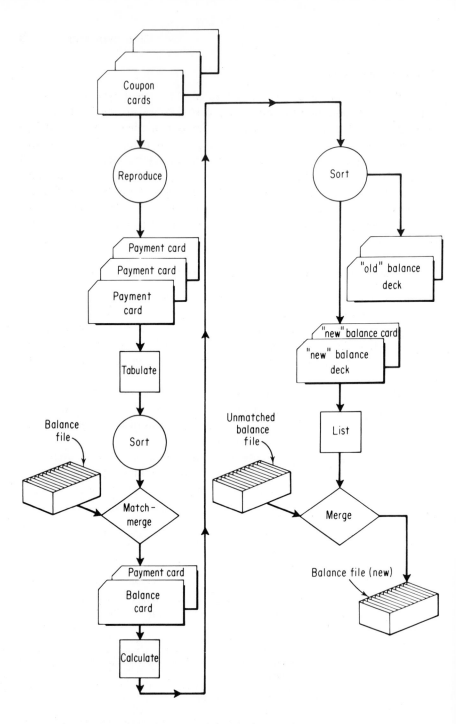

Fig. 12-10. Flow chart illustrating eight steps in the daily payments application

204

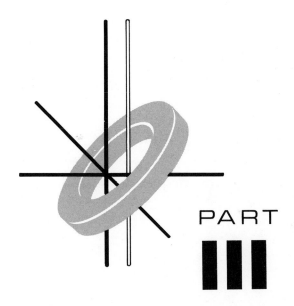

PART

III

Electronic Data
Processing-Systems
and Procedures

chapter

13

THE EFFECT
OF RESEARCH
ON BUSINESS
DATA-PROCESSING
SYSTEMS

ADVANTAGES AND DISADVANTAGES OF COMPUTERS
IN DATA PROCESSING

THE FIVE *M*s OF MANAGEMENT

PUNCHED-CARD DATA-PROCESSING SYSTEMS and the equipment associated with them are in wide use today and most likely will be used by business firms for a long time to come. Consequently, the question arises as to why there is any demand for automatic computers to process business data already processable by punched-card machines. To answer this question we must turn in our study of data-processing systems to a relatively advanced processing routine, still in its infancy, which involves the use of electronics. Such a routine is designed to serve business firms in a much more efficient, more accurate, more economical manner than the punched-card routine. The development of computer systems for business data processing, side by side with the improvement and perfection of punched-card systems, is a perfect example of how rapid technological change can be in new industries and of what is meant by the statement that "what is new today may become obsolete tomorrow."

Although electronic systems are a decided improvement over punched-card systems, the fact remains that, until more is known about how to adapt them to all types of situations economically, punched-card systems remain the most practical for business firms where the volume of repetitive paper work is such that their installation can be justified. Although the "old" is serving to alleviate the present situation, research, experimentation, and actual size of the "new" systems forge ahead in those industries which find electronic systems economical. Whether one will displace the other, or whether they will supplement each other, only time will tell. The "new" improves on the basic ideas behind business data processing in use by the "old," just as the "new" punched-card systems supplanted the "old" manual methods.

Thus, to give students a well-rounded picture of all developments in the business data-processing field, a description and analysis of the development of the "Babbage" ideas on a practical basis in modern computer systems are essential. A computer system is usually installed when this becomes economically feasible. Thus, as research progresses, the everyday use of computer systems in business continues to widen. When today's students enter business, they will be likely to find themselves involved in either an actual operation, or a consideration of the feasibility of a computer installation. Hence their need for understanding the ideas involved in both punched-card and electronic systems stands out in clear relief.

The purpose of Part III is not to prepare anyone to become a systems analyst or a programmer. It is, instead, to instill understanding about electronic data processing in the student's mind by showing: (1) why there is so much interest in electronic computers, and (2) how an electronic computer works. A clear-cut picture of the computer's basic elements, its language, the means by which it calculates and processes data, and how instructions are written so that it can perform its various calculations should enable students to think intelligently rather than "awesomely" about these machines and their purposes in business.

Advantages and Disadvantages of Computers in Data Processing

Digital computers used in business are built to aid man in doing the many required repetitive tasks that make up the course of his business. Computers boost man's productivity and improve the quality of his output, regardless of whether such output is a tangible product or an intangible service. An electronic computer operates more successfully than a punched-card system in four ways:

(1) By processing a greater number of items per second, the exact amount depending upon the type and size of the computer. Because the speed of the electronic computer is measured in thousands or millions of steps per second, it is, therefore, faster than any other type of machine designed to do similar work.

(2) By processing business data more accurately than alternative methods. A clerk, *at his best,* makes at least five mistakes per 100 manual calculations, whereas the computer's rate of error is a fraction of 1/10,000 of 1 per cent, or 99.999+ per cent accuracy. A punched-card system operates with a much higher degree of accuracy than any manual system, but it cannot operate with as great a degree of accuracy as an electronic system, because it is composed mostly of mechanical parts. Although electricity is used to operate most punched-card systems, the fact that they are mechanical makes their operation subject to slightly greater error than a computer system which operates by means of electronic circuitry.

(3) By allowing more time for creative and intelligent planning than is provided by a punched-card system. A computer's greater versatility in performing millions of operations tirelessly frees even greater amounts of time for more productive use.

(4) By lowering costs. The cost of each application processed by a computer, in general, is lower than when alternative machine methods are used. Although the initial cost of obtaining the computer is high, the saving resulting from its speed and accuracy in many cases justifies the decision to install it.

Interest in the practical use of electronic systems developed for various reasons, among which the following are significant. A hundred years ago, electronic computers were not really needed for the comparatively slow pace of events characteristic of an agricultural economy. If they had been, there would have been interest in building them, because the ideas governing their operation and behavior were already known, as was brought out in Chapter 2. However, as economies were transformed from basically agricultural ones to predominantly manufacturing or industrial ones, the need for machinery and the adoption of automated techniques to mass-produce for expanding markets became more and more apparent. Business executives have become very conscious that, if they are to compete in rapidly growing competitive markets, they must have essential business data regarding their products and have it as quickly as possible and in usable form. Therefore, the elements of time, speed, and accuracy in data preparation become more important, rather than less important, as economies grow and markets expand. The saving of time through speed can be, and is, solved by increasing clerical help to process and handle paper work. However, increasing the clerical staff results in the generation of new problems. (1) A firm must hire supervisors to organize and direct the many plans and procedures handled by clerks, and this results in an increase in the cost of data-handling tasks. (2) Morale problems increase with the increase in human help. Many office workers become bored with the repetitive nature of their work, and its monotony causes them to brood about many things, at the expense of their accuracy and efficiency. (3) Storage becomes a problem, because all business data must be filed daily.

Even though the problems of time and speed are solved in this manner, the high costs associated with such a solution are illustrated by the fact that clerical workers receive approximately one dollar out of every eight paid for wages and salaries in the United States. The basic problem of lowering the cost of data handling and data processing, thus, remains. To solve it, some industries have moved ahead successfully in the areas of punched-card and electronic data processing. The banking industry, for instance, processes, on the average, ten billion checks every year. Each of these checks is handled several times and must go through a tedious routine before it is finally paid and returned. At present, more and more of the larger banks are using magnetic character sensing by reader-sorter machines which read the depositor's account number and other related data printed in magnetic ink on the face of the check. Checks are sorted into the desired classifications or sequence in a fraction of the time needed to do it manually.

The Five Ms of Management

As economies have grown industrially, progressive business firms have expanded their operations. The emergence of the large firm with many branches is well known. This requires the intelligent use and coordination of the five *M*s of management, that is, *money, men, methods, materials,* and *managerial talent,* in order to operate profitably. Productive use of these elements demands greater amounts of data. For example, the obtaining of *money* involves contacts with financial institutions and the presentation of financial statements and plans for the purpose of establishing lines of credit for the negotiation of loans. The mounting need for labor (*men*) requires the gathering together and processing of various forms for interviewing, testing, screening, and selecting the men best suited to the various kinds of jobs. *Methods* must be constantly devised and procedures prepared so that the firm's goal can be attained. *Materials* used in the manufacture of the product must be ordered. None of the foregoing factors are of much use to a firm without *managerial talent.* Because management is basically defined as "getting things done through people," executives with a background in the literature of management are in great demand to coordinate and synchronize the work of many people who follow *preplanned* methods and procedures.

Maintaining relationships with workers and their supervisors, on the one hand, and being informed about the performance of the equipment, the quality of the products, the status of the raw materials, and the level of production, on the other, require that accurate facts be made available quickly. Each and every report must be prepared in such a way that it aids management in making better decisions. The speed and accuracy with which these reports are prepared and disseminated to key executives give a firm a better chance for survival in the business community, provided the information is put to intelligent use by the top-management officials who receive it. To meet competition, by utilizing their physical plants to capacity, many firms diversify their products. Ford Motor Company, for instance, introduces each year a variety of different-sized and different price-level automobiles in addition to their basic model. The consumer can choose between two or more sizes, colors, and price ranges. Engines of different power ratings are available upon request. Accessories can be easily provided for, including colored whitewall tires or hubcaps to match the owner's attire. Other automobile companies do the same. The introduction of a variety of basically similar, yet different, products on the market increases the need for data for analysis and comparison so that decisions can be made as to the competitive advantage to be derived from such "differentiation." Can the company justify the mass production of a given product, considering the initial manufacturing and marketing costs? What portion of the market does it hold? How does it rate when compared with a competitor's product of similar specifications? How long is the product expected to be in demand? How long would it take before a breakeven point is reached? All these and other questions must be answered. Management cannot plan wisely without access to all the basic data pertaining to its products. Unlike the Spartans who did not question the number of the enemy but only asked where it was, a business firm must measure its own strength against that of its competitors in order to prepare the right "weapons" for the competitive "battle."

Punched-card data-processing systems and equipment became commercially available in the 1930s and are still in widespread use today. They are a big step ahead of manual methods in the area of business data processing. However, continuous research for better ways to save time and money has shown that electronics can make even greater gains in business data processing, and electronic systems are being built on a practical basis for industries where the volume and kind of data to be handled justify the expense of their installation.

In many operations, manual systems of handling data are used because managements cannot justify the installation costs of either punched-card or electronic systems. Although machine methods provide cheaper handling once the systems have been installed, each firm must be able to justify the initial costs on the basis of the nature of its operations and the mass of data generated by them. Thus, manual, punched-card, and electronic systems exist side by side in the modern business world. In all systems, the same basic processing steps must be followed. Because this text is concerned primarily with machine methods of data handling, attention is, therefore, focused on a description and analysis of punched-card and electronic systems so that students can develop an awareness of the significant developments in machine handling in the rapidly changing business data-processing field.

REVIEW QUESTIONS

1. "What is new today may become obsolete tomorrow." Do you agree with this statement? Write a 200- to 400-word report to defend your answer.
2. In how many ways can an electronic data-processing computer help a business firm boost productivity and/or improve the quality of its products? Explain each way briefly.
3. What are some of the disadvantages of increasing clerical help in a manual system? Explain.
4. Explain briefly each of the five Ms of management.
5. How can speed and accuracy of report preparation help key executives increase the chance of their firm for survival?

chapter

14

BUSINESS COMPUTER SYSTEMS
Their Nature, Capabilities, Limitations, Types, and Make-up

THE AUTOMATIC BUSINESS COMPUTER

ESSENTIAL CAPABILITIES OF A BUSINESS COMPUTER

Ability to handle information   Ability to handle repetitive tasks
Self-operational ability   Ability to communicate effectively
Ability to "make decisions"   Ability to check on the correctness
of its own work   Ability to do new and additional tasks

LIMITATIONS OF A DIGITAL COMPUTER

Inability to handle unprogrammed information   Inability to make
decisions independently   Occasional breakdowns   Impracticality
of use on nonrecurring or nonrepetitive calculations

ELEMENTS OF A BUSINESS DATA-PROCESSING
COMPUTER SYSTEM

THE HUMAN THINKING PROCESS   Communication   Holding information and making decisions   Using arithmetic   Producing
reports   THE ELEMENTS COMPRISING A BUSINESS COMPUTER
SYSTEM   Communication   Storage   Decision making   Arithmetic computation   Report preparation   The stored program

CLASSIFICATION OF COMPUTER SYSTEMS

PURPOSE   Special-purpose computers   General-purpose computers   CAPACITY   Desk-size computers   Small-size computers
Medium-size computers   Large-scale computers

AN AUTOMATIC BUSINESS COMPUTER IS DEFINED as a machine that manipulates bits of business information within its main unit, based on a predetermined series of steps or sets of instructions, with a minimum of human intervention. To be more exact, a better name for a business computer is "Automatic High-speed Electronic Business Data-processing Digital Computer." [1]

The Automatic Business Computer

The term *automatic* is synonymous with *self-directing,* because, once the computer receives a set of instructions, which tells it what to do and how to bring about the desired results, it performs all the required work independently of human intervention. In this respect, the computer is referred to as being *automatic* or *self-directing.* Its self-direction is limited, however, by the instructions made available to it by a human programmer.

The term *high-speed* represents the ability of the computer to perform needed operations at the speed of light. The average speed of most computers ranges from a minimum of 100 operations per second up to 500,000 per second. Only a few computers are found beyond this limit.

The term *electronic* explains why a computer is referred to as a high-speed machine. "Electronics" relates to the flow of electrons behaving as signals in the circuitry of electronic equipment. These signals are manipulated to represent codes, which can be numeric, alphabetic, or special. The electron's high speed causes electronic computers to operate efficiently, as a result of which information flows thousands of times faster than it does through mechanical or electromechanical machines.

The term *business data processing* refers to the manipulation of known business facts for the purpose of obtaining a desired result such as are used in printed financial reports or other business statements.

The term *digital* refers to the type of computer. Such a computer utilizes counting devices and numbers for expressing variable quantities as well as for calculations. In contrast, the analog computer transforms physical flows, such as temperature or pressure, into electrical quantities in solving a given problem.

[1] Ned Chapin, *An Introduction to Automatic Computers,* 2nd ed. (Princeton, N.J.: D. Van Nostrand Co., Inc., 1963). The idea for the approach used in this chapter has been adapted from Chapter 2.

The term *computer* is used to designate a machine that can be used to solve problems in their entirety, and not merely the arithmetical operations which can be performed on any calculator. Although referred to as a "human brain," a computer is no more human than an electric saw or an automobile. A computer is assembled from many different parts. However, the manner in which it processes data is seemingly "human," primarily because it is designed to follow the same routine that a human being would have to follow in solving the problem.

Essential Capabilities of a Business Computer

1. *Ability to handle information:* A digital computer which is designed to process business data is capable of storing (remembering) the data being worked on, and of transferring it from a given part in storage to any other desired location in the system at high speed. The speed is usually measured in one-thousandth of a second, referred to as a *millisecond* (abbreviated ms), in one-millionth of a second, referred to as a *microsecond* (abbreviated μs), or in one-billionth of a second (*nanosecond*).[2] With this capability, a business firm can conveniently update each and every record, because actual calculations take very little time.

2. *Ability to handle repetitive tasks:* In general, a business computer is designed to handle any repetitive, recurring problem using different data as long as it follows the same prescribed procedures.

3. *Self-operational ability:* The business computer is capable of storing temporarily, or permanently, both business data and the set of instructions, called a *program,* that tells it what to do. These are stored in a common storage so as to effect direct access to the data. This constitutes a self-operating situation with a minimum of human intervention.

4. *Ability to communicate effectively:* As an effective and useful means of communication, a business computer is capable of accepting information and, after performing the desired routine, of giving correct results.

5. *Ability to "make decisions":* A computer cannot do anything a man could not do if he had the time. A digital computer is capable of following instructions stored in it and of modifying any of those instructions if necessary. In other words, the computer is preset so that it can choose

---

[2] Despite its fantastic speed, however, the computer manipulates processes of certain applications (for example, real-time situations) where solutions are not produced as fast as expected.

between alternative courses of action to perform the right routine. In this respect, the act is referred to as "decision-making." However, the choice between alternatives is limited to those prepared for it by the programmer. The computer can decide on the correct sequence of steps necessary to solve a given problem on the basis of conditions occurring in the interim. In computer terminology, this is referred to as *feedback*.

6. *Ability to check on the correctness of its own work:* A business computer is capable of checking on the accuracy of its own work by means of a "code check." In this, the computer counts the number of characters it has in storage and keeps track of every character as a result of an arithmetical, or other, operation.

7. *Ability to do new and additional tasks:* A computer can be instructed to do additional tasks, such as the printing of an order every time the stock level of a given item falls below a desired minimum. By the same token, it can print a list of all the items currently available in stock with a specific color, size, and/or other specifications. It can tabulate or summarize quantitative information more effectively than any human clerk because it is not subject to "boredom."

Limitations of a Digital Computer

1. *Inability to handle unprogrammed information:* A computer can handle the business information it has been programmed to handle, and can communicate the information to the user. It cannot do anything beyond this limit. In other words, it cannot make a decision in situations where *qualitative* factors are involved. A computer, for instance, can show certain expense items which exceed a desired maximum, but it cannot take action to stop the expense.

2. *Inability to make decisions independently:* A computer can neither make its own program nor determine its own course of action. Because it is made of metal, it has to be told in a very detailed manner how to do any given job. All alternative courses of action are predetermined and stored as a part of the program by a human programmer. The computer can choose a desired routine only if it is provided for in the program.

3. *Occasional breakdowns:* Even though a computer processes business data close to perfection, it cannot be perfect. Anything made by man is subject to occasional breakdown. A computer occasionally develops "bugs." An amusing story is told of a digital computer that sold the wrong stocks, because of a slipped cog. Another concerns the computer operated by the army that ordered shipped to Europe millions of dollars' worth of

items which were never required. These stories, while anecdotal, do point out that environmental, technical, and human factors can contribute to the failure of a computer. All manufacturers prescribe the manner in which their computers are to be treated and operated. A workable series of steps are outlined that lead to the attainment of the results desired. When the instructions are followed exactly by the user, a computer's accuracy, compared with that of a human being, is almost perfect. Computers are now being built to perform over nine billion operations without an error.

4. *Impracticality of use on nonrecurring or nonrepetitive calculations:* The best justification for the use of a computer in business lies in its application to routine, continuous, repetitive tasks. A computer should not be expected to do nonrecurring or nonrepetitive calculations on small amounts of data. As was mentioned previously, every application requires the preparation of a program to tell the computer what to do and how to go about reaching a solution to the problem. It is normally anticipated that, with the expenditure of human effort and time in the preparation of the program, the application will be used over and over again. The many hours involved in writing the program become only a matter of minutes to the computer when it processes the complete application. Therefore, programming effort should be applied toward routine and recurring applications and not toward those jobs that involve *many exceptions* and which are *not to be processed frequently.*

Elements of a Business Data-processing Computer System

The Human Thinking Process

The elements comprising a business data-processing computer system are a copy of those comprising the human thought processes involved in any kind of data processing. For this reason, we will outline the manner in which a human being solves problems, and review the steps involved in the attainment of the correct result. For example, assume that George Cook, a freshman student at a local community college, was asked on an accounting exam to determine the amount of the new cash balance of ABC Company, by adding the previous balance of $30.00 to today's receipts of $5.00. What elements are required for a correct solution to this problem?

    1. *Communication.* The student cannot give the correct answer unless he is capable of communicating. Communicating is a transportation device. The instruction implying addition of the previous balance of $30.00 to today's receipts of $5.00 must be accessible and properly visualized (Fig. 14-1).

2. *Holding information and making decisions.* After the instruction (*add*) and the amounts to be added (*30* and *5*) are visualized, they are retained in the mind (memory) of the student. Memory retains the desired data as long as they are needed. In memory, logical decisions are also made concerning the problems. The student determines whether both amounts have positive signs, checks to ascertain that no fractions are ignored, and decides whether the amounts in memory are sufficient data for a satisfactory answer (Fig. 14-2).

3. *Doing arithmetic.* The next step is to add *30* plus *5* to realize the sum, $35.00—the new cash balance (Fig. 14-3).

4. *Producing reports.* Upon arriving at the sum ($35.00), the student writes down the answer on the exam paper, along with the proper description (Fig. 14-4).

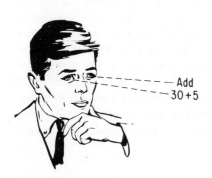

Fig. 14-1. Communication

Fig. 14-2. Holding information and making decisions

Fig. 14-3. Doing arithmetic

Fig. 14-4. Producing reports

The Elements Comprising a Business Computer System

You will note from the foregoing illustration of the human thought process that the brain cannot work effectively without the aid of its auxiliary units or organs. The eyes, for instance, read the data written on the blackboard and communicate (transport) the instruction (*add*) and the amounts, *30* and *5,* to be added by the brain. After addition, the hand communicates the answer to the instructor by writing it on the examination paper.

Like the human brain, the business computer cannot function effectively without the aid of its auxiliary units. That is the reason why we speak in terms of a computer system rather than of a single computer. The main elements comprising any business data-processing computer system are:

1. *Communication.* In order to work on business problems, a computer, like the human brain, must be capable of receiving business data in an orderly manner. The business information is called *input* (Fig. 14-5). Data are placed in a unit called the *input* unit, which is the "eye" of the computer. It reads the desired data and communicates (through cables) to the memory unit of the computer (see the square in the middle of Fig. 14-5).

2. *Storage.* Once read by the input unit, data are transferred to the primary storage section of the computer, called *memory.* They are held there until arithmetic is performed. We should remember that primary storage is the heart of the computer. It is analogous to the "human brain." (See the square in Fig. 14-5.)

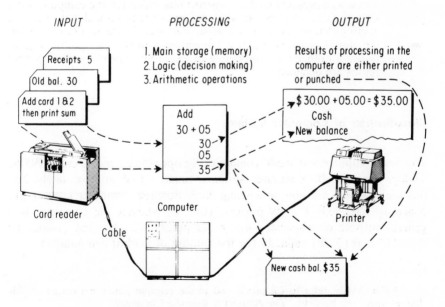

Fig. 14-5. Computer communication

3. *Decision-making.* The computer has the ability to compare two values "logically" to determine whether they are equal or unequal, distinguishing between a positive and a negative value and determining whether a number is greater or less than zero. These important capabilities take place in the central processing unit.

4. *Arithmetic computation.* The computer, referred to frequently as the *central processing unit,* contains an arithmetic unit where a part of the memory is used for arithmetical calculations. The computer has a very basic mathematical education. It can only add, subtract, multiply, divide, and compare. Its ability to compare makes the computer useful. It can tell whether a number is positive, negative, or zero. Only in the central processing unit are calculations of any kind performed. The external units are merely assisting units that facilitate transmission and storage of information. Elements two, three, and four constitute the heart of the computer, referred to from now on as the *central processing unit* (C.P.U.).

5. *Report preparation.* The final element of a computer system is the preparation of reports based on the calculations made in the central processing unit. This step is referred to as *readable output* and is usually expressed in the form of a printed report. Nonreadable output is usually expressed either in the form of a punched card or of magnetic tape. In certain systems, punched paper tape is also available as a form of output. In the example involving the human being, the examination paper is the output medium and the pencil is the output unit or device.

6. *The stored program.* If the computer system is to read, remember, make decisions, calculate, and write, it must do them in proper sequence. The stored program contains instructions which tell the computer what steps to take, what data to work on, and what to do with the results. A control element instructs the computer what instructions to use from the stored program which a human programmer has prepared. This causes all other units to operate in the proper manner so that correct results are obtained.

Classification of Computer Systems

The first computer was made commercially operational in the early 1950s. Today, over 25,000 computer systems, made up of approximately 300 different models, are now processing data. Business computer systems are generally classified: (1) by purpose (that is, whether the computer is a general-purpose or a special-purpose computer), (2) by type (analog or digital),[3] and (3) by capacity (or the amount of work it can handle).

---

[3] For details, refer to Chapter 1 and to the relevant paragraph earlier in this chapter under the heading, "The Automatic Business Computer."

Purpose

Special-purpose computers

Special-purpose computers are designed to solve specific type of problems and usually are tailored to the specific needs of a single customer. Some computers have built into them detailed operations to do the job for which they are specifically ordered. Many of the computers built for the airlines and the military are of this type. Examples include those which are used for traffic control, airline reservation systems (Fig. 14-6), satellite tracking, and collection of highway tolls.

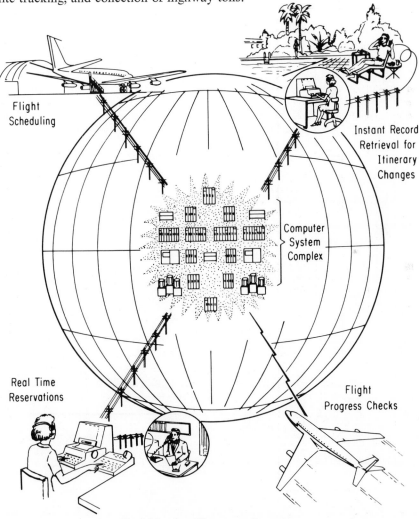

Fig. 14-6. An airline reservation system

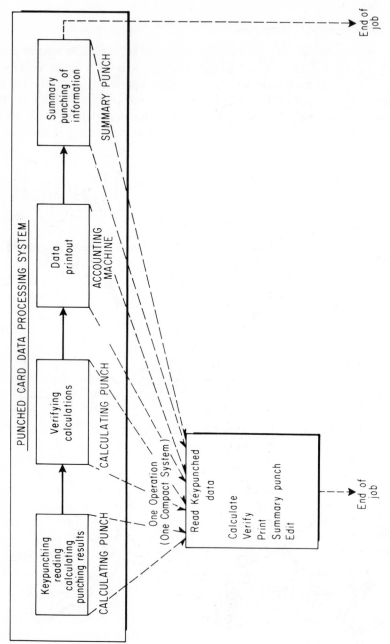

Fig. 14-7. Advantage of a small computer system over conventional punched-card data-processing systems

General-purpose computers

General-purpose computers are built to handle a variety of jobs by executing stored sets of instructions. This characteristic permits more versatility in working out diversified routines, such as payrolls, sales analysis, accounts receivables, and inventory control, thus incurring lower cost per application and better service. On the other hand, diversification means some sacrifice of speed and some limitations imposed by the size of the computer's primary storage.

Capacity

Computer capacity refers to the volume of data the computer can handle. Earlier computers' capacities were perceived to be a function of their physical size; the larger the computer the more volume of work it was expected to handle. Later, technological advancements in terms of miniaturization (transistorizing) of modern computers' primary storage permit us today to measure a computer's capacity by the volume of work it can process. With that in mind, computer systems are classified as desk size, small size, medium size, or large scale. Size is determined primarily on the basis of processing speed and size of primary storage.

Desk-size computers

Desk-size computers (synonymous with a very sophisticated slide rule) are small devices used by engineers to work out small, relatively straightforward mathematical (computational) problems. No special installation facilities or specifications are usually required. Many computers of this size are binary machines. Others have relatively slow input/output media and devices.

Small-size computers

Small-size computers have more efficient input-output media and devices than those of desk-size computers. Many of the small-size computers were originally built to do the job of punched-card data-processing systems, thus replacing most of the sorters, collators, and accounting machines (Fig. 14-7). The UNIVAC 1004 (second generation), UNIVAC 9200 (third generation), and the IBM 360 (Model 20) computer systems are examples (Figs. 14-8 to 14-10). They provide the advantages of stored programming to users who are ready to change from a punched-card system to a more powerful and flexible solution to their problems. The system consists mainly of a central processing unit (core storage capacity from 4,096 to 20,000 positions), a punched-card input/output device, two to four magnetic tape units (optional), and a printer. Depending on the optional features included, rent ranges from $1,000 to 5,000 per month.

Fig. 14-8. The UNIVAC 1004

Fig. 14-9. The UNIVAC 9200 system

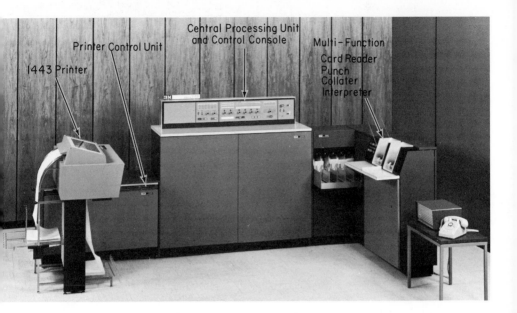

Fig. 14-10. The IBM 360, model 20

Medium-size computers

Medium-size computer systems are the most widely used systems. Compared to small computer systems, medium-size installations provide the advantages of: (1) faster operating speeds, (2) larger memory capacity (between 16,000 and 250,000 positions), (3) faster input/output devices (usually magnetic tape units) for efficient handling of data, and (4) printers for producing reports at high speeds. The Burroughs 3500 (Fig. 14-11) and the IBM 360, Model 40 (Fig. 14-12) are examples. Depending on the optional features included in the system, rent ranges between $5,000 and $20,000 per month.

Large-scale computers

Large-scale computers (Figs. 14-13 and 14-14) incorporate the features of medium-size computers, have separate consoles to manipulate the system and its peripheral equipment, more optional and faster input/output devices, faster and larger processing units, and storage capacity between 131,000 and 1,000,000 positions capable of handling random processing. Monthly rental is over $20,000.

Fig. 14-11. Burroughs 3500 computer system

Fig. 14-12. IBM 360, model 40

Fig. 14-13. Burroughs 6500

Fig. 14-14. IBM 360, model 65

GLOSSARY OF TERMS

CODE CHECK: A summation check for accuracy in which binary bits representing each character are converted and their sum maintained throughout a processing cycle.

DIGITAL COMPUTER: An electronic device which processes data represented by combinations of discrete information. Also, a device which executes sequences of arithmetic or other operations based on a program stored in memory.

FEEDBACK: A self-correcting or control feature involving the part of a closed-loop system which automatically brings back relevant data regarding the routine or process under control.

GENERAL-PURPOSE COMPUTER: A computer that can be used to solve a large class or a variety of applications.

INPUT: Incoming data; or data to be transferred from an external *input* device into the central processing unit of the computer.

LOGIC: A computer characteristic involving the computer's ability to compare two values for equality; distinguishes between a positive and a negative value and determines whether a number is greater than or less than zero.

MEMORY: Synonymous with storage; a device in which data can be stored and retrieved for later use.

MICROSECOND: One-millionth of a second ($\frac{1}{10}^6$ sec.).

MILLISECOND: One-thousandth of a second ($\frac{1}{10}^3$ sec.).

NANOSECOND: One-billionth of a second or millimicrosecond ($\frac{1}{10}^9$ sec.).

OUTPUT: The result of processed information.

PROGRAM: A set of sequential instructions designed to solve a specific problem.

SPECIAL-PURPOSE COMPUTER: An electronic device designed to solve a specific class or type of applications.

REVIEW QUESTIONS

1. What is meant by the term *computer?* What is meant by the term *digital?*
2. List and explain in detail the essential capabilities of a business computer.
3. "A computer cannot do anything a man could not do if he had the time." Do you agree with the statement? Defend your answer.
4. In what respect is a computer referred to as "making decisions"?
5. What is meant by *code check?*
6. What are the four limitations of a digital computer? Explain each limitation briefly.
7. What are the elements which comprise a business data-processing system? Explain each element in detail.
8. What elements constitute the central processing unit?

9. What does an electronic data-processing installation normally consist of, if it is to operate as a complete system? Why? Explain. (See Fig. 14-5.)

10. Does a stored program differ from logic? Explain.

11. What are the three classifications of business computers? Explain each briefly.

12. What distinguishes a small-size from a desk-size computer? A medium- from a small-size computer? A large-scale from a medium-size computer?

chapter

15

CENTRAL PROCESSING UNIT
Primary Storage

INTRODUCTION

PRIMARY STORAGE

CHARACTERISTICS OF PRIMARY STORAGE   Immediate Access to
Data Stored in Memory   Reusability   Permanent Recording of
Data Already in Storage   Automatic or Self-checking Ability
Durability   Compact Size   MAIN TYPES OF PRIMARY-STORAGE
DEVICES   Magnetic-core Storage   *Advantages of Magnetic Core
Storage   The Binary Mode   Data Storage   Reading a Mag-
netic Core   Writing-in a Magnetic Core*   Thin-film Memory
Cryogenic Memory

Introduction

THE CENTRAL PROCESSING UNIT is the computer. It is the center of all data computations; without it, processing cannot be done. Its role in a computer system is analogous to the relationship of the human memory to man, or of the engine to the automobile. All computations and decisions that are made affecting the daily activities of the person involved are made in the human memory. The only difference in the case of a computer is that the computer has to be instructed in detail by a human programmer before it *acts as* a human brain. The computer is, then, really more analogous to a reference book than to a human being's memory. Despite this, the term *memory* is used to describe it.

The central processing unit is the primary working mechanism in which needed data are stored as a first step in processing. Next, a decision is made about the type of computations to be performed on the stored data. Storage of data in the central processing unit itself is referred to as internal, or *primary,* storage; storage of data anywhere else is referred to as external, or *secondary,* storage. The following example illustrates the difference between primary and secondary storage.

Every retailing firm, regardless of its size or sales volume, orders merchandise in quantities which often exceed its present needs or anticipated volume during a given period of time. Savings to be had through quantity purchasing, seasonal drop in the price of the merchandise, or price discount on quantities beyond a certain limit, say 100 items, would induce the retailer to order in large quantities. A common procedure followed is to fill the shelves on the sales floor with the merchandise they will hold and to store the rest in a stockroom. Merchandise placed on the sales floor is said to be in *primary storage,* whereas the extra merchandise stored in the stockroom is said to be in *secondary storage.* If a customer should want an item which is in secondary storage, the salesman must ask the customer to wait until the merchandise is delivered from the stockroom before the sale can be made. This process, although workable, is impractical, because it takes extra time and results in inconvenience to the customer. Therefore, to make sales efficiently, the salesman and the customer should have direct access to the merchandise.

The central processing unit, like the retail store, must have the needed information in internal storage, to which it has convenient access, before any decisions can be made with regard to the type of computations to be performed. It receives initial data from an input device in the same manner as the salesman on the sales floor receives merchandise from the stockroom at the beginning of the business day and more during the day, if needed. The average time the computer requires to locate data or to recall information from any given memory location is called *average access time*. In primary storage, average access time is less than that in secondary storage, because data in primary storage is already within the computer, thus reducing the time needed to recall any information.

The "stockroom" of the central processing unit can be a punched-card reader, a magnetic-tape unit, a magnetic-disk machine, or other devices designed to transfer the information which the central processing unit might need later in the processing routine. The external-storage (or file-memory) devices will be explained in the next chapter.

Primary Storage

Regardless of the kinds of devices available, primary storage is any device into which business and related information can be placed which will retain information temporarily or permanently until used, and out of which the same information can be obtained any number of times. It is often referred to as "working memory," because computations and other processing routines are "worked" in it. Data stored outside the computer system are usually in a file cabinet. The external devices retaining such data are called *file-storage devices*. Therefore, external storage is called *file storage* or *file memory*.

Characteristics of Primary Storage

Immediate access to data stored in memory

For the arithmetic and logic units to operate efficiently, the stored information in working memory should be accessible immediately at high speed. In other words, the access time to data in primary memory should be as close to zero as possible in order to keep the speed of delivery as high as possible.

Reusability

The primary-storage device, whether it is a magnetic core, magnetic drum, or other kind of device, should be capable of erasing unneeded data and storing new data in its place. In other words, it should act in the same manner as a tape recorder which is capable of erasing previous recordings every time a new recording is made on the same tape. Most of the primary-storage devices have this characteristic.

Permanent recording of data already in storage

In cases of electric failure, the primary-storage device should be capable of retaining any data permanently regardless of the presence or absence of electrical power. A processing unit cannot be expected to produce results unless the memory of the computer is designed to retain vital data if the electricity goes off. It should be able to retain data until they are no longer needed, at which time they may be erased purposely by the introduction and storage of other needed information by a human operator. Most primary-storage devices used in commercial computers retain data permanently.

However, some primary-storage devices lose their stored data temporarily during readout; that is, when certain information is read from storage to be used elsewhere for processing purposes. This is referred to as *destructive readout*. Since primary-storage devices are designed to retain the original data permanently and correctly, they restore the original information automatically as it is being "read out."

Automatic or self-checking ability

In order to ascertain the accuracy of the data represented in storage, a primary-storage device should have an automatic self-checking feature. This is called *parity check*. The computer counts the number of bits of information in storage in such a way that, upon the destruction or loss of any single bit, it signals on the console that an error has been made, thus stopping the computer. The operator can then determine the type of error and its location by manipulating certain switches.

Durability

Unlike a punched card, which wears out in time, primary-storage devices are built to last permanently in spite of the constant storing and restoring of data in them. It is neither convenient nor cheap to the user to replace, or frequently repair, a primary-storage device.

Compact size

A primary-storage device should be physically small, yet capable of storing a large amount of data, because space is always at a premium. Although it is the most expensive such device, magnetic-core memory is the most compact.

Main Types of Primary-storage Devices

Magnetic-core storage

This is a very popular and practical storage device, and one that is used in most commercial computers. A magnetic core is a doughnut-shaped ring of ferromagnetic material that measures about one-sixteenth of an inch on the outside diameter. *Ferro* hints at the presence of iron, and the word *magnetic* indicates that the material can be magnetized. A magnetic core can be magnetized quickly and is highly retentive, capable of retaining its magnetism almost indefinitely, unless demagnetized.

Owing to the importance of speed, cores are made very small, because they can thus switch faster and require less magnetizing force to change their status. The magnetizing force is generated by running a heavy current through two wires, usually called X and Y, passing through the core (Fig. 15-1).

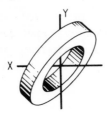

Fig. 15-1. A magnetic core with two current-carrying wires

ADVANTAGES OF MAGNETIC-CORE STORAGE.

1. *Dependability:* A magnetic core can be magnetized easily to represent data. Data stored in it are an indestructible part of the permanent memory.
2. *Durability:* A magnetic core does not wear out or deteriorate with age because it is an immovable part which does not rely upon physical motion for its operation.
3. *High-speed Access:* Access time is faster in magnetic-core memory than in any of the other memory devices. In a magnetic core, the output of the desired data is not under a "read" head, as is usually the case in using a magnetic drum, for instance. Each bit of information is stored in a separate magnetic core ready to read or write. Fast switching of a core is one of its characteristics.
4. *Low-cost Operation:* The operating cost of a magnetic core is considered low. It does not use any power to retain the data it stores. The only time it uses power is when new data are being stored.
5. *Large Capacity:* Because each magnetic core measures about one-sixteenth of an inch, there are a great number of cores in the primary storage of the computer. Memories with 100,000 cores or more are not uncommon in large-sized computers.

THE BINARY MODE. Most computers store data by using the binary mode. This is a numerical system that uses only two digits, namely, *0* and *1*. It can be compared to a light bulb which can be either energized (turned on) or de-energized (turned off).

The use of digits *0* (zero) and *1* (one) can represent any value in the decimal system by their position. When a value greater than one is desired, two or more positions are needed. For instance, *1 0* (one, zero) in binary means that the first digit position does not have any value, while a *1* in the second position designates two. The number is two, because the first digit on the right occupying the first position is equal to zero, while a *1* in second position is equal to two, since one times the position is equal to two.

You should remember that the position of a zero or a one enables these two binary digits to represent equivalent values in the decimal system. Because *0* × the position equals zero, *1 1* (one, one) in binary means *1* × the position (1) = *1, plus 1* × position (2) = *2;* or a total of *3.* When a value greater than three is required, a third-place position is added, having a value of four, because *the value of each position after the first increases in multiples of two.* See Fig. 15-2.

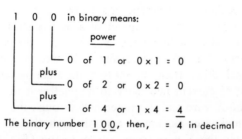

Fig. 15-2. Position values in the binary system

In the binary system, values of digits increase by a *multiple of two* as they are added from right to left, instead of ten, as is true in the decimal system. For a further discussion of the binary mode, see Chapter 19.

The magnetic core, used in computers as a storage device, has only two definite states: the *0* (zero) and *1* (one). A core can store either a one-bit or a zero-bit of information. If values greater than one have to be stored in core, then more than one core is needed. For example, to store a decimal value of two, two cores are needed: one to represent the zero-bit and one to the left of the first to represent a one-bit, because in binary "two" means *1 0* (Fig. 15-3). Data stored in a magnetic core are referred to as *bits.* The word *bit* is a condensation of the words binary digit.

Fig. 15-3. Two magnetic cores representing the decimal value 2 in the binary mode

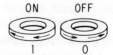

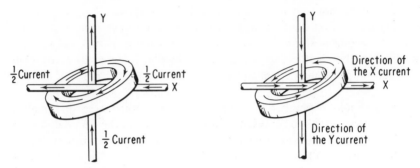

Fig. 15-4. A magnetic core in a one-bit status

Fig. 15-5. A magnetic core in a zero-bit status

DATA STORAGE. Data are stored in a core by the use of magnetism. A core can be magnetized in either of two directions: clockwise or counterclockwise. When it is magnetized clockwise, it is said to be ON, as it represents a one-bit (Fig. 15-4). When it is magnetized counterclockwise, it is said to be OFF, because it represents a zero-bit (Fig. 15-5).

Cores are arranged in the manner of a matrix strung on a screen of wires, the horizontal ones being the X wires and the vertical ones, the Y wires. Each core has an X wire and a Y wire running through it at right angles to each other. It can be set to a one state by sending one-half of the total amount of current necessary to magnetize it in that way (clockwise) through the X wire and the other half through the Y wire. To magnetize a core clockwise, current is sent through the X wire from right to left and through the Y wire from bottom to top (Fig. 15-4). The core can be set to a zero state by sending the flow of current through the X and Y wires in the opposite directions (Fig. 15-5). The polarity, that is, the clockwise or counterclockwise direction of magnetization, of a core depends upon the direction of the current flowing through the X and Y wires.

These bits of information (cores) are used to represent either a digit, a letter, or a special character. The C.P.U. can be programmed to select any one of these without disturbing the others. Such an arrangement of wires is referred to as a *magnetic-core plane* (Fig. 15-7).

READING A MAGNETIC CORE. When a particular core is read, one-half of the total amount of necessary current is sent through each of the X and Y wires. In Fig. 15-7, one-half of the current was sent through the X^2 wire, and one-half of it through the Y^2 wire. *Only the core at the intersection of the two wires receives the full current.* That particular core is said to be *selected.* All other cores strung on the X^2 wire retain their status, because each of them receives only one-half of the current necessary to magnetize them, that is, X^2 current only. They are said to be *half-selected.* Fig. 15-6 shows a blown-up schematic of the "selected" core at the intersection of the X^2 and Y^2 wires.

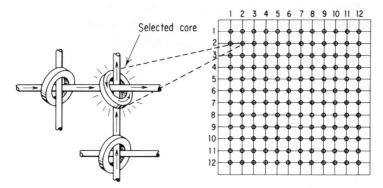

Selected core

Fig. 15-6. A selected core

Fig. 15-7. A magnetic-core plane (*IBM*)

The destructive aspect of the readout process requires the use of a third wire (inserted through each core) called a *sense wire* (Fig. 15-8). When a particular core representing a one-bit of data is read, it clears to zero. This action induces current in the sense wire which signals that the one-bit should be restored to that particular core. Then the circuitry immediately writes in the one-bit by reversing the current flowing through the X and Y wires of that core, so that the core is once again magnetized in a clockwise direction. However, if the selected core originally stored a zero-bit, no current enters the sense wire, and the core retains its status. The sense wire is activated only in a reading operation where a magnetic core originally representing a one-bit was cleared to zero as a result of readout.

WRITING-IN A MAGNETIC CORE. The process of writing data in a magnetic core is somewhat more complex. Writing-in a core involves either restoring the information previously stored in it or replacing the data with new information. When data are written-in a core, one-half of the necessary current is sent through each of the X and Y wires in *exactly the opposite direction of that used in readout*. That is, to write-in information, the current travels from left to right through the X wire and from top to bottom through the Y wire. To read out information, the current travels in the opposite directions through the X and Y wires.

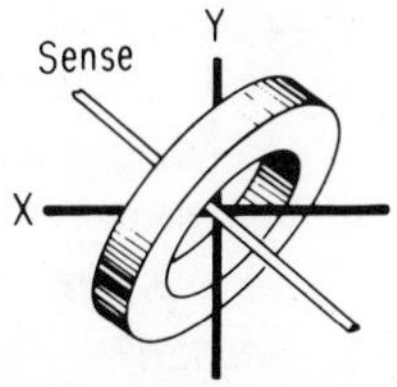

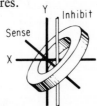

Fig. 15-8. A magnetic core showing the X, Y, and sense wires

Fig. 15-9. A magnetic core showing the inhibit wire

The *X* and *Y* wires cannot distinguish between *0*s and *1*s. They merely carry current. Because at times certain cores must be coded to represent a zero-bit, some technique is required so that these cores can be kept in this state. This necessitates the addition of a fourth wire, called the *inhibit* wire (Fig. 15-9). It is inserted parallel to the *Y* wire and extends through every core in storage. Its main function, if activated, is to maintain the status of the zero-bit cores by preventing one-bits from being written-in them, as would be done normally if the procedure were not interfered with.

For example, the normal write-in procedure causes one-half of the current to flow through the *X* wire from left to right and the other half through the *Y* wire from top to bottom. To preserve the zero-bits in their original states, only one-half of the current can be allowed to flow through them, because they would be magnetized clockwise if the full charge were permitted to pass through them. To accomplish this, the computer passes one-half of the amount of the necessary current through the inhibit wire from bottom to top. This flow neutralizes the one-half current flowing through the *X* wire, with the result that the zero-cores have only the current from the *Y* wires flowing through them. Because this is not sufficient to disturb their original magnetization as zero-bits, this procedure, using the inhibit wire, preserves them as zero-bit cores. If it were not used, they would become one-bit cores (Fig. 15-10).

In summary, then, the function of the four wires is:

1-2. *X* and *Y* wires are used for readout and/or writing-in magnetic cores.
3. The sense wire is used only in a read operation to determine if a given core is in a one-bit or a zero-bit state.
4. The inhibit wire is used in the write operation only if it is decided that a given core is to represent a zero state.

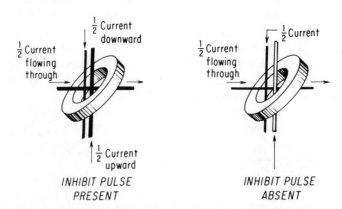

Fig. 15-10.   Left—the presence of an inhibit current; right—the absence of an inhibit current

Thin-film memory

A very rapid and reliable storage device, magnetic thin-film memory, is a recent attempt at faster access to and miniaturization of primary storage. It was developed by a process of depositing a nickel ferrite substance on a nonconductive base such as glass or plastic. These metallic spots, connected by ultra-thin wires, make up planes of memory cores that are much smaller than the doughnut-shaped magnetic core (Fig. 15-11).

Fig. 15-11. Example of magnetic thin-film memory (*Burroughs*)

Thin-film memories are now in operation at an access time of 0.4 microseconds. New techniques of vacuum depositing brought the present cost of making thin-film memory within a practical price range. Further improvements and miniaturization are likely to continue in the future.

Cryogenic memory

Still relatively new, the cryogenic-memory technique deals with a super-conducting memory set at a very low temperature, which makes it extremely fast and small. Development of a technique to reduce production cost is needed before it can be commercially available.

GLOSSARY OF TERMS

CRYOGENICS: The study and use of devices utilizing properties of materials near absolute zero in temperature.

FILE MEMORY: (See secondary storage.)

INHIBIT WIRE: One of four wires strung through a magnetic core. It is used in a *write* operation if it is decided that a given core is to represent a zero state.

MAGNETIC CORE: A configuration of magnetic material that is, or is intended to be, placed in a spatial relationship to current-carrying conductor and whose magnetic properties are essential to its use.

PARITY CHECK: A *check* that tests whether the number of ones (or zeros) in an array of binary digits is odd or even. Synonymous with odd-even check.

PRIMARY STORAGE: An area or a device in the central processing unit where required data are stored until needed.

SECONDARY STORAGE: An area or a device (other than the central processing unit) that stores relevant information until needed. Also called file memory.

SELF-CHECKING CODE: Same as *error-detecting* code.

SENSE WIRE: One of four wires strung through a magnetic wire and used in a *read* operation to determine if a given core is in a one-bit or a zero-bit state.

THIN-FILM MEMORY: Primary-storage unit, made up of layers of magnetic material, usually less than one micron thick.

REVIEW QUESTIONS

1. Explain the difference between primary and secondary storage. Give an example to illustrate.
2. What are the characteristics of primary storage? Explain each characteristic briefly.
3. What is meant by *destructive readout?* What is *parity check?*
4. Describe a magnetic core.
5. What are the advantages in the use of a magnetic core for primary storage?
6. Explain briefly the difference between the decimal and the binary systems.
7. "A magnetic core has only two definite states." What are they? Explain.
8. Draw a magnetic core, showing clockwise magnetization.
9. What is a *magnetic-core plane?*
10. How can a given magnetic core be set to a zero-state? To a one-state?
11. If the X and Y wires are used to carry current, then what is the purpose of the sense wire?
12. When is a magnetic core referred to as a *selected* core?
13. How are data read from magnetic cores?
14. How are data written in a magnetic core?
15. In what case does current flow through the inhibit wire? Explain.
16. What is the difference between thin-film and cryogenic memory? Explain.

chapter

16

CENTRAL
PROCESSING UNIT
Secondary Storage

WHY EXTERNAL MEMORY?

SEQUENTIAL-ACCESS FILES—MAGNETIC TAPE

WHY MAGNETIC TAPE? TYPES OF MAGNETIC TAPE REPRESENTA-
TION OF DATA ON MAGNETIC TAPE Seven-bit Character Code
Parity Check THE MAGNETIC-TAPE UNIT DENSITY OF THE RE-
CORDED INFORMATION FORMAT OF A MAGNETIC TAPE Load
Point End-of-file Indicator Main Information GROUP MARKS
PROCESSING MAGNETIC-TAPE FILES SORTING DATA ON MAGNETIC
TAPE ADVANTAGES VERSUS DRAWBACKS OF MAGNETIC TAPE Ad-
vantages of Magnetic Tape *Saving in Storage Space* *Ease of
Handling* *More Efficient Unit Record* *Saving in Recording
Data for Storage* *Correction of Errors* *Cost Advantage* *High
Speed* Drawbacks of Magnetic Tape *Slow Access Time
Physical and Environmental Weaknesses* *Tape Breakage* *Print-
through Effect* TAPE HANDLING AND STORAGE

RANDOM-ACCESS FILES

MAGNETIC-DISK STORAGE Types of Magnetic Disks Sectors and
Tracks Low-activity and High-activity Data Processing Real-
time Processing On-line Systems Summary MAGNETIC-DRUM
STORAGE Data Storage and Processing on Magnetic Drums
Advantages of Magnetic-drum Storage *High Storage Capacity
No Acceleration Problem* MAGNETIC-CARD STORAGE

Why External Memory?

BUSINESS DATA-PROCESSING APPLICATIONS involve thousands of transactions and a great amount of related data. A large-scale computer cannot store all these data internally and still have enough room for processing them. Even if the computer were built large enough to accommodate them in primary storage, it would be impractical, because the computer can only work on one transaction at a time. Although access time would be much faster if all the related facts were available in primary storage, the cost of building a computer large enough to eliminate the need for secondary storage would be prohibitive. In the retail-store example of the last chapter, the firm could build a sales floor large enough to accommodate all available merchandise and do away with the stockroom. This would, however, be impractical, because the salesman deals with only one or two customers a day for any particular item, and unnecessary storage on the sales floor would limit the amount of efficient working space. Thus, to attempt to eliminate the use of secondary storage, the stockroom, would be both impractical and unnecessary. The same is true in the case of secondary storage in a computer system. In both cases, the advantage gained in access time would be reduced drastically, if not lost altogether, because of the new problems created by such a solution.

Sequential-access Files—Magnetic Tape

Why Magnetic Tape?

One of the major characteristics of a large-scale commercial data-processing computer system is its ability to process data and move any pertinent information into and out of the machine at high speed. This is accomplished by the use of a medium called *magnetic tape,* which is much faster than the punched card, paper tape, or almost any other secondary-storage medium. Magnetic tape is used as a chief source of input and output, its role being to store information until it is needed by the computer. Magnetic tape is used, then, mainly in three areas: (1) as an input medium, (2) as an output medium, and (3) as a secondary-storage medium. In any of these areas, magnetic tape is regarded as external memory, because its main function is to store information for later processing by the computer.

Types of Magnetic Tape

Have you ever seen the plastic tape used in home tape recording? Magnetic tape used for electronic data processing is similar to the regular tape used in a home tape recorder. The only difference is that the former is much wider and is of better quality than the latter. Magnetic tape used in electronic data-processing machines is one-half to one inch wide and 1,200 to 3,000 feet long per reel of tape.

IBM magnetic tape is a plastic tape coated with a metallic oxide on one side only. It is one-half inch wide and comes in three popular lengths: 1,200, 2,400, and 3,600 feet. It is mounted on reels ranging from eight to twelve inches in diameter.

Magnetic tape is a *sequential*-file storage medium, which means that the first record written on it must be read before the second record, the second before the third, and so forth. Assume that we have 10 records written on tape in the proper numeric sequence, that is, 01, 02, 03, 04, 05, 06, 07, 08, 09, and 10. If, for instance, record 06 is needed for processing, records 01, 02, 03, 04, and 05 must be read before record 06 moves under the reading head. Sequential-file storage is ideal where regular updating of records, such as customers' accounts, is necessary. Access time of each record to primary storage for processing purposes is faster in sequential-file storage than is the case with other secondary-storage media. Time is not wasted as the computer does not have to search for the desired record, because each customer's account is in alphabetic or numeric sequence on the tape. In applications that require reading records scattered here and there on the tape, access time is slower than in a continuous operation such as periodic updating of every account.

Representation of Data on Magnetic Tape

Seven-bit character code

Numeric, alphabetic, or special characters are represented on tape by means of a coding technique similar to that of the punched card. This technique is called the *seven-bit character code* (Fig. 16-1).

Data are recorded on the seven parallel, horizontal channels, or tracks, along the tape. The seven recording channels are labeled *1, 2, 4, 8, A, B,* and *C*. Positions across the width of the tape represent one column of data or one character. The seven-bit positions are recorded by means of read-write heads, each of which is assigned to one of the seven channels. In Fig. 16-1, a dash (I) in a given square stands for the presence of a magnetic spot, which means the same as a one-bit in the binary mode.

Numeric characters can be recorded on tape by using the lower four-bit positions; that is, bit positions *1, 2, 4,* and *8*. Each of these bits cor-

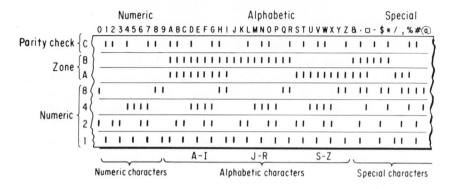

Fig. 16-1.   The seven-bit character code (*IBM*)

responds to a position value in the binary mode. For example, numeric character 6 is represented by the presence of two magnetic spots: one spot in 4 and another spot in 2 or a total of 6. Zero may be coded arbitrarily as 8 plus 2, although other combinations may be used. The manner in which it is coded depends upon the make of computer under consideration. The top channel (parity check) will be discussed later.

Alphabetic characters are represented on tape in a manner similar to that used to represent them in a punched card. Each letter is represented by a combination of numeric and zero-bit positions. The alphabet is divided into three sections:

1. Each of the letters *A* through *I* is represented by zone bits *A* and *B*, in addition to the use of the numeric bits. For example, letter *A* would be represented by three magnetic spots: one each in *A* and *B* zones and one in numeric one-bit position. (See Fig. 16-1.) In a punched card, letter *A* is represented by one punch in zone twelve (zone punching position) and another punch in digit one (digit punching position).
2. Each of the letters *J* through *R* is represented by zone bit *B*, in addition to the use of numeric bit values one through nine. For example, letter *J* would be represented by two magnetic spots: the *B* zone bit and another spot in numeric one-bit position (Fig. 16-1). In a punched card, *J* is represented by two punches: one punch in zone eleven (zone punching position) and another in digit one (digit punching position).
3. Each of the letters *S* through *Z* is represented by zone bit *A*, in addition to the use of the numeric bit positions *1, 2, 4,* and *8*. For instance, letter *S* is represented by means of two magnetic spots, one in zone bit *A* and another in the two-bit position. Letter *S* in a punched card is represented by a zero punch (zone) and a two punch (digit). In writing, spacing between columns is done automatically by the magnetic-tape unit. Special characters can also be coded. The code selected for each special character should be clear and entirely dissimilar to that of any other coded character.

Parity check

The six channels discussed are adequate for recording numeric, alphabetic, and/or special characters. Why, then, is there a need for the top, or seventh channel? This channel is used for checking the coding of the others. Magnetic spots on tape can be erased accidentally or obscured because of dust, dirt, or cracking of the oxide coating. To ascertain the correctness of data during tape reading or tape writing, the number of magnetized spots, or one-bits, representing each character are counted. This is called *parity check.*

In Fig. 16-1, the number of magnetized spots, or one-bits, in channels *1, 2, 4, 8, A,* and *B* is counted vertically. If the total is odd, a magnetic spot is made in the parity check (*C*) channel on the top. However, if the total number of one-bits in the six channels is even, nothing is recorded in the "check" channel. This technique is called even parity check or *even parity.* The goal is to have each character represented on the tape by an even number of one-bits, because the computer cannot operate if they are odd.

As an illustration, a description of the formation of digit *7* follows. Digit *7* is represented by three one-bits: one-bit of *4* plus one-bit of *2* plus one-bit of *1.* The machine counts the one-bits in *4, 2,* and *1.* Because the total (*3*) is odd, it adds one more bit to the "check" position in channel seven to make the total even. This parity check is made on both alphabetic and numeric information. If a bit is lost—for example, while data are being transferred from one device to another in the system—the signal for error appears and the machine stops, because the remaining bits equal an odd number.

A question commonly raised is what would happen if two bits were lost for one character instead of one bit, in which case the count would be even and the computer could not detect the loss by an even parity check. Although such an occurrence is rare, it can be avoided by using a horizontal parity check on each record. In this instance, the machine counts the number of one-bits in each of the seven channels. At the end of the record, a check character is added to each channel that contains an odd number of one-bits. Therefore, during readout, parity check is active vertically per column and horizontally per channel.

Instead of even parity check, some machines follow odd parity check. The idea is the same, except that a check character is made in the check channel only when the total number of one-bits representing a given character is even. In this case, an even number of bits causes the machines to signal an error and stop the operation.

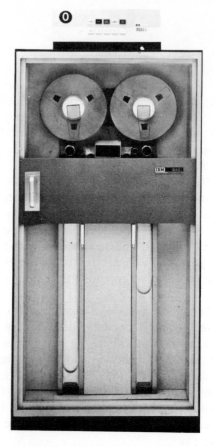

Fig. 16-2. IBM 2401 magnetic tape unit

The Magnetic-tape Unit

The magnetic-tape unit is used both as an input device and as an output device. It transports tape from one reel to another as it passes the read-write head in the actual reading or writing of information (Fig. 16-2).

In preparing the reading or writing operation, the data tape, or file-tape reel, is mounted (loaded) on the left side and an empty reel, called the *take-up reel,* is mounted on the right side. The tape from the left reel is threaded past the read-write head to the take-up reel. Because of the high speed involved in starting and stopping, a loop in the tape drops (floats) in the two vacuum tubes acting as buffers against tape breakage. The slack that this permits absorbs tension during the sudden burst of speed generated by a read instruction from the computer. As the tape

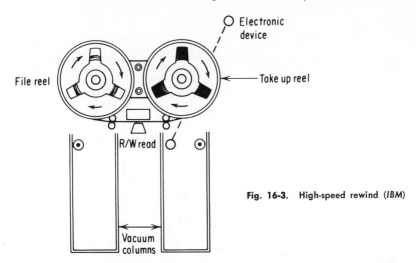

Fig. 16-3. High-speed rewind (*IBM*)

in the left vacuum tube is drawn by the take-up reel, it is replenished by the file reel immediately above it. As the tape loop in the right vacuum tube begins to reach the bottom, an "electronic eye" actuates the take-up reel to take up the slack automatically.

When a reading or writing operation is completed, the data tape is wound around the take-up reel. The operator must rewind the tape and store it on the original reel, leaving the take-up reel empty for another application. The take-up reel is commonly referred to as a *machine reel.*

When rewinding takes place, the tape is drawn from the vacuum tubes and fed directly from the take-up reel back to the file reel, that is, from right to left (Fig. 16-3). During the initial part of the rewind operations, the machine goes into a high-speed rewind until it reaches a predetermined distance from the end of the reel. At this point, the machine stops immediately and pauses for an instant. During the pause, a tape loop drops in both vacuum columns and then, at low speed, the machine rewinds the few feet of remaining tape (Fig. 16-4). The latter part of the rewind operation is considered a safety measure which prevents the machine from rewinding the entire tape at high speed, subjecting it to a possible break.

The machine is stopped just before the end of the tape by an electronic device. The device emits a beam which, at the beginning of the rewind operation, is blocked by the tape on the take-up reel (Fig. 16-3). When enough tape is rewound on the file reel, the electronic beam makes contact with another device underneath the reel (Fig. 16-4). This causes the tape unit to stop, forces the tape into the vacuum tubes, and throws the rewind operation into low speed. When the machine reaches the end of the tape, it stops automatically.

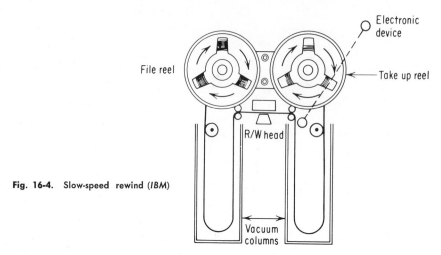

Fig. 16-4. Slow-speed rewind (*IBM*)

Density of the Recorded Information

Depending upon the type of magnetic-tape unit used, data may be recorded at a density between 100 and 800 bits per channel and a tape speed of from fifty to 200 inches per second.

Density is defined as the greatest possible number of columns of data that can be recorded on a unit length of tape. The unit used is usually an inch. The present densities used by IBM magnetic-tape recording units are 200 or 556 columns per inch of tape. The former density is referred to as *LO* density; the latter, as *HI* density. At a HI density of 556 columns per inch of tape, for example, the contents of about seven punched cards of eighty columns each can be stored; that is, eighty times seven equals 560. Some tape-recording units are capable of writing on tape at a super-HI density of 800 columns per inch. The faster the speed and the higher the density used, the greater is the rate at which data are transferred—that is, read from, or written on, tape. Steady improvements in transfer rate have been made over the years. Today's tape systems are built with a transfer rate of well over 200,000 characters per second.

Format of a Magnetic Tape

The format of a magnetic tape is similar to the table of contents of a speech or a term paper. The first part is usually the introduction; the second part, the main body of the paper; and the third part, a summary of the report. Similarly, the contents of a magnetic-tape run are typically as follows: (1) the load point, (2) the end-of-file indicator, and (3) the main information.

Load point

The load point is a reflective spot coated on one side with magnetic material and having adhesive on the other side. It measures about one inch by three-sixteenths of an inch. It is located on the top edge of the shiny side where recording is not done (Fig. 16-5). Photoelectric cells in the tape unit sense the label and interpret it as the beginning of the usable portion of the tape where writing or reading is to begin. A space of at least ten feet from the beginning of the tape is recommended for the load point location. Usually, it is located between twelve and fifteen feet from the beginning of the tape.

End-of-file indicator

The end-of-file indicator is also a reflective spot, or marker, coated on one side with magnetic material and having adhesive on the other side. It, too, measures one inch by three-sixteenths of an inch. It differs from the load point in that it is used to indicate the end of the reel or when writing is to stop. It should be placed about eighteen feet from the end of the tape. It is located on the shiny side of the tape and on the side farthest from the person looking at it (Fig. 16-16).

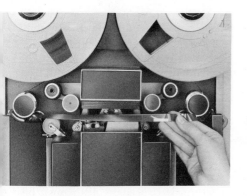

Fig. 16-5. Load point *(IBM)*   Fig. 16-6. End-of-file indicator *(IBM)*

Main information

The data to be written on tape can be located anywhere between the load point and the end-of-file indicator. Records on tape are not restricted to fixed length, as is the case in a punched card. A record can be of any length within the area of the tape allowed for writing records. One record is separated from another record by a space which is referred to as an *interrecord gap,* abbreviated *IRG* (Fig. 16-7).

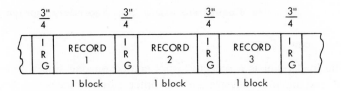

Fig. 16-7. Example of interrecord gap and single-record block

Fig. 16-7. Example of interrecord gap and single-record block

The interrecord gap serves two purposes: (1) to separate one logical tape record from another logical tape record; (2) to allow for the waste of tape caused by acceleration and deceleration every time a new record is read. The interrecord gap measures about three-fourths of an inch. The tape unit wastes about three-eighths of an inch every time it decelerates to a stop and also three-eighths of an inch when it accelerates to read or write the next sequential record: a total of three-fourths of an inch. The gap between records is made automatically. Each logical record on a tape is considered as one block and is called a *single-record block.*

Normally, a record is at least fourteen characters in size. For purposes of clarity, assume that each record on a given tape averages fifty-five characters and can be written at a density of 550 characters per inch. This means that each record is stored on one-tenth of an inch of tape bordered by two interrecord gaps (one before and another after the record), occupying a total of one and one-half inches of tape. Clearly, a lot of the tape consists of interrecord gaps or blanks. To solve this problem, a technique is used whereby a group of logical records is written in one block with an interrecord gap before and after the data. This technique is called *multiple-record block.* The term used is *blocking.* Compare Fig. 16-8 with Fig. 16-7 and note the savings in tape as a result of blocking records. There is not only a saving of tape, but also a saving in time, because the tape-recording unit will accelerate and decelerate less frequently. All the recordings in a given block are read before the machine pauses.

Group Marks

In the use of multiple-record blocking, a mark is used to distinguish between the different records in each block. It is a tape character and is referred to as a *group mark.* A group mark is part of the programming.

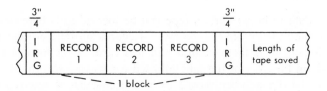

Fig. 16-8. Example of a multiple-record block

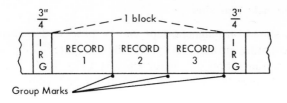

Group Marks

Fig. 16-9. Example of a multiple-record, block, showing group marks

Its purpose is to tell where one record ends and another record begins within the block (Fig. 16-9).

One or more tape reels may be required to record a business application. A tape reel may contain one, or more than one tape record. A tape record may consist of one or more logical records. A logical record, the smallest unit on the tape reel, contains basic information and is stored for further processing by transferral to primary storage. Figure 16-10 presents a schematic of an accounts receivable application in order to show the points mentioned in this paragraph.

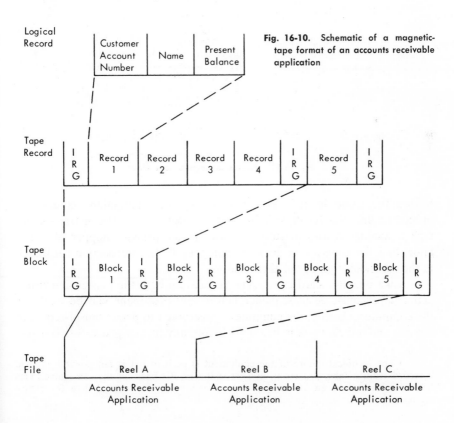

Fig. 16-10. Schematic of a magnetic-tape format of an accounts receivable application

Processing Magnetic-tape Files

Master data stored on magnetic tape can be processed against *transaction* data by a collating process, in which the computer compares a master record with a transaction record for equality (Fig. 16-11). Unequal master records are merely copied on an output tape,[1] while master records

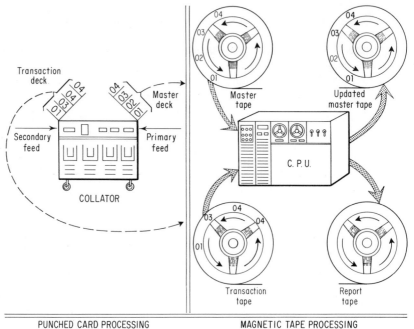

PUNCHED CARD PROCESSING   MAGNETIC TAPE PROCESSING

Fig. 16-11.   Processing magnetic-tape files

having the same identification number as the transaction records are processed and the result written on the output tape. The master-record tape is analogous to a master-card deck in the primary hopper of a collator, and the transaction deck is analogous to the transaction-card deck in the secondary hopper of the collator.

Like punched-card processing, records on both the master and transaction tapes must be in sequence before any processing can be made by the computer. Usually, the computer is instructed to detect out-of-sequence records and handle them individually before any further processing is made.

---

[1] The technical nature of the equipment is such that it is not possible to read a record from a tape, process it, and write the results back on the same tape. This limitation turns into an advantage: that of preserving the original data for future reference.

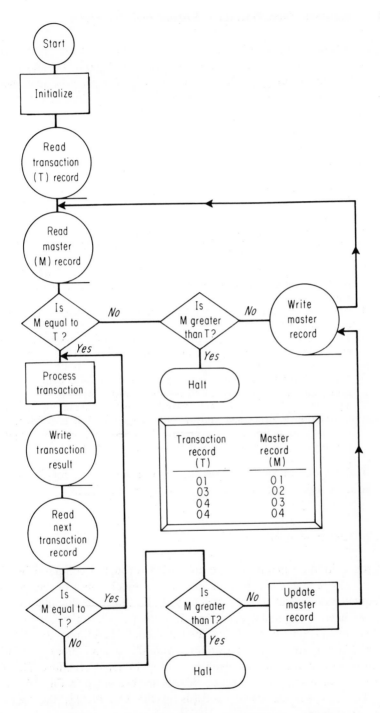

Fig. 16-12. General block diagram of magnetic-tape processing

To illustrate magnetic-tape processing, assume that the master-record tape consists of four logical records identified as 01, 02, 03, and 04, and the transaction-record tape consists of four logical records, identified as 01, 03, 04, and 04 (Fig. 16-11). Processing these records requires the preparation of a computer program similar in general form to the one shown in Fig. 16-12.

When the program is loaded and the operation begins, the following steps take place:

1. $T(01)$ and $M(01)$ are read and their identification number is compared for equality. Being equal, the transaction is processed and an output record of it is written.
2. $T(03)$ is read and, having a greater identification number than $M(01)$, causes $M(01)$ to be updated, and master record $M01$ to be written on the output tape.
3. $M(02)$ is read and $T(03)$ is compared with $M(02)$. $M(02)$, having a smaller identification number than $T(03)$, is copied on the output tape and $M(03)$ is read.
4. $T(03)$ is equal to $M(03)$. So, the transaction is processed and an output record of it is written.
5. $T(04)$ is read and, having a greater identification number than $M(03)$, causes $M(03)$ to be updated, and master record $M(03)$ to be written on the output tape.
6. $M(04)$ is read and $T(04)$ is compared with $M(04)$. Being equal, the transaction is processed and an output record is written.
7. The last $T(04)$ is read. $T(04)$ and $M(04)$ are again equal. So, the transaction is processed and an output record of it is written. Being the last transaction and the end of the operation, $M(04)$ is updated, and master record $M04$ is written on the output tape.

Today's output tape becomes tomorrow's input tape for file processing. Today's input tape is filed away for future reference.

Sorting Data on Magnetic Tape

Records written on magnetic tape are sorted through a computer by interfiling blocks of sequential records into longer blocks until one large block or sequence of logical records is achieved. To illustrate this method, suppose we have a magnetic tape, containing two blocks of twenty records: the first block consists of eleven logical records pertaining to customers whose accounts are in good standing; and the second block consists of logical records pertaining to customers with delinquent accounts. The identification numbers of each of those records are presented in Fig. 16-13.

To sequence the twenty records in the two blocks, the following passes are taken:

Pass one: Break input tape *A* into two tapes (*B* and *C*), as shown in Fig.
16-14. Note that each of the five records, the next six records, and the
remaining nine records are in sequence. The procedure involves writing
the first batch of five sequential records on tape *B* and then switching to
tape *C* for writing the next batch of six sequential records. The next
(last) nine sequential records are switched to tape *B*, thus completing
the first pass. In an operation involving many batches of sequential
records, switching from one tape to another tape continues until the last
batch has been written.

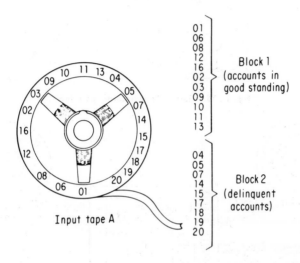

Fig. 16-13.   Two blocks of records on tape A, before interfiling

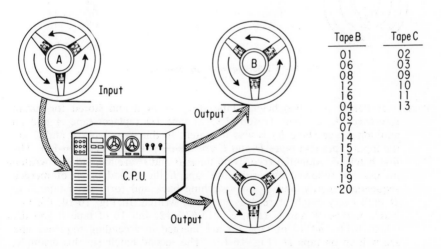

Fig. 16-14.   Sorting tape records—pass one

Tape D	Tape E
01	04
02	05
03	07
06	14
08	15
09	17
10	18
11	19
12	20
13	
16	

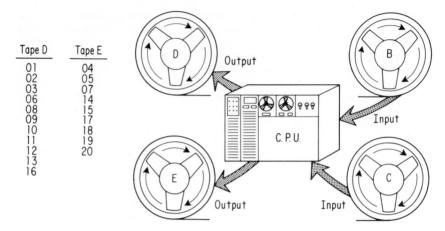

Fig. 16-15. Sorting tape records—pass two

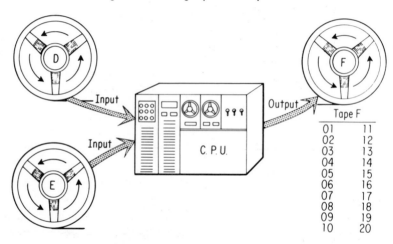

Tape F

01	11
02	12
03	13
04	14
05	15
06	16
07	17
08	18
09	19
10	20

Fig. 16-16. Sorting tape records—pass three

Pass two: Before pass two begins, tape *A* is removed and stored for future reference. A new tape (referred to as tape *D*) replaces tape *A* and an additional tape (tape *E*) is also mounted. In this pass, tapes *B* and *C* are the input tapes and tapes *D* and *E* are the output tapes (Fig. 16-15). The first batch of sequential records on tapes *B* and *C* are merged and written on tape *D,* followed by writing on tape *E* the second batch of merged sequential records, and so on, switching back and forth from tape *E* to *D* until every batch of records has been written. In Fig. 16-14, the first batch of tapes *B* and *C* (that is, 01,06,08,12, and 16 of tape *B* and 02, 03,09,10,11, and 13 of tape *C*) are merged in ascending sequence and are written on tape *D* (Fig. 16-15). The second batch (in this example, the remaining nine records of tape *B* in Fig. 16-14) are directed to be written on tape *E*.

Pass three: A third pass is needed to merge the two sets of records in tapes *D* and *E* into one sequence. Tapes *D* and *E* now become the input tapes and a new tape (tape *F*) becomes the output tape. Since there is only one batch of sequenced records on each tape, they are merged in one final pass and are written on tape *F* (Fig. 16-16).

Advantages Versus Drawbacks of Magnetic Tape

Advantages of magnetic tape

SAVING IN STORAGE SPACE. The compactness of magnetic tape permits data to be written at a common density of 556 characters per inch of tape, or the equivalent of the contents of seven cards. A 2,400-foot reel of tape can store up to 14,000,000 characters, and the reel can be stored in one drawer of a file. If these data were stored permanently on punched cards, 175,000 would be required. A number of file cabinets, and floor space to put them in, would be needed. The saving in storage space gained by using tape is evident.

EASE OF HANDLING. Cards, although of convenient size, appear bulky when compared with tape. It is much easier to handle a reel of tape than thousands of cards. Too, recording on tape is much easier than recording on cards owing to the fact that each card must be handled separately either by the machine or by a human operator.

MORE EFFICIENT UNIT RECORD. The use of a punched card is limited to eighty columns in which a total of eighty characters can be punched. The use of magnetic tape as a unit record is more flexible; more freedom is gained because each record can be as long or as short as desired. The only limiting factor is the length of the tape itself.

SAVING IN RECORDING DATA FOR STORAGE. A punched card, once punched with certain data, cannot be used again for recording different data. In contrast, magnetic tape can be erased and used over and over again for recording any kind of data, which means considerable saving in the cost of recording data for storage.

CORRECTION OF ERRORS. In key punching, once a hole is punched in a given column, it cannot be removed. If the wrong character is punched, the card must be destroyed and a new one used in its place. The correct character, along with any other information in the card, must be repunched. On magnetic tape, if a mistake is made, it can be erased easily and the correct data written in instead. Any other data in the record in which the mistake occurred need not be rewritten or duplicated, as is the case in the punched card.

COST ADVANTAGE. The density of tape makes it a low-cost storage medium. In order to store equivalent amounts of data on any other storage medium, a substantially larger investment would be required. For instance, in our previous example, the cost of one reel of tape would be about $38.00. Storing the same data in punched cards would cost about $175.00, as punched cards sell for about $1.00 per 1,000 cards.

HIGH SPEED. Magnetic tape is the fastest form of direct input medium and output medium available to users of computers. It is, typically, one of the components of a large-scale computer system. High speed is attained despite the limitations imposed on all forms of input and output equipment by the mechanical parts used in their construction, which, by their very nature, are bound to be slower than electronics.

Drawbacks of magnetic tape

SLOW ACCESS TIME. A magnetic tape is often described as a very long, thin memory. That is, in order to find specific data on the tape, a single reading head must start scanning the tape from the beginning each time new information is desired. This takes time. The only data immediately available to the computer are those which are located under the reading head. Also, the tape itself must be started every time information stored on it needs to be read. This, too, takes time. Naturally, if a single reading head is replaced by a dozen or more reading heads, each designed to read a section of the reel of tape, the time taken to locate wanted data on tape will be considerably reduced.

PHYSICAL AND ENVIRONMENTAL WEAKNESSES. *Dust* is one of the great enemies of magnetic tape. Particles of dust can, under pressure, wipe out magnetized spots on tape or widen the gap between the tape and read-write heads. Either can cause reading or writing errors.

Heat and *humidity* can cause the separation of the oxide coating from the plastic base of the tape, destroying the data completely. For this reason, a computer department in which magnetic tape is used for input and output must install air-conditioning in the computer room and provide constant control over humidity, temperature, and freedom of air from dust or any other foreign particles that might damage the data stored on tape. A "No Smoking" sign is popular in most computer departments. Ashes can contaminate the tape with foreign matter, and, in some cases, cause permanent damage if they touch the oxide coating on which data are recorded.

TAPE BREAKAGE. When tape breaks, regardless of how neatly and carefully it is spliced, some data will be destroyed, because of the density at which they are recorded. Because of this fact, permanent splicing is not recommended.

PRINT-THROUGH EFFECT. When magnetic tape is wound on a tape reel, it is subject to *print through*. That is, magnetic attractions can cause magnetic patterns on one coil to be copied on adjoining coils of tape within the reel. This distorts and obscures the data recorded on the tape, causing confusion and the processing of inaccurate data. To forestall this possibility, the operator should wind the tape loosely and somewhat slowly. The tape should also be rewound about once a month and stored in a cool place.

Tape Handling and Storage

A business firm converting from punched-card or other systems to a tape system frequently retains its employees to operate the new equipment. Because of the special characteristics of tape, the company must give intensive retraining and constant supervision to all the personnel engaged in handling the new tape system in the computer department. This retraining includes instructions in the proper handling, control, and storage of tape. Some of the main points to consider in tape storage and tape handling are:

1. Accidental dropping or careless handling of the reel of tape can cause nicks or kinks. This, in time, will affect the quality of recording or reading the data recorded on it. A damaged tape is as inferior as a chipped or a broken phonograph disk.
2. When not in use, a magnetic-tape reel should be supported at the hub. If this is not done, especially when the reel is in storage, it may warp, thus reducing its efficiency.
3. While in operation, the door of the tape unit must always remain closed. This should be done in order to prevent any foreign particles entering and interfering with the processing of the stored data. Even when the tape is on the machine, the plastic tape container must remain closed in order to prevent dust or dirt from accumulating in it. If it becomes dirty or if dust particles collect inside the container, it should be cleaned immediately either by using a vacuum cleaner or by washing it with a regular house detergent.
4. The top of the tape unit must not be used for a working area. Doing so is inadvisable because the objects left on it might hamper the effectiveness of the cooling system, and the materials placed on the tape unit themselves would be exposed to dust and heat driven out by the blowers of the tape unit.
5. In tape control, some form of visual identification should be made. A typical computer department may have hundreds of reels of tape involved in its many processing applications. To the human operator, one reel of tape looks the same as any other reel of tape on file. Unlike the punched card, for instance, which can be read manually, the magnetic tape does not show any data that can be understood directly by an operator. It must be read by a machine.

    In order to distinguish one reel from another, an external label is used to describe the data contained in the tape. The label shows the tape serial number, reel number, date of the application, type of application (payroll, accounts receivable, accounts payable, and so forth), number of times the tape has been passed through the machine, and the name of the programmer who made up the program to be stored in it. In this way, the tape can be easily identified without the need for taking it out of the container or reading the contents on the tape itself. An index can be made, by serial number or by type of application, of all the reels of tape available. When a processing run is necessary, the librarian, or the programmer, would look for the proper identification on the label in order to find the correct reel to be used.

6. In order to avoid any accidental destruction of data on tape when new information is written, each reel of tape must have a special plastic "ring" attached to it before any recording can be performed by the tape-recording unit. The saying, "No ring—no write," among console operators simply means that the tape unit always reads data from tape unless a plastic ring is inserted in its groove which allows the tape unit to write data on tape. This precautionary feature controls the read and write operations in such a way that accidental writing is impossible (Fig. 16-17).

Fig. 16-17. An IBM file protective ring

7. As a further precautionary feature in tape control, a programmer should record the description of the label to be placed in the reel at the beginning of each tape. When this is done, if the external label should be torn out, the description is always available at the beginning of the tape. When the program is loaded into the computer, the first instruction in it commands the computer to record the description of the reel of tape, to see if it is a payroll tape, for example. The tape unit causes the reel to rotate and the tape moves under the reading head, which reads the description. If the description read is the same as the one written in the program, the application continues and the data on that reel of tape will be processed. However, if it is not the same, the computer stops and the programmer will have to determine the nature of the error. If the tape used pertains to a different application, he will have to rewind the tape, take it out of the unit drive, and replace it with the correct tape.

Random-access Files

Magnetic-disk Storage

Unlike magnetic-tape storage, which is referred to as *sequential-access files,* magnetic-disk storage, referred to as *random-access* (or direct-access) *files,* is made up of a vertical stack of magnetic metal disks similar to the musical records in a juke box. Random-access files are characterized by the ability of the system to skip around within the file and read or write specific data with no particular regard to the sequence in which the reading or writing is performed.

Types of magnetic disks

A magnetic disk is a thin metal disk coated on both sides of its flat surfaces with a ferrous oxide recording material. This material is much the same as that used on magnetic tapes. Each magnetic disk has flat surfaces on both sides. Data are represented by a six-bit code (*1,2,4,8,A,B*) and are stored in tracks on either side by means of magnetic spots caused by a read-write head.

A magnetic disk is separated from the adjacent ones above and below it, in order to allow small read-write heads to read from or write informa-

Fig. 16-18.   IBM head-per-disk magnetic-disk file

tion on it. A selected access arm (controlling the read-write head) is directed by the program to manipulate data on a specific section of the disk. Earlier disk models had one large access arm that served a stack of twenty-five or fifty immovable files. Since the arm required some time to reach its destination, designers later introduced the two access-arm model: one arm to process a specific transaction at a given storage position, while the other arm moved toward the next record.

The latest magnetic disk file includes a comb-shaped access mechanism which moves in and out between the disks. Enough movable read-write heads are attached so as to allow each disk its own read-write head, thus reducing average access time to a fraction of a second (Fig. 16-18).

Disk packs have recently become very popular. A disk pack (with an average capacity of 1,400,000 words) is a stack of six magnetic disks which are handled as a unit (Fig. 16-19). They have an edge over original disk files, in that if the computer breaks down or when the user wishes to process the data stored in the disk file on another computer system

Fig. 16-19. IBM disk pack

located on a distant site, the disk pack can be easily removed from one drive unit and inserted in the drive unit of another system. Furthermore, replacement of one disk pack by another in the same system takes less than one minute.

Early in 1967, Burroughs Corporation introduced a head-per-track design which couples the recording economies of magnetic disks with the programming simplicity of magnetic-core storage (Fig. 16-20). There are no moving read-write heads or access arms. Thus, there is no time requirement for mechanical positioning over desired information tracks on the

Fig. 16-20. Burroughs No. 1029030 head-per-track disk design

disk surfaces. Instead, individual read-write heads are permanently positioned over each information track on each surface of each disk. Only the disks move, spinning at a constant speed under the read-write heads. Heads are air-flown to within a few millionths of an inch of the vertical disk surface, and they store or extract information at rates ranging from 100,000 to over 500,000 characters per second. Fig. 16-20 shows a portion of the head-per-track array of read-write heads poised over the surface of one disk in a Burroughs disk file.

Sectors and tracks

In order to have better control over the location of data in a specific track, the magnetic disk is divided into five equal pie-shaped areas, called *sectors* or *segments* (Fig. 16-21). The addresses (location numbers) of the five segments on one side are: 00, 01, 02, 03, and 04. The five segments of the other side of the same disk are numbered 05, 06, 07, 08, and 09. As shown in Fig. 16-21, the numbers in parenthesis denote the segment

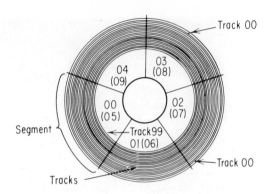

Fig. 16-21. Segments and tracks of a magnetic disk (*IBM*)

numbers of the bottom of the disk. The others denote the numbers of the five segments of the top side of the disk.

A specific record location is normally identified by the disk number, the segment number, and the track number within the sector. The track located within a segment is of fixed length and is referred to as a *record*. If each record holds 200 characters of information, then how much storage would a file of 100 disks hold?

To answer the question above, the following steps may be taken:

$$
\begin{aligned}
1 \text{ disk} &= 2 \text{ disk faces} \\
100 \text{ disks} &= 200 \text{ disk faces} \\
1 \text{ disk face} &= 5 \text{ segments} \\
200 \text{ disk faces} &= 1{,}000 \text{ segments} \\
1 \text{ segment} &= 100 \text{ records (track within the segment)} \\
1{,}000 \text{ segments} &= 100{,}000 \text{ records} \\
1 \text{ record} &= 200 \text{ characters} \\
100{,}000 \text{ records} &= 20{,}000{,}000 \text{ characters}
\end{aligned}
$$

Another way to arrive at the storage capacity of a 100-disk file is to begin with the smallest unit and work out. That is, if each record stores 200 characters, a segment containing 100 records (tracks within the segment) can store $200 \times 100 = 20{,}000$ characters per segment. There are five segments per disk face. So the total characters that can be stored on each disk face is $20{,}000 \times 5 = 100{,}000$ characters. Because each disk has two disk faces, then $100{,}000 \times 2 = 200{,}000$ characters that can be stored per disk. There are 100 disks in the file. The total storage capacity of the file, then, is $200{,}000 \times 100 = 20{,}000{,}000$ characters. Twenty million characters are equivalent to the contents of the five telephone books of the boroughs of New York City.

Low-activity and high-activity data processing

Some applications (for example, various billing systems) require processing of a relatively limited number of input transactions against a very large master file. The use of random-access devices allows retrieval of any single record without extensive searching or examining of others in storage. Disk storage is equally effective in high-activity applications (for example, payroll of 5,000 employees) involving a comparatively small number of records updated frequently. The random-access approach allows direct access to all types of tables and other relevant data without the need for batching or extensive searching through the data files.

Real-time processing

Many business applications require processing data as they become available. This type of processing is called *real-time* or *in-line* processing. High-capacity, randomly accessible disk-storage devices make real-time processing feasible. Thus, one can now process data in the sequence in which transactions take place. Furthermore, the user can easily process intermixed and nonsequential input data for multiple application routines and maintain up-to-date records for diversified applications.

On-line systems

On-line systems refer to the functioning of the units or devices (for example, on-line printer) under the direct control of the central processing unit. The unit(s) may or may not be physically located near the C.P.U. The latter case is made possible through remote links to facilitate proper communication (referred to as teleprocessing). The airlines have been using on-line teleprocessing for many years. Random-access equipment is compatible with this technique, for without it, access to and updating of flight data would be time consuming and difficult. Thus, *on-line* input/output devices make *in-line* processing possible. Details on teleprocessing are found in Chapter 18.

Summary

The RAMAC system (random-access method of accounting and control) can update all accounts quickly without having them in sequence. A disk file is used most commonly in business applications which require an immediate response, if the incoming data enter the system in a random manner. Updating and/or obtaining information on certain accounts in the file can be performed faster, because access to these accounts is made easier with the availability of these accounts on a number of individual disks. If, instead, the information on these disks is stored on magnetic tape, obtaining the same information would be time consuming. The reason for this is that, when work on an account somewhere in the middle of the magnetic tape is desired, the tape has to be read and unwound until the location of the specific account is reached. Tape is, therefore, considered an efficient operation only when each and every account in the file need to be read sequentially. However, when certain accounts in random locations must be read, the disk-file device is the better system. One can go to any record in the disk file at any time, because each record is individually and directly addressable; that is, it has a separate location number.

Magnetic-disk storage accommodates the storage of a large amount of data. One disk unit has a storage capacity equal to that of two average reels of magnetic tape. Its storage can be further increased by adding additional units to the system.

Finally, a magnetic disk is very durable, and it is manufactured to serve for a long time. Furthermore, data can be erased from the magnetic disk, which makes the storage of secondary information in the magnetic disk less costly in the long run than would be the case if the other random-access secondary-storage devices available were used. The disk file is one of the latest developments in automatic data-processing memory.

Fig. 16-22. UNIVAC mass storage subsystem

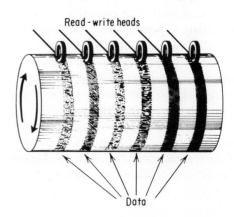

Fig. 16-23. Schematic of magnetic drum and read-write heads

Magnetic-drum Storage

The second type of random-access storage device is the magnetic drum (Fig. 16-22). A magnetic drum is a high-quality, precision steel cylinder enclosed in a copper sleeve. The copper sleeve is coated with a magnetic material on which data may be written at high speed (Fig. 16-23).

Data storage and processing on magnetic drums

Reading from and writing on a magnetic drum are accomplished by devices called *read-write heads*. A series of parallel read-write heads, each of which is capable of reading and writing binary configuration as a result of electrical pulses received by it, are placed so that the drum revolves beneath them. Once written, the data may be read back indefinitely. Recording on magnetic drums is basically the same technique used as for the audio tape recorder, except that the latter machine records an audio signal, whereas the magnetic drum records electrical pulses (Fig. 16-24).

A HOME TAPE RECORDER   *MAGNETIC DRUM RECORDING*

Fig. 16-24.   Left—home tape recording; right—magnetic-drum recording

In a writing operation, as the drum rotates at constant speed, a current passes through the coil of a particular *write head*. This sets up a magnetic field (flux) and places a magnetic spot on the surface of the drum. The presence of a magnetic spot represents a one-bit of data. The absence of a magnetic spot represents a zero-bit of data. Written information on the surface of a magnetic drum is in the binary mode.

In a reading operation, the magnetized spot on the surface of a magnetic drum passing under the head induces an output signal through the coil. The coil transfers the signal to the operating circuitry. In this way, reading recorded data on a drum is made possible. Data are retained and read back as many times as necessary. Reading from a magnetic drum *is not destructive,* because the condition of a magnetic spot representing the one binary digit is not changed or erased when it passes under the *read head*. Therefore, magnetic-drum storage is permanent, and data can be so stored indefinitely even when power is turned off. The only time that data are destroyed is when new data are written in the same location.

A magnetic drum is divided into several channels across its length (Fig. 16-25). Each channel has a read-write head which performs the reading and writing operations of all the storage locations in it. In other words,

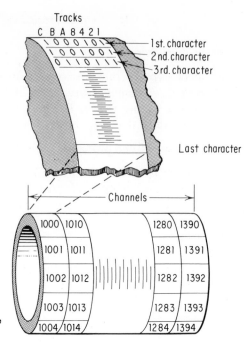

Fig. 16-25. Schematic of a drum storage

the binary digits representing data are stored in parallel tracks. The address (location number) of any given data depends on its physical location on the drum.

A magnetic drum contains a specific number of storage locations, each of which can be addressed by the computer. This is possible owing to the fact that each location has a specific number or address (Fig. 16-25). Each channel contains many characters (for storage) around the drum. If the contents of location number (address) 1004 is desired, for instance, the head designated to that particular channel which includes 1004 is activated. The time needed to begin reading the data (access time) varies, depending upon many factors: (1) the distance to be traveled by that location to the head, (2) the physical dimensions of the magnetic drum, (3) the number and types of heads used, (4) the arrangement of data, and (5) the speed of rotation of the drum.

Advantages of magnetic-drum storage

HIGH STORAGE CAPACITY. A magnetic drum is a short, fat memory. Its high capacity to store data is one of its main advantages. Its speed is moderate, the most popular being 3,600 revolutions per minute (r.p.m.), although ultra-fast drums, rotating at a little less than 10,000 r.p.m., have been developed. This speed is considered adequate in small-sized computers, but not as satisfactory in large computers that demand access time of a fraction of that of the magnetic drum.

NO ACCELERATION PROBLEM. A magnetic drum rotates at a constant speed, a fact which eliminates any acceleration problem. The latter problem often occurs in other storage devices during reading and/or writing operations, an example of which is the acceleration problem that arises with the use of magnetic tape.

Magnetic-card Storage

Another random-access storage method is through the use of mylar magnetic cards. A magnetic card is a flexible plastic strip with a magnetizable coating. It offers features similar to those of magnetic disks, in that it is capable of storing a large volume of randomly accessible information. Fig. 16-26. Data are recorded on or read from any of the seven individually addressable tracks. Each track can accommodate up to 3,100 alphanumeric characters, giving a total of 21,700 (3,100 × 7 tracks) alphanumeric characters.

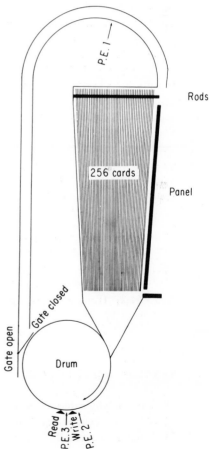

Fig. 16-26.   NCR card random-access memory unit, with schematic (*National Cash Register Corporation*)

Magnetic cards are usually arranged in packs, each consisting of several hundred cards. A randomly selected record is obtained by selecting from the pack the card storing the information. The card is wrapped around a rotating drum where seven read-write heads process the data it contains. When released, the card is returned to its original location for future processing.

Some of the good features of this random-access storage file are its low storage cost per digit, availability of a large number of records at any given time, and the ease with which the card packs may be removed, stored, and/or replaced.

GLOSSARY OF TERMS

BLOCKING: Combining two or more records into one block.

DENSITY: The maximum possible number of columns of data which can be recorded on a unit length (usually one inch) of tape.

END-OF-FILE INDICATOR: A code which indicates the last record of a data file has been read.

IN-LINE PROCESSING: (See real-time processing.)

LOAD POINT: A tape marker, indicating the beginning of the usable portion of the tape when writing or reading is to begin.

MAGNETIC TAPE: A tape coated with magnetizable material, on which information may be recorded in the form of magnetically polarized spots.

ON-LINE SYSTEMS: Functioning of the peripheral devices under the direct control of the central processing unit.

PARITY CHECK: A *check* that tests whether the number of ones (or zeros) in an array of binary digits is odd or even. Synonymous with odd-even check.

RANDOM ACCESS: Pertaining to a storage device in which the *access time* is effectively independent of the location of the data.

REAL-TIME PROCESSING: Data processing in which transactions are processed as they actually occur.

SEQUENTIAL DATA PROCESSING: A technique by which items to be processed must be collected into groups prior to processing.

REVIEW QUESTIONS

1. Explain why external memory is needed in business data processing.
2. What is magnetic tape? In what three areas is it used?
3. What is sequential-file storage?

4. Assume that twenty-five customer records are stored on magnetic tape. If only record *25* (the last record) is needed for processing, does the machine have an immediate access to it? Explain.

5. Explain the seven-bit character code.

6. Assuming the use of even parity check, determine the status (zero-bit, or one-bit) of the parity-check core in the representation of the following characters: *3, 4, 5, 6, A, C, J, L, S, T, V, X, Z.*

7. Why are vacuum columns used in a magnetic-tape unit? Explain.

8. What is meant by the term *density?* What is the difference between HI density and super-HI density?

9. Define the following terms:
   (a) Load point
   (b) Trailer label end-of-file indicator
   (c) Interrecord gap
   (d) Single-record block
   (e) Multiple-record block
   (f) Group mark

10. List and discuss briefly the advantages and disadvantages of magnetic tape.

11. What physical and environmental factors should be considered and controlled when a tape system is used? Why?

12. What is meant by *print-through* effect?

13. List and explain briefly the steps to be taken in tape handling and storage.

14. What are the three different ways in which a data reel is distinguished? Explain.

15. When and why is a plastic ring used in the tape-recording unit?

16. What is the difference between sequential- and random-access files?

17. What is a magnetic disk? What advantages does RAMAC file have over magnetic tape? Explain.

18. What are high- and low-activity data processing?

19. Distinguish the difference between on-line and in-line processing. Give an example to illustrate.

20. What is a magnetic drum? Draw a schematic, showing a magnetic drum and the location of five read-write heads.

21. What is the primary difference between audio and magnetic-drum recording?

22. Explain briefly the recording and reading operations on a magnetic drum.

23. Is reading from a magnetic drum destructive? Why?

24. Describe the uses and function of a magnetic-drum channel.

25. What factors determine the access time for reading the data from a magnetic drum?

26. List and explain briefly the two main advantages of a magnetic drum.

27. Explain how a magnetic card stores data. In what respect is it similar to a magnetic disk?

28. How is collating performed on magnetic tape? Give an example.

chapter

17

INPUT
AND OUTPUT DEVICES

Introduction

ONE OF THE MOST IMPORTANT ASPECTS of processing business data by a computer is to prepare related raw data accurately and in the proper sequence. One should bear in mind that all incorrect information used as input will result in inaccurate output. For example, in anticipation of the sum *3* for an answer (output), only certain digits or a combination of digits can be used (input). The alternatives can be either $3 + 0$, $2 + 1$, $2 + 1 + 0$, or $1 + 2 + 0$. Using a combination such as $3 + B$, or $A + 2$, and so forth, as input, obviously will not result in the correct output of *3* unless *B* is coded to have a value of *0,* or unless *A* is coded to have a value of *1*. Personnel in the business data-processing field use a humorous, unofficial abbreviation *"G I G O,"* interpreted as "Garbage In, Garbage Out," to emphasize the need for the presentation of accurate and logical input if accurate and meaningful output is to be expected.

The main characteristic of business data-processing applications is the performance of simple and limited amounts of computations on large amounts of data. The credit department of a large business concern, for instance, uses a computer to update each customer's account by adding to the customer's old balance all purchases made by him on account and subtracting from the sum all payments which he made during a given period, in order to arrive at a new balance for the period. This application involves basically one addition and one subtraction—functions which are extremely easy. However, the fact that thousands of customers' accounts need updating frequently means that these two simple operations must be repeated thousands of times. Thus, a great volume of data flows into and out of the computer in the process of the comparatively simple operation of updating. This makes the input and output equipment the busiest part of the system, because it has to read and print the information speedily.

Generally speaking, input and output units (called peripheral equipment) perform translation and communication functions. These units do not do the actual processing but, rather, prepare the data for processing in the central processing unit. For this reason the input and output units are under the direct control of the central processing unit. Can you explain the meaning of the phrase: "latigid retupmoc"? Your response is an emphatic *NO!* until you are told that it is "digital computer" spelled backward. The computer finds it just as difficult to process data if the language representing the data cannot be easily interpreted by it.

The machine language is read by input devices, which then transfer the data to the computer for processing. If the output is needed immediately by management, it is put back into human language by an output device called the *printer*. If the output, on the other hand, is to be stored for future processing by the computer, this can be done by using various kinds of other output devices, that is, punched cards, punched paper tape, or magnetic tape.

To summarize, then, input equipment *translates* the machine language and transfers it to the computer. It *reads* data into the storage unit of the computer. The term to *read in* means to "put in." The data "read in" or "put in" are called *input*. Output equipment *translates* machine language to human language. It provides a means of communication between the computer and the outside world. Output equipment *writes* data out of the storage unit. The term *to write out,* then, means "to put out." Thus, the data "written" or "put out" are referred to as *output*. Each different type of computer has its own individual machine language and utilizes different input and output devices. Thus, we must examine the different input and output media that computers use in order to comprehend more fully the implications involved in the various processing systems and to understand how "Garbage In, Garbage Out" can be prevented from occurring.

Reading Devices—Punched-card Reader

The punched-card reader is one of the most popular input devices in use today. It is designed to transfer the data punched in each card to the central processing unit for processing. In Fig. 17-1, data cards are placed in the feed hopper on the right. The holes in the card are interpreted into electrical impulses which go to the central computer unit for processing. Although cards go inside the card reader to be read, they do not go inside the computer proper.

The two types of punched-card readers are: (1) the brush type, and (2) the photoelectric type. Fig. 17-1 is a brush-type punched-card reader. The punched-card reader reads one card at a time. A stack of cards is first placed in the read hopper nine-edge first, face down. The first card in sequence passes underneath the first set of eighty reading brushes, called the *read-check* station. (See Fig. 17-2.) The brushes take a *hole count,* that is, they keep track of the number of holes in the card for checking purposes. Then the same card moves underneath the next set of eighty read brushes, which, after verifying the hole count made by the read-check

Fig. 17-1. IBM 2540 brush-type card reader (right) and card punch (left)

brushes, direct the data electrically into the computer unit. Then the card drops into the stacker marked "normal read." The second card in sequence goes through the same procedure, and so forth, until the whole file is read. All the cards are finally dropped into the radial stacker (Fig. 17-1).

The left side of the card reader shown in Fig. 17-2 is used to punch the results of processing (output) in blank cards placed in a hopper on the left. The greatest speed of this specific card reader is 1,000 cards per minute. The angular device in the read hopper shown in Fig. 17-1 is called a *file feed,* which facilitates the feed of as many as 3,000 cards at a time.

The photoelectric-type punched-card reader is the same as the brush type in that both machines sense holes in a card. The main difference, however, is in the method of sensing. The latter machine uses brushes to sense holes in a card, whereas in the former, eighty photoelectric cells are activated as the punched card passes over a main light source. Fig. 17-3 presents the IBM 2501 card reader. It reads cards serially (column by column) by a light-sensing unit at the rate of 1,000 cards per minute and is capable of detecting invalid, off-punched, and mispositioned codes. This input device typically goes with the IBM 360, Model 20 system.

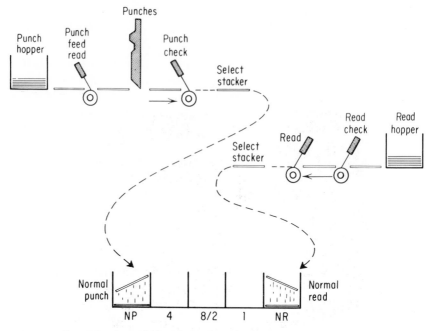

Fig. 17-2. A punched-card "read" and "punch" schematic of brush-type reader

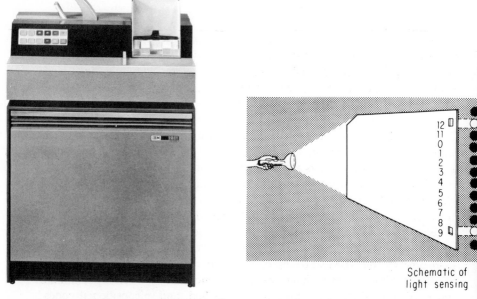

Schematic of light sensing

Fig. 17-3. IBM 2501 card reader and schematic of light sensing

Punching Devices

The left side of the punched-card reader (Fig. 17-1) is used to punch the results (output) from the central processing unit into blank cards fed into the punch hopper. A blank card moves automatically under the punch dies, and the output is punched. The punched card then moves under a set of eighty brushes to check on the accuracy of the punch dies. If they are correct, the card ejects into the radial stacker below it. Otherwise, the machine stops, indicating an error. The IBM 2540 punches up to 300 cards per minute. Faster machines especially designed for card punching are also available.

Printers

All computers process and produce information which, when received, represents the last step in a business application. The way the result is received depends on the output device (hooked to the system in use) and on the specific features it includes. Most output devices are capable of presenting the same result in various forms.

The machine which is used exclusively in business applications as a means of output is referred to as the *printer*. It provides a permanent visual record of information as computer output. A printed statement is the most popular output medium to be presented to the user—usually, to management. Depending upon the type of printer, its speed varies from 10 to 2,000 characters per second or up to 1,285 lines per minute.

The primary printing devices used in printing computer output are the wire-matrix, the wheel, and the chain printer.

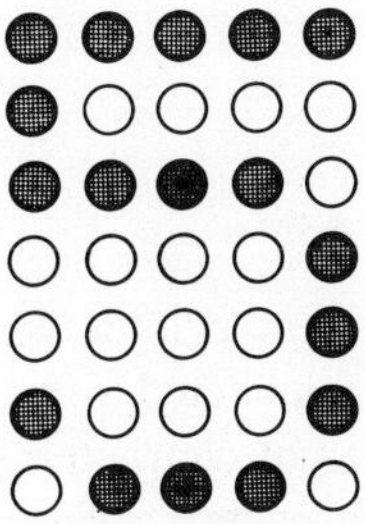

Fig. 17-4. Wire arrangement of wire-matrix printer

Wire-matrix Printer

In the wire-matrix printer, small wires are arranged in the form of a rectangle usually in a 5×7 matrix (Fig. 17-4). The matrix moves along the line of the paper to print alphabetic, numeric, or special characters. The ends of the selected wires are pressed by a hammer against an inked ribbon, resulting in the printing of the data on paper.

Wheel Printer

The wheel printer consists of 120 print wheels, each of which contains ten digits, twenty-six letters, and twelve special characters (Fig. 17-5). The 120 printwheels are aligned horizontally along the width of the paper and, upon printing, are positioned to print the desired information simultaneously. This means that the parallel method of printing is used and that up to 120 characters can be printed on a given line.

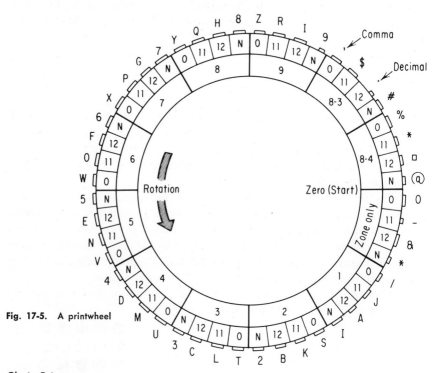

Fig. 17-5. A printwheel

Chain Printer

The chain printer is an electromechanical printer which utilizes five sections connected together to form a chain. Each of the sections contains forty-eight characters, to print ten digits, twenty-six letters, and twelve special characters (Fig. 17-6). The chain revolves horizontally and is positioned behind the inked ribbon. The hammers, upon firing against the back of the paper, cause a character in the chain to press against the ribbon, resulting in the printing of that character on the form. Fig. 17-7 shows the 1403 printer, which prints the output produced by the IBM 1401 and 360 computers.

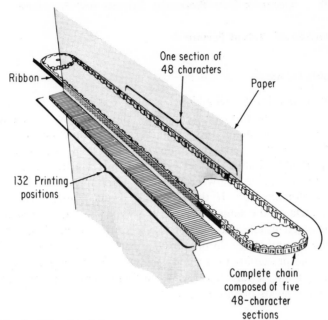

Fig. 17-6.   An IBM print chain

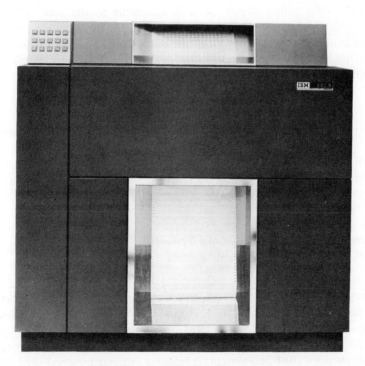

Fig. 17-7.   The IBM 1403 chain printer

Selection of Output Format

Usable Format

The output format should be usable. If a balance sheet is required, for instance, it should have the name of the company, the name of the statement, and the date. Each of these items would occupy a separate line and be centered correctly. Following this group, the assets section should be presented. Liabilities and proprietorship data follow next, after enough spacing is allowed between the total asset amount and the liabilities and proprietorship title. If the computer, instead, presented all these necessary facts on the same line or in the wrong order, the result would not be considered usable. In such a case, an adjustment should be made either in the output device, in the program itself by changing certain instructions, or in the presentation of the data input. The change in any of these three areas should be directed toward the improvement of the output format to meet the needs of the user.

Understandable Output

The output information should be understandable to the user. This can be accomplished either by training the user to learn the machine language or to direct the computer to produce the output in simple form which can be easily understood. The latter alternative would be the more logical solution to the case, because it would be easiest for the user.

Relevant and Complete Output

The output information must be relevant and complete. If, after examination of the output information, some data are found to be lacking, the input information can be resequenced or revised in such a way as to aid in a more complete processing, leading to the attainment of more correct, more relevant, and more complete output information.

An Electronic Data-processing Card System— IBM 360, Model 20 Card System

The foregoing input/output components work with the central processing unit to form a computer *system*. A typical example of a system, utilizing punched-card components, is the IBM 360, Model 20 (Fig. 17-8). The Model 20 punched-card processing system is a low-cost, compact version of the all-purpose IBM 360 system. It features familiar punched-card data-

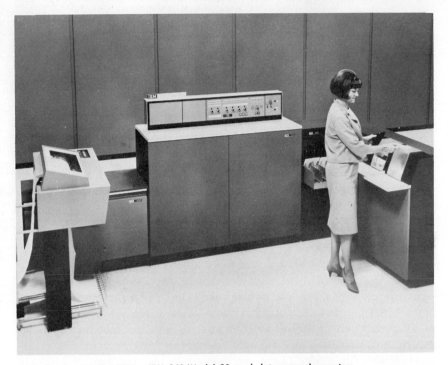

Fig. 17-8.   IBM 360/Model 20 card data-processing system

handling concepts and familiar input/output functions, and offers rapid transition from conventional punched-card equipment. The units discussed below make up this system.

IBM 2020 Processing Unit

The IBM 2020 stores all data and instructions and is the heart of the system. It comes with either 4,096, 8,192, 12,288 or 16,384 positions of core storage. Under program control, the 2020 makes all logical decisions, performs all required arithmetic calculations, and tells attached card-handling machines what to read, punch, or print, and when to do it. Over-lapped operation of processing and card input/output functions allows computation to be made concurrently with reading, printing, and punching.

IBM 2560 Multi-function Card Machine (MFCM)

The MFCM offers a new concept in punched-card processing. This unit permits a high degree of card-handling flexibility for the Model 20. It combines the functions of a collator, gang punch, reproducer, sorter, and interpreter. Cards from two separate hoppers are read, then merged into a single-card path where they are punched, printed, and selectively stacked. File maintenance can be accomplished in only one pass of a master-card file. Cards are read at speeds of up to 500 per minute and punched at the rate of 160 columns per second.

IBM 2203 Printer

This component provides high-speed printed output for the Model 20 system. It prints up to 425 alphanumeric or 750 numeric lines per minute. The 2203 features interchangeable typebars which permit the character arrangements to be varied as required. All data to be printed are controlled by the processor's stored program.

Other Components

Other card-punching and card-reading components available for the Model 20 include the IBM 1442 card punch, Model 5, which punches from ninety-one to 270 cards per minute, depending upon the number of columns being punched, and the IBM 2501 card reader (Fig. 17-3) which reads cards at either 600 or 1,000 cards per minute depending upon the model. A combination of these components can form the basic input/output functions for Model 20, or can be used to augment the 2560 MFCM for greater system performance, versatility, and flexibility.

Tape Devices

Magnetic Tape

A single computer can be used to control one or more tape units as input or output. A tape unit is similar to a tape recorder. At the input stage, it reads the coded data to the computer. At the output stage, it writes (records) the results for storage and future reference. Magnetic tape and magnetic units are used most often for either secondary storage or temporary storage of data which might later be read back into the computer when needed (Fig. 17-9).

As an input/output medium, magnetic tape is preferred over the punched card, primarily because of its speed, its ability to store on one inch of tape data punched in several cards, and its ability to be reused indefinitely to record new data on it. It is one of the fastest forms of input or output available.

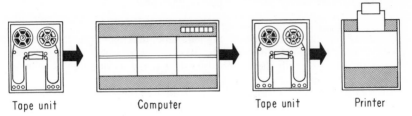

Tape unit   Computer   Tape unit   Printer

Fig. 17-9. The use of a magnetic-tape unit as an input/output medium

Paper-tape Reader

A paper-tape reader is used to provide direct input to a computer, by reading prepunched data in paper tape. A tape-punch machine is also used to provide output from a computer by punching output information in paper tape (Fig. 17-10). Data on paper tape are recorded in holes patterned along the length of the tape. The basic classification of paper tape is according to the number of channels on it. Fig. 17-11 shows the eight-channel tape, one of the most commonly used. A channel is an imaginary line which runs parallel to the edge of the tape. From the bottom, in an eight-channel tape, the channels are *1, 2, 4, 8, K, O,* and *X.* A numeric, alphabetic, or special character is represented by one or a combination of holes in a given vertical column. The columns in a paper tape are similar to those in punched cards.

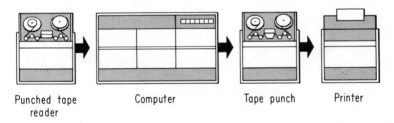

Punched tape   Computer   Tape punch   Printer
reader

Fig. 17-10. The use of a paper-tape unit as an input/output device

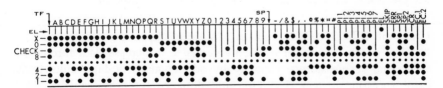

Fig. 17-11. Paper-tape eight-channel code *(IBM)*

Disadvantages of punched paper tape are:

1. Compared to magnetic tape, it is very slow.
2. Unlike the typewriter or magnetic tape, making corrections or inserting additional items in it is difficult.
3. Compared with the punched card, it is not as durable, neither is it as convenient to store, to file, or to handle.
4. Reclassifying information is difficult without first duplicating its contents into another form of unit record, such as the punched card.

Primary advantages of paper tape are:

1. It is used on several IBM machines (Fig. 17-12). However, use as an input or output medium is somewhat limited in the business field.
2. It is inexpensive and fairly cheap to produce (about twenty-five cents per 100 feet).
3. It is easier to mail than the punched card, and much lighter to handle.

Fig. 17-12. IBM 382 paper-tape reader

An Electronic Data-processing Tape System—An Example

Using the IBM 360/Model 20 as a basic example, the smaller business firm for which this model is usually geared can increase data throughput speed and record-storage capacity by adding magnetic-tape units to its card-processing system. The tape unit designed for it is the IBM 2415 magnetic-tape unit (Fig. 17-13).

Fig. 17-13.   IBM 360/Model 20 tape system

With magnetic-tape units added to the system, the input/output speed requirements are increased. To match this increased speed, a faster printer is usually recommended. Generally, the IBM 1403 printer is installed in lieu of a 2203 printer (the standard printer for the Model 20 card system) to achieve printing speeds of 600 or 1,100 alphanumeric lines per minute. Furthermore, for high-speed card punching, the 2560 MFCM can be replaced by: (1) IBM 2520 Model A1 card read punch which reads and punches 500 cards per minute, and (2) Models A2 and A3 card punch units which punch 500 and 300 cards per minute, respectively.

Random-access Devices

IBM 2311 Disk-drive Unit

Magnetic-disk units are normally used as input/output auxiliary devices in medium- to large-sized installations or for those applications requiring large-volume master-data records with immediate accessibility. The unit consists of a number of thin magnetic disks covered by magnetizable coating for storing information. As the disks spin around, the unit can be

Fig. 17-14. IBM 2311 disk-drive unit

instructed by the computer program to read from (input) or write on (output) any disk when necessary (Fig. 17-14).

IBM 2316 Disk-pack Assembly

As mentioned in the previous chapter, disk packs are becoming more popular each year. A disk pack is a compact device that weighs between eight and fifteen pounds and contains a specific number of disks on which information is recorded. To illustrate, an IBM 2316 disk-pack assembly that weighs about thirteen pounds goes into the IBM 2311 disk-drive unit (Fig. 17-14). It is composed of eleven disks (each fourteen inches in diameter) mounted one-half inch apart on a vertical shaft. The disks provide twenty surfaces on which data can be recorded. The entire assembly rotates at a speed of 2,400 revolutions per minute in a Model 2314 disk unit.

An Electronic Data-processing Disk System—An Example

As mentioned earlier, magnetic-disk units are usually used with medium-to large-sized computer systems. In 1966, a magnetic-disk drive became available on the IBM 360/Model 20 in order to enable smaller businesses to add direct-access storage capacity in millions of characters and to provide record access in a matter of a few milliseconds (Fig. 17-15). The use of the Model 1316 disk packs in the 2311 disk units expanded the direct-access capability of the system. Master records can now be implemented on disks and updated as soon as a transaction enters the system, with no batching or presequencing required. A disk-oriented system should improve record-keeping techniques in various applications. Retail companies, for example, can realize more efficient processing of their payroll, accounts payable, sales audit, billing, and the like. Likewise, manufacturing companies can use this relatively small disk-oriented system in accounting, in

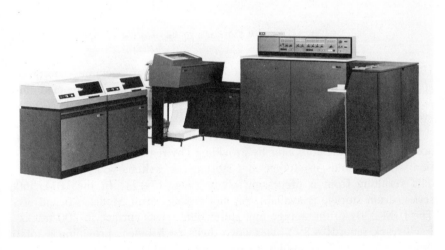

Fig. 17-15. An IBM 360/Model 20 disk system

determining bill of material, and in inventory management, shop status, and routings.

For companies whose requirements warrant it, maximum capacity of the Model 20 system can be achieved through combining card processing, magnetic-tape storage, and disk storage (Fig. 17-16). This is considered the most powerful system of the three versions. Larger systems, such as

Fig. 17-16. An IBM 360/Model 20 disk/tape system

IBM 360/Models 30, 40, 50, and 65 are much faster, accommodate more special-purpose input/output devices, and are normally justified by medium-sized to large companies with constant need for speed and real-time processing.

The *magnetic-drum* unit is another random-access device, capable of accommodating the computer by providing (by reading) required information which it holds in storage and storing (or writing—output function) data resulting from a processing phase (Fig. 17-17). In the IBM 360 series, drum storage is available on any model except Models 20 and 30. The IBM 2301 drum storage unit stores data on its surface in 800 tracks. Each track records 4,892 bytes (two digits each byte), providing a total drum capacity of 3.91 million bytes (4,892 × 800) or 7,820,000 packed digits.

Input/Output Devices Summarized

The foregoing pages covered some of the primary and most widely used input and output devices. Each of these components perform in an *auxiliary* capacity to aid the central processing unit perform its *primary* function

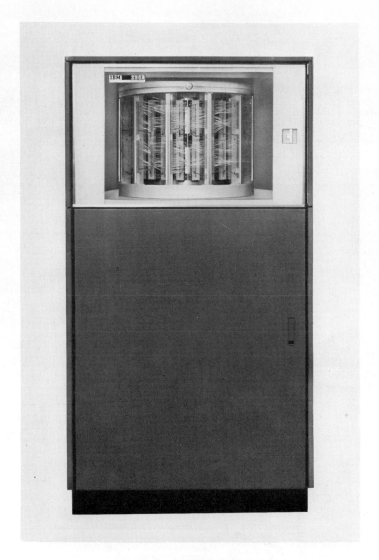

Fig. 17-17. IBM 2303 drum storage

of processing incoming data and turning out useful output. Fig. 17-18 serves as an illustration of the types of peripheral components which can be used in a computer system. Additional special-purpose input/output devices and other data-communication components can also be added to a system (referred to as a real-time computer system). These aspects will be discussed in the next chapter.

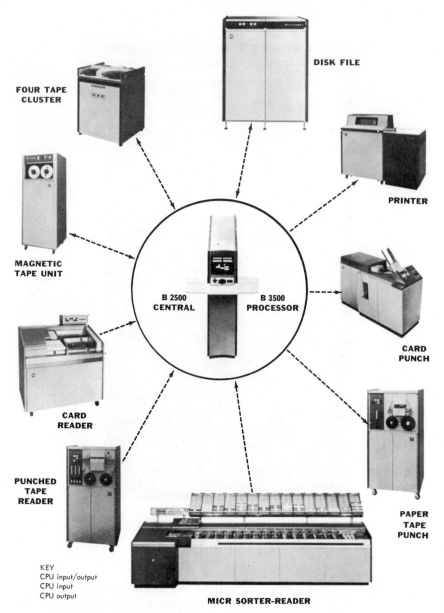

DISK FILE

FOUR TAPE
CLUSTER

PRINTER

MAGNETIC
TAPE UNIT

B 2500
CENTRAL

B 3500
PROCESSOR

CARD
PUNCH

CARD
READER

PUNCHED
TAPE
READER

PAPER
TAPE
PUNCH

KEY
CPU input/output
CPU input
CPU output

MICR SORTER-READER

Fig. 17-18. Types of input/output devices used in a computer system (*Burroughs Corporation*)

GLOSSARY OF TERMS

DISK PACK: A device containing a set of magetic disks for storing secondary information.

INPUT DEVICE: A component designed to bring the data to be processed into the central processing unit, for example, the card reader.

OUTPUT DEVICE: A computer component designed to translate electrical impulses representing data processed by the central processing unit into an intelligible and presentable format (result).

PERIPHERAL EQUIPMENT: Components which work in conjunction with, but are not a part of, the central processing system, for example, a card reader, printer, and so forth.

READ CHECK: An inspection-type unit in an input or output component that ascertains the accuracy of the data handled.

WIRE-MATRIX PRINTER: A type of printer which uses a 5 × 7 configuration of small wires to print alphabetic or numeric characters.

REVIEW QUESTIONS

1. What are the roles of the input and output devices in a computer system? Explain.
2. What are the two types of punched-card readers? What is the difference between them?
3. Explain how a punched card is read by a brush-type card reader. What is the function of the first read-check brushes? Why?
4. How is a punched-card reader used as an output device?
5. Describe a magnetic tape; a punched paper tape.
6. List and explain the advantages and disadvantages of paper tape.
7. What are the primary media that can be used for storing either input or output data?
8. What device is used exclusively as an output device? Describe it.
9. What is a wire matrix?
10. Describe the chain printer and tell how it operates.
11. What type of output format is considered the best? Explain.
12. What is a multi-function card machine?
13. Discuss the difference between and the advantages of IBM 360, Model 20:
    a. card versus tape system
    b. tape versus disk system
    c. disk versus card system
    d. tape/disk versus disk system
    e. tape/disk versus card system
14. What is a disk pack? Why is it preferred over other types of disk devices?

chapter

18

MAN-MACHINE INTERFACE
The Computer System Revolution

The Evolution of Real-time Processing [1]

PRIOR TO THE DEVELOPMENT of direct communications to a central computer or on-line communications, the majority of computer operations were performed by bulk processing, or the grouping of data into batches of similar or associated information. The data were accumulated until sufficient volume was collected to justify the amount of computer time required for processing. Data were forwarded for processing in the form of original documents or copies, or punched into cards or tape, or added as supplementary data to the cards received prepunched. Following this, further off-line handling was required to sort and sequence the file data in the required order for processing. The cutoff for processing usually reflected the accounting cycle under which the processing was controlled, such as a weekly or monthly period.

The cumulative process associated with establishing each batch, combined with the fixed cutoff, resulted in peak load requirements, often necessitating around-the-clock operations to obtain the desired results and special reports. These peak processing periods frequently led to the establishment of oversized systems to absorb the peak volume at costs far in excess of the overall productivity realized.

As the use of data processing was expanded for multi-plant or multi-office operations, data-collection problems grew more complex. This led to the multi-system approach involving systems of different sizes located in the various departments, divisions, and offices. Data from these systems were then sent to the main site for organizationwide processing and analysis. This method worked in some instances, but serious problems of data collection persisted.

At this stage, the physical transfer of data and documents by mail or similar means slowed down computer operations. Attention logically turned to public telephone and teletypewriter facilities. Teletypewriter facilities, which offered the advantage of printed copies of each communication, were rented from common carriers such as American Telephone and Telegraph Company and the Western Union Telegraph Company.

The first use of data transmission, using punched tape for additional speed, was limited to administrative messages between different locations.

---

[1] This section was adapted by permission from UNIVAC Division, Sperry Rand Corporation.

Later, operational data were transmitted over telegraph lines to the computer site, where they were converted to compatible form for the data-processing system. The next step was the development of data-communications units that could transmit information directly from punched cards, or magnetic tape, thus eliminating conversion from paper tape.

The combination of semiautomatic electrical data communication with the multi-system approach yielded a partial solution to the problem of data collection and processing. However, the actual processing of data was still being performed on a batch basis, which meant that transactions were transmitted only periodically. As a result of this processing time lag, data for management were historic rather than current. What was lacking was the ability to operate upon a transaction as it took place.

To understand this problem more fully, assume that a sales office at a remote location receives an order from a customer. As the first step, the clerk will consult the inventory listings. If the listings indicate that the required items are available, an order will be placed and the customer can be informed when delivery will be made. There is, however, one flaw in this arrangement. The inventory listings used by the sales office may not reflect the true current status of the inventory at the time the order is placed. This situation results from the fact that the inventory listings are updated at the computer site only on a periodic basis and are, therefore, correct only on the date they are processed. Between updatings, orders may be placed for items that are not actually available, with the result that these items will later have to be back-ordered and the customer will not receive them on the date promised.

To close this gap in time between actual transactions and the updating of the master file, the new concept of *real-time processing* was pioneered by UNIVAC. The real-time system combines data processing with communications. This unique method of operation involves direct communication of transaction data between remote offices and the central computer, thus allowing the data to be processed almost simultaneously with transmission (Fig. 18-1).

To explain more fully the capabilities and implications of a real-time system, let us refer to the previously mentioned sales application. The remotely located sales office would be supplied with an inquiry/answer device capable of communicating directly with the computer itself (Fig. 18-2). To place an order, the required information is entered into the system by the input device. Since the device is connected directly to the computer, complete information including the availability and status of the item ordered is confirmed in seconds. If the items are available, the invoice is printed automatically, along with associated shipping information, at the sales office, indicating to the salesman that the order has been filled as requested. If any particular item on the order depleted the inventory

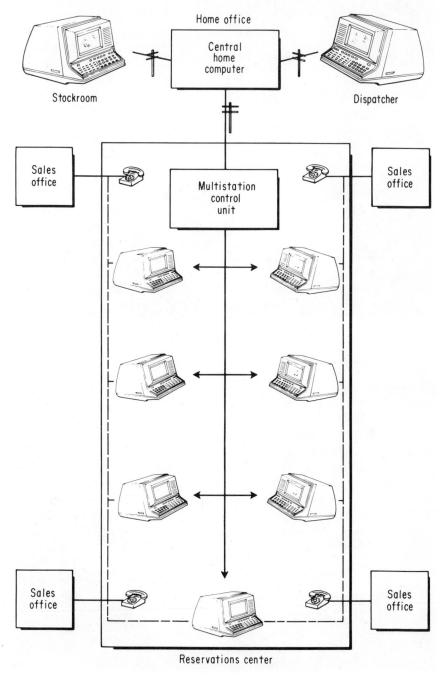

Fig. 18-1. Real-time processing (*UNIVAC*)

Fig. 18-2. Inquiry/answer device (*UNIVAC*)

Fig. 18-3. The IBM real-time computer system

to the reorder point, the computer automatically sends a message to the reorder source, connected directly to the computer, requesting an updating in inventory. All these operations are accomplished in a matter of seconds. Fig. 18-3 is an example of the IBM (SABRE) real-time computer system.

Display Devices

Need for a Visual Display

Original real-time computer systems used the keyboard/printer as the universal means of feeding input data to the computer and recording the output data from the computer. Many of the applications automated by a real-time computer system were dynamic applications with no requirement to preserve the output data once they had been interpreted by the human operator. The requirement to automate dynamic applications, increasingly more important in recent years, has necessitated the search for a substitute for the traditional keyboard/printer which, in addition to being slow, was not a very satisfactory man/machine interface.

The logical substitute for the keyboard/printer is a visual display which can be coupled to the operator by means of the keyboard and display (Fig. 18-2). Like a TV screen, the display device (sometimes called a plotter) generally is a *cathode-ray tube* which flashes graphs, numbers, or messages on the screen. A new-product concept, visual-display devices *extend man's cognition* and are useful for those applications which require direct operator interaction with a centralized computer system. Information generated by the operator is displayed on the device prior to transmission to the computer, so that any required changes or editing can be made where necessary. Furthermore, data transmitted from the computer are displayed to the operator for interpretation and understanding.

Other than UNIVAC, IBM, Burroughs, RCA, Sanders Associates, Bunker-Ramo Corp., and Control Data Corp., among others, offer similar display devices (Fig. 18-4).

Dynamic Applications for Visual Display

The applications for display devices all imply necessity, speed, and human intervention. The feeling exists that operations and profits could be better if the quality and timeliness of the available information were better. These applications are dynamic.

Since the applications are so varied, cover so many industries, and include a myriad of functions, it is impossible to describe them in detail and also difficult to put them into categories. A discussion of two cate-

Fig. 18-4.   IBM 2250 display unit, Model 2

gories, however, will provide an adequate breakdown for examination of the broad ideas involved in applying display devices. These categories are information retrieval and direct data input. If any particular installation were to be examined, we would probably find that these categories overlap or that both were being covered. *Applications for a visual communication terminal or cathode-ray tube display are becoming universal.*

Information retrieval

A corporation can benefit immensely by using visual-display devices in a computer communication system for information retrieval (Fig. 18-5). Before the information can be retrieved, it must be streamlined, concise, and to the point. This means that the data-gathering function will be standardized, selected input data will be reduced, and the controlling program will make the clearest presentation.

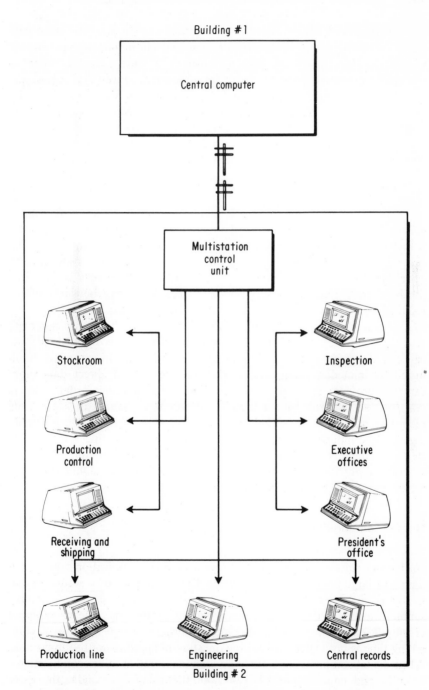

Fig. 18-5. Network of single control points within one building *(UNIVAC)*

Applications where information retrieval can be gainfully used with respect to management problems, services, and file inquiry are as follows: (1) *Management problems:* presents up-to-the-minute picture of financial reports, competitive position, program milestones, inventory status, deliveries, and product development. (2) *Services:* for use in banking, insurance, and information industries; to answer customers' requests, to centralize records, to monitor and simplify work flow, and to deploy personnel. (3) *File inquiry:* immediate presentation of retail credit or inventory status, medical case histories and references, and library applications.

Direct data input

Direct input of source data is finally becoming a reality after many years of unsatisfactory unit-record manipulation. To a large degree, this is becoming possible because access to mass storage and computer power can be accomplished through multi-access communication systems. Key punching, with its slow production rate, is no longer the only choice; and the high error rate of the key-punching technique may be substantially reduced with a visual-display communication subsystem. The display-device operator can immediately proofread and verify his input statement after he completes it, and edit it completely before it is transmitted. Because of the direct interface with computer power, human errors are minimized by immediate computer validation. The ease of direct data input can thus provide: (a) *simplified file maintenance:* updating a data base in real time so that subsequent inquiries or running changes to accumulate records can be made immediately; and (b) *new data entry:* that is, ability to take new input data directly from the source, eliminating several entry steps and thereby avoiding possibility of human errors, eliminating necessity for intermediate storage of bulky source material, and eliminating need for expensive off-line data-manipulating machines.

The Console Inquiry Station

An inquiry station is used for man-to-machine communication with a medium- to large-scale computer system. The console inquiry station is basically a character-at-a-time, *on-line* typewriter (Fig. 18-6). Although simple, the typewriter is not generally used as the chief means of input or output, except in small-sized computer systems where the cost of computing time is not expensive and the question of speed is not too important. When digital computers operate at a speed measured in milliseconds, microseconds, and nanoseconds (1/1,000,000,000ths of a second), the typewriter, which operates at ten characters a second, is too slow to make the best use of the computer's capabilities. In all other types of computers, especially large-sized ones, the typewriter is used as an auxiliary, manual method of input or output.

The typewriter's most common use, then, is as an inquiry station. The computer is interrupted during the processing of given data and inquiry is made by asking the computer to disclose the balance or other data concerning a specific account. "Asking" the computer is done by typewriting the code that tells the computer what to do and where to find the desired

Fig. 18-6. IBM/360, Model 30 showing inquiry station

information. With the manipulation of certain physical switches or buttons, the inquiry takes place and accurate results are obtained. Other uses include giving the computer proper substitution for invalid data, inserting missing or new operating instructions into the stored program, resetting the system when an error condition causes the computer to halt, and instructing the console to select different input/output devices. The usefulness of the typewriter, then, lies mainly in notifying the computer of these conditions and exceptions.

Data Synchronizers

Generally, most central processing units operate at a much greater speed than their input/output devices. In order to maximize the efficiency and capability of the C.P.U., data synchronizers are often used to act as a *buffer*-storage device between the computer and its input/output devices.

In Fig. 18-7, the buffer unit at the input stage provides (holds) input data while the C.P.U. is processing other information. When the C.P.U. is ready to process more input data, the buffer provides instant feedback, thus minimizing the time normally needed to transfer required data from the input device to the central processing unit. Likewise, the buffer at the output stage stores output information beyond what the printer is currently capable of handling, thus relieving the computer of the time it otherwise has to wait before the required output is retrieved.

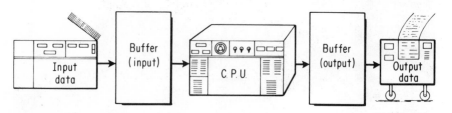

Fig. 18-7. Data synchronizers as a buffer-storage device

On-line Teller System—An Illustration [2]

On-line computer systems have the common trait of permitting direct access to a computer, including the pertinent records stored in its electronic memory. This direct access may come from one or many inquiry stations, of various types, which may be located either close by the computer or miles away, connected to the computer over various communication devices such as telephone or telegraph lines. In on-line teller systems, all tellers are in direct communication with, and are under complete control of, a computer that is connected, via communication lines, to each teller console (Fig. 18-8).

[2] This illustration has been adapted from Burroughs *On-line Teller System Manual* number 1024544, pp. 2-33.

Fig. 18-8. On-line teller system in operation *(Burroughs)*

Major Elements

A typical on-line teller system has several major elements:

1. *Teller consoles* accept keyboard-indexed messages for transmission to the processing center and print processed replies received from the center to passbooks, tickets, and transaction journals (Fig. 18-9 [1]).

2. Teller consoles may communicate with the center over telephone lines through a single *remote terminal unit* (RTU) which converts information for transmission and monitors the input and output status of each teller console (Fig. 18-9 [2]). Standard telephone-company data sets (*data-phones*) at each end of the telephone line convert signals from the RTU and CTU (central terminal unit) into "tones" for transmission over the line. Conversely, the data set converts "tones" received from the lines into signals for the terminal units (Fig. 18-9 [3]). Furthermore, *a central-office bridge* in the nearest telephone company central office combines information from separate offices onto one line, significantly reducing data-set and line-mileage charges (Fig. 18-9 [4]).

3. *The central terminal unit* (CTU) supervises communication between the teller consoles and the processing center. It receives incoming messages at random intervals, stores them until the central processor is ready to process them, and returns the processed replies to the teller consoles which originated the transactions (Fig. 18-9 [5]).

4. Attached to the central terminal unit is the *data communications control unit* (DCCU) which scans the CTU buffers for transaction messages, transfers the next message to the central processor when requested, and returns the processed reply to the same CTU buffer. The DCCU and CTU greatly simplify central-processor programming since the program has been freed of communications, control, queueing, and storage of messages and replies (Fig. 18-9 [6]).

5. The *heart* of the on-line system is the *central processor,* which performs the computations and makes all logical decisions required in the processing of on-line transactions. All transactions are recorded chronologically on magnetic tape throughout the day and, at the end of the day, are sequenced and printed out in pertinent reports (Fig. 18-9 [7]).

6. The account records and related information, such as holds and no-book transactions, are stored in the random-access *disk file* (DF). Since access time to the disk file is fast (average of one-fiftieth of a second), its storage provides a virtually unlimited extension of core memory. Consequently, there are virtually no limits to the number of tellers for whom proof totals can be maintained, the variety of transactions which can be handled, the variations in transaction processing that individual institutions require, and the variety of passbook formats that are used (Fig. 18-9 [8]).

Benefits

Some of the major benefits derived from an on-line teller system are as follows: (1) The teller remains at the window to serve customers: ledger and other record references, dividend posting, previous no-book transaction posting, and all other teller operations are handled automatically through the window machine. Consequently, customers are served more rapidly, even at peak periods. (2) Computer-to-teller communication is outstanding. Alphanumeric messages, status lights, and an audible signal combine to advise the teller on inquiries and rejected postings. (3) Although immediately accessible up-to-the-second transaction totals and other management information reduce the significance of many printed reports, the on-line system provides daily teller, transaction, and exception reports; periodic delinquent and to-date historical reports; monthly trial balances; quarterly and semiannual dividend and to-date historical reports; annual statistical reports, borrowers' statements, and tax form 1099s; and other reports at the institution's discretion.

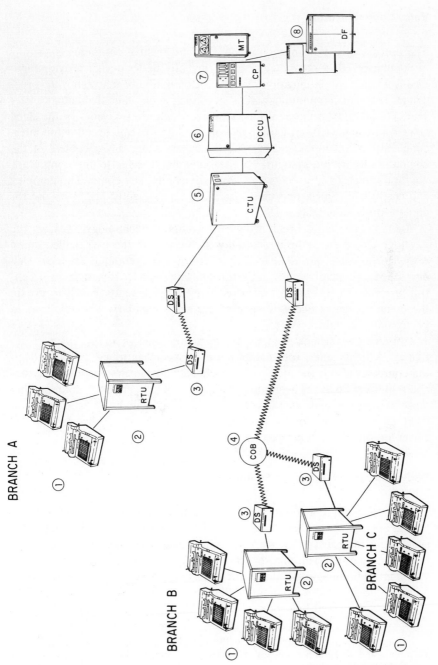

Fig. 18-9. A typical on-line teller system *(Burroughs)*

Voice Communication

The use of voice transmission of data to and from a computer is gaining in popularity. Most computer systems currently under design provide facilities for voice-communication channels. Compatibility between data processing and data communication is becoming more complementary every year. We hear of on-line real-time systems which are two sides of the same coin. As explained in an earlier section, on-line systems account for interconnection of all input and peripheral devices under direct control of the computer. Real-time systems, on the other hand, refer to the computer's ability to collect and process data immediately as they come. The complex and costly nature of a real-time system do not presently justify its use for all data-processing systems.

One of the latest breakthroughs in computer technology has been the development of the computer's ability to "talk" with the user, called *audio response* or *voice output*. Earlier aspects of this technique are now well developed and involve the user's transmitting a coded message to a central processing unit and in return receiving a voice reply. For it to do so, the computer gains access to a prerecorded vocabulary which it uses in giving out a certain answer.

Voice-answerback systems are currently used in many business activities. A bank teller, for example, uses a special terminal unit to talk to the computer about the status of a particular customer's account (say account number 5678). The computer locates and answers back in an audible voice a message such as: "Account number 5678 balance to date seven eight nine point one one." The answer is usually heard through the receiver or through a loudspeaker nearby.

Wider Variety of Terminal Equipment [3]

Since data communications in its present form became available in the late 1950s, an increasing variety of terminal equipments have been designed and introduced for use with communications lines. This variety of terminal apparatus will almost certainly continue to increase in the coming years as additional applications for data communications are developed. Some of the newer developments in the area of terminal equipment, among others, are discussed below.

[3] From "Data Communications in Business." Copyright © 1965 by American Telephone and Telegraph Company. Used by permission of the American Telephone and Telegraph Company.

PICTUREPHONE Service

PICTUREPHONE service is a recently developed service that permits the calling party to see as well as to hear the person with whom he is talking on the telephone. A long distance "booth-to-booth" service was established in 1964 on a trial basis between New York, Washington, and Chicago. "See-while-you-talk" calls were on an appointment basis.

While today only a head-and-shoulders image of a person is transmitted, the future holds many interesting possibilities. Someday we may be able to transmit finely detailed printed material with clarity. Although a great deal of development work must be completed before this service is acceptable for any type of data transmission, its potential is evident.

MICR Transmission

MICR (magnetic ink character recognition) is a technique for electrically reading coded characters printed on documents (such as bank checks) in magnetic ink. Today, most bank checks are automatically sorted by machines that recognize the MICR characters. As yet, however, machines are not able economically to read these characters and transmit the information directly over a communications line. See Fig. 18-10.

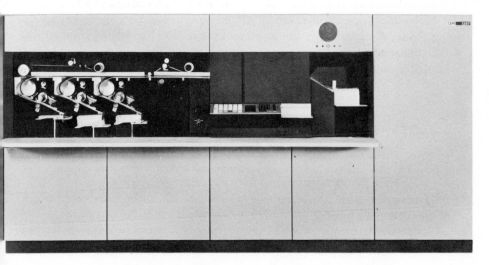

Fig. 18-10.   IBM magnetic ink character reader

High-speed Facsimile

The high-speed transmission of graphics is now practical with the use of wideband [4] communications service. Considerable work is also under way to enable the transmission of high-speed facsimile over regular voice-grade channels. Although a technological breakthrough is first required, conceivably documents and pictures will someday be transmitted over such channels in less than one minute per page.

Remote Meter Reading

One of the current challenges in the utility field is to develop a technique for automatically reading residential electric, gas, and water meters. A number of systems have already been designed and special terminal equipment has been developed. The cost of the service, however, is not yet low enough to be generally competitive with manual reading.

Microfilm Transmission

During the last few years a need has arisen for the transmission of images that are recorded on microfilm records. Work has already progressed in this area, and a few terminals of this type are available today.

Optical Scanning

Another needed service is the facility to scan printed documents, convert the information to a code, and transmit it over a communications channel. Techniques for optical scanning of certain types of documents have been perfected for some time, but at present the required wideband communication channels that must be used do not transmit the information in a reasonable length of time. Subsequent developments will probably permit the use of telephone channels for transmission.

GLOSSARY OF TERMS

BUFFER: An internal portion of a computer system, serving as intermediary storage between two components with different access times.

CATHODE-RAY TUBE: An electronic vacuum tube containing a screen on which information may be displayed or stored.

INQUIRY: A technique by which the contents of a computer's storage may be interrogated through a keyboard.

---

[4] Wideband channel refers to a channel wider in bandwidth than a voice-grade channel.

MICR: Magnetic ink character recognition—a form of input for a computer system using certain characters printed with ink which can be magnetized for processing.

OPTICAL SCANNING: A technique for machine recognition of characters by their images.

REAL-TIME PROCESSING: Synonymous with real-time system—data processing in which transactions are processed as they actually occur.

REVIEW QUESTIONS

1. Explain the difference between batch processing and real-time processing.
2. Summarize the stages that led to the present use of real-time processing.
3. What is a display device? Why is it needed? In what types of applications is it used?
4. What two categories provide ideas regarding applications of display devices? Explain briefly each category.
5. What benefits can be derived from direct-data-input facilities?
6. What is a console inquiry station? How is it different from a display device?
7. What is meant by data synchronizers?
8. Briefly summarize the on-line teller system (that is, its elements, benefits, and so forth).
9. How does a voice-answerback system work? Explain.
10. List and briefly explain the wider variety of terminal equipment for use with communication lines.

chapter

19

THE CENTRAL
PROCESSING UNIT
Coding Systems

THIS CHAPTER PRESENTS the primary decimal and binary systems and their role as symbols for representing various quantities in arithmetical computation and for storage purposes. The specific numbering system in use depends upon the type and design of the computer.

The Decimal System

When man first began to count, he relied on his ten fingers. He lifted three fingers when he wanted to stress three units or three values. He added two more fingers to show a total of five units, and so forth. In the *decimal system,* using ten digits, the *base* used is ten and the value attributed to a number is determined by its position. The first position to the right has a value of one; the second to the left, ten; the third to the left, 100; the fourth to the left, 1,000, and so forth. As each position is added, note that it is placed to the left of the preceding one. Number *111,* for example, shows the character *1* in three different positions. The decimal value of number *111* is determined as shown in Fig. 19-1.

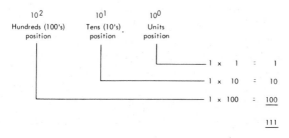

Fig. 19-1. Decimal value of number *111*

The Binary System

Because the decimal system is the most commonly used system for arithmetical operations, we have learned to add, subtract, multiply, and/or divide according to its rules. In fact, until recently, it has been the only system taught in our schools. Many call it "ten-finger arithmetic."

Unfortunately, however, "ten-finger arithmetic" is not suited to the operation of electronic digital computers in business. For one reason, the computers, being electronic, and being made up of vacuum tubes and switching devices, have two definite states. They are either energized (on) or de-energized (off). To convert these two states to numeric characters, it was decided to use the binary system so that, when the tube was on, it would represent a value of *1,* and when it was off, a value of *0* (zero). Therefore, tubes would represent *1* (one) or *0* (zero), because these are the only numbers used in binary arithmetic. The binary system is sometimes referred to as "two-finger arithmetic." It is much easier and faster to use than the decimal system when it is understood clearly.

Whereas the decimal system uses base ten, because of its use of ten digits, the *binary system* uses *base two* because of its use of two digits. The value of each binary number is dependent upon its position, as is true of digits *0* through *9* in the decimal system. The value of each position in the binary system doubles as it is added from right to left, that is, *1, 2, 4, 8, 16, 32, 64,* and so forth.

We can easily write the value of zero or the value of one. In the decimal system, we are not forced to add a position until we reach nine. We are forced, however, to do so in the binary system when we go past one. We add the next position to the left, which is called the *twos* (2s) position, because it is a multiple of two (2 × 1). A value of two is registered in this second position if represented by one (Fig. 19-2).

A *3* is recorded by placing a *1* in the second position, which has a value of two, together with a *1* in the first position, which has a value of one. The total of the two positions is three (Fig. 19-3). When *4* needs to be recorded, we have to use a third position, which has a value of four, because numeric values increase by multiples of two. Thus, *4* is represented by placing a *1* in the third position, *0* in the second position, and *0* in the first position (Fig. 19-4). With these three positions, numbers up to seven can be represented. Thus, a fourth position is added having a value of eight. To represent *8* in binary, we record *1* of position eight, *0* of position four, *0* of position two, and *0* of position one. With these four positions, numbers *1* to *15* can be expressed (Fig. 19-5). With a fifth position, num-

Place Value of 2	Place Value of 1
1	0

Fig. 19-2. A decimal value of 2 in binary

Place Value of 2	Place Value of 1
1	1

Fig. 19-3. A decimal value of 3 in binary

Place value of 4	Place value of 2	Place value of 1
1	0	0

Fig. 19-4. A decimal value of 4 in binary

bers *1* through *31* may be written. For numbers higher than this, additional positions must be added. Decimal equivalents of binary numbers *0 0 0 0 1* to *1 1 0 0 1* can be read from the table. To familiarize yourself with the binary mode, finish the table to the decimal equivalent of *31* in binary.

From the previous description, the method of determining the decimal equivalent of the binary number *1 1 1 0 1,* for example, is as follows:

$$
\begin{array}{llll}
1 \text{ in the} & \text{1s position (or } 1 \times & 1) = & 1 \\
0 \text{ in the} & \text{2s position (or } 0 \times & 2) = & 0 \\
1 \text{ in the} & \text{4s position (or } 1 \times & 4) = & 4 \\
1 \text{ in the} & \text{8s position (or } 1 \times & 8) = & 8 \\
1 \text{ in the} & \text{16s position (or } 1 \times & 16) = & 16
\end{array}
$$

Therefore, 1 1 1 0 1 in binary (base 2) is equal to   29 in decimal (base 10).

Note, from the values in Fig. 19-5 that two digits are required in the decimal system (base ten) to express a value of *29,* whereas five digits are required in the binary system (base two) to express the same value. The use of more digits in binary does not present any problem to the computer because of the speed with which its electronic switches operate.

Decimal Equivalent	Place Value 16	Place Value 8	Place Value 4	Place Value 2	Place Value 1	Decimal Equivalent
1					1	1
2				1	0	2
3				1	1	3
4			1	0	0	4
5			1	0	1	5
6			1	1	0	6
7			1	1	1	7
8		1	0	0	0	8
9		1	0	0	1	9
10		1	0	1	0	10
11		1	0	1	1	11
12		1	1	0	0	12
13		1	1	0	1	13
14		1	1	1	0	14
15		1	1	1	1	15
16	1	0	0	0	0	16
17	1	0	0	0	1	17
18	1	0	0	1	0	18
19	1	0	0	1	1	19
20	1	0	1	0	0	20
21	1	0	1	0	1	21
22	1	0	1	1	0	22
23	1	0	1	1	1	23
24	1	1	0	0	0	24
25	1	1	0	0	1	25

Fig. 19-5. A binary representation of twenty-five decimal values

The electronic switch can go on and off (two states) hundreds of thousands of times in one second. Thus, a great number of binary digits is immaterial to the computer.

Decimal-to-binary Conversion

One method of converting a number from decimal to binary is to divide the decimal number by two successively. Fig. 19-6 shows the conversion of the number *39* from decimal to binary.

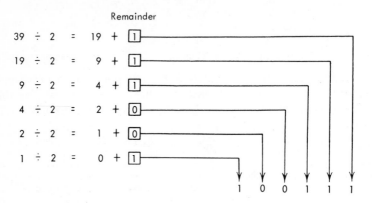

Fig. 19-6.   Conversion of a number from decimal to binary

Fig. 19-7.   Conversion of a number from binary to decimal

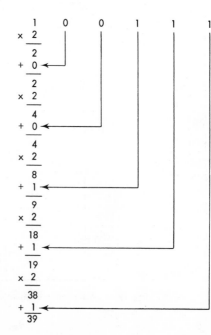

Therefore, decimal number *39* is equivalent to *1 0 0 1 1 1* in binary: that is, the sixth position, having a value of *32,* plus the first three positions, totaling a value of *7.* Zeros in the fourth and fifth positions, having values of *8* and *16,* respectively, of course, signify *0.*

Binary-to-decimal Conversion

Binary-to-decimal conversion follows the opposite procedure. Each binary character (beginning with the left digit) is multiplied by two and its product added to the next digit until the entire binary amount is converted. For example, to convert the binary value 1 0 0 1 1 1 (the result of the preceding illustration) the procedure in Fig. 19-7 takes place.

Coding Systems

The coding system is a technique which utilizes a set of different symbols to represent (code) all the incoming data (input data), whether they are numeric, alphabetic, or special characters. The symbols are not the data but represent data by one-bits in a fixed number of binary combinations determining the code of the data. For example, numeric, alphabetic, and special characters can be stored (written) on magnetic tape by the presence or absence of magnetic spots in a given column. The presence of a magnetic spot symbolizes a one-bit. Its absence symbolizes a zero-bit. However, regardless of the number of one- or zero-bits representing any given character, the total is limited to seven binary bits per character.

This chapter describes some of the most commonly used computer codes. They are: (1) the binary coded decimal; (2) the seven-bit alphanumeric code, (3) the octal code, and (4) the bi-quinary code.

The Binary Coded Decimal (BCD Code)

Even though most computers operate in the binary mode, some of them use straight binary representation as a coding system. A straight binary machine represents data by translating a decimal number, regardless of its size, into one binary combination. For example, a decimal value of 954 is symbolized by the straight binary representation shown in Fig. 19-8.

Place Value	512	256	128	64	32	16	8	4	2	1	
Binary Equivalent	1	1	1	0	1	1	1	0	1	0	= 954

Fig. 19-8. Straight binary representation

For purposes of facilitating arithmetical computations, straight binary representation is more suited to scientific calculations than to commercial data processing. In business data-processing computer systems, each code digit should be instantly recognizable. Therefore, a special coding technique is required. For easy representation of decimal digits, coded-decimal techniques are more popular. The most popular coded-decimal technique is referred to as "the binary coded decimal" or BCD code.

Uses

The binary coded decimal is used in computers which are a compromise between pure binary and pure decimal computers. The technique simply takes each decimal digit and codes it in a fixed number of binary bits. We have ten digits in the decimal system. A combination of two one-binary bits (1 1) will represent only a maximum equivalent of *3* in decimal. A combination of three one-binary bits (1 1 1) will represent a maximum equivalent of *7* in decimal. Therefore, four one-binary bits (1 1 1 1) are needed to represent any of the one-decimal digits (0 through 9). The BCD code of the ten decimal digits is shown in Fig. 19-9.

Decimal equivalent	Binary coded decimal
0	0 0 0 0
1	0 0 0 1
2	0 0 1 0
3	0 0 1 1
4	0 1 0 0
5	0 1 0 1
6	0 1 1 0
7	0 1 1 1
8	1 0 0 0
9	1 0 0 1

Fig. 19-9. The BCD code of the ten decimal digits

Using the information in Fig. 19-9, we see that a fixed number of four binary bits, or digits, are needed every time a decimal digit is represented. Fig. 19-10 shows the decimal value 954 represented in BCD.

Advantages

The main advantage of the binary coded-decimal technique is that the binary coding of decimal digits is easily and clearly understood. Anyone who has an understanding of the binary values of the ten decimal digits can recognize and interpret the decimal equivalent of any specific binary coded-decimal number (Fig. 19-10).

Fig. 19-10. The binary coded-decimal value of *954*

Disadvantages

The primary disadvantages of the BCD are: (1) its inefficiency; (2) the difficulty in doing arithmetic when compared with the binary system; and (3) the need to perform two types of arithmetic in each arithmetical operation.

1. The BCD system is inefficient because, although the four fixed binary digits (8, 4, 2, 1) can represent up to the decimal equivalent of *15*, they are, however, employed to represent only the first ten decimal digits.

2. In arithmetical operations, the BCD encounters difficulty with regard to the decimal carry. When an addition requiring a carry is made, it does not provide a carry. Instead, it represents the sum of two or more decimal digits in one binary combination. For example: 9 + 4 = 13. In binary:

Decimal		*BCD*
9		1 0 0 1
+	+	
4		0 1 0 0
13		1 1 0 1

3. The arithmetic section must perform the double function of binary and decimal arithmetic. In other words, binary addition within those binary digits being added, and decimal addition when the number of decimal digits added exceeds two.

We can see that the binary coded decimal does not provide for the required decimal carry. In *13,* the sum *3* (0 0 1 1) and a carry should be obtained. Instead, the system represents the whole sum (13) in one decimal digit. Computers which use the BCD code need some corrective techniques of representing the desired carry.

Where no carry is required, however, addition in the BCD is very easy and convenient. For example, add 6 + 3 = 9.

Decimal		*BCD*
6		0 1 1 0
+	+	
3		0 0 1 1
9		1 0 0 1

The decimal sum in this example does not require a carry. The sum is one digit. The BCD system works well, because the sum represents one decimal digit only.

The Seven-bit Alphanumeric Code

From the presentation of the BCD code, one can conclude that only numeric information (essentially, decimal digits *0* and *1* through *9*) can be represented. Some mention was made, however, in Chapter 16, of how nonnumeric data are written on magnetic tape. The seven-bit alphanumeric code used to write numeric and alphabetic data on tape follows the same pattern as that used by automatic commercial computers in storing the same information internally.

The seven-bit alphanumeric code is, in fact, an outgrowth of the BCD. That is, for alphabetic data coding, two additional digits, called *A* and *B,* are added to the four fixed binary combinations (8, 4, 2, 1), with a seventh bit for parity check (Fig. 19-11). The two additional digits (*A* and *B*) are equivalent to the zone punching positions (*0* and *11*) in punched-card alphabetic coding. The third-card zone punching position is represented by combining *A* and *B*.

C	B	A	8	4	2	1
parity check bit	zone bits		numeric bits			

Fig. 19-11. Seven-bit alphanumeric code

The check bit in the seven-bit alphanumeric code system stands for *even parity check*. Each coded character must have an even number of one-bits when they are added in the alphabetic and numeric zones. If the sum of one-bits in the alphabetic and numeric zones representing a given character is odd, the check bit is turned on or one check bit is added to make it even. Otherwise, the check bit is always zero. If, during processing or the transfer of data, a one-bit is destroyed, remaining one-bits become odd. The computer signals an error, which prevents further processing until it is corrected.

Numeric representation (Fig. 19-12) uses the four binary combinations of the BCD code (8, 4, 2, 1). Note that zero is coded as 1 0 1 0. This is done in order to make possible the coding of a blank, which is coded as 0 0 0 0. Also note that, for coding numeric characters, bits *A* and *B* are always zero.

Decimal digit	Check bit	Zone bits	Numeric bits
	C	B A	8 4 2 1
0	0	0 0	1 0 1 0
1	1	0 0	0 0 0 1
2	1	0 0	0 0 1 0
3	0	0 0	0 0 1 1
4	1	0 0	0 1 0 0
5	0	0 0	0 1 0 1
6	0	0 0	0 1 1 0
7	1	0 0	0 1 1 1
8	1	0 0	1 0 0 0
9	0	0 0	1 0 0 1

Fig. 19-12. The seven-bit alphanumeric code system, showing the coding of decimal digits 0, and 1-9

Like the punched-card code, when alphabetic characters are coded, they are divided into the following three categories: Letters *A* through *I* are coded by the presence of two one-bits in *A* and *B* alphabetic zones, in addition to numeric values *1* through *9*, respectively (Fig. 19-13).

Alpha. char.	Check bits	Zone bits	Numeric bits
	C	B A	8 4 2 1
A	1	1 1	0 0 0 1
B	1	1 1	0 0 1 0
C	0	1 1	0 0 1 1
D	1	1 1	0 1 0 0
E	0	1 1	0 1 0 1
F	0	1 1	0 1 1 0
G	1	1 1	0 1 1 1
H	1	1 1	1 0 0 0
I	0	1 1	1 0 0 1

Fig. 19-13. The seven-bit alphanumeric code system, showing the coding letters A through I

The second category involves the coding of letters *J* through *R*. Letters *J* through *R* are coded by the presence of one *B*-bit in the alphabetic zone bits, in addition to numeric values *1* through *9*. The *A*-bit in the alphabetic zone in this category is always zero (Fig. 19-14).

Alpha. char.	Check bits C	Zone bits B A	Numeric bits 8 4 2 1
J	0	1 0	0 0 0 1
K	0	1 0	0 0 1 0
L	1	1 0	0 0 1 1
M	0	1 0	0 1 0 0
N	1	1 0	0 1 0 1
O	1	1 0	0 1 1 0
P	0	1 0	0 1 1 1
Q	0	1 0	1 0 0 0
R	1	1 0	1 0 0 1

Fig. 19-14. The seven-bit alpha-numeric code system, showing the coding of letters *J* through *R*

The third category involves the coding of letters *S* through *Z*. These last eight letters are coded by the presence of one *A*-bit in the alphabetic zone, in addition to numeric values 2 through 9. The *B*-bit in the alphabetic zone in this category remains zero. Note that letter *S* has a numeric value of 2, based on the coding used in the punched cards (Fig. 19-15).

Alpha. char.	Check bits C	Zone bits B A	Numeric bits 8 4 2 1
S	0	0 1	0 0 1 0
T	1	0 1	0 0 1 1
U	0	0 1	0 1 0 0
V	1	0 1	0 1 0 1
W	1	0 1	0 1 1 0
X	0	0 1	0 1 1 1
Y	0	0 1	1 0 0 0
Z	1	0 1	1 0 0 1

Fig. 19-15. The seven-bit alpha-numeric code system, showing the coding of letters *S* through *Z*

The Octal System

The *octal* is a *base eight* (in contrast with the binary—base two) system and is used specifically in scientific-oriented computers. It uses three bits (1, 2, 4) to represent a maximum decimal value of 7. Thus, the octal is similar to the BCD code (8, 4, 2, 1), except that the fourth bit (8) is not used. Decimal number *8* and more are represented by adding a digit to the left of the previous one. Each digit is a multiple of eight and is similar to the binary digit which increases by a multiple of two (base two), and the decimal digit which increases by a multiple of ten (base ten). Fig. 19-16 shows a comparative representation of decimal digits, in BCD and octal codes.

Decimal digit	BCD 8 4 2 1	Octal
0	0 0 0 0	0
1	0 0 0 1	1
2	0 0 1 0	2
3	0 0 1 1	3
4	0 1 0 0	4
5	0 1 0 1	5
6	0 1 1 0	6
7	0 1 1 1	7
8	1 0 0 0	10
9	1 0 0 1	11

Decimal value	Octal Place Value 64 8 1	Octal Notation	Explanation
14	1 6	16_8	(1x8) + (6x1) = 14
15	1 7	17_8	(1x8) + (7x1) = 15
16	2 0	20_8	(2x8) + (0x1) = 16
75	1 1 3	113_8	(1x64) + (1x8) + (3x1) = 75

sub 8 indicates that the number 113 is an octal number

Fig. 19-16. Comparison of decimal digits in BCD and octal codes

Octal-to-decimal conversion

Octal-to-decimal conversion is done by multiplying each octal position (beginning with the left octal digit) by eight and adding its product to the next number, and so on, until the last digit is added (but not multiplied). For example, 467 in octal is converted to decimal as follows:

$$
\begin{array}{r}
4 \quad 6 \quad 7 \\
\times \underline{8} \\
32 \\
+ \underline{6} \\
38 \\
\times \underline{8} \\
304 \\
+ \underline{7} \\
311
\end{array}
$$

Decimal-to-octal conversion

Decimal-to-octal conversion is performed by successively dividing the decimal amount and succeeding quotients by eight until no further division is feasible. For example, 418 in decimal is converted to octal, as follows:

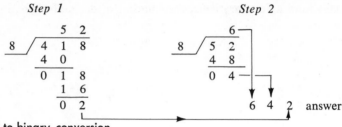

| Step 1 | Step 2 |

Octal-to-binary conversion

Octal-to-binary conversion is made by assigning to each octal digit a fixed number of three binary digits. For example:

```
                            octal
Octal value      ⌈ 4        6        3 ⌉     is equivalent
   to            \1 0 0    1 1 0    0 1 1/    in binary.
                            binary
```

Binary-to-octal conversion

Binary-to-octal conversion involves dividing the binary value (beginning with the right binary digit) into a fixed number of three bits each (the opposite procedure followed in the octal-to-binary conversion). For example:

```
                            binary
Binary value ─→ ⌈1 0 0    1 1 0    0 1 1⌉   is equivalent
   to ────→      ⌊ 4′       6′       3′⌋    in octal.
                            octal
```

The Bi-quinary Code

The bi-quinary code requires seven binary positions to symbolize each of the ten decimal digits. In the name of this code, the *BI*nary part stands for two bits *with arbitrarily assigned values* (0 and 5) and the *QUI*nary [1] part stands for five bits with arbitrarily assigned values of (0, 1, 2, 3,

---

[1] Recall that in the decimal system, *quin* means 5. A well-known popular version of this meaning is used in the word *quintuplets* to mean five children born at the same time.

and 4)—a total of seven bits. Two of these seven bits must be one-bits, one binary bit and one quinary bit. The remaining bits must be zero-bits. The position values of the bi-quinary code are, then, from left to right, 0, 5, 0, 1, 2, 3, 4 (Fig. 19-17).

The primary advantage of this code is that it is easy to understand. It is also convenient as a code check because of the constant presence of two one-bits out of seven making up each bi-quinary combination. The absence of a one-bit from any such combination is immediately detected. The system is considered inefficient, however, because each combination uses seven positions, which, in binary, could be used to represent 127 different decimal numbers, but which in bi-quinary represent only ten of them.

Decimal Digit	Bi-Quinary code system Bi / Quinary 0 5 / 0 1 2 3 4	
0	1 0	1 0 0 0 0
1	1 0	0 1 0 0 0
2	1 0	0 0 1 0 0
3	1 0	0 0 0 1 0
4	1 0	0 0 0 0 1
5	0 1	1 0 0 0 0
6	0 1	0 1 0 0 0
7	0 1	0 0 1 0 0
8	0 1	0 0 0 1 0
9	0 1	0 0 0 0 1

A decimal value 35, for example, is represented in the bi-quinary code as follows:

3	5
1 0 0 0 0 1 0	0 1 1 0 0 0 0

Fig. 19-17. The bi-quinary code system

GLOSSARY OF TERMS

BI-QUINARY: A two-part representation of a decimal digit made up of a binary portion (values *0* or *5*) and a quinary section with values *0, 1, 2, 3, 4.*

BINARY: A system using two as its base and using only digits *0* and *1.*

BINARY CODED DECIMAL: An element of a notation system where a decimal digit is represented by a fixed number of binary positions.

OCTAL: A number using the equivalent of the decimal integer *8* as a base.

PARITY CHECK: A check which tests whether the number of bits representing a given character meet the established odd or even standard.

REVIEW QUESTIONS

1. What is a "coding system"?
2. What is the difference between straight binary and binary coded-decimal representation?
3. "The decimal system uses base ten, whereas the binary system uses base two." Explain this statement in detail.
4. Explain some of the disadvantages of the BCD code.
5. Describe the seven-bit alphanumeric code. How does it differ from the BCD code?
6. Why are four binary bits used in the BCD code to represent the decimal digits?
7. What is the procedure used in converting values from binary into decimal? Give an example to illustrate.
8. Using the seven-bit alphanumeric code, code the following data:
   a. 14728
   b. Business education
   c. Product number 6K 4821
9. What is the octal code? How is it different from the binary code? The decimal code? Give an example illustrating the method used in converting an octal value into these two codes.

chapter

20

THE CENTRAL
PROCESSING UNIT
Arithmetic

BINARY VERSUS DECIMAL ARITHMETIC

TYPES OF ARITHMETIC

SERIAL METHOD   PARALLEL METHOD

BINARY AND DECIMAL ADDITION

BINARY AND DECIMAL SUBTRACTION

THE DECIMAL TENS COMPLEMENT METHOD OF SUBTRACTION
THE DECIMAL NINES COMPLEMENT METHOD OF SUBTRACTION
BINARY SUBTRACTION

BINARY AND DECIMAL MULTIPLICATION

PROCEDURE   THE DECIMAL METHOD OF BINARY MULTIPLICATION
THE SHIFT METHOD OF BINARY MULTIPLICATION

BINARY AND DECIMAL DIVISION

PROCEDURE   RESTORING METHOD OF DETECTING A REMAINDER

Binary Versus Decimal Arithmetic

BECAUSE ARITHMETICAL OPERATIONS, in most computers, are performed in binary, the data in the decimal system to be worked on (input) are converted automatically into the binary system when they enter the computer. The results (output) then are made available to us in the decimal system by a conversion process from binary to decimal within the computer. It would be embarrassing, indeed, if, for example, an employee's pay check of $8.00 for one day were written by the computer in the binary, which is $1,000.00. The employer could not expect the bank to read the amount and pay the employee in binary, because the decimal system is the accepted form of communication. The binary combination 1 0 0 0 is converted to the decimal *8,* so that the *8* appears on the pay check as the result.

Unfortunately, however, the conversion process in a binary computer is both awkward and complex, and is performed at the sacrifice of considerable time. There are computers, on the other hand, that are considered decimal computers which do not use binary arithmetic. Their primary advantage is that they are not involved in the complex conversion problems. One of the drawbacks, however, is their comparatively slow processing of decimal data. Additional circuitry and related parts can be integrated to speed up the arithmetic operation, but this creates additional cost to an already expensive machine. For this reason, the remainder of this chapter presents the methods of addition, subtraction, multiplication, and division used in the arithmetical units of both decimal and binary computers.

Types of Arithmetic

Depending on the type of computer, variable word length or fixed word length, arithmetic is performed by one of two methods: (1) serial, or (2) parallel operation.

Serial Method

In *serial* addition, one position in a decimal number is added at a time. This procedure follows the manner in which addition is performed manually with pencil and paper. For example, adding *113* and *177* would involve the following steps:

	Step 1	*Step 2*	*Step 3*
Augend	113	113	113
	+	+	+
Addend	177	177	177
Carry	1	1	
Sum	0	90	290

In step one, the figures in the units position are added. In step two, those in the tens position plus the carry from step one are added. In step three, the figures in the *100*s position are added.

Parallel Method

In *parallel* addition, all the decimal positions of a decimal number are added in one step at the same time. Using the example presented for serial addition, the step involved in adding *113* and *177* in parallel is as follows:

	One step
Augend	113
	+
Addend	177
Carry	1
Sum	290

Serial addition takes more time than parallel addition. The total time involved depends primarily upon the number of places used. If the numbers are six places long, the serial adder would take about twice as much time as it would take adding numbers three places long. In serial addition, a computer has lower speed but less equipment; whereas in parallel addition, a computer has greater speed but more equipment. To add two three-place numbers, like the above, for example, would require the use of three one-position adders in parallel addition which operate simultaneously. The serial addition of the two three-place numbers would require the use of one adder which goes through three consecutive steps to add the units, tens, and the 100s digits of the two numbers.

Binary and Decimal Addition

Nearly all arithmetical operations are performed by computers through addition. One number is placed under another number and the two are added. In decimal addition, we carry a number from one column to the next, if the sum of the first column exceeds 9. In binary addition, we carry a number from one column to the next, if the sum of the first column exceeds one. Let us add two numbers together (in decimal and binary) and see how each works:

	Binary Numbers		*Decimal Numbers*
Addend	1 1 1 0	=	1 4
	+		+
Augend	0 1 0 1		5
Carry	1		
Sum	+ 1 0 0 1 1		+ 1 9

Note that in binary, two ones added together equal *0* with a carry of *1*. Starting from the right bit:

right bit 0 + 1 equals *1*
2nd bit   1 + 0 equals *1*
3rd bit   1 + 1 equals *0* and carry *1*
4th bit   1 + carry 1 equals *0* and carry *1*

Therefore, the sum is *1 0 0 1 1* or 19 in decimal. As you can see, the addition rules in binary are few and simple. They are summarized as follows:

$$
\begin{array}{cccc}
0 & 1 & 0 & 1 \\
+ & + & + & + \\
1 & 0 & 0 & 1 \\
\hline
1 & 1 & 0 & 10
\end{array}
$$ (zero and carry *1*)

Take a larger binary number to apply the binary addition table further:

	Binary Addition	*Decimal Addition*
Addend	1 1 1 0 1	2 9
	+	+
Augend	1 0 0 1 1	1 9
Carry	1 1 1 1	1
Sum	1 1 0 0 0 0	4 8

In Binary:

first bit   1 + 1 = 0   and carry 1
second bit 0 + 1 = 1   1 + carry 1 = 0 and carry 1
third bit   1 + 0 = 1   1 + carry 1 = 0 and carry 1
fourth bit 1 + 0 = 1   1 + carry 1 = 0 and carry 1
fifth bit   1 + 1 + 1 = 1 and carry 1

Note that three *1*s added equal *1* + a carry of *1*. Therefore, the sum is 1 1 0 0 0 0, or 48 in decimal.

Binary and Decimal Subtraction

A popular method of subtraction by computers is performed by complementing the subtrahend (the lower number) and then adding that complement to the minuend (the upper number) to arrive at the remainder.

In the decimal system, the tens or the nines complement is used. In the binary system, the same method is referred to as the "twos complement" or "ones complement," respectively.

The Decimal Tens Complement Method of Subtraction

In using the tens complement, the complement of a number is the amount that must be added to that number to make a total of the appropriate power of ten. For example, the complement of *4* is *6* ($10 - 4 = 6$). The complement of *19* is *81* ($100 - 19$); of *10, 90* ($100 - 10$); and so forth. Let us take two decimal numbers and subtract one number from another by the use of the tens complement.

Minuend	9
Subtrahend	− 3
Difference	+ 6

Step 1: Complement the subtrahend. The tens complement of *3* is *7*.
Step 2: Then add the minuend, *9,* and the complement *7*. If the sum results in a carry in the high-order position, replace the carry by a plus sign.

Therefore:

$$9$$
$$+$$
$$7$$

① 6   The difference of $9 - 3$, then, is equal to $+ 6$.
+ 6

If no carry develops in step two above, this means that the remainder is in complement form, and that the final answer will be negative. If the remainder is in complement form, this means that it is not the true remainder. To get the true remainder, it must be complemented. For example:

Minuend	4
Subtrahend	− 7
Difference	− 3

Step 1: Complement the subtrahend *7*. The tens complement of *7* is *3*.
Step 2: Then add *4* plus the complement *3*.

$$4$$
$$+$$
$$3$$
$$+ 7$$

Step 3: Since there is no carry in the high-order position in step two, 7 is the complement remainder. The tens complement of *7* is *3*, and its sign is negative, since a carry is absent. The answer, then, is equal to − *3*.

The Decimal Nines Complement Method of Subtraction

The nines complement method of subtraction is similar to that of the tens complement, except that the complement of the subtrahend is the amount that must be added to that number to make a total of 9. That is, the complement of 5 is 4, the complement of 3 is 6, that of 62 is 37 (99 − 62), that of 621 is 378 (999 − 621), and so forth. Let us take the following two numbers:

Minuend	61
Subtrahend	32
Difference	+ 29

Step 1: Take the nines complement of the subtrahend:

The appropriate place value total of 9 is: 99

Minus the subtrahend	32	
The difference	+ 67	is the nines complement of the subtrahend.

Step 2: Add the complement to the minuend:

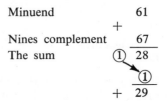

Minuend	61
	+
Nines complement	67
The sum	① 28
	①
	+ 29

Step 3: If a carry in the high-order position of the sum develops in step two above, add it to the units digit and give the total value a plus sign. Therefore, the remainder of 61 − 32 is + 29.

However, if no carry develops in step two above, it means that the sum developed is not a true remainder. It is, instead, in complement form. It must be recomplemented and a negative sign given the difference. For example:

Minuend	64
Subtrahend	78
Difference	− 14

Step 1: Take the nines complement of the subtrahend:

The appropriate power of 9 is   99

Minus the subtrahend	78
The difference	+ 21

Step 2: Add the complement to the minuend:

$$
\begin{array}{lr}
\text{Minuend} & 64 \\
& + \\
\text{Nines complement} & \underline{\;21\;} \\
\text{The sum} & +\;85
\end{array}
$$

Step 3: If no carry develops, as is the case in step two above, recomplement the sum and add a − sign to the true remainder. The nines complement of 85 is 14. The true remainder is, then, − 14.

Binary Subtraction

Like decimal subtraction, which is performed by the use of the tens complement, binary subtraction is done by the use of the ones complement. The subtrahend is complemented simply by changing all zeros (*0*s) to ones (*1*s) and all ones to zeros, and then adding. For example:

$$
\begin{array}{lcr}
\text{Minuend} & 1\,0\,0\,1 & 9 \\
& \overline{} & \overline{} \\
\text{Subtrahend} & \underline{0\,1\,1\,0} & \underline{6} \\
\text{Difference} & +\,0\,0\,1\,1 & +\,3
\end{array}
$$

Step 1: Complement the subtrahend by reversing its numbers, and then add:

$$
\begin{array}{ll}
\text{Minuend} & 1\,0\,0\,1 \\
\text{Plus subtrahend} & \\
\quad \text{in complement} & + \\
\quad \text{form} & \underline{1\,0\,0\,1} \\
& 1\,0\,0\,1\,0
\end{array}
$$

Step 2: If a carry in the high-order position develops, add it to the units position and give the result a plus sign.

$$
\begin{array}{r}
1\,0\,0\,1 \\
+ \\
\underline{1\,0\,0\,1} \\
①\;\;0\,0\,1\,0 \\
\underline{1} \\
+\,0\,0\,1\,1
\end{array}
$$

The difference, then, is 1 1 in binary, or a decimal value of + 3.

However, if no carry develops, the result is a negative remainder in a complement form. It must be recomplemented and a negative sign added to get the right answer. For example:

$$
\begin{array}{lcr}
\text{Minuend} & 0\,1\,1\,1 & 7 \\
& \overline{} & \overline{} \\
\text{Subtrahend} & \underline{1\,0\,1\,1} & \underline{11} \\
\text{Difference} & -\,0\,1\,0\,0 & -\,04
\end{array}
$$

Step 1: Complement the subtrahend by reversing its bits, and then add:

$$
\begin{array}{r}
0\;1\;1\;1 \\
+\quad 0\;1\;0\;0 \\
\hline
1\;0\;1\;1
\end{array}
$$

Step 2: If no carry develops, recomplement the result in step one and give it a negative sign.

1 0 1 1 in complement form becomes 0 1 0 0.

The true difference, then, is − 1 0 0, or the decimal equivalent of − 4.

Note that, in binary subtraction, both the minuend and the subtrahend must have equal length.

$$
\begin{array}{l}
9 \text{ in binary is } 1\,0\,0\,1 \\
3 \text{ in binary is } \qquad 1\,1
\end{array}
$$

Before complementing the subtrahend and subsequently performing subtraction, the subtrahend must be filled with zeros to equal the number of bits of the minuend.

Therefore,   1 0 0 1   1 0 0 1
   −   becomes
       1 1   0 0 1 1

After complement, it becomes   1 0 0 1
                                  +   Step 1
                                      1 1 0 0
                              ① 0 1 0 1
                                         1   Step 2
                                      0 1 1 0   or 6 in decimal

Binary and Decimal Multiplication

Procedure

In the decimal system, multiplication by *ten* can be done by placing a zero to the right of the number. For example,

$$21 \times 10 = 210$$

Likewise, in the binary system, multiplication by *two* can be done by placing a zero to the right of the number. For example,

$$1\,1 \times 1\,0 = 1\,1\,0$$

The binary multiplication table involves four basic steps:

$$0 \times 0 = 0$$
$$0 \times 1 = 0$$
$$1 \times 0 = 0$$
$$1 \times 1 = 1$$

In the binary mode, multiplication is done by either of two methods: (1) the decimal method, or (2) the shift method.

The Decimal Method of Binary Multiplication

The decimal method simply utilizes the technique which we follow when we multiply manually, using pencil and paper. That is, we multiply by each bit of the multiplier and then add. Note the similarity in the following illustration:

	Decimal System		*Binary System*
Multiplicand	5		1 0 1
	×		×
Multiplier	3		1 1
Product	+ 15		1 0 1
			1 0 1
			1 1 1 1 = 15

Multiplicand	7		1 1 1
	×		×
Multiplier	5		1 0 1
Product	+ 35		1 1 1
			0 0 0
			1 1 1
			1 0 0 0 1 1 = 35

The Shift Method of Binary Multiplication

Multiplication is performed, using the shifting method, by multiplying the multiplicand by the first left-hand bit of the multiplier and then shifting left one position and adding zero. The same procedure follows on the second-position bit of the multiplier, and so on until the operation is complete. For example:

Multiplicand	3		1 1
	×		
Multiplier	3		1 1
Product	+ 9		1 0 0 1

Step 1: Multiply the multiplicand by the first left bit of the multiplier:

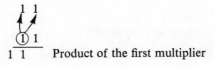

1 1   Product of the first multiplier

Step 2: Shift left one by adding zero (0) to the right: The product (1 1) of step one becomes 1 1 0.

Step 3: Multiply the multiplicand by the next bit of the multiplier.

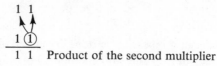

1 1   Product of the second multiplier

Step 4: Add the product attained in step three to the shifted product in step two. Or:

$$
\begin{array}{r}
1\ 1\ 0 \\
1\ 1 \\
\hline
1\ 0\ 0\ 1
\end{array}
$$

1 0 0 1   The final product

Multiplication on a computer is performed in a similar way. A device called an *accumulator* is used to record the steps illustrated above.

Binary and Decimal Division

Procedure

In either the decimal or the binary system, division is performed by successive subtraction. It is, in fact, the opposite of multiplication, which is a series of successive additions. When we divide, the quotient is the number of times subtraction of the divisor is made from the dividend. For example:

$$15 \div 3 = 5$$

$$
\begin{aligned}
15 - 3 &= 12 \text{ Result of 1 subtraction} \\
12 - 3 &= 9 \text{ Result of 1 subtraction} \\
9 - 3 &= 6 \text{ Result of 1 subtraction} \\
6 - 3 &= 3 \text{ Result of 1 subtraction} \\
3 - 3 &= 0 \text{ Result of 1 subtraction}
\end{aligned}
$$

The quotient, then, is 5

In binary, the same procedure is followed. For example:

$$
\begin{array}{r}
1\ 0\ 1 \text{ (5) the quotient} \\
1\ 1\ \overline{)\ 1\ 1\ 1\ 1} \\
1\ 1 \\
\hline
0\ 0\ 1\ 1 \\
1\ 1 \\
\hline
0\ 0
\end{array}
$$

Restoring Method of Detecting a Remainder

As mentioned, division is performed by successive subtractions. A computer does not know when to stop subtracting until it has gone too far—

in fact, one step too far. This takes place in an operation when the dividend does not go an even number of times into the divisor, as is the case in $14 \div 4 = 3$ and remainder 2. When a remainder of two is arrived at by the computer, the computer keeps on subtracting until it encounters a negative remainder, at which time it restores the last subtraction and considers the result as a true remainder. This method is referred to as the *restoring* method. For illustration, assume the decimal division of $14 \div 4$:

Step 1:	14	
	− 04	1 subtraction
	+ 10	
Step 2:	04	1 subtraction
	+ 06	
Step 3:	04	1 subtraction
	+ 02	True remainder
Step 4:	− 04	Unnecessary under our manual method
	− 02	Negative remainder
Step 5:	+ 04	Reversing step 4
	+ 02	Restored remainder

Total number of subtractions is equal to 3—the quotient.

The last step which is taken unnecessarily by the computer can be avoided if the remainder of each subtraction is compared with the divisor for equality. The operation can be programmed to halt any further subtraction when the first unequal compare is detected. However, this would involve complex controls and the aid of auxiliary equipment.

GLOSSARY OF TERMS

PARALLEL ADDITION: Applies to adding in one step all the decimal positions of a decimal number.

SERIAL ADDITION: Relates to adding decimal digits, one digit at a time.

TENS COMPLEMENT: A decimal method of subtraction.

chapter

21

THE
BLOCK DIAGRAM

AN ELECTRONIC COMPUTER is dependent on man. Although it aids his work, it cannot replace him. The degree of its aid is limited to the degree of experience and knowledge of the human programmer. To follow an old adage, "The stream can be no greater than its source."

Preparing to Program

A program is a part of a problem-solving cycle which, when done carefully, saves time as well as money for the user. In order to provide an overall understanding of the problem-solving process, we shall explain in this chapter the steps involved in preparing to program the problem. These steps must be properly planned and carried out before any program can be written. Like the links in a bicycle chain, each step represents a link which, if detached or weakened, can ruin the effectiveness of the other links.

Steps in the Problem-solving Process

Working out a solution to a business problem follows the same steps as those used in working out a solution to a scientific problem. The "scientific" method includes: (1) defining the problem, (2) organizing the required data, (3) devising a procedure for a desired solution, (4) writing the program and testing the procedure, and (5) carrying out (documenting) the program.

Problem Definition

The goal of a computer system is the realization of meaningful information as output. Problem definition involves the advance determination of what is needed as input to obtain the information desired as output. The first necessary step in problem solving, then, is a clear, detailed definition of the type of information needed. The objective of each step must be determined. No procedure can be deemed pertinent that will not lead directly to the attainment of a predetermined goal. The following quotation from *Alice in Wonderland* brings out the basic idea that the objective must be set before effective action can be taken:

> "Cheshire Puss, would you tell me, please, which way I ought to go from here?"
> "That depends a good deal on where you want to get to," said the cat.
> "I don't much care where—," said Alice.
> "Then it doesn't matter which way you go," said the cat.

Such aimless wandering cannot be condoned in problem solving because it wastes time and costs money. A sufficient amount of time must be allowed for defining the specific problem as well as for gathering together the specific information to be used in its solution. If the objective is not clearly defined, or if the goal is determined too hurriedly, the steps followed will lead to meaningless results.

When the goal has been determined, the personnel responsible for its achievement should keep in mind the capabilities and limitations of their particular computer system. The type of output information expected must be within the capabilities of the system. Through experience and observation on the job, one can determine the details of what the computer installation can and cannot do. If such an installation is the result of status seeking by the firm without regard for the value of the computer in helping to do repetitive work, or if the wrong type is installed, the firm has an expensive layout which cannot be justified. It becomes entirely purposeless when management does not receive the hoped-for information. The blame cannot be put on the computer, because this is the result of bad judgment on the part of humans. The computer is the "victim," not the "villain," in such a case. System design, the degree of experience of the programmers, and other factors involved in the planning, such as the way in which data are received and produced, are all related closely to the success or failure of a computer data-processing system. The failure of a computer installation to be of value to a business organization is either the result of the inability of humans to recognize precisely the organization's need for it or the failure of those in charge to utilize fully the capabilities of the system.

Data Organization

After the problem is defined, the next logical step involves the organization of the proper source data to be used in the application and the preparation of the program for the computer system so that the data can be processed. The term *organize* is synonymous with the terms *arrange, institute,* and *bring into being.* It involves the preparation of the basic component parts and their relationships to each other in such a way that they contribute effectively toward the realization of the predetermined goal.

In a payroll application, for instance, the problem can be defined as the determination of the employee's pay for the period covered, including the computation of taxes to be withheld and the preparation of pertinent statements to support such computations. Problem organization, in this respect, involves the preparation of the time cards (the source data), the employee's regular base rate and his overtime, his number of withholding exemptions, and other related factors which would affect the amount of his paycheck for the period covered. The results of data organization begin with recording the source data by punching them into cards and verifying them to ascertain their accuracy. In order to do this, the systematic recording of specific data in a given location in the card is a "must." Next, the file must be sorted and classified in a given order before processing can take place effectively and correctly.

The above example stresses the importance of the punched card for temporary data storage. We should bear in mind, however, that the punched card is neither necessarily the best type of direct input in a computer data-processing application nor the only means used in business-computer installations. Although the punched card was the technique used originally and it is still in popular use today, the increasing popularity of optical scanners makes the need for punching data in a card for input a matter of choice. However, regardless of the exact input medium used, data must be punched into a card originally so that the human language in the source documents can be converted into the machine language that an input device can understand.

The steps presented thus far can be properly labeled the "collection stage." The source data must be accurately recorded, properly classified, and checked out as the proper data for accomplishing the objective for which an application is being run.

The Development Stage

The next stage in problem solving is referred to as the *development* stage. Although general, the term nevertheless includes the remaining steps leading to the output results. Those who are responsible for the results to be procured compare these results with the objective in a "trial run" in order to satisfy themselves concerning the accuracy and reliability of the future computer output. This stage, thus, is a corrective step for a better output in future applications.

One of the main steps in the development stage is devising a procedure which will convert the input data into meaningful results. A *procedure* is defined as "a specific way of doing something." To devise a successful procedure one should bear in mind the information needed on the final reports, the form which the report should take, the sequence leading to its preparation, and the extent of detail it should contain. To illustrate, the procedure involved in admission to college follows a specific series of steps. When you decided to go to college, you followed a procedure which involved certain steps, that is, writing a letter to the registrar or an admissions officer, mailing a transcript of your high school grades, asking one or more of your teachers for a recommendation, possibly visiting the college or meeting a representative of the college for a personal interview, and taking a series of entrance examinations. Finally, if everything was considered acceptable, you were notified of your acceptance to commence college work at that particular institution. This procedure was constructed after the objectives of the institution were determined—which, in their turn, were based on the college's knowledge of your aims with regard to a college education. The objectives must be in harmony with those of the prospective student, because he cannot expect to learn something that is not available to him in the college of his choice.

What is a block diagram?

In preparing a program, a procedure is devised by the technique of the block diagram, consisting of a number of blocks each containing an instruction which the computer must execute, in proper sequence. A block diagram is essential in that it enables one to write the program in an orderly manner.

A block diagram, also called a program flow chart, is in effect a detailed outline giving the steps which must be performed by the computer for the accurate processing of the data involved. The diagram or chart places emphasis upon "how" the computer is to go about solving a problem. It is a graphic representation of operations, decisions, and the order in which they are to be made. This aids the programmer in visualizing the sequence of the necessary operations. The diagram acts not only as a visual aid, but also as a guide to coding the symbolic language which it contains into machine language. The programmer's main interest is to mechanize a specific application. He uses various blocks and builds a diagram which he feels would be the best approach to an efficient solution of the application. Once the program is "debugged" and proved workable, it is kept on file for future reference either to be used as is or to be modified if experience with it shows that this should be done.

A block diagram, then, is a means of outlining a given problem. The author recalls how his speech instructor outlined on the board the steps involved in delivering a speech: that is, (1) "stand up," (2) "speak up," and (3) "shut up." Each of these steps can be expanded to show other detailed substeps leading to a complete speech. A term paper follows a similar basic series of steps: namely, the introduction, the main body, and conclusions. Many ideas can be presented under each of these three headings, particularly the middle one. These three headings constitute a *general flow diagram*. When the details are included, the diagram is called a detailed flow diagram or *block diagram*. Figure 21-1 presents an example of a block diagram of "How to get to school in the morning." This will serve to illustrate that plans of action for our daily routines are really "block diagrams" which are repeated so often that they are "written" in our memory. We are likely to become upset if anything interferes with

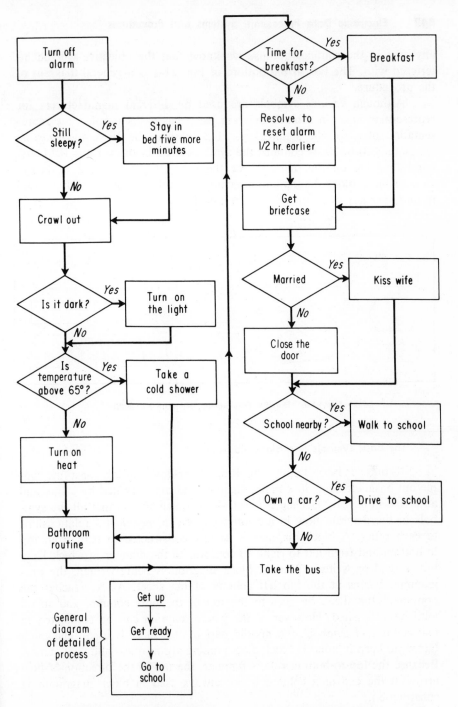

Fig. 21-1. A detailed block diagram and a general diagram of "How to get to school in the morning"

any step in the routine, because we know that the objective will be interfered with. The box at the bottom of Fig. 21-1 is a general diagram of the procedure.

Although various symbols are used by different manufacturers for representing ideas in a block diagram, each has as its purpose the representation of a specific action. Fig. 21-2 presents the IBM flow-charting template X20-8020. It contains the symbols used in the various IBM systems available on the market. For the sake of presenting a bird's-eye view of basic block-diagramming techniques, only the main symbols used in outlining any program will be explained.

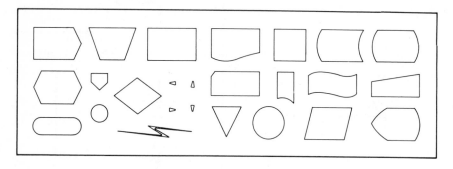

Fig. 21-2. The IBM flow-charting template X20-8020

The basic symbols of a block diagram

1. DIRECTION OF FLOW. The direction-of-flow symbols constitute simple but basic elements in a block diagram and are indicated by a line and an arrow (Fig. 21-3). They connect any two symbols so that all the symbols in the diagram flow in a related pattern in meaningful relationships to each other. A block diagram is usually constructed to read from top to bottom and from left to right, to conform to the manner in which English is read or written. When a block diagram is being written, the programmer begins at the top left column of the sheet. As he reaches the bottom of the sheet, he goes to the top of the next column, and so on until he is finished. However, if the whole diagram can be completed in one column of symbols, the middle part of the sheet is used. The main factors to keep in mind in block diagramming are neatness and consistency. Because the top-to-bottom rule is familiar, the use of the direction-of-flow arrow at the end of a column is not always used in block diagramming construction.

2. THE INPUT, OR OUTPUT, SYMBOL. The input, or output, symbol stands for an instruction to an input, or an output, device (Fig. 21-4). The

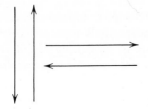

Fig. 21-3.   Direction-of-flow symbols used in block diagrams

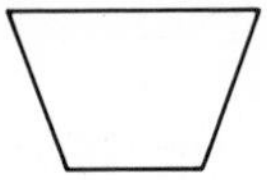

Fig. 21-4.   The IBM input/out-
put symbol

input device transfers the input data to the computer for processing. The output device prepares the result of the processed information for the user. These symbols are usually shown on either end of a complete block diagram. At times, other symbols are shown before the input symbol to instruct the computer to form what is referred to in programming as "house-keeping," or the preparation of the system for a new application. Examples of input/output steps are seen in Fig. 21-5.

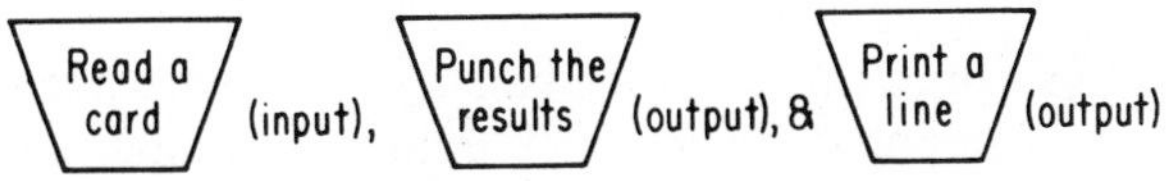

Read a card (input),   Punch the results (output), &   Print a line (output)

Fig. 21-5.   Input/output steps

The "read-a-card" instruction simply tells the card reader to read the first card in sequence and to transfer its contents to the central processing unit. Without this step, it would be impossible for the computer to do any work, unless other means were used to move the data into its primary storage.

The "punch-the-results" instruction is an output instruction and is usually the last step before the computer stops or loops (branches) back to the beginning of the program to repeat the steps on another account. This instruction causes the punching unit of an output device, that is, an auxiliary machine connected by a cable to the computer, to punch in a card the results of the processing routine.

The "print-a-line" instruction is another output step. The printer receives the output data from the computer and prints them on a form. Output can be presented to the user either in printed or in punched form. The former method is the one used when management wants the results immediately; the latter, when the data are to be stored for future use in the processing cycle.

Both punching in a card and printing the same data on a line can be performed simultaneously in the machine run if desired. The only exception is that the printer has preference (in terms of timing) over the punching unit.

3. THE PROCESSING SYMBOL. The processing symbol denotes an operation involved in the actual processing of data. It is represented by the symbol shown as Fig. 21-6. Some examples of processing are shown in Fig. 21-7.

Fig. 21-6. The processing
symbol

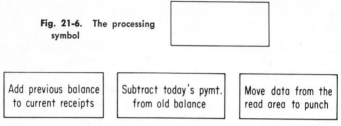

Fig. 21-7. Examples of processing symbols

These steps are carried out in the central processing unit. The symbol is referred to, then, as the "stored-program" symbol.

The following problem will illustrate the use of the symbols discussed thus far.

Problem: The problem is one of balancing accounts receivable. Assume the use of a computer system which utilizes card input and card output. Fig. 21-8 shows the card input for the problem. Given this input, block diagram the following steps for solving the problem: Previous balance − Cash received + Additional sales on account = Present balance.

The construction of a block diagram follows the same reasoning, obviously, as if the application were to be done manually.

a/c No.	Previous balance	Cash received	Sales on account

Fig. 21-8. Card input of accounts receivable problem

Because a number of accounts, all following the same repetitive procedure, are to be processed, we must design the program in such a way that the computer can go through the same necessary procedures for each of the accounts to be processed without stopping after each has been completed. To do this, a technique called *looping* is used. In Fig. 21-9, after the computer executes the last instruction of the program, "punch the new balance," on the first account card, it loops back to the first instruction,

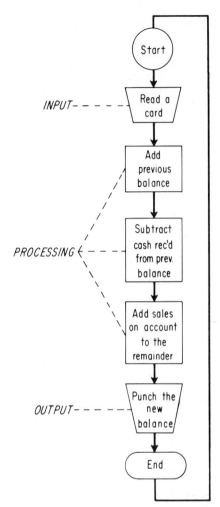

Fig. 21-9. Looping technique

"read a card," which causes the second account card to be read and the same procedure applied to it. One and only one program for the whole file of accounts receivable cards has to be prepared. If the computer were unable to *loop,* the only other alternative would be to store as many complete programs as there are accounts to be processed, which would not be practical in updating the accounts because the programs might occupy most of the primary storage unnecessarily.

4. THE DECISION SYMBOL. One of the more important capabilities of an electronic computer is its ability to choose among several alternatives, when programmed to do so. This is done by comparing two values and consequently following an instruction which tells it to use a certain routine in a specific case. The decision, or *logic,* symbol is represented in Fig. 21-10.

Fig. 21-10. The decision symbol

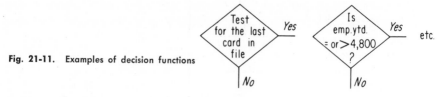

Fig. 21-11. Examples of decision functions

Some examples of decision functions are shown in Fig. 21-11. Although in a computer system utilizing punched cards as input the card reader stops the operation automatically at the end of the program, the computer would check to see if the card processed is the last card. Two alternatives exist: If it is the last card, the operation should halt. Otherwise, it would loop back and start from the beginning in order to process the next card in sequence. When this decision symbol is added to the example in Fig. 21-9, the diagram would then look like that in Fig. 21-12.

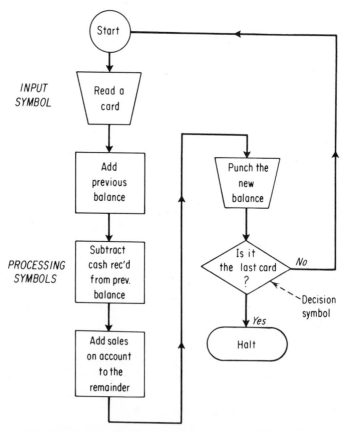

Fig. 21-12. A block diagram showing the use of a decision symbol

A decision symbol does not have to be in any specific location in the block diagram. In the case of Fig. 21-12, it is located toward the end, because its purpose is to check for a last card and to cause the system to halt if it is the last card. A decision symbol is usually located somewhere between the input and the output symbols, depending on the type of decision that must be made. It is also very likely that a block diagram will contain more than one decision symbol. The number of decision symbols desired depends on the number of alternative courses of action demanded by the program. For the purpose of illustrating the use of decision in a block diagram, other than testing for a last card, assume the following problem.

Problem: A group of cards in a file representing both employees and their supervisors are to be processed. Fifty ($50.00) dollars are to be added to each of the employees' current pay. In the event that the card represents a supervisor, an additional $40.00 is to be added. The output is to be printed. In order to distinguish an employee's card from that of a supervisor's an X punch is made in column seventy-six of the supervisor's card. The input card is divided into the fields shown in Fig. 21-13.

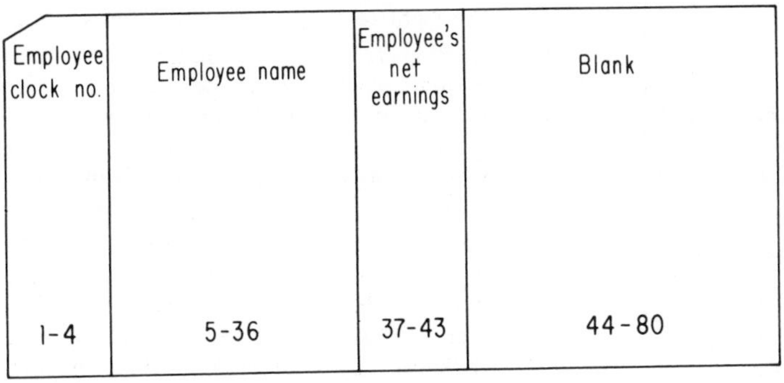

Employee clock no.	Employee name	Employee's net earnings	Blank
1-4	5-36	37-43	44-80

Fig. 21-13. Input card

The block diagram is designed to instruct the computer to read the first card in sequence. Next, it is instructed to add $50.00 to the earnings field. In this case, it makes no difference whether the earnings field is that of the employee or the supervisor, since either is entitled to the initial $50.00. The third symbol commands the computer to identify the card to which $50.00 has just been added. Identification in this case is done by the detection of an X punch in column seventy-six. Only a supervisor's card contains an X punch in that column. When an X punch is detected, the computer interprets it as a supervisor's card and then takes the next instruction in sequence, which is, "Add $40.00 to the earnings field." However, if no X punch is detected in column seventy-six, the card is an employee card. In this case, the computer "branches" to block five of the program and moves the data in the card to the print area, where the results are printed (Fig. 21-14).

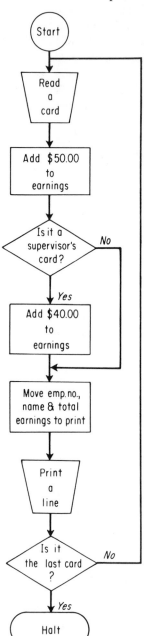

Branching is like a road detour. It bypasses the regular route for a logical reason. The computer branches by bypassing block four only when the card is an employee card. Otherwise, it follows the program from top to bottom as presented, one instruction at a time. The last decision symbol tests for a last card. If the answer is *No,* it loops the program back to the beginning for the processing of the remaining card(s) in the hopper. If the answer is *Yes,* it halts.

General block-diagramming hints

Some of the points considered helpful in constructing a block diagram are:

1. The steps constituting the diagram should start at the top of the sheet and flow down and toward the right to the lower right-hand section.

2. Each page should be numbered sequentially, and enough space should be allowed for the title of the business application, the name of the programmer, and the data from which the diagram was constructed. The title should be short and clear.

3. The language used in describing each of the steps in the block diagram should be in English, not machine language. This is desirable because it contributes to a better understanding of the instructions by people other than the programmer, people who may not know the system used in working the machine language.

4. In each instruction, all the writing should be clearly written within the symbol. If too many words are in the symbol, it tends to be confusing, especially if abbreviations are used. When you construct a block diagram, put yourself in the position of an uninformed reader. This will help you to see the problems involved.

5. Use a standardized template with clearly recognizable symbols, because the diagram will then look neater and more presentable than if a hand-drawn diagram is employed.

Fig. 21-14. The use of decision in a block diagram

Writing the Program and Testing the Procedure

The coding stage

Once a block diagram has been prepared, the programmer writes (codes) the program either in a computer language or in a language that can be translated into an appropriate one. Coding simply involves the translation or conversion of each of the instructions in the block diagram into language understandable to the computer. At this point in the developmental stage, the coding process contributes to the processing of data by preparing a guide to the precise location of various fields of data in memory so as to enable one to address them when necessary. Coding does not take a great amount of time if the block diagram, methods of input and output, and the location of various fields in memory are determined in advance. In most cases, coding can be done automatically. Automatic programming involves utilization of the computer itself to aid in coding the instructions written by a programmer. The utilization of the computer to do the clerical part of the coding reduces coding time and is much faster than doing it manually.

The "debugging" stage

The term *debug* means to locate and then correct any errors that may have been made in preparing the program. A program must be debugged to the extent that it is certain to attain the results for which it was constructed. Debugging should take place as each of the major steps in writing the program is completed. The more frequently the problem-definition stage and data-organization stage are worked over, or debugged, the fewer are the errors that are likely to occur when debugging of the block diagram and its coding are done. The problem of debugging increases geometrically as the size of the program increases arithmetically. In other words, considerably more time is required to debug a program consisting of several hundred instructions than one which contains thirty instructions. In some cases, a complex program can take days or even weeks to debug thoroughly. Delays in processing will be kept to a minimum if the program is written as accurately as possible in the first place. Thus, valuable time, and money, will be saved.

Two major types of errors are likely to be detected in the debugging stage: (1) logical errors, and (2) clerical errors. A logical error occurs as a result of poor interpretation of a phase of a problem or of lack of knowledge of some part of the data-processing setup. For example, the failure to take into consideration the fact that no employee should be paid at regular rates for more than a maximum forty-five hours a week is considered a logical error. In the absence of instructions to control this factor in the program, the computer will go ahead and multiply an employee's reported sixty-five hours worked for the week by the regular rate per hour to arrive at his gross pay. The result of this calculation is obviously inaccurate, owing to the fact that the man who wrote the program did not take overtime rates into account.

A clerical error is another type of error that occurs in programming and, especially, in the coding stage. A programmer, for instance, may assign, by error, two unrelated values to the same memory location, or he may assign the wrong address of the data needed in processing a certain application. An example of the latter case is assigning address 7128 instead of 7218. The use of automatic programming aids in reducing the error of assigning more than one character to a given address. When assignment of addresses to data is made manually, use of the debugging technique to locate and correct all types of errors within the shortest time possible is especially important. Again, in this case, however, the cost factor is of importance. If debugging of a given program causes too great a delay before the final program can be made ready to be stored in the computer, the processing job may be delayed so long that the results obtained may not be delivered in time for the knowledge to be effectively used by management.

The testing stage

Once the program is debugged and errors eliminated, the next logical step is to test its effectiveness. The program is loaded into the computer. Input data are loaded into the input device. The computer is started and the program begins to process the data. Answers to data being processed for testing purposes must have been worked out in advance by the programmer or his supervisor so as to compare them with those arrived at by the computer. If these results match, the program is considered clear of errors. The rest of the input data can then be processed with a high degree of confidence. However, if the answers are inaccurate, the program must be analyzed and worked on further. The overlooking of one factor, however minor it may be, at any stage of working out the problem will be greatly amplified at the programming stage. The purpose is to locate the error that is preventing the program from processing data correctly. In a complex program, which includes hundreds of instructions, the search for an error or errors is as difficult and time consuming as searching for a needle in a haystack. Great patience, experience, and technical know-how are necessary before a program of this size can be put to use in a reasonable length of time. The programmer should review the program for the correction of logical, as well as clerical, errors.

The program, when completed, is stored for future use. If future input data pose exceptions for which the program is unprepared, it should be modified or changed sufficiently to handle the "new" input data.

Documentation

Once a program becomes operational, some form of program documentation should be kept on file. A documentation record is essentially a "carbon copy" of the work performed on the program. The life of the program is separate from the tenure or the length of time committed by the programmer to his employer. In the event the author involved is transferred or later resigns, good documentation puts someone else in a helpful position to answer questions and to modify or otherwise service the program.

Some of the specific details included in a program-documentation file are: (1) preflow-charting data, (2) a copy of the master block diagram, (3) the methodology used in data collection and related procedures, (4) detailed description of input data preparation, (5) master list of details in connection with the record layout and code forms used in writing the program, (6) an adequate program run manually, listing the instructions the console operator must follow in running the program on the computer, and (7) a sample of tested data.

With the availability of the foregoing details, the data-processing manager can easily assign the task of periodic modifications to a qualified programmer, thus minimizing the likelihood of a major program overhaul.

GLOSSARY OF TERMS

BLOCK DIAGRAM: A graphic representation of the sequence of procedural steps for processing data.

CODING: An ordered list of computer instructions (in computer code) representing successive computer operations designed to solve a specific problem.

DEBUGGING: Locating and correcting mistakes made in preparing a computer program.

DOCUMENTATION: The process of gathering, organizing, storing, and dispensing documents or the information they contain.

PROCEDURE: A specific way of performing a given job.

REVIEW QUESTIONS

1. Why is the problem-definition stage important in problem solving? Explain.
2. What is involved in data organization? Discuss.

3. What is meant by the *development* stage? How is it different from the collection stage?

4. What is a block diagram? Explain in detail. Give an example.

5. Block diagram a project or a routine of interest to you. Explain the steps which you have included.

6. Explain briefly the following block-diagramming symbols:
   (a) Direction of flow
   (b) Input/output
   (c) Processing

7. What is *branching?* When and why is it used in a block diagram?

8. Explain the debugging stage and the testing stage.

9. What is the difference between a logical error and a clerical error? Give an example of each.

10. Why should debugged programs be documented? What is involved in documentation?

11. What specific items are included in a program-documentation file?

chapter

22

THE CENTRAL
PROCESSING UNIT
The Control Unit
and The Stored Program

THE CONTROL UNIT

THE STORED PROGRAM

WHAT IS A STORED PROGRAM? PLANNING THE PROGRAM Define input and procedures Use suitable language Make program accurate Prepare and produce precise instructions Provide complete sequential directions to the computer Make self-operative PROGRAM STORAGE AND COMPUTER MEMORY Storage Address The Word Mark ACTIVITIES RELATED TO THE STORED PROGRAM Block Diagramming (Review) *Input and Output Symbol The Processing Symbol The Logic or Decision Symbol* Coding *Symbolic Language Machine Language*

PROGRAM LOADING AND INSTRUCTION EXECUTION

THE PROBLEM THE INSTRUCTION FORMAT Operation Code Operand Digit Modifier AN EXAMPLE OF A SYMBOLIC PROGRAM Reserved Areas in Memory Storage of Instructions Interpretation and Execution of Program Instructions *Internal Registers* The instruction register The data register *Machine Cycles—Instruction One* The instruction phase The execution phase *Machine Cycles—Instruction Two Machine Cycles— Instruction Three Machine Cycles—Instruction Four* Looping

COMPILER LANGUAGE PROGRAMS

THE COBOL LANGUAGE THE FORTRAN LANGUAGE

VARIABLE VERSUS FIXED WORD-LENGTH COMPUTERS

BY NOW YOU HAVE LEARNED the various primary steps through which data must go in the electronic-processing cycle, ending in the attainment of the desired reports as a form of output. Input and output media or devices have been discussed. The primary- and secondary-storage devices and concepts have also been explained. In Chapters 17 and 18, some of the computer coding systems have been presented with emphasis upon their role in arithmetic operations. The previous chapter brought out block diagramming and its basic techniques. The study of electronic business data-processing concepts will be complete only when the heart of the matter has been discussed, that is, the control unit and the stored program.

The Control Unit

The control unit of a computer determines the path through which given data must move in order to be used in performing the various operations that take place. To do this, the control unit must first select the specific data related to a given operation before it determines the path along which the selected data must move. The control unit is similar to a railroad-switchyard control tower. The operator of the control tower decides which train should be routed where and then determines the track (path) over which it should travel. Once these decisions are made, he throws a switch which allows the train to make the desired transfer to the proper track safely.

The control unit of a computer can also be compared to a chief cook in a large restaurant. The cook supervises the number and kinds of ingredients that are to be mixed in a recipe. He directs his assistants to select the right temperature and the use of the proper utensils in preparing a pie or an exotic meal. His job is vital in that his knowledge of what goes on in his department enables the restaurant to render service and to offer the meals listed on the menu.

Like the cook, the control unit of the computer tells the input device *when* and *what* information to transfer to the memory section of the computer and when to do it. Once the selected data reach memory, the control unit tells the memory where to store them. The control unit also tells the computer what arithmetic operation to do, where in memory to locate the data, and what to do with the results after the arithmetic is performed. Further, the control unit tells the output device *what* to print and *when* to stop printing. If output is in punched form, it tells the punch device *what* to punch and *when* to stop punching.

Not only does the control unit select the data and properly connect the units that work on them so that the procedure is self-operating, but it also constantly watches over the operation as a whole to ascertain that every step is done according to schedule and on time. This "traffic director" is one of the most significant parts of a commercial electronic digital computer. For it to do its job, however, it in turn gets its "briefing" from what is called the *stored program*.

The Stored Program

What Is a Stored Program?

Do you still recall the series of events that took place during your high school commencement? The main activities on that day very likely went something like this:

1. Processional—*Pomp and Circumstance*.
2. National anthem—Audience please stand.
3. Prayer—Remain standing.
4. Opening remarks—Audience seated.
5. Main speaker.
6. Speeches of those awarded honors.
7. Awarding of diplomas—Audience will hold applause until all diplomas are awarded.
8. Recessional—Audience will remain seated until graduating class has exited.

These steps, including pertinent details, were printed and copies distributed to students, parents, and guests. They were called the commencement *programs*.

A program, then, is a series of acts, or a set of instructions, on how to carry out a particular operation or event. It presents the necessary instructions in a sequential, clear, and detailed manner. The term *sequential* means that the instructions are to be followed in the exact order in which they are presented. In the example of the commencement program, the diplomas could not have been awarded without the speeches of the honors graduates. Their speeches, in turn, could not be delivered before that of the main speaker. The main speaker could not deliver his speech until after the national anthem, the prayer, and the opening remarks had been completed. None of these things could be done until the completion of the processional which set the stage for their occurrence. In this example, the program began with the processional and ended with the awarding of the diplomas. The seniors to be graduated can be thought of as "input," and the awarding of the diplomas, as "output." The processional can be considered the "input device." The activities in between "input" and "output" represented the "processing" steps that led the audience and the speakers (the "computer") through the exercises ("operation"), in an orderly manner, so that a successful commencement was conducted.

Computer programming demands skill and knowledge of the subject matter, as was true of the people responsible for the conduct of your commencement. The required skill is related to the aptitude level and degree of experience of the human programmer. The more experience and talent a given programmer possesses, the more likely he will be to succeed in presenting a factual, informative, clear, and otherwise well-prepared program. Although it is highly desirable for his educational background to include the fundamental fields of business administration, that is, finance, production, accounting, marketing, and management, this is not absolutely necessary. Many successful programmers do not have a college education but have gained their knowledge in those fields by experience. However, knowledge of the principles of management, and experience in dealing with the field of human relations, will brighten his prospects for becoming the manager of the department in which he works as a computer programmer, should the opportunity present itself.

Planning the Program

If a computer control unit is to direct the various processing steps correctly, plans must be made in advance. In successful planning, the following steps are necessary.

1. *Define input and procedures:* The meeting place of all the graduating seniors for the starting of the procession, the doors through which they will pass, the hallways through which they will march, the side of the auditorium they will enter and exit, the specific seats in which they will sit, and the side of the stage they will approach upon receiving their diplomas are all a part of what is known, in the language of computers, as the *procedure.* The graduating seniors are considered as input. No program can be worked out satisfactorily without someone knowing what the input is to be and then preparing the "input" to act immediately upon the beginning of the strains of *Pomp and Circumstance* and instructing "it" what specific procedure is to be used so that the result may be a dignified and orderly "output"—in this case, the awarding of diplomas.

2. *Use suitable language:* Because English is the language understandable to the members of a graduating class in this country, if the program were communicated in Spanish, for example, translation into English would have to be completed before any activity of the commencement exercises could be initiated properly. In data processing, a program must also be written in language understandable to the computer before

the computer can follow instructions successfully. This language is referred to as "machine" language. Because programs are outlined in human language, translation into suitable machine language has to be completed before any processing can be conducted.

3. *Make program accurate:* An accurately produced program is the result of the way in which a computer operates as well as of the job the computer is to be directed to process. By analogy, a vacationing motorist would need to know where he wants to go before a local resident could give him accurate directions as to how to get there. Also, the preparation of accurate instructions demands that the programmer have basic understanding and sound knowledge of the particular computer to be programmed, because computers differ from one another. Again, by analogy, the directions given to a vacationing motorist are likely to be different from those given to a truck driver, even though each of them is heading for the same destination.

4. *Prepare and produce precise instructions:* Computers require that programs be precisely directed and contain clear, definite, detailed instructions. The kind of precision differs because of differences in computers and also because of the types of applications.

5. *Provide complete sequential directions to the computer:* A computer must have access to a program which offers complete instructions in the proper order and yet is brief enough to be considered efficient. The brevity of a complete program depends on the type of application.

6. *Make self-operative:* Once the computer is provided with a program containing clear, accurate, detailed, sequential instructions written in machine language, it must execute those instructions well. The control unit takes orders on the basis of the program. It takes one instruction at a time from the program and executes it, until it reaches the last instruction. It executes the last instruction and stops automatically, unless the last instruction tells it to start again from the beginning. If the latter is the case, the control unit starts from the beginning of the program and follows its instruction for "traffic directing" in the same manner as it did previously.

Program Storage and Computer Memory

Before a computer can process a problem, it must have direct access to the program, which contains the necessary instructions. The instructions tell it *what* to do and *how* to do it. Each instruction represents a command to the computer. The program is read into, or loaded into, the memory of the machine. As soon as it is stored, the execution of instructions and the primary processing of the data can begin.

Because of its continued use in business data-processing applications, the IBM 1401, a 4,000-storage-position computer, will be used to explain further the memory characteristics of a computer and, later, the program cycle. The understanding of one digital computer aids greatly in learning the workings of other computers, because most electronic digital computers operate in the same way. The memory section of the IBM 1401 computer has different storage capacities. Some are built to store 1,400 characters; others, to store 2,000, 4,000, 8,000, 12,000, or 16,000 characters.

Storage address

The memory of a medium-sized 1401 computer is divided into 4,000 storage locations. Each of these storage locations has a location number, called an *address*. They are arranged in a regular order ranging from location number (address) 0000 to 3999. This arrangement is similar to a coat checkroom which can store a certain number of coats. The coat checkroom contains several racks, each of which has a separate number. The racks are arranged in regular order, for example, from 01 to 99. Each of these numbers is called an *address,* which is printed on a card to be given to the owner of the coat. Without this means of identification, the coat-check girl would have difficulty returning the proper coat to its rightful owner. After all, who would want to have a $29.95-quality coat substituted for a $189.00 tailor-made imported coat!

The programmer, too, should be able to keep track of the program instructions and other related data which he loads into the memory section of the computer. When he needs to process certain data or to tell the computer where to find them, he would simply give it (the computer) the address (location number) of the data. The same is done with the coat-check girl. When a particular owner demands his coat, he hands the girl the ticket number, which represents the address of his coat in the coat checkroom. She, in this case, occupies the role of a computer which stores the data and later on fetches them for the programmer whenever they are needed.

The memory of the IBM 1401 under discussion is composed of a number of planes stacked vertically in such a way that they are capable of storing a total of 4,000 characters (Fig. 22-1). Each character position contains eight magnetic cores. The top seven cores are the seven-bit alphanumeric code system. The BCD (1,2,4,8) can be used to store numeric digits. The BCD bits and the A- and B-zone bits can be coded to store alphabetic and special characters. The top bit is used for parity check.

The word mark

The bottom, or eighth, bit available in each of the 4,000 storage locations in the memory of this particular computer is referred to as the *word mark.* As you will recall from the section on punched cards, a punched card can be divided into different areas, each of which may be used for representing a specific type of information and each of which is called a *field.*

Once the contents of a given punched card are read into memory, the data should be stored by *fields.* In the event that only a part of the data needs processing, the identification of each particular field by the computer becomes necessary. The *word mark* is used as a "field definer."

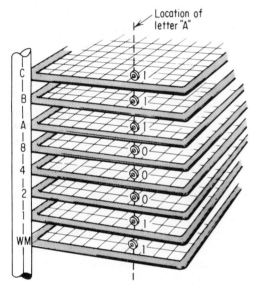

Fig. 22-1.   The location of letter A in the IBM internal storage

The term *word* is often synonymous with *field.* A *word* is a group of characters which are treated or handled as a complete unit. A customer account number is an example. The term *field* is usually used in the punched-card processing routine, whereas the term *word* is used in the electronic-computer programming routine. However, either term can be applied. A *mark* is a sign which defines the limit of the word. The eighth bit in Fig. 22-1 is a magnetic core which is turned on to represent a one-bit every time the programmer must define the limit of a given word. For example, assume that a customer's name is in storage location 412-426 and that the balance outstanding is stored in location 427-431. If during processing we wish to take the balance from storage to the arithmetic unit to be added to or subtracted from a different number, we must have a word mark which will separate the "balance outstanding" word from that of the customer's name. Therefore, a word mark is "set" in the high-order (left) position (Fig. 22-2).

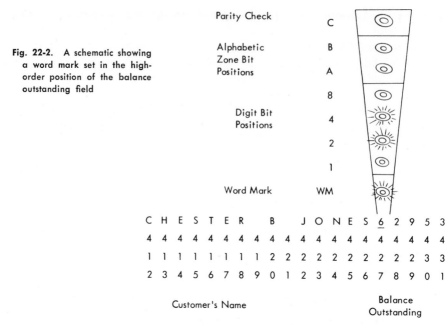

Fig. 22-2. A schematic showing a word mark set in the high-order position of the balance outstanding field

Parity Check   C

Alphabetic Zone Bit Positions   B   A

8

Digit Bit Positions   4

2

1

Word Mark   WM

C	H	E	S	T	E	R		B		J	O	N	E	S	6	2	9	5	3
4	4	4	4	4	4	4	4	4	4	4	4	4	4	4	4	4	4	4	4
1	1	1	1	1	1	1	1	1	2	2	2	2	2	2	2	2	2	3	3
2	3	4	5	6	7	8	9	0	1	2	3	4	5	6	7	8	9	0	1

Customer's Name   Balance Outstanding

From Fig. 22-2, the following points stand out:

1. The address of a word identifies its location only and *not* its contents. The address tells us *where* a character is stored. It does not give any indication whether the character is a digit, a letter, or a special character.

2. The address of a data word is always identified or located in the low-order (right) position. In Fig. 22-2, the "balance outstanding" field is located at the address 431. The reasons for this will be explained later. The location to the far right in a word is referred to as the *low-order* position. The location to the far left in a word is referred to as the *high-order* position.

3. Whereas the *address* of a data word is in the *low-order* position, the word mark separating it from another word is always located in the *high-order* position. In Fig. 22-2, we had to separate the "balance outstanding" field from the "customer's name" field. Therefore, a word mark (represented on paper as a dash) was set in 427. If, for some reason, a word mark should be set anywhere else in memory, it can be done by an instruction to the computer, containing the address and the code for setting a word mark. Clearing a word mark can also be done by giving the appropriate instruction to the computer.

4. Either data to be processed, or instructions, can be stored in the memory of a computer. Both are stored in the same manner. Processing data need not be stored in one section of memory while instructions are stored somewhere else in memory. As long as the programmer keeps track of the addresses of both the data to be processed and the instructions, any storage location can be used. However, instructions are usually stored in sequential ascending locations in an available gap in memory large enough to store the whole program. This is primarily a matter of convenience to the programmer.

Activities Related to the Stored Program

Before a program is written, a programmer takes two basic steps. They are: (1) block diagramming, and (2) coding.

Block diagramming (review)

A block diagram is one means of outlining the steps in the problem. It presents in graphic form the steps which the computer is expected to take before a proper solution can be achieved. It is a technique used in outlining a plan for action by which data are to be processed by a computer. Each of the steps shown in a block diagram is an instruction, which, when coded in machine language, tells the computer how a given job is to be done. A more complete explanation of the block diagram was presented in the previous chapter. For purposes of illustrating stored-program concepts and the functional units of a computer memory, familiarity with and emphasis upon the following symbols are desirable:

1. INPUT AND OUTPUT SYMBOL. Near the beginning of a block diagram one usually sees an input symbol (Fig. 22-3), which means that data must be read first from an external source into the internal memory of the machine before any processing is possible. The symbol for input is also used to represent output, after processing has been performed on the input data. The use of magnetic tape or other media of input and output would, at times, change the symbols.
2. THE PROCESSING SYMBOL. After the input data are received into storage, processing can be done on them. This includes moving data from one place to another in storage and doing arithmetical operations, such as adding, subtracting, multiplying, or dividing. The symbol (Fig. 22-3) used for processing is rectangular in shape.
3. THE LOGIC OR DECISION SYMBOL. The logic symbol (Fig. 22-3) is a decision function which involves a comparison between two values to determine whether one value is greater than, equal to, or less than another value. The result of a comparison is a selection between two alternatives, referred to as *branching*.

Fig. 22-3.   Block-diagramming symbols

In conclusion, therefore, each block diagram includes an input symbol, a processing symbol, a logic or decision symbol if necessary, and an output symbol.

Coding

After the block diagram is completed and "debugged," or checked out, the next step in the preparation of a program is coding. Coding involves translating, or converting, each of the steps in the block diagram into an instruction coded in language understandable to the computer. Programs can be written in two different languages:

1. SYMBOLIC LANGUAGE. Symbolic language is using symbols or mnemonics. The term *mnemonic* means any code that aids memory. Mnemonic, or symbolic, language uses codes that aid the memory of the programmer. For example, letter *A* stands for *add, S* for *subtract, M* for *multiply, D* for *divide, P* for *punch, W* for *print* or *write, R* for *read,* and so forth. The program in this chapter will be written in symbolic language, because the purpose of this presentation is to show how a program is developed and, later, executed by a computer, and not to teach coding language.
2. MACHINE LANGUAGE. When a program is initially written in symbolic language (called the source program), it must be converted into machine language (called the object program) before it can be loaded into computer memory to be used satisfactorily when needed. A special program is used to translate the program's symbolic instructions (called one-for-one conversion) into machine language automatically. First, the assembler is loaded into the computer. As the source program is read, the assembly program automatically translates the source program into a machine-language program, recording either on magnetic tape, punched cards, or another secondary storage medium. See Fig. 23-7 in the next chapter for a schematic. In the 1401 computer, the equivalent machine-language codes for a few of the symbolic codes are shown in Fig. 22-4.

Fig. 22-4. A presentation of some symbolic and machine-language codes used in the IBM 1401 computer programming

English Term	Symbolic Term	Machine Language
Read	R	1
Punch	P	4
Print (write)	W	2
Set Word Mark	SW	,

As is evident, symbolic language is easier for the programmer to use than machine language, because it is more similar to the English language than is machine language. The majority of programmers, therefore, write their programs first in symbolic language. A few write directly in machine language and claim that it is just as fast and easy as symbolic language. In this event, translation is not necessary.

Program Loading and Instruction Execution

A simplified program is presented in this section to show, step by step, the method of loading the program and of executing the instructions it contains.

The Problem

The program to be presented is for an accounts receivable application. The idea is to instruct the computer to update each customer's record, using the formula: "previous balance, less today's payments, equals balance outstanding." A punched card is used as an input device for the input, "previous balance." Its details are shown in Fig. 22-5.

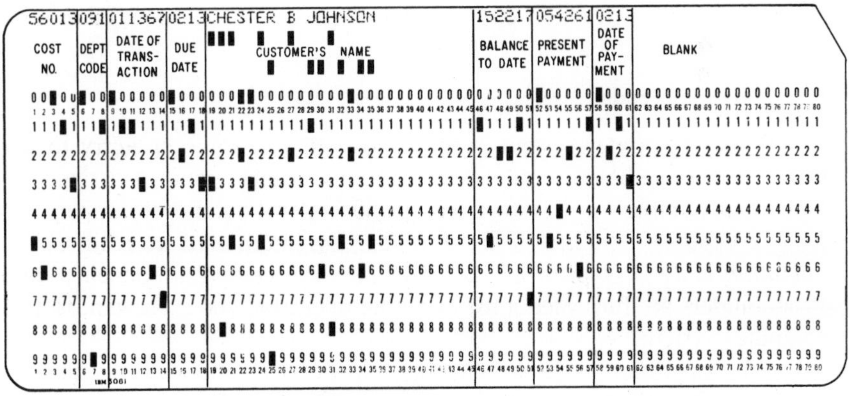

Fig. 22-5. Punched-card input

"Balance outstanding" is the output. The steps to be considered are:

1. *Input.* The program begins with an instruction to the card reader to read a card and transfer its contents to the computer.
2. *Processing.* Another instruction tells the control unit that today's payment is to be subtracted from the "balance to date," and that the answer is to be moved from its location to the punch area so that it can be punched in a blank IBM card.
3. *Output.* The last instruction tells the unit to see that the answer in the punch area is punched in a new card.

A block diagram showing all these steps in graphic form is presented in Fig. 22-6. Once a block diagram is prepared and "debugged," the next step is to convert each of the steps into more definite instructions to the computer. In order to understand this, one must have basic knowledge about the instruction format.

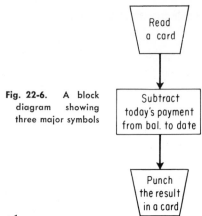

Fig. 22-6. A block diagram showing three major symbols

The Instruction Format [1]

Generally, each instruction consists of two parts: (1) the operation code, and (2) the operand.

Operation code

Every computer system is equipped with electronic circuitry to perform various arithmetic and other functions. Each circuit is assigned an individual number (code) to do a specific operation. For example, to a 1401 computer, *operation code 1* is directly interpreted as read a card; *operation code 2* as print a line; and *operation code 4* as punch a card. Programmers are furnished a list of all the operation codes relevant to their computer system.

The operation code is generally expressed symbolically as the first character of a written instruction to be performed. For example, in our accounts receivable example, we need to use instructions containing operation codes to tell the computer to *read* (*R*) a customer card, to *subtract* (*S*) today's payment from the previous balance, to *move* (*MCW*) the answer to the punch area, and lastly to *punch* (*P*) the results in a new card. Each of the italicized words is a separate instruction for a different operation. The letters in parenthesis represent the operation code for each of these instructions in symbolic language. In preparing a program for the 1401, the operation code consists of one character only for each instruction. The

---

[1] Computer systems have different programming requirements stemming from the specification of any one of several instruction formats. The two-address format is explained in this section. The single-address instruction format consists of an operation code and one operand address ⟨ Op. code ‖ Address ⟩. In addition, for instance, the computer has to be instructed to move the first value to an accumulator, add the second value to the accumulator, and move the sum to a selected address. The three-address instruction format consists of an operation code and three addresses ⟨Op. code ‖ Address 1 | Address 2 | Address 3⟩. In an "add" operation, the value stored in the first address is added to the value stored in the second address, and the sum is moved (stored) to the third address.

symbolic language describing the instruction can be up to three characters in length.

Operand

The operand is the remaining part of the instruction. It designates the address of the data needed for a given operation. In programming the 1401 computer, the operand section consists of two addresses, that is, the A-address and the B-address, both of which are referred to as *data addresses*.

The A-address represents the location of the word in storage *from which* it is to be moved.

The B-address represents the location of the area *to which* the word is to be moved. Each of the addresses is three characters in length in machine language or four characters in length in symbolic language. For example, 0 1 7 is a three-character address in machine language, whereas in symbolic language it is four characters, that is, 0 0 1 7. When a programmer writes his program in symbolic language, he uses a four-character data address. In the final conversion to machine language, all four-character addresses are coded as three-character ones.

Digit modifier

The last part of an instruction format is referred to as the *digit modifier* (D-modifier). In the present connection, its role of strengthening the operation code is the significant one. The presence of the D-modifier in an instruction adds more power and flexibility to the type of operation to be performed by a computer. It is always a one-character code.

An instruction, then, may contain up to four different parts:

1. The Operation Code.
2. The A-Address.
3. The B-Address.
4. The D-Modifier.

OPERATION CODE	A-ADDRESS	B-ADDRESS	D-MODIFIER
X	X X X	X X X	X

Fig. 22-7.   The IBM 1401 instruction format

The computer being programmed can handle instructions of varying lengths. For example, a "read" instruction consists of operation code *R* only. This code causes the contents of a given punched card to be read into memory in one step. Other instructions contain more than one character code as we shall see later.

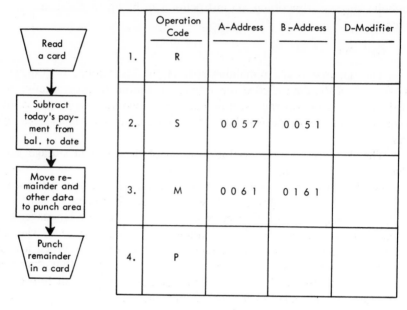

		Operation Code	A–Address	B –Address	D–Modifier
Read a card	1.	R			
Subtract today's pay-ment from bal. to date	2.	S	0 0 5 7	0 0 5 1	
Move re-mainder and other data to punch area	3.	M	0 0 6 1	0 1 6 1	
Punch remainder in a card	4.	P			

Fig. 22-8. Program instructions in symbolic language

An Example of a Symbolic Program

Having developed essential knowledge about block diagramming and the instruction format, our analysis of the accounts receivable application program can be continued.

The block diagram shown in Fig. 22-6 is amplified in Fig. 22-8.

Before the program can be loaded in the memory of the computer, the symbolic language must be converted to machine language to replace the "human" program with a "machine" program. The conversion is shown in Fig. 22-9.

	Op. Code	A–Address	B –Address	D–Modifier
1.	1			
2.	S	0 5 7	0 5 1	
3.	M	0 6 1	1 6 1	
4.	4			

Fig. 22-9. Program instructions of Fig. 22-8 converted into machine language

"Loading the program into memory" means that the instructions have to be read or put in. The four instructions are punched in four separate cards and fed into the card-reader input device which, upon the depression of a "load" button (and with a load program) will load the program (contents of four cards) in the first available positions in memory. The program occupies sixteen positions. They are determined as follows:

Instruction 1. One position for the operation code *1*, which stands for "read" a card.

2. Seven positions: one for the operation code *S* for subtract plus three for the address of the payment word (A-address) plus three for the address of the previous-balance word (B-address).

3. Seven positions: one for the operation code *M* for move plus three for the address of the move word (A-address) plus three for the address of where to move it—punch area (B-address).

4. One position for the operation code *4* meaning punch (what to do in the punching area).

Reserved areas in memory

The IBM 1401 computer memory reserves certain areas at the beginning of storage for making input and output easier. In the processing of data, input information is held temporarily in an area called the *read* area. The read area consists of the first eighty positions in storage; thus, it can store the maximum number of characters in any given punched card numbered 001-080. Every time data are received from an external source as input, they enter the read area and await further instruction. If a program, for example, includes two consecutive read instructions, the input data from the first read instruction are automatically destroyed upon storage of data from the second card as a result of the execution of the second read instruction. Therefore, the data from only one card must be dealt with at a time while the data are held in the read area. No other information should be allowed to enter the read area until the present information is either moved to a permanent storage location or processed satisfactorily (Fig. 22-10).

Another eighty-character area is reserved in storage for output numbered 101-180. It is called the *punch* area (Fig. 21-10).

If the output is to be in the form of punched results, results must be moved to the punched area. A "punch" instruction (symbolic *P*, machine language *4*) tells the control unit that the data in the punch area are to be transferred electronically to the punched card.

A third reserved area is called the *print* area (Fig. 22-10). In order that the results of a given problem can be printed, they must be moved to it. Then, by means of a print instruction (symbolic *W,* machine lan-

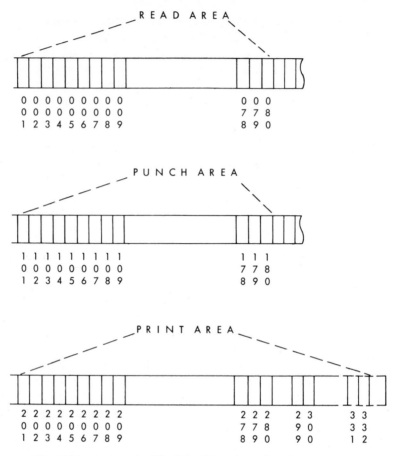

Fig. 22-10. A schematic of the IBM 1401 read, punch, and print areas

guage 2), the data in the print area are printed. The print area occupies position numbers 201-300, but in some printers they go as high as 332. The reason for the latter capacity is that the printer is able to print up to 132 characters on a line. If this is to be done, however, the print area must be larger to accommodate the storage of the additional thirty-two characters.

Storage of instructions

Assuming that we wish to store our program, which consists of four instructions, in the first available storage positions, instruction one will be stored in position number 333, instruction two in position numbers 334-340, instruction three in position numbers 341-347, and instruction four in position number 348. (See Fig. 22-11.)

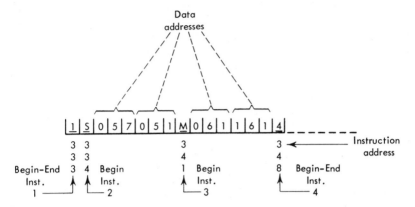

Fig. 22-11. A schematic showing the storage of a four-instruction program

Fig. 22-11 brings out several points:

1. Each instruction begins with an operation code. The operation codes in Fig. 21-11 are: *1* (read a card), *S* (subtract two values), *M* (move data), and *4* (punch a card).

2. Because only one instruction is handled at a time, a word mark must be used to separate each instruction. Therefore, a word mark (represented on paper by a dash) is set in the high-order (the left) position in the instruction word. Fig. 22-11 shows word marks denoting the presence of four different and separate instructions in storage positions 333 to 348.

3. The address of an instruction word is opposite to that of data words. The address of the operation code of each instruction is in the instruction's high-order position, because it identifies the instruction. An instruction word is read in storage from left to right, whereas a data word is read from right to left.

4. The location number of an instruction is referred to as an *instruction address*. For example, in Fig. 22-11:

333 is the address of instruction one
334 is the address of instruction two
341 is the address of instruction three
348 is the address of instruction four

Interpretation and execution of program instructions

INTERNAL REGISTERS. The computer goes about its work of interpreting and executing instructions by the use of registers. A register is a storage-unit device. Depending on its size, it can receive information, retain it, and later transfer it to a designated location. A register is named after the operation it performs. There are two types of registers: that is, the instruction register and the data register.

1. *The instruction register.* It holds the address of the instruction to be executed. For example, if instruction one pertaining to reading a card into memory is desired, the computer consults the contents of the instruction register (abbreviated *I-register*) to locate it. The I-register would contain ⎡0│3│3│3⎤. Unused positions are filled with zeros. Because it has the capacity of storing up to a four-digit address, it is referred to as a four-character I-register.

2. *The data register.* The data register stores the address of the data to be worked upon. In the IBM 1401 computer, the data register can store up to a four-digit address. The principal data registers used are the *A-address register,* which stores only the address of the data in the A-field, and the *B-address register,* which stores only the address of the data in the B-field. If instruction two were being interpreted, for example, the A-address register would contain ⎡0│0│5│7⎤ and the B-address register, ⎡0│0│5│1⎤.

MACHINE CYCLES—INSTRUCTION ONE. A computer operates in two consecutive phases: (1) the instruction phase, and (2) the execution phase.

1. *The instruction phase:* The instruction, or *I-phase,* locates and interprets an instruction. Using the prepared program (Fig. 22-11), the machine is started and the address of the first instruction is shown in the instruction register (0333). The computer goes to storage location 333 and finds *1* with a word mark. The machine language *1* is an operation code and, therefore, it is loaded in the operation register (Fig. 22-12). It will remain there until the instruction is completely executed.

The presence of a word mark in 334 tells the computer that instruction one is a one-character instruction. After operation code one is loaded

I-Register

Fig. 22-12. A schematic of the *I*-phase, pertaining to a read instruction in Fig. 21-11

Operation Register / A-Address Register / B-Address Register

in the "op-register," the instruction phase is ended. No data have been moved yet. Only the instruction has been loaded in the proper registers to prepare for its execution.

2. *The execution phase:* The execution, or *E-phase,* carries out the instruction. When operation code one enters the op-register, it is interpreted to mean "read a card." The card reader containing the data cards

reads the first card and transfers its contents to the "read" area of the computer memory. The customer's account number, *56013*, punched in columns one, two, three, four, and five (Fig. 22-5), is stored in position numbers 001, 002, 003, 004, and 005 of the "read" area (Fig. 22-21). Other data columns in the card, if any, are transferred to their corresponding locations in the "read" area also.

After the card is read, and its contents stored in the "read" area, the machine cycle pertaining to instruction one is ended. It starts again by loading instruction two into the registers.

MACHINE CYCLES—INSTRUCTION TWO. During the *I*-phase of instruction one, the I-register was automatically incremented by one, thus holding the address of the operation code of the second instruction. The *I*-phase of instruction two begins by referring to the contents of the *I*-register $\boxed{0\ 3\ 3\ 4}$. The computer goes to storage location 0334 and finds letter *S*. Being the first character in instruction two, it is interpreted to be the operation code. Therefore, it is loaded in its register, the op-register. Next, the computer takes the following three characters of the second instruction and automatically loads them in the A-address register. It checks for the presence of a word mark, and, finding none, it loads the next three characters into the B-address register. The computer is built so that it will interpret the first three characters as the A-address and the next three characters as the B-address.

Next, the computer attempts to load letter *M* (operation code of instruction three), but, detecting a word mark, it considers the letter *M* as a part of the third instruction. This ends the I-phase of instruction two. No data have been processed yet (Fig. 22-13).

I-Register

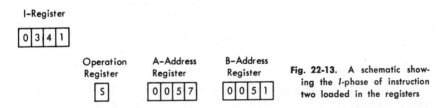

| Operation Register | A–Address Register | B–Address Register |

Fig. 22-13. A schematic showing the *I*-phase of instruction two loaded in the registers

The E-phase of instruction two begins by subtracting today's payment from the previous balance. Letter *S* in the operation register is interpreted to mean "subtract." In this operation, the contents of the A-field (today's payments) are subtracted from the contents of the B-field (previous balance). The remainder is stored in place of the previous balance (the B-field). The A-field is located by referring to the contents of the A-address register (0057). The B-field is located by reference to the contents of the B-address register (0051) (Fig. 22-14).

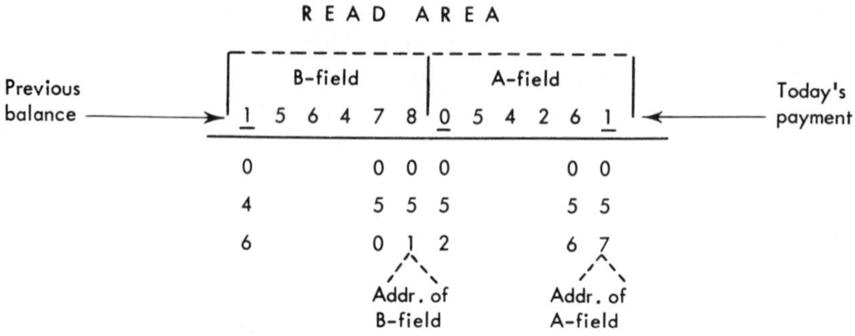

READ AREA

```
Previous          ┌─ ─ ─ ─ ─ ─ ─ ─ ─ ─ ─ ─ ─ ─ ┐
                  │   B-field    │    A-field     │           Today's
balance ────────►│ 1  5  6  4  7  8│0  5  4  2  6  1│◄──────── payment

                     0           0  0  0      0  0
                     4           5  5  5      5  5
                     6           0  1  2      6  7
                                  / \          / \
                                 Addr. of     Addr. of
                                 B-field      A-field
```

Fig. 22-14. A schematic showing the A- and B-fields
in the read area

Subtraction is performed in the same manner as it is manually, that is, one digit at a time from right to left. The steps taken by a computer to subtract the two values are:

Step one. The character stored in address 057 (*1*) is subtracted from the character stored in address 051 (*8*). The remainder (*7*) is stored in the place of *8* in the B-field.[2] The result is shown in Fig. 21-15.

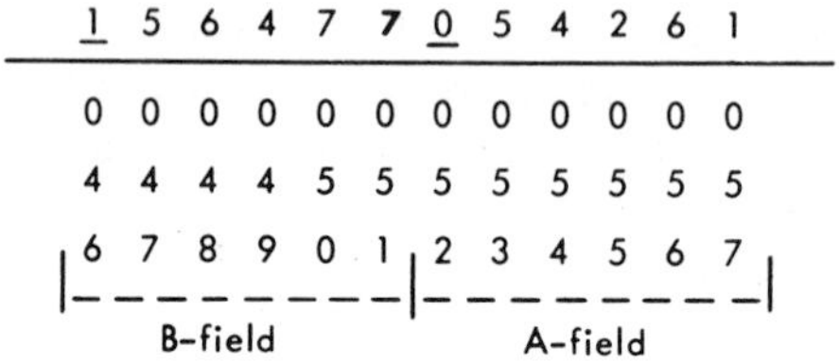

```
 1  5  6  4  7  7  0  5  4  2  6  1
─────────────────────────────────────
 0  0  0  0  0  0  0  0  0  0  0  0
 4  4  4  4  5  5  5  5  5  5  5  5
│6  7  8  9  0  1│2  3  4  5  6  7│
│─ ─ ─ ─ ─ ─ ─ ─│─ ─ ─ ─ ─ ─ ─ ─│
      B-field         A-field
```

Fig. 22-15. Subtraction—step one

Step two. During the subtraction in step one, the contents of the A- and B-address registers are decremented by one, that is, 0056 and 0050, respectively. This is done automatically so as to prepare the computer for the next subtraction. In the absence of a word mark, subtraction continues.

The computer subtracts the data in 056 (*6*) from the data in 050 (*7*). The remainder (*1*) is stored in the place of *8* in the B-field.[2] The result is shown in Fig. 22-15.

[2] Remember that throughout the subtraction routine, the value stored in the A-field remains unchanged, while the value in the B-field will be replaced by the *remainder.*

```
1  5  6  4  1  7  0  5  4  2  6  1
────────────────────────────────────
0  0  0  0  0  0  0  0  0  0  0  0
4  4  4  4  5  5  5  5  5  5  5  5
|6  7  8  9  0  1 |2  3  4  5  6  7|
|─ ─ ─ ─ ─ ─ ─ ─|─ ─ ─ ─ ─ ─ ─|
      B-field          A-field
```

Fig. 22-16. Subtraction—step two

Step three. During the subtraction in step two, the A- and B-address registers are decremented by one; that is, 0055 and 0049, respectively. The computer subtracts the character stored in 0055 (*2*) from the character stored in 0049 (*4*). The remainder (*2*) is stored in the place of *4* in the B-field. The result is seen in Fig. 22-17.

```
1  5  6  2  1  7  0  5  4  2  6  1
────────────────────────────────────
0  0  0  0  0  0  0  0  0  0  0  0
4  4  4  4  5  5  5  5  5  5  5  5
|6  7  8  9  0  1 |2  3  4  5  6  7|
|─ ─ ─ ─ ─ ─ ─ ─|─ ─ ─ ─ ─ ─ ─|
      B-field          A-field
```

Fig. 22-17. Subtraction—step three

Step four. No word mark has been detected as yet. Thus, subtraction continues. The A- and B-address registers are decremented by one. They now contain 0054 and 0048, respectively. The character in 0054 (*4*) is subtracted from the character in 0048 (*6*). The remainder (*2*) replaces digit *6* in the B-field. The result is seen in Fig. 22-18.

```
1  5  2  2  1  7  0  5  4  2  6  1
────────────────────────────────────
0  0  0  0  0  0  0  0  0  0  0  0
4  4  4  4  5  5  5  5  5  5  5  5
|6  7  8  9  0  1 |2  3  4  5  6  7|
|─ ─ ─ ─ ─ ─ ─ ─|─ ─ ─ ─ ─ ─ ─|
      B-field          A-field
```

Fig. 22-18. Subtraction—step four

Step five. No word mark is detected, so subtraction continues. The A- and B-address registers are decremented by one. They now contain 0053 and 0047, respectively. The computer uses the address 0053 in the A-field to locate digit *5*. It uses address 0047 in the B-field to locate *5*. It subtracts the first *5* from the next *5*. The remainder (*0*) replaces the *5* in the B-field. The result is seen in Fig. 22-19.

```
    1  0  2  2  1  7  0  5  4  2  6  1

    0  0  0  0  0  0  0  0  0  0  0  0
    4  4  4  4  5  5  5  5  5  5  5  5
   |6  7  8  9  0  1| 2  3  4  5  6  7|
    -------------- --------------
       B-field          A-field
```

Fig. 22-19. Subtraction—step five

Step six. Because no word mark has been detected yet, subtraction continues. Each of the A- and B-address registers is decremented by one. They now contain 0052 and 0046, respectively. The character stored in 0052 (*0*) is subtracted from the content of 0046 (*1*). The remainder (*1*) replaces *1* (actually it remains the same) in the B-field. The result is seen in Fig. 22-20.

```
    1  0  2  2  1  7  0  5  4  2  6  1

    0  0  0  0  0  0  0  0  0  0  0  0
    4  4  4  4  5  5  5  5  5  5  5  5
   |6  7  8  9  0  1| 2  3  4  5  6  7|
    -------------- --------------
       B-field          A-field
```

Fig. 22-20. Subtraction—step six

The detection of a word mark in the B-field (in address 052 and 046) indicates to the computer that the end of each of the A- and B-fields has been reached. This ends the E-phase of instruction two. The new balance (1,022.17) is now available in the B-field, which previously contained the old balance of 1,564.78. You will have noted by now that *data words* are *processed* or picked up from storage *one character at a time from right to left* in the same manner as is done manually. You will have noted also that *instruction words,* on the other hand, *are picked up* from storage (one character at a time) *from left to right* (Fig. 22-11).

The "read" area of the computer memory after instruction two is executed would be as seen in Fig. 22-21.

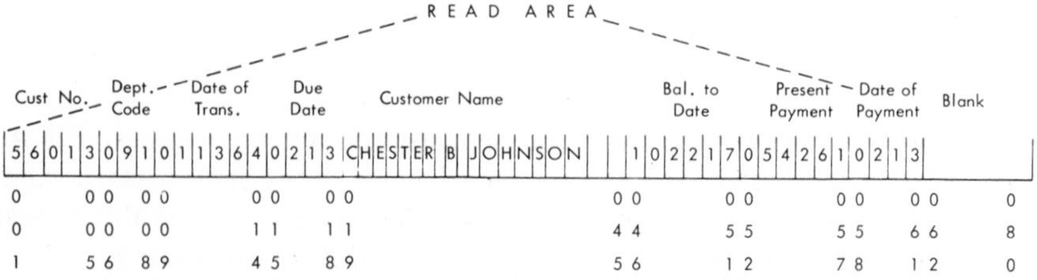

Fig. 22-21. The contents of the read area after subtraction of payments from previous balance is performed

MACHINE CYCLES—INSTRUCTION THREE. Like the first two instructions, instruction three goes through an I-phase and an E-phase. During the E-phase of instruction two, the I-address register was incremented by 7, the length of instruction two, showing address 0341, the address of instruction three. The computer finds letter M in 0341 which is loaded in the op-register. The next three characters (data address 061) are loaded in the A-address register, and data address 161 in the B-address register.

Assuming that the two word marks have been cleared, the computer begins moving the entire contents of the "read" area one digit at a time, beginning at address 061, to the "punch" area. That is, data in 061 are moved to 161 ("punch" area), data in 060 to 160, data in 059 to 159, and so forth, until every character stored in the "read" area is moved to its corresponding position in the "punch" area (Fig. 22-22).

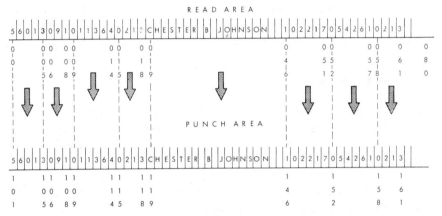

Fig. 22-22. Instruction three transfers contents of the read area to the corresponding number in the punch area before punching takes place in instruction four

MACHINE CYCLES—INSTRUCTION FOUR. The computer loads machine code 4, meaning "punch a card," from its address, 0348, into the op-register. This instruction causes all the characters moved into the "punch" area to be punched into a blank card by the "punch" end of the card reader. The machine stops automatically upon the detection of the last card.

LOOPING. The program presented in this chapter illustrates the cycle completed by the computer on each customer's account in an accounts receivable application. The computer is programmed to continue until the last account has been processed. This is done by instructing it to go back (loop or branch back) to the beginning of the program and execute each of the four instructions over again. This cycle is followed in processing the rest of the accounts. The instruction to branch the program is shown in Fig. 22-23.

Op. Code	I-Address
B	3 3 3

Fig. 22-23. Branching instruction

B stands for "branch," and 333 is the address of the first instruction of the program. The instruction address 333 is written in the A-field, because the A-field can be used to store *either* the data address, as we have seen in the "move" instruction, or the instruction address, as shown in the branch instruction above. Like the first four instructions, the branch instruction must also be programmed and stored in memory. Usually, its storage location will be one following the fourth instruction. In the illustration, it would then occupy position numbers 349 to 352.

Branching causes continuous processing until all the cards are read. The cycle described above is repeated as many times as there are accounts. In this way, an entire accounts receivable file containing thousands of accounts can be updated frequently, quickly, and inexpensively.

Compiler Language Programs [3]

Assembly languages, although better than machine-language programming (coding), are not as practical as the *higher-level languages.* Higher-level languages are more English-like or mathematically oriented than either the assembly or machine language.

The program that changes the higher-level language into machine language is called a *compiler.* A single statement in such a language may cause the *compilation* of a whole subroutine of instructions, and this is where it differs from assembly languages, in which one symbolic instruction caused the generation of one machine-language instruction.

The most popular scientific language is called FORTRAN (*FOR*mula *TRAN*slation) and the most popular business language is COBOL (*CO*mmon *B*usiness *O*riented *L*anguage). Quite a number of other higher-level languages are in fairly common use (ALGOL, NELIAC, JOVIAL, and SIMSCRIPT to name just a few), but FORTRAN and COBOL are by far the most commonly used. Another new language that is moving into some prominence is PL1 (*P*rogramming *L*anguage *1*) developed by the IBM Corporation. It is of special interest because it attempts to override the differences between scientific and business languages, and it can be used for both types of programming.

[3] The text and illustrations for the balance of this chapter (with the exception of the illustration on p. 379) are taken from J. A. Saxon and W. W. Steyer, *Basic Principles of Data Processing* (Englewood Cliffs, N.J.: Prentice-Hall, Inc., 1967) and reprinted by permission of the authors and the publisher.

Each computer has its own unique machine language. By this we mean *type* of computer, not each individual computer. Therefore, for a higher-level language to be operable on any particular type of computer, a compiler must be written for it.

Let us examine what this means a little more closely. If an installation has an IBM 1620 computer and the programmers wished to write FORTRAN programs to be run on this computer, the installation must obtain a FORTRAN compiler for the IBM 1620 computer. If another installation had a UNIVAC 1107 computer and they wanted to write FORTRAN programs, a FORTRAN compiler would be required for the UNIVAC 1107. This is because the machine language of the 1107 is entirely different from the machine language of the 1620. Each compiler must translate the original FORTRAN program (source program) into the language of the computer which will run the translated (object) program.

Although each different type of computer must have its own compiler, the source program written in FORTRAN (or one of the other higher-level languages) does not have to be rewritten to run on different computers. Usually only minor modifications are required plus a recompilation of the source program to the object language of the other computer.

This has a very important advantage. A great deal of programming effort is needed to produce operational runs that accomplish the data-processing requirements of an installation. If the programs are written in a higher-level language and the computer equipment is changed, the programs are still useful on the new equipment after recompilation. Otherwise years of effort and many thousands of dollars would be wasted, and all new programs would have to be written for the new equipment.

Special programs, such as compilers, are generally termed *software,* as opposed to *hardware,* which refers to actual computer equipment. In the past few years, software has become almost more important than hardware, and manuafacturers vie with each other to produce more and more sophisticated software packages to help sell their hardware.

The COBOL Language

The programs developed on the previous pages consisted of instructions that were made up for demonstration purposes but were similar to real machine-language and assembly-language instructions. The material to be covered in this and the following section is actually the way the languages are used.

COBOL programs are written in four separate and distinct parts, called *divisions.*

1. *Identification Division.* This division is used to identify the name of the programmer, title of the program, current date, and any pertinent

information about the process. It has a very specific format but is quite simple and needs no further explanation.

2. *Environment Division.* Since COBOL is written in the same manner for any computer, basic information about the machine configuration is described here. Each computer that has a COBOL compiler comes equipped with a special publication which spells out how the equipment is to be referenced in the program. This is also quite straightforward and needs no further amplification.

3. *Data Division.* Each kind of data used in the program is described in this division. All of the input and output files used in the program must also be defined in this division. The division is separated into two parts, *working storage* and *constant* sections. This is usually the first division to be written in the program, and a number of special rules must be followed. Although the data division is fairly detailed, assimilating the rules necessary to write the data division of a program is not too difficult.

4. *Procedure Division.* This division is the heart of the system. It describes the operations to be performed, and it is not oriented to any machine. It details what the program is expected to accomplish.

Usually, a special program-writing form is used. It is divided into eighty little blocks so that a key-punch operator can easily punch up cards from the work sheets used by the programmer. Fig. 22-24 is a sample COBOL work sheet. Note the eighty columns of information which correspond to the eighty columns of a card.

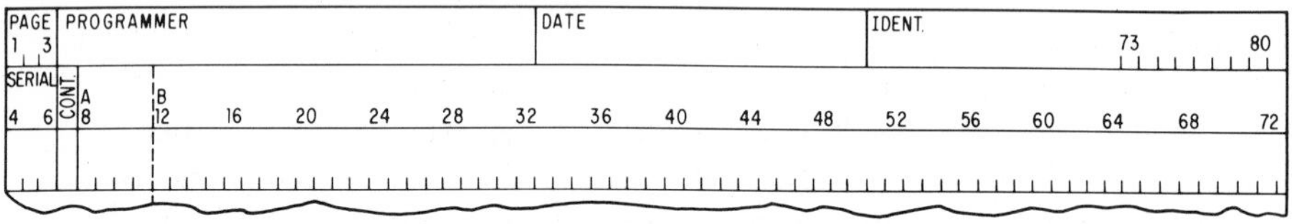

Fig. 22-24. COBOL work sheet

The programmer always prints (in capital letters) on the form to make it easier to read and because writing one character to a block in long hand is practically impossible.

Certain letters of the alphabet resemble numerics very closely. The key-punch operator must know, without doubt, exactly what the programmer desires. For this reason, a standardized method of printing has been adopted by most programmers. The letters *I, O, S,* and *Z* resemble very closely the numbers *1, 0, 5,* and *2.* Also, *U* and *V* are sometimes hard to tell apart. Therefore, the following method of printing these letters is suggested:

I   O   S   Z̸   U   V

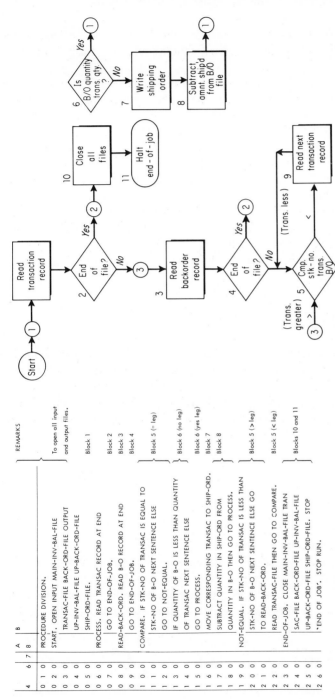

Fig. 22-25. Procedure division of a COBOL program and accompanying flow chart

4	6	7	8	B	REMARKS
0	1	0		PROCEDURE DIVISION.	
0	2	0		START. OPEN INPUT MAIN-INV-BAL-FILE	To open all input
0	3	0		TRANSAC-FILE BACK-ORD-FILE OUTPUT	and output files.
0	4	0		UP-INV-BAL-FILE UP-BACK-ORD-FILE	
0	5	0		SHIP-ORD-FILE.	Block 1
0	6	0		PROCESS. READ TRANSAC RECORD AT END	
0	7	0		GO TO END-OF-JOB.	Block 2
0	8	0		READ-BACK-ORD. READ B-O RECORD AT END	Block 3
0	9	0		GO TO END-OF-JOB.	Block 4
1	0	0		COMPARE. IF STK-NO OF TRANSAC IS EQUAL TO	
1	1	0		STK-NO OF B-O NEXT SENTENCE ELSE	Block 5 (= leg)
1	2	0		GO TO NOT-EQUAL.	
1	3	0		IF QUANTITY OF B-O IS LESS THAN QUANTITY	Block 6 (no leg)
1	4	0		OF TRANSAC NEXT SENTENCE ELSE	
1	5	0		GO TO PROCESS.	Block 6 (yes leg)
1	6	0		MOVE CORRESPONDING TRANSAC TO SHIP-ORD.	Block 7
1	7	0		SUBTRACT QUANTITY IN SHIP-ORD FROM	
1	8	0		QUANTITY IN B-O THEN GO TO PROCESS.	Block 8
1	9	0		NOT-EQUAL. IF STK-NO OF TRANSAC IS LESS THAN	
2	0	0		STK-NO OF B-O NEXT SENTENCE ELSE GO	Block 5 (> leg)
2	1	0		TO READ-BACK-ORD.	
2	2	0		READ TRANSAC-FILE THEN GO TO COMPARE.	Block 5 (< leg)
2	3	0		END-OF-JOB. CLOSE MAIN-INV-BAL-FILE TRAN	
2	4	0		SAC-FILE BACK-ORD-FILE UP-INV-BAL-FILE	Blocks 10 and 11
2	5	0		UP-BACK-ORD-FILE SHIP-ORD-FILE. STOP	
2	6	0		'END OF JOB'. STOP RUN.	

This program is courtesy of J.A. Saxon. COBOL: A Self-Instructional Manual. Prentice-Hall, Inc. Englewood Cliffs, N.J., 1963.

379

To identify the numeric zero from the letter *O,* some installations insist on a slash through the zero (ø), others prefer the slash through the letter (Ø).

Punctuation is extremely vital in COBOL. The omission of a period could cause the program not to run. Also, when names are used in several places in the program, the spelling must be very carefully observed since once a name is defined in the data division, no variation is permitted.

To demonstrate a COBOL program, the following flow chart will be used. Only the procedure division will be shown. Notice how easily one can read the program. With a little more careful examination, the program segments can be related to the individual blocks of the flow chart.

The sentences in the *compare* and *not-equal* paragraphs were separated to simplify the association of sentences with flow-chart blocks. Normally, no large blank spaces would be left.

The literal *end of job* on line 260 will print the words *end of job* on the display unit.

The FORTRAN Language

FORTRAN programming is used for the solution of scientific and mathematical problems. This language attempts to stay with normal mathematical notation as much as possible, but certain special rules must be observed.

For example, in normal algebraic notation *AB* means *A* times *B* (the times sign is implied). In FORTRAN, all arithmetic symbols (called *operators*) must be specifically shown.

Add	+
Subtract	−
Multiply	*
Divide	/
Exponent	**

A times *B* would have to be written A * B.

Another important point is the order of execution. If you were to write: A + B * C / D, you might mean: Add A + B, multiply the sum by C, and divide the product by D. But the computer works on a specific order of preference, and all formulas must be written with this order in mind.

1. Expressions enclosed in parentheses
2. Exponentiation
3. Multiply and divide
4. Add and subtract

All other things being equal, execution will be from left to right. To get the desired result for the formula above, it would have been written:

$$(A + B) * C / D.$$

FORTRAN has the ability to operate in either fixed-point or floating-point mode. Floating point is advantageous because the computer automatically places the decimal point. If there is a decimal point in your number, it is considered by the compiler to be a floating point; and, if there is no decimal point, it is a fixed-point number.

As in COBOL, or any other language, a number of rules must be learned. No shortcut method can be used. You must know the rules to use the language. For example, the equal sign has a special meaning in FORTRAN:

$$A = B + C$$

Replace the contents of *operand* A with the result of the calculation B + C. Equal, then, means *is replaced by* rather than *is equivalent to*.

The constants and variables used in a FORTRAN program are called *operands*. They are separated by the *operators* (+, −, *, and so forth) mentioned above.

Even as in COBOL, the writing of FORTRAN programs is accomplished on a special work sheet divided into eighty sections. This is used for ease in key punching the FORTRAN programs. Fig. 22-26 shows a sample of such a work sheet.

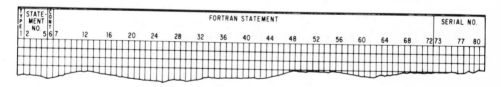

Fig. 22-26.   FORTRAN work sheet

A brief FORTRAN program will be demonstrated based on the following formula:

$$X = A + (B * C) ** D / (E + 16.0)$$

Assume that the data are on cards and the program will halt when the last card has been processed; also, that there is a special punch on the last card to identify it from the other cards. Fig. 22-27 shows the flow chart, and the program solution.

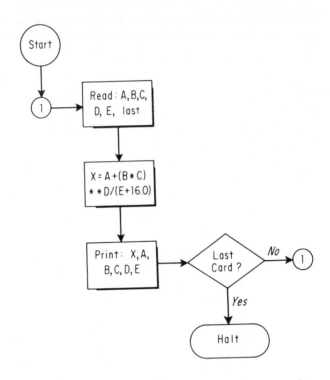

Program Solve   *Remarks*

```
10 READ 20, A, B, C, D, E, LAST
20 FORMAT (5 F 10.2, I 10)


   X = A + (B * C) ** D / (E + 16.0)
   PRINT 30, X, A, B, C, D, E
30 FORMAT (6 F 10.2)


   IF (LAST) 40, 10, 40
40 CONTINUE
   END
```

Read cards with format at 20.
Five fields, flt. pt., 10 place fields, two
  places to right of decimal; one field
  integer 10 places.
Formula.
Print, format at 30.
Output format, 6 fields, flt. pt., 10
  place fields, 2 decimal places.
Test for last card.
Continue to end if last card.

Fig. 22-27. Flow chart and program solution for FORTRAN program

Variable Versus Fixed Word-length Computers

Computers are of two types: (1) variable word-length, where there
is no limit to the size or number of characters making up a word in storage,
and (2) fixed word-length, where the number of characters making up a
word is fixed in length. The 1401 computer is a *variable* word-length ma-

chine. Each character in storage is individually addressable (has a specific address). Any character (represented by six or more bits) [4] can be pulled out of storage and processed with other characters through proper programming instructions (Fig. 22-28).

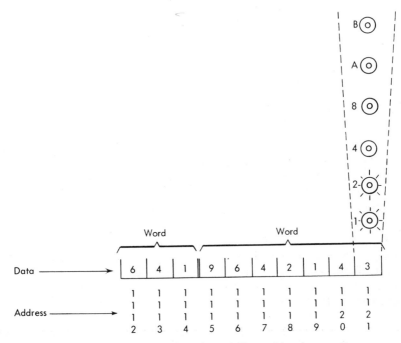

Fig. 22-28. Example of a variable word length

The second type of computer is the *fixed* word-length machine, where the number of characters comprising a word is fixed in length and is handled as a group. Each word has only one address, is picked up as a unit, and contains as many characters as every other word. For example, the numeric characters in Fig. 22-29 make up two five-character words. The first word is referenced by only one address, 1425, and the second word is referenced by only one address, 1430.

---

[4] The term *byte* is used to represent an arbitrary number of bits. It is a part of a computer's internal function as it deals with input/output devices during data transmission routines. Programmers refer to data being transmitted from an input device to core storage in terms of so many bytes, rather than bits as individual elements. For example, assuming an assignment of nine bits per byte, and a fixed word length of thirty-six bits, the data transmission rate by an auxiliary device to core storage is in increments of four bytes per word.

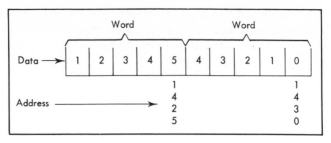

Fig. 22-29. Example of a fixed word length

GLOSSARY OF TERMS

ADDRESS: A name, number, or label which identifies a location in storage.

ASSEMBLY PROGRAM: A computer program which translates symbolic input data into machine instructions.

BIT: An abbreviation of "binary digit"; a character in a binary number.

BRANCHING: Selecting one of two or more alternative paths under control of a routine.

BYTE: A group of binary numbers, generally operated on as a unit.

COBOL: *CO*mmon *B*usiness *O*riented *L*anguage; a coding language by which business data-processing procedures may be described in a standard form.

CODE: (1) A set of rules used to convert data from one representation to another. (2) The assignment of meaning to a character or a group of characters.

COMPUTER MEMORY: The part of a computer which stores the program and holds intermediate results until needed.

COMPILER: A computer program which performs the translating function and replaces certain input information with a series of instructions (subroutines).

CONTROL UNIT: The part of a computer which determines the interpretation and execution of instructions in a logical sequence.

DATA REGISTER: A hardware device used to store data until needed.

DIGIT MODIFIER: A part of an instruction used to strengthen the operation code.

FIELD: A number of consecutive columns reserved for a particular purpose.

FIXED WORD-LENGTH COMPUTER: Used to refer to a computer in which the word addressed always consists of a fixed number of characters or digits.

FORTRAN: *FOR*mula *TRAN*slator; a programming language which can be translated into algebraic notation.

HARDWARE: A colloquial term applied to the mechanical and electronic features of a data-processing system.

INSTRUCTION FORMAT: Allocation of characters of a computer instruction to do specific functions.

INSTRUCTION REGISTER: A hardware device that stores the instruction currently governing a computer operation.

MACHINE LANGUAGE: A set of instructions written in a language directly understandable to the computer.

MNEMONICS: Elements (terms) which assist the memory.

OPERAND: A quantity which is operated upon in an instruction. It may be the address portion of an instruction or the location of the next instruction. Also the constants and variables used in a FORTRAN program.

OPERATION CODE: A code that represents specific operations. Synonymous with *instruction code*.

OPERATOR: The *what to do* part of an instruction; for example, the arithmetic symbol in a FORTRAN program.

STORED PROGRAM: A series of instructions stored in a computer to direct it in performing specific operations.

SOFTWARE: A colloquial term applied to programs or routines which extend the capabilities of a computer; for example, assemblers, compilers, subroutines, and the like.

SYMBOLIC PROGRAM: A set of instructions written in a language using mnemonic codes.

VARIABLE WORD-LENGTH COMPUTER: Used to refer to a computer in which the number of characters or digits addressed vary by the data or instruction.

WORD: A number of characters which have one address and are treated as one unit.

WORD MARK: Used in programming to define the length of a field.

REVIEW QUESTIONS

1. What is the function of the control unit? Explain how it manipulates the operation of the complete system.
2. What is a stored program? Explain the difference between the control unit and the stored program.
3. List and explain the necessary steps for program planning.
4. What is the importance of the self-operational feature of a computer?
5. Why must the programmer keep track of the location of data in storage?
6. What is a word mark? Why is it used in programming? When present in a field, in which position is it located?
7. Distinguish the difference between an address and data.
8. What is a block diagram? Why do we use a block diagram?
9. Explain the input/output symbol, the processing symbol, and the logic symbol.
10. What is meant by the term *branching?* The term *debugging?*
11. Differentiate between symbolic language and machine language. Which language is usually written first?
12. What is an operation code? An operand? Give an example of each.

13. Describe the two- and three-address instruction formats.

14. For what are the A- and B-fields used? Which field is also used to hold an instruction address?

15. What are the three reserved areas in a 1401 computer? For what are they reserved? Briefly explain each area.

16. If card output is desired, to which area in the central processing unit must the data be moved first?

17. What is the difference between a data address and an instruction address?

18. Explain in detail the instruction phase. When does the execution, E-phase, start?

19. What is the primary difference between variable and fixed word-length computers?

20. What is a compiler language? In what respect is it different from assembly language? Machine language?

21. What is the difference between software and hardware?

22. What is COBOL? What are the main divisions in COBOL? Name the two most important divisions.

23. What is an operator?

24. What is FORTRAN programming? Show the FORTRAN symbols for five different operators, and name each symbol.

25. List the order of execution of FORTRAN formulas.

chapter

23

BANKING
APPLICATION
Proof of
Irregular-payment Loans

ALTHOUGH THE COVERAGE of the basic ideas explained in Part III of this text is generally comprehensive, at this point we should benefit from a study of the following case. It illustrates clearly the steps leading to the development of a program in a banking application, using a 1401 computer system. Although most programs written for business applications are lengthy and include advanced programming techniques, the brief application presented in this chapter is a simplified program but one which illustrates the basic ideas with helpful clarity.

One of the chief services of a commercial bank is the extension of loans of various types. Loans are ordinarily paid in a given number of equal monthly installments. For example, a loan for $1,800 extended to customer A can be paid back in six installments at $300.00 each installment, or twelve payments at $150.00 each payment, or eighteen payments at $100.00 each payment, and so forth. No longer unusual, however, is it for a customer to dictate his own terms with regard to the method and amount of payment of the loan. A bank finds it only practical, and in some cases profitable, to arrange for "irregular" payments of loans by certain customers.

The following is a step-by-step description of the development of a program constructed for the purpose of verifying payment coupons (the total of which equals the amount of the loan) before they are mailed to the customer to accompany his future payments.

Background Information

On January 1 Mr. Julius Wilson, a senior programmer at a local firm, walked into the main office of a commercial bank and applied for a personal loan of $950.00. His eighteen-year-old daughter, Caroline, had recently been accepted by a Midwestern university to begin her undergraduate study in the department of business administration. Because her application for a scholarship was not favorably considered, her father decided to secure enough funds for payment of her expenses during the first year.

When the application for the loan was approved the next day, Mr. Wilson asked the bank to arrange the payments in eleven monthly installments, beginning in February. The interest on the loan plus other charges increased the amount due from $950.00 to $1,000.00 (Fig. 23-1). The loan card is shown in Fig. 23-2. Mr. Wilson's method of payment is irregular, in that he wishes to repay the loan in eleven installments of unequal amounts, instead of the regular method of repaying in six, twelve, eighteen, twenty-four, thirty, or thirty-six monthly installments of equal amounts.

Payment No.	Due Date	Amount Due
01	Feb. 28	$ 90.00
02	Mar. 31	50.00
03	Apr. 30	90.00
04	May 31	90.00
05	June 30	90.00
06	July 31	90.00
07	Aug. 31	90.00
08	Sept. 30	90.00
09	Oct. 31	90.00
10	Nov. 30	90.00
11	Dec. 31	140.00

Total amount due $1,000.00

Fig. 23-1.   Mr. Wilson's payment schedule

Various reasons exist for the irregular payment of a loan. In the case of Mr. Wilson, his living expenses in March go up slightly on account of the Easter holiday. For him to be permitted to pay only $50.00 at the end of that month is a helpful break. However, he is in a good position to pay the balance of the loan ($140.00) on December 31, because his firm pays its usual yearly Christmas bonus to its employees during that month. Therefore, the bank approved Wilson's terms and sent the necessary data to the consumer credit department for processing.

The first step required in the processing of Mr. Wilson's loan is the conversion of loan detail from the form which he signed to a punched

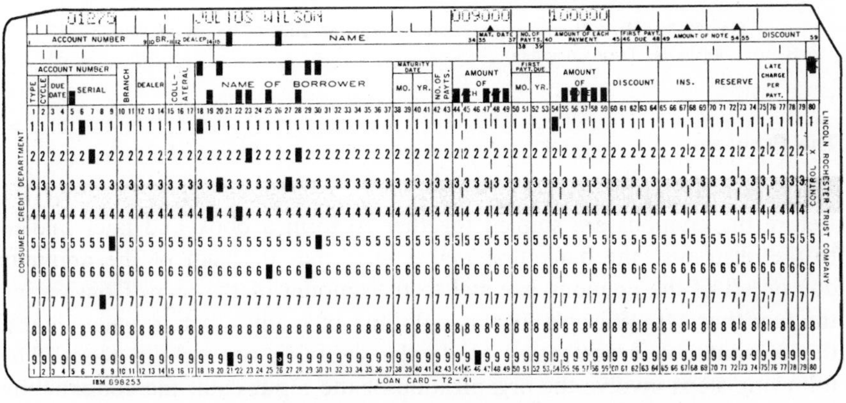

Fig. 23-2.   Mr. Wilson's loan card (*Lincoln Rochester Trust Company*)

card, called the *loan card* (Fig. 23-2). The loan card is punched with a serial number assigned to the specific loan, the name of the customer, the amount of each payment, and the amount of the loan (including interest and service charge). The $50.00 payment in March and the $140.00 payment in December are treated as exceptions in comparison to the majority of the payments represented by $90.00 each payment. These exceptions are dealt with in a different program when the "balance outstanding" on the loan is determined.

Next, the key-punch operator punches eleven payment coupons with Mr. Wilson's account number (01275) and the amount due ($90.00). The coupons are fed into an interpreter which is wired to read the holes in the coupon card and to print their meaning in the proper boxes on the top of it. Fig. 23-3 shows the payment No. 01 coupon with the account number and the amount due.

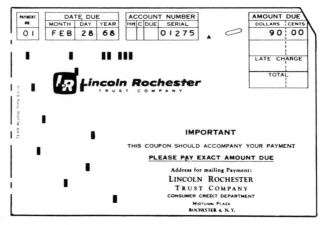

Fig. 23-3. Mr. Wilson's payment No. 01 coupon card (*Courtesy of Lincoln Rochester Trust Company*)

The Problem

Before the coupons are stapled together to form a book and later mailed to the customer, the bank first makes sure that the sum of the amounts due on all of the coupons is equal to the amount of the loan. Considering the fact that Mr. Wilson's loan is only one of many other irregular loans, the computer is programmed to do the verifying on each of them. The following steps involve the organization of the input data, the construction of a program to "proof" the irregular-payment loans, and debugging and testing the program.

Data Organization

In order to prepare the input data for verification by the computer, the collator is used to merge behind each loan card all the coupons belonging to it. The loan cards are fed into the primary hopper and the coupon cards are fed into the secondary hopper. The control panel of the collator is wired so that a comparison is made between the account number of the loan card and that of the coupon. The result, in the case of Mr. Wilson's loan, is shown in Fig. 23-4.

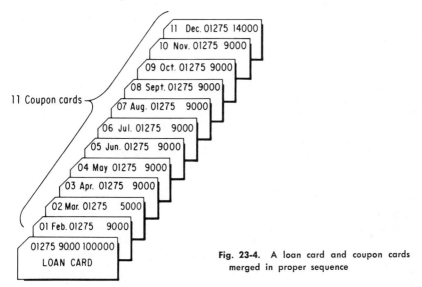

11 Coupon cards

11 Dec. 01275 14000
10 Nov. 01275 9000
09 Oct. 01275 9000
08 Sept. 01275 9000
07 Aug. 01275 9000
06 Jul. 01275 9000
05 Jun. 01275 9000
04 May 01275 9000
03 Apr. 01275 9000
02 Mar. 01275 5000
01 Feb. 01275 9000

01275 9000 100000
LOAN CARD

Fig. 23-4. A loan card and coupon cards merged in proper sequence

The Development Stage

Up to this point, the key punch, the interpreter, and the collator have been used for the preparation of the data for input for a computer application. A program should be written, next, to instruct the computer to do the following steps:

1. To read the first card (the loan card). Each loan card should have an X punch in a specific column to distinguish it (being a loan card) from the coupon cards following it. An X in column eighty is arbitrarily chosen in this application. The coupon cards should not have an X punched in column eighty. The program should include an instruction which would cause the computer to halt in the event an X punch is not detected in column eighty.
2. Assuming that the first card is read and an X punch is detected in column eighty, the computer is to move the amount of the note field

(columns 54-59) to a storage area. The card will remain there until the subsequent payment-coupon cards pertaining to the loan are read and the sum of the amount due on them is compared for equality with the amount of the loan. The serial number of the loan (columns 5-9) is also placed in a specific location for comparison with the serial number on the coupon card to make sure that the coupon card is related to the loan card.

3. Next, coupon-payment number 01 is read. The account number is compared with that of the loan card serial number. If they are equal, this means that the coupon is a payment coupon for the loan card placed in storage. The amount due is added to a counter. The amount due from all other coupon cards is also added to the same counter.

4. All coupons belonging to a specific loan card are added to the counter. The next loan card, having a different serial number, will cause the computer to ignore it momentarily. It compares the sum of the counter, to which the amount due from all coupon cards bearing the same serial number are added, to the amount of the loan. If they are the same or equal, this would mean that the coupons contain a total equal to that of the loan. In the case of Mr. Wilson, the amount due in his eleven coupon cards should add up to $1,000.00. However, if they are not equal, then a subtraction is performed by the computer. The discrepancy, along with the serial number of the customer, is printed. This can be shown later to the key-punch operator for the purpose of alerting her to the mistake(s) made.

The Block Diagram

The foregoing four steps can be performed by a computer if a suitable program is constructed and eventually coded into machine language. But first the programmer would draw a block diagram in order to have a visual means of expressing a solution to the problem of "proofing the irregular-payment loans."

The block diagram shows all the input, processing, and output details pertaining to the application in question. The programmer should, at the block-diagramming stage, attempt to modify and otherwise prepare the steps as correctly as possible. Any logical errors should be eliminated here, because by doing so less time is needed for debugging the program at the remaining stages.

The Coding Stage

The common procedure followed by most programmers is to write the program instructions in language other than the machine (absolute) language. The language used in the preparation of this program is referred to as the *Symbolic Programming System* (SPS). As was explained in Chapter 22, the use of mnemonics or letters or codes that aid the memory constitute the approach followed in the use of the symbolic language. For example, letter *R* stands for *read, A* for *add, W* for *print,* and so forth. Most programmers prepare a program first in language such as the symbolic language and next use an automatic program coder (or a compiler) to convert all the instructions into machine language.

Standard forms are used in writing instructions in symbolic language. Fig. 23-5 is an IBM 1401 Symbolic Programming System coding sheet.

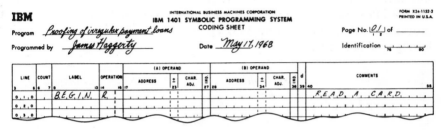

Fig. 23-5. The IBM 1401 SPS coding sheet

It is divided into various vertical areas making up the necessary parts of a complete instruction. Horizontally, the SPS coding sheet contains twenty-six lines, each of which is used to write one instruction which will be punched in a single card. Therefore, the maximum number of instructions which can be written on any given coding sheet is twenty-six. If the program consists of thirty instructions, for instance, another sheet (marked page *02*) would be used for writing the last four instructions. Fig. 23-5 is a coding sheet showing the standard headings and the first three lines of the SPS sheet. Instruction one of the symbolic program (Fig. 23-6) is also shown.

In an attempt to explain the subsequent steps in this computer application, a brief description of the parts of the SPS coding sheet pertaining to the application should be helpful.

On the top of the sheet, the title of the program, the name of the programmer, the date at which the program is written, and the page number are written. This information identifies the specific program in such a way that, when filed, the program would be unique in relationship to the other programs.

The extreme left-hand heading in the main frame shows the line number. Each line when filled in represents one instruction. The line number occupies three columns when punched in a punched card. They are columns three through five. The rest of the vertical columns on the sheet correspond to the card columns to be punched.

The *count* columns (columns six and seven) are filled with the number of characters that the declarative instruction on that line will occupy. The *label* section (columns eight through thirteen) is used for the purpose of writing a word description of the instructions on that line. Because, in symbolic programming, addresses are used to specify the location of any given instruction, the label becomes useful in that it stands for the address of that instruction. When an assembly program converts the instruction from symbolic to machine language, it replaces the label with an address (called "instruction address") which will identify the instruction in the program. In the case of the first instruction, its operation codes were stored in location number 333 in the primary storage, for instance. In this case, then, the word *BEGIN* is replaced by that address (333) in the machine-language deck. If the word *BEGIN* is used elsewhere in the program, it is also replaced by 333. To clarify this point, assume the following symbolic instructions:

Label	*Op. Code*	*A/I Address*	*B-Address*	*d*
BEGIN	R			
	:			
	B	BEGIN		

The first instruction simply means "read a card." The second instruction is interpreted as "branch" to an instruction that has a label *begin,* or back to the first instruction. When these two instructions are converted into machine language, assuming that program storage begins in 333, they are converted as follows:

Instruction Location	*Op. Code*	*A/I Address*	*B-Address*	*d*
333	1			
334	B	333		

Because the word *begin* in the symbolic program identified the location of the first instruction, and because the letter *R* (converted to *1* in machine language) is stored in memory location 333, the word *BEGIN* in the A/I address of the second instruction is automatically converted to 333. The second instruction means: "branch to 333 or to the first instruction to read another card."

The *A-operand* section (columns seventeen through twenty-seven) contains the A-address information. For the purposes of the application, it would suffice to say that columns seventeen through twenty-two of the A-operand are used for writing the A-address of the instruction. The *B-operand* section (columns twenty-eight through thirty-eight) contains the B-address information. Columns twenty-eight through thirty-three are used for writing the B-address of the instruction.

Column thirty-nine is reserved for a digit modifier code which, when present, can strengthen the operation of code by causing the computer to branch, halt, or do other required functions. In this application, we want the computer to halt if an X is not detected when a loan card is read. This conditional storage, when coded properly, constitutes the D-modifier; and in the above example, upon the failure of the computer to detect the presence of X in column eighty in the loan card, it halts immediately.

The *comments* section (columns forty through fifty-five) can be used for printing any informative comments which would tend to clarify an instruction. The programmer should comment on the instructions which seem clear only to him. If another programmer continues this operation or tries to complete the program begun by the first programmer, the absence of comments can make the job difficult to complete or to process. The author heard of an unfortunate incident in a case which involved the preparation of a complex program for a large business application. Two programmers spent several weeks constructing the program and finally succeeded in applying it to process the desired data according to the plan. A week later, they accepted a more attractive position with a competitor. Much to the surprise of management, they left behind a program with no comments, explanation, or any indication of how it was constructed. When the program needed modification as a result of some changes in the input data, the newly hired programmer preferred to rewrite the program from the beginning. This, naturally, duplicated the work of the former programmers unnecessarily, not to mention the delay in data processing and the expense incurred as a result of such an avoidable mistake.

Before the program is converted from a symbolic to machine language, each of the instructions on the SPS coding sheet is punched in a card. Fig. 23-6 shows instruction one punched in an IBM card. Therefore,

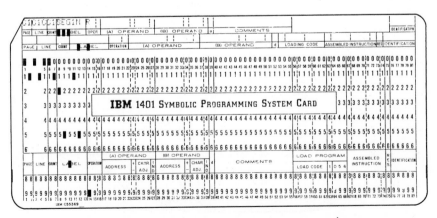

Fig. 23-6. An IBM symbolic programming system card

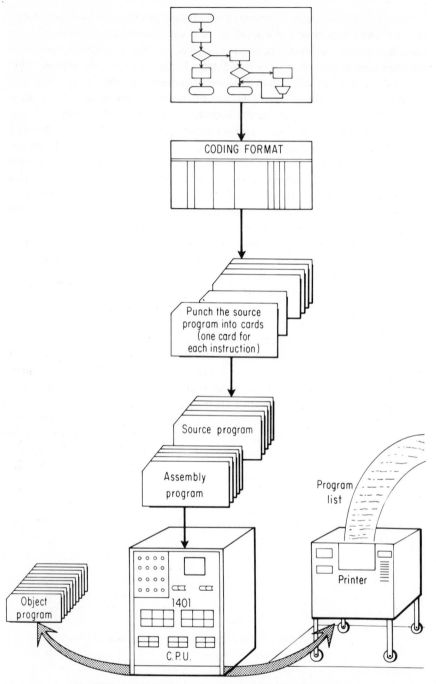

Fig. 23-7. A schematic showing the steps in the coding process

the number of cards representing a symbolic deck should be equal to the number of instructions written on the coding sheet.

Translating a symbolic deck (source program) into machine language is done through the *assembly program*. Because the object is to arrive at a deck of cards containing the instructions in a machine language, the latter deck is referred to as the *object program* (Fig. 23-7).

The assembly deck is placed in the card reader first, and behind it is fed the symbolic deck. In the punched end, a number of blank cards are fed into the punch hopper. The assembly program is not a machine. It is a deck of cards each of which is coded in such a way that the instructions contained tell the computer, in machine language, how to convert a symbolic instruction. When the card reader is started by the depression of the load button, the assembly-program instructions are transferred and loaded into the computer. Next, the symbolic deck is read, one card (one instruction) at a time. The result is the punching of a blank card with the symbolic instruction on the left side and the machine-language equivalent on the right side. (See Fig. 23-8.)

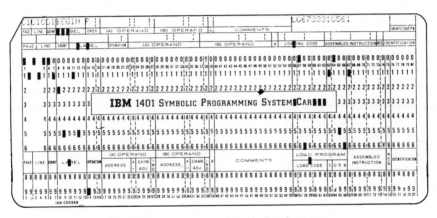

Fig. 23-8. A program card in absolute language

Post-listing

When all the cards are finally punched with machine language, they are fed behind a special assembler for the purpose of post-listing them through the use of the printer. For the purpose of convenience, the most practical method is to interpret and check the program in printed form rather than from punched cards (Fig. 23-9). At this stage, the programmer can make any necessary modifications or check on any phase of the program.

PG	L/N	CT	LABEL	OP	A OPERAND	B OPERAND	D	LOC	INSTRUCTION COMMENTS
1	010	1	BEGIN	R				0333	1
1	011	8		BWZ	GOON	C080	K	0334	V 349 080 K
1	012	7		H	0001	C001		0342	. 001 001
1	020	4	GOON	SW	0005			0349	, 005
1	030	7		MCW	0009	STR		0353	M 009 512
1	040	4		SW	0054			0360	, 054
1	050	7		MCW	0059	ACCUM		0364	M 059 501
1	060	1	START	R				0371	1
1	070	8		BWZ	TOTAL	C080	K	0372	V 410 080 K
1	080	7		SW	0038	CC44		0380	, 038 044
1	090	7		C	0042	STR		0387	C 042 512
1	100	5		B	TOTAL		/	0394	B 410 /
1	110	7		A	0049	CTR		0399	A 049 507
1	130	4		B	START			0406	B 371
1	140	7	TCTAL	S	CTR	ACCUM		0410	S 507 501
1	142	4		S	CTR			0417	S 507
1	145	7		MZ	0081	CTR		0421	Y 081 507
1	150	7		MZ	0081	ACCUM		0428	Y 081 501
1	160	7		C	ACCUM	ZERO		0435	C 501 518
1	170	5		B	GOON		S	0442	B 349 S
1	180	7		MCW	ACCUM	C220		0447	M 501 220
1	190	7		MCW	STR	C208		0454	M 512 208
2	010	1		W				0461	2
2	020	4		CS	0280			0462	/ 280
2	022	4		S	ACCUM			0466	S 501
2	024	7		MZ	0081	ACCUM		0470	Y 081 501
2	025	8		BWZ	GOON	C080	K	0477	V 349 080 K
2	040	7	ERROR	H	0002	C002		0489	. 002 002
2	060	6	ACCUM	DCW	*			0501	
2	070	6	CTR	DCW	*			0507	
2	080	5	STR	DCW	*			0512	
2	090	6	ZERO	DCW	*		C00000	0518	
2	100			ENC	BEGIN				/ 333 080

33 CARDS

Fig. 23-9. Post-listing of the program from the machine language cards

If the program appears to be in good order, it is tested: it is loaded into the computer, and then data cards are fed into the card reader for processing. The results obtained from the computer are checked against those arrived at either by the use of another system or by a manual system. If they are the same, the program is found to be in good processing order. Otherwise, further modification(s) or debugging should be performed.

chapter
24

SYSTEM
ANALYSIS AND DESIGN

THE TERM *system* is generally referred to as the result of dovetailing all the operations, one with another, to make the firm a productive business organization. The term *systems design or systems study,* as commonly used, rarely refers to this meaning, however, but is, instead, used to refer to any *disciplined framework of reference which requires proceeding in an orderly fashion to accomplish the work demanded by an activity and insure that the objectives of the activity support the objectives of the firm in the best possible way.* Hence, "systems" is used in this chapter in a broad sense and describes the firm's activities in terms of a system made up of sub-systems.

The basic activities, or functions, that characterize all firms are: (1) production, (2) marketing, (3) accounting, (4) finance, and (5) management of men, money, materials, and equipment. The first two are sometimes referred to as *principal activities,* the latter three as *supportive activities.* Branching off from these broad basic classifications are activities that reinforce the work of each specialized class or function. Hence, a shipping and receiving department reinforces the work of the marketing activity as well as the work of the production activity and the accounting activity. An employment office reinforces the work of the personnel activity as well as the work of all other activities, and so forth. If an activity is described as a system making up an integral part of the firm, then the reinforcing activities may be described as *subsystems.* Subsystems, thus, make up the system.

The Need for a Data-processing System

As we saw in Chapter 3, a subsystem is the organization of the required manual and machine-related procedures for generating the results of data in connection with a given project. Any application must be worked out in a systematic form if the data produced are to be meaningful. While one may logically assume that the amount of data to be processed is dependent upon the size of the organization, companies of all sizes find themselves faced with the necessity for processing data at regular intervals. A large department store, for example, processes data involving thousands of customer accounts daily. A small shoe repair shop checks the quantity and the sale price of each material on hand at least once a week. Regardless of the frequency with which it is done, and the volume involved, however, manipulation of data in an orderly and logical manner requires the development of disciplined framework to guide men in reaching a desired objective.

Primary Functions of a Data-processing System

A data-processing system serves two primary functions: first, it creates data files with respect to a specific organizational activity; and, second, it allows for extraction, manipulation, and reporting of any part of a file of data requested, that is, file maintenance.

Creation of Data Files

In a manual system, hand-posted cards constitute a file. In an electro-mechanical system (such as the window-posting machine used by bank tellers), machine-posted standard-sized documents, for example savings books, constitute a data file.[1] In a punched-card system, a deck of punched cards containing specific account information make up a data file, while in an electronic system, a set of magnetic-tape reels storing specific data are referred to as data files.

File Maintenance

The second function served by a system is purposive extraction, manipulation, and reporting of any part of the data in a file, when necessary. This is referred to as *file maintenance*. File maintenance is necessary because of the day-to-day changes that take place in the records of an organization. A department store, for instance, in handling its accounts receivable, has to update the accounts of all customers to allow for: (1) payments against their outstanding balances, or (2) increases in the amounts owed because of additional purchases on credit. Likewise, the data in the file of a payroll system must be updated to account for changes in the status of current employees and to provide details on new employees. File maintenance requires updating routine data because the information is used to produce significant output data, such as payroll checks.

The Meaning of Systems Procedure

In order to produce the desired output, procedural routines must be set up. For the purpose of this discussion, a *procedure* is defined as an orderly way of handling a task. It comprises all steps required to accomplish a particular job. The illustrations of procedures presented in earlier chapters regarding payroll and daily payments of installment loans involve specific,

---

[1] A *file* is defined as a collection of data records, each consisting of information regarding a specific activity (for example, accounts receivable).

detailed steps performed in logical and sequential order, culminating in the production of a desired output.

To further illustrate systems procedures, assume that two weeks after the beginning of the school quarter (or semester), you have decided to drop a course from your schedule. Upon making this decision, you are likely to be instructed by, or be handed, a written outline from your advisor, prepared by the registrar, describing the steps you must take to drop the course. The *system* set up by the registrar might be made up of the following *procedure:*

1. Pick up a drop slip form from the registrar.
2. Fill out the details (such as course number, department number offering the course, course title, number of credit hours, and so forth).
3. Have your advisor sign the card.
4. Withdraw the course card from the instructor teaching the course.
5. Submit the drop slip and the course card to the registrar.
6. Pay a fee (if required).

The Role of the Systems Analyst

Systems analysis and design is a team effort, requiring that team members discuss together the problem(s) at hand for more effective results. Their work involves some combination of: (1) identifying the objective(s) of the system; (2) determining the system's requirements; and (3) designing the sequential pattern to be used in carrying them out. Stated somewhat differently, the role of systems analysis is a combination of designating the data to be used (data collection); showing how it is to be handled (data analysis); and creating the routine pattern to be used in attaining the objective (systems design).

The systems analyst is the key figure in the systems concept. He directs those in charge of developing the procedures for achieving desired results; designates which of the management techniques presently used —for example, program evaluation and review technique (PERT)—are to be used to inform management of the status of the information system; explores new techniques for designing a more effective system; and keeps himself current regarding the capabilities and cost of different types of equipment on the market. He must justify the need for current reports, eliminate any unnecessary procedures, and switch people from routine to creative roles insofar as this is possible.

Identify the Objectives (Output) of the System

Systems objectives such as smoother operation, more prompt reports, and improved economy of operation are usually identified through examining:

(1) the type of information expected from the system; (2) the reportorial format in which it should be presented; and (3) the time between collection of raw data and the date on which the results of their processing are to be reported.

Identifying the objectives of a system is synonymous with defining a problem. In studying a given problem, the analyst must distinguish between "problems" and "symptoms" as he gathers data from various departments. For example, a "bottleneck" *problem* of the shipping and accounting departments in handling large numbers of orders during the last few days of each month might turn out to be a *symptom* of the *real problem* which may be caused by salesmen withholding orders because they figure it is better to place them all at once instead of as they are received. An analyst must discover, therefore, what the actual problem is through detailed evaluation of each activity before he makes a decision as to why the present system is not accomplishing its objectives satisfactorily. In the example given, the system functioned imperfectly because the procedure followed by the salesmen interfered with the objective of smoothing out operations so customers could receive efficient service on their orders. To accomplish all of the system's objectives, the salesmen must be instructed to change their procedures in handling the orders they receive.

Data collection

Data collection is done by means of *written documents* or *interviews*. In carrying out this phase, the systems analyst must determine the sources in the organization which make the data available, since the sources of data vary depending on the type of information demanded. The personnel department creates data on employees such as their qualifications, academic and practical backgrounds, ages, aptitudes, and the like. The accounting department builds up data in connection with material costs, taxes, packing and shipping costs, and operating expenses. The sales department creates information regarding the volume of sales, behavior and attitude of clients, and so forth. The production department is the source of information on production planning, production procedures, material handling, and quality control. The systems analyst is, of course, dependent on the departments involved for the information he needs in any specific case.

Data collection through interviews is a specialized field. Unlike written documents, people are bundles of emotions, possessing high degrees of sensitivity. The analyst can obtain desired information from members of the organization only when an atmosphere of mutual trust prevails. He must avoid all appearances of being a "snooper," by making clear what he must know and why he must have the information he is after. He must be detached and objective about what he is doing and not become emotionally involved over any difficulties he may face in doing it.

In interviewing, the interviewer faces the possibility that interviewees will give him the answers which they feel would please him. For this reason, he should be able to differentiate between *opinion* and *fact*. If the employee who is being interviewed is resentful toward the current system, the interview, to him, is an opportunity to air the reasons for his hostility. In this case, the interviewer should encourage the interviewee to suggest improvements rather than to voice adverse criticism only.

Structural information

To summarize the first phase of systems analysis, a systems analyst's first function is to understand thoroughly the problem to which he must find a solution (for example, increasing sales volume by 20 per cent, preventing expensive bottlenecks, or realizing a specific percentage return on investment). He must understand also the attitudes and philosophies that dominate management in realizing its objectives, as well as details connected with the current system. This would suggest gathering structural

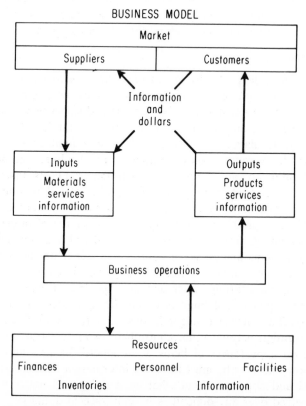

Fig. 24-1. Basic elements of structural information (*IBM F20-8150 Basic System Study Guide*)

information describing the interaction between the business organization's external environment and its resources. Fig. 24-1 emphasizes the three basic elements connected with structural information: (1) the company's outputs, in terms of its products and markets; (2) its inputs, in terms of materials and supplies; and (3) its resources (finances, personnel, facilities, and information). Structural information helps the systems analyst to acquire a broader understanding of the organization involved which in turn helps him in performing the system design work ahead.

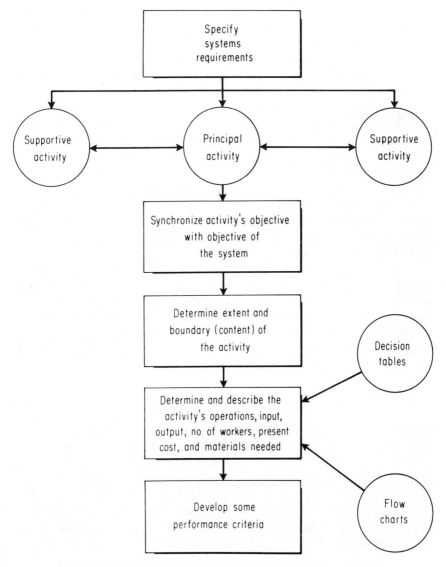

Fig. 24-2. The elements involved in determining the system's requirements

In addition to the foregoing, we should stress that the systems analyst does not set, but rather defines for management a set of meaningful goals on which agreement can be reached. When the goals are defined to everyone's satisfaction, the analyst is free to begin the work outlined on the following pages.

Determine and Define the System's Requirements

Once the objectives (output) of the system have been determined, the next step to be taken is determining what the system is required to do, via a study geared to finding out *how* (procedure), *who,* and *what* current work is being done. The study examines the input data at hand, the data files, the type of information necessary for their up-to-date maintenance, the output data being produced by the present system, and the physical and informational resources it must use.

This phase results in a plan: (1) specifying the primary characteristics of the proposed new system, (2) specifying all related supportive or reinforcing activities; and (3) indicating the inputs, outputs, and human, financial, and physical resources of the principal activity needed to better the present system or replace it with a new one (Fig. 24-2). It is highly recommended, then, that keen evaluation and, if necessary, modification of the present *goals* be made before modifications of the procedures making up the activities, or the development of new ones, are executed. In other words, do not "change for the sake of change" but change only for the sake of meeting the overall objectives of the firm.

Before concluding the second phase, we should remember that no system design is considered adequate without prior specification of some performance criteria which the new system is expected to achieve, followed by specification of ways of measuring these criteria. Once the performance criteria are specified, the system designer should be in a position to design a system which best satisfies the demands of the organization and maximizes the gains the system produces.

Tools used by the analyst

SYSTEMS AND PROCEDURES FLOW CHARTS. One of two tools used by a systems analyst in organizing and describing the decision logic of his findings (that is, outlining the flow of data and operations) is the systems and procedures flow chart. Like a computer block diagram, the systems and procedures flow chart presents in a logical sequence the procedures which make up the application of the system under consideration and is used to show the application of manual, mechanical, and/or computer operations to the processing of the data generated. The symbols used are standard and are shown in Fig. 24-3.

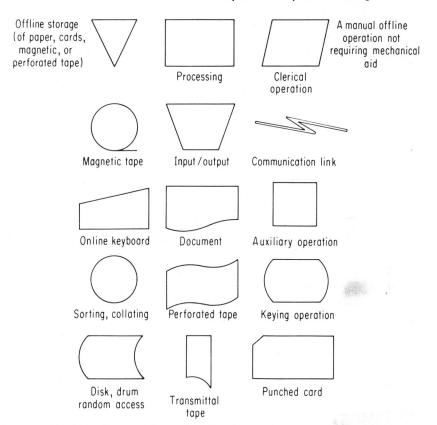

Offline storage
(of paper, cards,
magnetic, or
perforated tape)

Processing

Clerical
operation

A manual offline
operation not
requiring mechanical
aid

Magnetic tape

Input / output

Communication link

Online keyboard

Document

Auxiliary operation

Sorting, collating

Perforated tape

Keying operation

Disk, drum
random access

Transmittal
tape

Punched card

Fig. 24-3. Systems and procedures flow-chart symbols, IBM template form
X 20-8020

One of the drawbacks of the flow chart is that there is no standard method of learning its construction. Furthermore, during the process, a programmer often finds himself under strain with a long list of ideas and data, most of which are directly interrelated. The drawback is further compounded by the fact that flow charting involves other personnel in the department. Communication problems and the lack of speed and accuracy of related data acquisition could be significant.

DECISION TABLES. The other tool used by a systems analyst in describing cause-effect relationships is a decision table. A decision table is a documentation technique which is considered as effective, if not more so, than a flow chart. It provides a more concise and simpler form of data analysis than the flow chart. It was introduced to data-processing analysts about 1962, probably because of the limitations of the flow-charting techniques.

A decision table is divided into an upper left section (called *condition stub*) which sets forth the conditions that may exist and a lower left section (called *action stub*) which outlines the action to be taken to meet each condition (Fig. 24-4).

Condition stub	Condition entry
Action stub	Action entry

Fig. 24-4. The elements of a decision table

The right part of a decision table is also divided into an upper section, called the *condition entry,* and a lower section, called the *action entry.* Other details involve: (1) the availability of a number of columns in the condition-entry section, each representing a condition (an alternative plan); and (2) a number of rows in the condition stub, each representing a logical question answerable by yes (Y) or no (N). The same logic applies to the columns and rows of action entry and action stub: that is, the action entry shows completion of the action statement, and the action stub presents an indication of where to go next for each instruction or rule (Fig. 24-5).

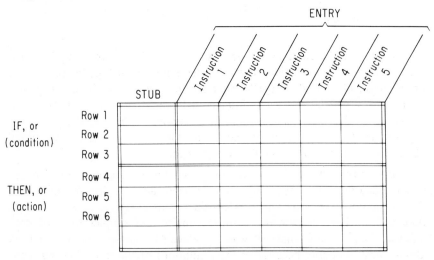

Fig. 24-5. A schematic of a detailed decision table

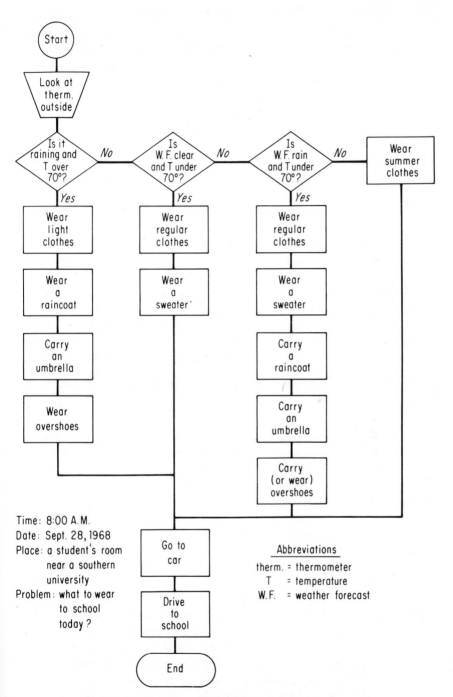

Fig. 24-6. Systems and procedures flow chart to determine what to wear to school

409

Application of analyst's tools to a problem

To illustrate the application of decision tables, suppose that early on September 28, 1968, a college student, either because of a change in the weather forecast, or in the weather itself, is faced with the problem of determining what to wear to school. Fig. 24-6 presents, in a flow-chart form, the decisions he would make in regard to the procedures to be followed. His usual system would have to be changed in favor of another. The problem is what system to choose. A look at either a flow chart or a decision table would give the answer immediately. The illustration shows the details that went into the construction of a simplified flow chart and a decision table. In the decision table, the condition constitutes the input, while the action is the output (Fig. 24-7).

The student looks outside at the thermometer, and, *IF* it is raining and the temperature is over 70 degrees with a forecast that these conditions will continue, reference to the table tells him that he should wear his light clothes, a raincoat, carry an umbrella, wear overshoes, go to the car, and drive to school. However, if the weather is clear and the forecast indicates clear skies and temperature under 70 degrees, the table tells him to wear regular-weight clothes, a sweater, go to the car, and drive to school. If the weather forecast calls for rain and temperatures under 70 degrees, the table shows that he would wear regular clothes, a sweater, carry a raincoat, an umbrella, and overshoes, go to the car, and drive to school. If the weather is clear, and the forecast is for a continuation of clear weather, with no change in temperature, the student would not have to make any decision because a problem would not exist. He would simply follow his usual system by proceeding to: (1) wear summer clothes, (2) go to his car, and (3) drive to school.

The construction of a flow chart for an actual business application, of course, is likely to involve more detailed logical and processing steps as well as several data computations. Once prepared, a programmer converts the steps into a language understandable to the computer, and, finally, debugs the program through testing it against actual (live) data. The decision table in Fig. 24-7 presents the same information as the flow chart in Fig. 24-6 in a form more easily read. The first column reads as follows: *IF* it is raining and the temperature is over 70 degrees, *THEN,* wear light clothes and a raincoat, carry an umbrella, wear overshoes, go to the car, and drive to school. The remaining columns are read in the same manner.

To summarize, decision tables stand out as excellent communication aids both to programmers and to other personnel of the organization and, in situations involving complex relationships between key variables, can be very effective, although relatively simple to construct and follow.

CONDITION ENTRY ENCOUNTERED

		Alternative one	Alternative two	Alternative three	Alternative four
IF, or (condition)	Raining and temp. over 70°	Y	N	N	N
	Forecast clear and temp. under 70°	--	Y	N	N
	Forecast rain and temp. under 70°	--	--	Y	N
THEN, or (action)	Wear light clothes	X	--	--	--
	Wear regular clothes	--	X	X	--
	Wear summer clothes	--	--	--	X
	Wear a sweater	--	X	X	--
	Wear a raincoat	X	--	--	--
	Carry a raincoat	--	--	X	--
	Carry an umbrella	X	--	X	--
	Wear overshoes	X	--	X	--
	Go to car	X	X	X	X
	Drive to school	X	X	X	X

ACTION ENTRY

Abbreviations

Y = yes
N = no
-- = irrelevant action (or condition)
X = completion of action statement

Fig. 24-7. Decision table to determine what to wear to school

Design the New System

System design is creative in approach and orientation. Like a tailor-made suit, each system is designed to meet the requirements of the problem involved. Creativity in system design implies inspiration on the part of the system designer to come up with unique ideas specifically aimed at solving a clearly defined problem.

Although there is no agreed-upon approach to system design, certain basic steps are commonly taken in its development. First, the system designer selects the key, or most crucial, activities (for example, input steps), and analyzes each activity separately, listing it in the order of its importance, or the role it plays in the performance of the system under study.

The designer examines the characteristics, and requirements, of input data. How should they be presented to the system? How important is the accuracy phase of input data? What time constraints are to be considered? Likewise, output data have their own characteristics. In terms of the format, which printout is called for, how many copies are required, how much is allowed to produce the output? Other data (primary or secondary) may be involved. What is the volume of the data? At what rate do the data grow? In what manner should data be filed (random versus sequential)? Finally, the process between input and output must be examined in terms of combining minor operations or splitting major ones for maximizing efficiency.

Second, the result of the first step helps in establishing alternative machine methods which may be used to meet the objectives of the system. The term *method* refers to how a given data-processing operation is performed. Any of the manual, electromechanical, punched-card, or computer techniques can be employed as methods to perform an operation. With the system's objectives in mind, the system analyst proceeds to array the methods in terms of their effectiveness and performance, and then selects the "hardware" that will best do the job.

Third, the analyst lists the alternative machine systems in terms of their relative appeal, economy, performance, and so forth, and, *for each alternative, he selects the data-processing equipment which best achieves the system's objectives* while meeting any constraints set by management. For instance, management may designate that the cost is not to be above a certain figure.

Fourth, for each "hardware" or "equipment" system, the analyst develops all necessary routine and special operational procedures, including machine runs which govern the manner in which certain data files must be organized. Once selected, all the necessary procedures with respect to designing the flow of required manual and machine operations must be developed. Some of the procedures include type, content, and format of input and output data.

Finally, a detailed report on the proposed machine system is prepared for management, linking its advantages, limitations, characteristics and description of capabilities, type and degree of effectiveness the system generates, type of application it can handle, the kind of changes in organizational and other areas it is likely to cause, the factors to be considered in its implementation (for example, programming, personnel, installation, and conversion problems), and a comparative cost analysis of the new and the present system. After the report is presented, management must take action to authorize the installation of the new system. The report is used as an authoritative and scientific document covering the matters presented in summary form in Fig. 24-8.

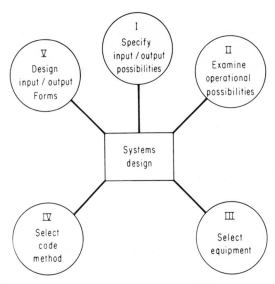

Fig. 24-8. Five steps in systems design

Selection of the Best System

In deciding on data-processing equipment, one should bear in mind that *the best machine system is one which produces the user's desired output most accurately, economically (both in terms of manpower and machine time), and at the rate of speed required.* With these factors in mind, the size and type of the system (that is, whether it is manual, electromechanical, punched-card, or computer) depend on the size of the firm, volume of data to be processed, degree of complexity of the operation(s), and accuracy, speed, and economy requirements. Fig. 24-9 presents a table, suggesting the type of data-processing system to be chosen, given the condition, as a function of the factors mentioned at the top of the six columns. To explain the method of reading the table, the first row reads as follows: A manual data-processing system would be used IF: (1) the size of the firm is small; (2) the volume of data is low; (3) accuracy requirements are low; (4) speed requirements are low; (5) economy requirements are low-to-medium, *and* (6) the degree of complexity of operation is low. The table can be used with the following as guidelines:

1. A manual system (with mechanical aid) is used to process nonrepetitive, simple applications.
2. From the economy standpoint, a punched-card system is used in situations involving repetitive operations not requiring random processing (that is, daily or regular maintenance of current balances of file records), such as the case in the preparation of payroll.
3. A high volume of repetitive applications, requiring a substantial amount of calculating within each cycle, would suggest the use of a digital computer; *the more complex the operation and the larger the volume of data involved, the larger is the computer system needed.*

Type of Data Processing System	Size of Firm	Volume of Data	Accuracy Requirement	Speed Requirement	Economy Requirement	Degree of complexity of operation
Manual	Small	LO	LO	LO	LO - Med.	LO
Manual	Small	LO - Med.	LO - Med.	LO	Med.	LO
Manual-electro-mechanical	Small	LO - Med.	Med.	LO - Med.	Med.	LO
Electromechanical to punched card	Small	Med.	Med.	Med.	Med.	LO - Med.
Punched card	Small-medium	Med.	Med. - HI	Med.	Med. - HI	LO - Med.
Punched card	Medium	Med.	HI	Med.	Med. - HI	Med.
Computer (small)	Medium	Med.	HI	Med. - HI	HI	Med.
Computer (sm.-med.)	Medium	Med. - HI	HI	Med. - HI	HI	Med. - HI
Computer (medium)	Med.-large	HI	HI	HI	HI	Med. - HI
Computer (med.-large)	Med.-large	HI	HI	HI	HI	HI
Computer (large)	Large	HI	HI	HI	SUPER HI	HI

Fig. 24-9. Guide to selection of appropriate data-processing system

Occupational Specifications of Systems Analyst

Occupational Definition

Analyzes business problem, such as development of integrated production, inventory control, and cost analysis system, to refine its formulation and convert it to programable form for application to electronic data-processing system: Confers with project director, business data-processing department heads, and department heads of units involved to ascertain specific output requirements, such as types of breakouts, degree of data summarization, and format for management reports. Confers with personnel of operating units to devise plans for obtaining and standardizing input data. Studies current or develops new systems and procedures to devise work-flow sequence. Analyzes alternative means of deriving input data to select most feasible and economical method. Develops process flow charts or diagrams in outlined and then in detailed form for programing, indicating external verification points, such as audit trial printouts. May work as member of team, applying specialized knowledge to one phase of project development. May coordinate activities of team members. May direct preparation of programs.

Education, Training, and Experience

College graduation with courses in business administration and accounting usually is required for entrants without prior experience in data processing. Some employers, while requiring a college degree, do not require a specific major or course content. A successful college record is regarded as proof of ability to reason logically, which is considered more important for successful performance than knowledge of techniques acquired in any specific area. Many employers waive the formal education requirements for those workers employed in their establishments who have had several years' manual and machine systems experience prior to computer conversion. Business programers without a college degree can, through experience, acquire a background in business systems and procedures and may thereby advance into systems analysis. Currently, the trend is to require a knowledge of advanced mathematics because of the rapidly increasing sophistication of business systems. Continuing education, through specialized courses, self-study, and participation in activities of professional associations, is the rule rather than the exception in this occupation, as in all higher-level occupations related to the computer.

Special Characteristics

Aptitudes:

Verbal ability to discuss problems and progress, prepare reports, and make annotations for graphic representations of work.

Numerical ability to select from alternatives to develop optimum system, procedures, and methods. Mathematical investigation of such factors as variation in volume of input data, and frequency of appearance of exceptions to normal work flow in processing is often necessary. Level of mathematics varies from business arithmetic and algebra to differential equations.

Spatial ability to visualize, prepare, and review two-dimensional graphic representations of work flow.

Form perception to identify nonverbal symbols on records such as block diagrams and flow charts.

Clerical perception to avoid perceptual errors and recognize pertinent detail in the recording and identifying of letters and numbers that often occur in abbreviated or acronymic combinations.

Interests:

A preference for activities that are technical and analytical, and those that are abstract and creative in nature to devise new or to modify standardized computer-oriented systems to meet the specific needs of an organization.

Temperaments:

Ability to confer with personnel from other departments, develop flow charts, devise work-flow sequence, and prepare reports.

Required to deal with people in conference and interview situations.

Required to make judgmental decisions to select from alternatives when devising optimal system.

Required to make decisions on basis of factual data to design system within machine capability.

Physical activities and environmental conditions

Work is sedentary, with occasional standing and walking. Occasional handling of source documents, books, charts, and other records that seldom exceed ten pounds.

Talking and hearing to discuss and confer with management and technical personnel to devise suitable business systems.

Near visual acuity to prepare and review work-flow charts and diagrams.

GLOSSARY OF TERMS

FILE: An organized collection of information directed toward some purpose.

SUBSYSTEM: A part of a system; a component; a formal aspect of an organized routine.

SYSTEM: A collection of consecutive procedures, methods, or routines designed to form an organized whole. Also, a set of components related by some form of united interaction to form an organized whole.

SYSTEMS ANALYSIS: The analysis of an activity (business or other) to determine what must be accomplished and how the necessary operations may best be achieved.

REVIEW QUESTIONS

1. How is a subsystem related to a system? Give an example.
2. Explain why a data-processing system is needed?
3. What are the primary functions of a data-processing system? Give an example of each function.
4. Distinguish the difference between: (1) systems analysis and systems procedure, and (2) system and procedure.
5. What three primary steps are taken in systems analysis? Explain each step briefly.
6. How does a systems analyst collect data? Which source or method is superior?
7. What chief elements are connected with structural information?
8. What steps are involved in determining the system's requirements? Explain each step briefly.
9. What tools does a systems analyst use in outlining the flow of data or operation?
10. What is a decision table? Describe its components. Why is it used? How is it different from the flow chart?
11. List and describe the key steps in systems design.
12. What factors would you consider in determining the type and size of a data-processing system? Give an example to illustrate.

PART

IV

Data-processing
Management

chapter

25

MANAGEMENT PROBLEMS INVOLVED IN THE INTRODUCTION OF A DATA-PROCESSING SYSTEM

AS IS COMMON KNOWLEDGE, the majority of people in the United States constantly strive to reach a class level higher and more refined than any other level their associates have been able to attain. Whether this objective can actually be realized is not so important as the desire to aim in that direction. Most of us surround ourselves with symbols which represent a rank or a position, namely, a status higher than what we really have or are able to afford. This resembles the case of the Japanese specialty-shop owner who purchased a modern calculator and placed it in the shop window while instructing his bookkeeper to continue using the abacus for calculating purposes. He wanted to impress his customers that he was using modern equipment as a tool in preparing his financial matters.

Status-seeking Firms

A business firm is in no way different from other members of the community. It is made up of people, who also aim toward achieving a status higher than that of their competitors. Whether they are able to maintain that status seems, in many cases, less important than attaining it, regardless of the expenses incurred. Some business firms (both large and small) seem to be hypnotized by the glamor and prestige of a data-processing installation—especially, a computer installation. They hear about and believe in stories told about the fantastic potentials of computers in business. Some envision a computer which can solve all their problems, meet their needs and expectations, make decisions in major areas, and eliminate all the worries and frustrations that a manager often encounters. Such firms are said to have "computeritis."

Whereas a data-processing system appears to be a sign of progress and prestige resulting from the apparent ability of a company to purchase or rent the equipment, the introduction of the system itself is not necessarily the best approach to solving a given problem. The major part of the gain realized by the use of the equipment can be achieved under the presently used manual or semimechanized methods if they are changed periodically to meet the needs of the business. On the other hand, many firms neglect to modify or revamp their system, however old it is, as long as they realize a reasonable return on their investment. They grow in size and expand their operation over a number of years with a realization of a high margin of income. They thus reach a stage where they realize suddenly that their manual method of data processing is no longer adequate to do the job well. Some panic and conduct a hurried, and brief, feasibility study resulting in the installation of a punched-card, or an electronic data-processing system. Experience shows that most of those firms who awakened a bit too late to their need for improvement and alignment with the competitive business surrounding, after their hurriedly installed system is put into operation, begin to realize less than desirable results. In order to adjust the equipment to the procedures used by the various departments, additional auxiliaries are added. They find the system so unfit to do the work that must be done that they decide to revert to the previously used manual system.

What Types of Firms Buy Computers, and Why?

In order for a company to survive the competitive pressure and continue to make a profit large enough to remain in business and provide for expansion in the future, methods other than the manual techniques of information flow appear to be desirable. Companies are becoming more complex in their structure, organizational framework and relationships, diversity of products, and in the voluminous amounts of data to be worked on and rearranged daily. To a typical firm, production of quality products at a competitive price means a need for efficient and modern data-processing equipment to aid in the realization of that goal by processing the data needed for analysis quickly and cheaply.

Naturally, it is not an easy task to decide on the installation of a computer in business. Risks are involved which cannot be determined accurately. The unforeseen future makes many firms feel helpless if they do not have any way to use the tools of business forecasting or market research. When costly equipment is introduced, whether purchased or leased, the firm should make sure that such equipment has the capacity to handle present business needs, and also that it can be modified conveniently in the event that unexpected developments, such as a rise in production or sales or general expansion, should take place, making alterations necessary.

What should a business firm do with regard to the introduction of data-processing equipment? Can it afford to stand still and learn from the experiences of other firms, or should it initiate a complete and detailed survey of the available equipment with regard to the existing data-processing problems that need to be solved? The former alternative has merit in that a company can learn from the experimentation of other companies of similar size in the use of specific equipment. However, the firm experimenting with its new computer is not likely to divulge any information which would put it at a competitive disadvantage. The second alternative promises results if a thorough feasibility study is made and if enough time is allowed for research so that the right equipment to do the job for which such assistance is needed is obtained.

If top management is to take advantage of the advances in the field of data processing, decisions must be made relating to: (1) the overhauling of procedures used in order to discover exactly what they are and where they need correction; (2) the feasibility of using an installation in its operation; (3) acceptance of the installation by operative members of the firm, including its employees as well as its stockholders; (4) the willingness of all concerned to cooperate in the operation of the data-processing system after it is installed; and (5) the problem of retraining those of its employees affected by such an installation.

The procedure should be really "block diagrammed" in the minds of top-management members so that important details will not be overlooked in the transition from thinking in terms of manual performance. If each step is worked out carefully and painstakingly, time will be saved in the long run, because many of the problems incident to the installation of a computer system will have been foreseen and allowances will be made for them.

The types of firms that purchase computers are typically:

1. Those which can well afford to pay for them. The cost of the installation usually comes from funds which are not earmarked for any other particular or preplanned project. Such firms are usually medium-size to large-size ones that can use a computer to maximum capacity. The exception in this case is the small firm which cooperates with a neighboring firm or firms to purchase the computer, a charge being made by the contracting firm for its use. This approach is widely used also by educational institutions which reserve a certain amount of time per week for sale to local firms for the processing of their data.
2. Another factor which characterizes the firm that is likely to buy a computer is the employment of a large amount of clerical help for purposes of computation. The larger the firm, the larger is the clerical staff. Computations performed in business range from simple addition or subtraction in updating customer accounts in the credit department to more complex computations involving mathematical formulas used in research or the production-control area.
3. Not only is the type of computation a factor, but also the number of computations and the time required to complete them are significant in inducing a firm to install a computer system. Simple computations may take a few minutes each. By contrast, a complex scientific or mathematical computation may take hours to complete.

From the foregoing discussion, we can infer that some of the major objectives of an electronic data-processing installation would be:

1. To process progressively increasing volumes of data resulting from a company's expansion over the years which are not efficiently handled by the system presently used.

2. To deal with more complex computational problems which cannot be processed efficiently by manual methods.
3. To attempt to reduce the cost of computing complex applications, as well as that of processing voluminous amounts of data involving simple computations. Cost is important in that its reduction will result in a greater increase in the profit figure, assuming that all other factors remain fairly constant.
4. To provide a framework for decision-making by management based on the facts processed and produced by the installation. These facts play an important role in that an increase in their accuracy, along with a reduction in the time needed to process and prepare them in report form, will help management arrive at better conclusions in planning future courses of action for the firm.

The Feasibility Study

A feasibility study involves the survey and evaluation of the advantages of using a computer to work out a set of given applications for a firm.

In deciding whether a computer system should be installed, the character of a firm's operations, its present operational procedures, and its general objectives should be carefully reviewed in the light of the purposes that the processing machines are designed to serve. Management must formulate a sharply defined picture of its data-processing needs and of how a computer can fit into the organization to serve its various departments in this respect. *All should plainly understand that a computer is intended only as an aid to men.* Without this understanding, the whole character of the system when installed is likely to be misconstrued and frustrations caused by its failure to live up to expectations.

The steps involved in conducting a feasibility study are similar to those used in solving many of our personal daily problems.

To illustrate: After graduating from college, Ralph Bender, a business management major, accepted a position with a manufacturing concern. Considering the limited income of a management trainee, his new job, and the need to have a mode of transportation, Ralph purchased a used car for $95.00 from a friend who was answering the call from his local draft board. In time, Ralph advanced within the firm. He gained recognition and promotions steadily. A year and a half later he married and, during the same month, he was promoted to head a department in the manufacturing division of the main plant.

With a substantial increase in salary and a relocation to a suburban area, Ralph felt the old "jalopy" to be unsuited to his new status. The upkeep proved to be exorbitant because repairs had to be made frequently. It was *unreliable,* in that mechanical failure happened at inopportune times, often resulting in his late arrival at the plant. It was also *inefficient* with respect to the excessive gasoline and oil it consumed. It had a *shabby appearance,* and also was *hazardous* to drive at high speeds.

Knowing that his present car no longer met his needs, Ralph conducted a "feasibility study." He spent his free evenings shopping for a new automobile. He contacted dealers who sold various makes and models. He drove a few demonstration cars and obtained literature about the various models. To supplement his general knowledge about the merchandise, he contacted friends and associates to learn what their experience had been with the new automobiles they had purchased. He also read articles in independent magazines about the results of tests made on various makes.

After two weeks of survey and evaluation, Ralph considered his present position and his chances for further advancement with the firm. The chances looked good. He also considered the expenses involved with regard to his home mortgage, his living and other expenses, the amount of cash he had available, and the amount he needed to borrow to pay for a new car. He weighed the price of the car against the savings in gasoline and oil and the car's known reliability, efficiency, and speed. When his analysis was complete, to his wife's very apparent pleasure, he placed an order for the purchase of a specific make, size, power rating, and price range. He selected the dealer to whom he gave the order because of his reputation for guaranteed prompt delivery, courteous service, and extension of reasonable credit terms.

The feasibility study conducted by a business firm for determining whether to use a computer to serve its needs is similar to that conducted by Ralph in the determination, and the eventual purchase, of his automobile. The remaining part of this chapter explains the steps involved and the factors which should be considered in the installation of a computer system.

Impetus for a Feasibility Study

For a feasibility study to succeed, the following must occur: (1) the survey and evaluation must be made by competent, qualified personnel; (2) the study must guarantee savings in clerical and other related costs; and, most importantly, (3) it must be approved by top management, especially when the need for it is being recognized and supported by members of the lower ranks in the management organization. When top management initiates a feasibility study, their motive is generally a desire for experimentation, with less emphasis upon cost or the obtaining of funds. Their aim is to use a computer for producing information, such as sales analyses or business forecasting, which is useful to management and which is unobtainable under the present system. When interest in this is generated at the top level, the project gets under way fairly easily, because top-management people are already sold on the need for and the desirability of having a computer. More often lower management initiates the interest because of a known need for the use of faster methods in the processing of data in their departments. Regardless of who conceives the idea, top management must be sold on the need for its implementation. In the latter case, communications flow upward first, and all data pertinent to the problem which would be helpful in gaining the approval of superiors must be presented. Success in gaining the approval of top management is related, to a great extent, to their attitudes and personalities as shown in their dealings with lower management men. If the members of top management are young, aggressive, and willing to risk investment of money in new ideas, in new ways of doing things, and in applying the latest methods available for the purpose of meeting competition head on, then no great problem arises in gaining their support. On the other hand, if top management are conservative, unimaginative, insist on the presentation of all the facts regardless of their value, and spend an unreasonable amount of time deliberating on the matter, then the job of selling them the idea of introducing a new computer would be difficult. We assume in this discussion, however, that management is interested in knowing in some detail about the specific problems at hand, a description of the proposal, and the basic facts which would support the contention of the person presenting the need for the new system. That person would find it helpful if a survey were conducted to show the cost of the new system in comparison with the anticipated saving resulting from its installation and use.

The Mystery Period

At this stage, little is known of the uses and capabilities of, and the real need for, a computer to serve the needs of the company and, particularly, to solve the specific data-processing problem(s) in which a need is felt. An electronic computer is mysterious primarily because of the ignorance of the layman in understanding its real potentials and the ways in which it can be useful to him and his firm. In order to start the project, assuming that management approves, a preliminary survey is usually the first step.

The Project Team

Before any survey is made, whether preliminary or detailed, personnel from the various levels of the organization are appointed to assume responsibility for the project. They are referred to as the *project team*. The team usually consists of the various department heads, whose main job is to find out whether a data-processing system can perform various applications for the firm. The group is to keep in mind, not only the immediate problems and applications, but also the long-range applications. The new system must be capable of meeting an expanding business situation and, with the addition of the necessary components, process those applications the information from which is used to keep the firm in good competitive standing. Further, questions such as the following should be borne in mind: What is the basic objective of the computer? Is it feasible to centralize operations and reduce costs? What applications appear to be economical to run as a start, and what applications are economical to run after a computer is installed? Will the responsible people in the firm, as well as the employees, cooperate? How flexible is a specific computer with regard to adding more components for faster processing or more storage capacity? Attempting to answer these questions is not an easy task. The job becomes similar to that of an architect who must use all his resources and blend various facts in such a way as to bring about a good plan for the construction of a house or other type of building.

The desirability of forming a project team to initiate a feasibility study is based on the belief that man's background and know-how are limited to the favorable performance of certain familiar duties and that he is a less competent judge in regard to those about which he is unfamiliar. When a few men from various departments, encompassing vast knowledge in different areas, are grouped as a team, the benefit of their combined knowledge and experience should aid in bringing about better results.

Authority and responsibility of the project team

The project team should have authority commensurate with the responsibility which it agrees to assume. Its members should be authorized to contact line managers, as well as to seek information through the staff personnel for data-collection purposes. This cannot be done successfully unless top management are in full agreement about what the team is doing. Top management should be willing to be used to gain the cooperation of the operating units at lower levels so that the work of the team may be done with minimum loss of time. By the same token, all report findings, and other important information, should be reported to top management—preferably, to the chief executive of the firm. In the case of a very large firm, an executive vice-president in charge of manufacturing or finance would be a good substitute.

The project director

Regardless of the background and knowledge of the project team investigating the feasibility of introducing a new computer, its job can be done well only after someone has been appointed to supervise the study and synchronize the work of the team as it is related to the duties and functions of other people in the organization. Such a person is referred to as the *project director*. To "direct" means to issue directives, orders, and commands, and to supervise the work of his staff group so that it works within the plan set in advance toward the goal for which it was created. A project director is a management man with special abilities and above-average intelligence. He is imaginative and able to size up a problem quickly and to arrive at the alternatives, adapting the one that can provide a solution. He should have a wide background in business and specific knowledge in accounting and finance, because most business applications involve knowledge based on these two fields. A knowledge of accounting will help him to understand the accounting implications pertaining an application and to communicate more effectively with those personnel who are engaged in payroll, accounting, and other related departments. His finance background should help him to consider more seriously the matter of costs versus savings. Cost justification has to be made to management before a new installation can be approved. A firm's vice-president in charge of finance may become the project director, because he already possesses such knowledge. He is unlikely to have financial bias, because his work and position are independent of any department or division of the organization. His function is simply to determine the goals of the company and to find out how to introduce an electronic data-processing system to meet these goals.

Senior management committee

Personnel selection is usually headed by a *senior management committee* whose job is to disseminate information and maintain communications among the various executives about the findings of the project team, the members of which it is responsible for selecting. The senior management committee is used to level off any misunderstanding about the automatic data-processing system and to promote enthusiasm and interest for the use of the computer by the departments. Without that, the project may collapse. Therefore, the cooperation of all departments is necessary. The committee transmits all information it receives (feedback) to the project team and keeps it informed about other matters of concern to its members.

Personal qualifications of the project team

What are the desired personal qualifications of each of the project-team members? A team member is expected to be knowledgeable in and guided by the concepts and policies that management uses in operating the company. He should seek whatever information is necessary to understand how these policies and concepts are worked out. A knowledge of company procedures will provide the basis for an analysis and evaluation of the flow and transformation of data through the organization by the use of the current system. Without this knowledge, one could not select a computer that is tailored to solve the company's specific problem(s).

Above all, a project-team member must be experienced in human relations, because he will be dealing with other people at all times. His experience must guide him in communicating effectively to gain their co-operation and help in matters related to the study. Further, he must be creative, because data-processing systems demand new ways of doing things, owing to their flexibility. Imagination, hard work, and patience are needed to do detailed charts and to construct useful programs.

Part of the work of the project team involves the collection of cost figures on the present system. A team member should be unbiased, impartial, and able to evaluate clerical and other related costs and to utilize any other information which would help him to arrive at a true and clear survey and evaluation report.

When asked to serve on the team, some men may be reluctant to do so. The interest and attitude of the team members are also very important because they may not wish to learn a new and different field unrelated directly to their own. The sign of a mathematical formula, however basic or elementary it is, discourages some personnel from pursuing the field any further. Lack of knowledge is ignorance in a given area. Ignorance generates fear. Some personnel fear that the introduction of an electronic data-processing system, once installed, may fail to render the desired results. They feel fully responsible in view of the thousands of dollars that may be invested. That is where the project director, a leader with confidence and hope, can "water down," if not suppress, those fears and reservations in the minds of the members of the team. This can be accomplished by: (1) reducing as much as possible the amount of work that team members have to do on their regular jobs (preferably, they would be in a better position if all of their regular duties were assigned temporarily to someone else, thus allowing them to concentrate freely on the project); and (2) easing the deadline pressure (the director can emphasize a deadline of presenting their findings to management only *after* the team has had a chance to become familiar with the new computer field).

The team members may also not wish to put in the time and effort necessary, especially when the person in question is reaching retirement age or has in mind a transfer to a better position within the company or elsewhere. For these reasons, the project team should consist of men between the ages of thirty and forty-five. Generally speaking, those under thirty probably have not been with the firm long enough to understand it well or to have had experience in dealing with people effectively. By the same token, some of the men over forty-five years of age may have decided already to concentrate on a specific field and may have planned to use their talent and time in developing it further. Their hopes lie in moving ahead in an area with which they are already familiar. There are, of course, exceptions to these generalities. Many of those exceptions have proved invaluable to the more effective survey and evaluation of the project.

Technical qualifications of the project team

In addition to the personal qualifications described above, members of the project team should possess the proper technical knowledge needed in the job. A knowledge of accounting and a background in electronics are desirable. Problems are bound to arise when the project team is too heavily weighted in either direction. Personnel with a background in electronics tend to put more emphasis upon the aspects of a computer from the electronics viewpoint, such as speed, access time, and so forth, with too little emphasis upon the procedures used by the firm. On the other hand, personnel with an accounting background stress the procedures but put little emphasis upon electronics. The result of either extreme can only be the introduction of an inadequate computer system. Hence, the need for balance in the team's make-up between these two kinds of "experts" is obvious.

Members who have combined a broad background in the accounting system used by the firm and basic knowledge of electronics or electronic data processing appear to be ideal. If such men are not available in the firm, and a choice has to be made, those with the accounting background are preferred, because an accountant can be taught how to program a machine and how its parts work more easily than an expert electronics man can be taught accounting systems.

Companies have tried to solve the problem by pirating personnel with the desired background from other firms, luring them with attractive salaries and fringe benefits. Although this is done repeatedly, it is not considered exactly ethical and is not too productive. After all, a newcomer will have to acquaint himself with the procedures, the policies, objectives, and needs, and the data-processing problems of a firm with which he is unfamiliar. Because he has worked in the same field elsewhere, however, his learning period is bound to be shorter than that of a person who starts "from scratch."

The Preliminary Survey Stage

The foregoing discussion involved the selecting of personnel to form a project team headed by a director for the purpose of investigating the feasibility of introducing an electronic data-processing system to the organization. Once this stage is completed and management approves the project, the first stage to be carried out is a preliminary survey. Like Ralph Bender, the college graduate, after a need is felt for a new system in solving an existing processing problem, the members of the team should begin to contact and visit various computer manufacturers in order: (1)

to acquaint themselves with the computer field, (2) to have a visual view of the components on display, (3) to get a general orientation to the over-all capabilities of electronic data-processing systems, and (4) to gain impressions about the possibility of using one of the systems in their firm. Throughout the survey stage, the members should keep in mind the particular problem(s) of their firm as they learn more about the various systems. They are also to remember that no "cookbook" exists to guide them as to what to tell management in regard to which computer will solve their problem(s) satisfactorily.

The team members should contact more than one computer manufacturer. Like Ralph in his contacting of several dealers selling different makes of automobiles, the members of the team are interested in educating and exposing themselves to what is available on the market. This eliminates the bias factor for a specific computer manufacturer. However, some contend that, if a project team concentrates on one set of equipment put out by a given manufacturer, the members would learn to program well and do an application for testing purposes. In this case, less time would be wasted, especially because they would not run the danger of becoming confused by viewing too much of essentially the same equipment.

Although concentration on one manufacturer's equipment appears advantageous and time saving, the disadvantages might outweigh the advantages. Like any other manufacturer, a computer manufacturer is a sales-minded person. Occasionally a customer can be "high pressured" to purchase a computer system just as is true in buying other items. The team should, therefore, spend a reasonable amount of time looking at each offering in the market before they concentrate on any one model.

More Intensive Survey and Evaluation Stage

When the "acquaintanceship" stage is well under way, the project team should make frequent contacts with computer manufacturers and consult them with regard to whether the company's problem(s) can be processed electronically. Whatever type of computer system is recommended, the team should obtain cost data as well as a description of the specific types of application(s) that can be done on it. Pressures brought on the team members, whatever their source, should not be allowed to "hurry" the decision unduly.

In addition to consultation with computer manufacturers, a check on the success of other firms which have had experience with the same or a similar system would be helpful. As mentioned earlier in this chapter, obtaining such data may not be possible.

Small and medium-sized firms and, less frequently, large firms seek the aid of a management consultant for gaining information, advice, and direction in a feasibility study. Even though consultants' fees are high, smaller firms do use them, primarily because they (the firms) do not have skilled men within their organization to do the survey well. A consultant's chief duty is to guide a project team in planning and supervising the survey. Many consultants have little knowledge of electronic data processing, but they are experienced in analyzing and solving problems. They have leadership qualities and the ability to "size up" the situation well. No matter how well they may be able to "size up" the situation themselves, many organizations seek the aid of a consultant so as to have a third party's independent and unbiased views with regard to the recommendations presented by the project team. The idea of having outlined the solution to a problem based on a procedure supervised by a consultant commands respect, and often consent, by the operating heads and other levels within the organization. Organizations should be quite selective in hiring a consultant. When a project involves thousands of dollars of investment, care and caution, along with efficiency, should be exercised continuously throughout the study.

Other services of a consultant who is a specialist in electronic data processing include training in programming and education in how computers work. Some consultants also have a reliable background in systems design. They can be of great help in formulating a system tailored to the company's needs. A consultant can also provide technicians, programmers, and other temporary help to operate the new computer installation until the company trains or hires someone on a more permanent basis. Many computer manufacturers offer these services also, once their particular systems are chosen for installation.

Personnel Training

Acquaintanceship alone is insufficient either for arriving at a decision or preparing a valid recommendation to be considered and approved by management. Thus, the project team must undertake to learn more about the uses of data-processing equipment in solving processing problems generally and those that are prevalent in their own organization specifically. This education is available either in academic institutions or in educational training centers directed by computer manufacturers.

Many academic institutions of higher learning have already introduced courses at the undergraduate and graduate levels in electronic data processing. For the past few years, colleges and universities have felt the impact of the electronic computer upon industry. In a number of forward-looking educational institutions, programs in the business and science fields were tailored to include courses in data processing and programming. Members of the project team can benefit immensely from the computer facilities of nearby universities that have an installation.

The other alternative open for a prospective customer is attending a computer manufacturer's educational center. Most manufacturers of necessity believe in the "sale-through-education" approach. Courses ranging from "the basics of key punching" to those in advanced programming techniques for large-scale computers are available. In most cases, this education is rendered free to prospective customers. The project team should utilize this privilege and take a series of courses suitable for their needs. One popular series of courses progresses from the history of data processing through machine functions, flow charting and block diagramming, programming basics and techniques, and coding to the role of management in the field of electronic data processing.

When basic knowledge has been acquired and the team has learned some programming techniques, a good idea is to program a typical application of the firm. After the program has been written, it should be tested in order to judge whether a specific computer produces the desired results. This brings up the question: What application should be selected? Should it be a brief and easy application, with the purpose of speeding up the process of selecting a computer, once a specific computer has passed the test by processing the application successfully? Or should the application be a major, detailed company application to see if it can be processed properly, because it would occupy a substantial part of the computer time when the computer is installed? The latter alternative is preferred in most cases, provided that the steps in the application are systemized and well presented. Such preparation makes the job of programming the steps and testing the application as a whole less difficult.

Others argue that the application to be selected should involve the development of data which it is not feasible to process by the presently used methods. This would test the capability of a computer in producing results important to management for making better decisions. However, most of those who have had experience in undergoing a feasibility study will agree that an application from the "brute-force area" where a large number of personnel and much clerical work are involved would be the best to use. Economy and cost reduction are factors which are constantly stressed and are most likely to be the major factors which make many firms feel a need for conversion to an electronic data-processing system. In manufacturing, such "bread-and-butter" applications include inventory control, product control, factory scheduling, and so forth. In a bank, consumer credit loans and loan accounting are popular examples.

Electronic Data-processing Versus the Employees of the Firm

During the survey and evaluation stage, the employees should be informed of the possibility of introducing electronic data-processing equipment into the plant. Although the employees should not share in decision-making with regard to the installation itself, before any installation is considered seriously, the project team should investigate its effect upon them. Because of their lack of knowledge in the electronic data-processing field, they fear being replaced by a computer. They worry about their job security. Some begin to have a "mental inferiority complex" because of their apprehensiveness about working in a new and strange environment and expect the computer "to tell them what to do." If left unchecked, the net effect would be the employees' refusal to cooperate. Information begins to be withheld deliberately, and soon the system has been sabotaged altogether. For these reasons, management cannot afford to ignore the feelings and attitudes of its employees. The matter becomes worse in a unionized firm where the union can cause inconvenience and fight for the security of its employees. Management should publicize, educate, and distribute materials on electronic data processing to quiet replacement fears. The suggestion box is a useful safety valve which employees should be encouraged to use to air their grievances and suggestions with regard to the installation. Bear in mind that the grapevine is a great, though unofficial, line of communication. No executive can stop its use. It should be utilized to the best advantage of the firm by feeding needed information to the rank-and-file employees, especially those whose jobs may be affected. All that can be done should be done, in terms of instilling confidence and hope in the minds of the employees as far as job security is concerned. As is understandable, all people resist change, especially older employees. They dislike any innovation which they do not understand. If the majority of the firm's employees are older men and women, the job of selling them the advantages of a computer installation becomes more difficult.

Employees can be sold on the fact that: (1) the use of a computer means less physical as well as less mental effort; (2) it is a tool to aid them in doing their jobs with greater efficiency; (3) more opportunities are bound to arise of which they can avail themselves (the use of a second, and possibly a third, shift will open a new set of jobs for women, and especially housewives who cannot hold a job during the day); and (4) the inconvenience of unannounced overtime will no longer occur because of the speed at which routine data are processed within the regular shift.

What makes more difficult the job of selling the employees on the value of a computer system is the poor publicity which constantly frightens and threatens the layman. Newspaper and magazine cartoons sometimes depict a computer as superior intellectually to man. Employees take this to heart and add it to their fears and frustrations. This tends to cast suspicion on the real situation and increases the difficulty for management in selling the advantages of electronic data processing and getting the cooperation and willingness of employees to be educated and adjusted to the real meaning of the proposed installation.

Cost-analysis Stage

While the educational program is being carried out and an application is being programmed to test the effective use of a computer system, the project director should see that a cost estimate of the computer system is made. A comparison should then be made between this cost and that of the presently used system to see if any saving can be realized. Cost estimates are helpful in that they aid the project team in determining the amount and degree of savings from an automatic data-processing installation.

The estimated annual savings can be presented in the following condensed form (all figures and data are hypothetical):

Estimated cost of operating the present system	$1,250,000
Estimated cost of operating the new system (when installed)	500,000
Estimated gross saving	$ 750,000
Less estimated computer rental	420,000
Estimated net saving per year	$ 330,000

Costs incidental to a computer installation are as follows:

1. *Investment cost.* The cost of investing cash in the equipment and related factors is in addition to the rental price of the computer. Also included in investment costs are the costs of remodeling, purchase of furniture and fixtures, personnel training, systems design, installation of air conditioning, and the feasibility study.
2. *Operation cost.* This includes the cost of employing technical personnel, programmers, console operators, and coding and maintenance employees. Because the jobs of most of these employees are skilled, such personnel command higher salaries than those hired under the previous system. This can increase the cost of operating the new system to the extent that savings become negligible. Also included in the operation cost is the cost of input and output preparation. Data must be punched in cards or recorded on tape from punched cards for input. In the former case, a key punch is needed and a card inventory must be available for input preparation. In addition, the need arises for a sorter or a collator for classifying the data in a form suitable for the computer as input. In the latter case, data must be punched in a card or paper tape and, by the use of a converter, recorded on tape for input preparation.

    The cost of output involves primarily the use of punched cards, if the results are to be punched, or statement forms, if they are to be printed. Stocking cards and statement forms might cause confusion in the stockroom. In the event that a computer installation is decided upon, the stockroom should be cleared of any and all forms pertaining to the old system in order to avoid confusion and delay in finding the desired materials.

3. *Physical and technical obsolescence.* Obsolescence can be costly. In the case of companies that purchase the computer, an allowance for depreciation is made because of the gradual reduction in the value of the system. The depreciation range is generally between five and ten years. In some situations, however, this range reaches fifteen years. Technical obsolescence is inherent in the field of electronic data processing. Computer design, speed, and so forth, change constantly. A computer that appeared to be ideal two years ago may not be as efficient today. Again, in this case, the firm needs to look at its procedures, its short- and long-range objectives, its needs and requirements with regard to the data, and the way they must be processed. If the computer still serves these needs, one can conclude that, as far as the firm is concerned, the computer is still efficient.

In many cases, the discovery may be made that present manual methods are equal to, or superior to, the proposed method of mechanization. Unless there are large enough applications which require detailed, repetitive treatement (that can be done easily once the procedure is outlined), management had better think twice about spending money on a proposed electronic data-processing system. If the volume of data surrounding any one application is not large enough and requires too many exceptions in its treatment—which involve judgment—so much time may be needed to program on a computer that this type of installation would be out of the question. On the other hand, the application might be adaptable to a punched-card system. In examining procedures used to accomplish its objectives, management may find that these will have to be changed in some way if the processing is to be most rewarding. Some executives have found that, when they got their procedures really straightened out, there was no need for conversion to a better system as the presently used methods, once brought up to date, were quite adequate.

Another question that arises in this connection involves a value judgment: that is, whether the information to be provided by a computer system is really needed as quickly as it can be procured. This depends a great deal upon the type of decisions that management men are faced with making. Unless they demand information quickly in order that action on decisions may be speeded up, the rapidity of procuring data under a manual system of processing is probably adequate. If, on the other hand, the length of the waiting time for data is of paramount importance to the decision-making process, a mechanized system will probably be welcome. A good amount of thought should be given to this question of the real need for speed in the procurement of basic information, when justifying the acquisition of a data-processing system.

In summary, then, if the savings and the frequency of use of a computer system are not great, the adoption of a less expensive system, perhaps a punched-card system, would be a suitable substitute. Consideration will be directed, then, to the preparation of plans for consideration of the punched-card equipment.

Concluding the Feasibility Study

At this stage, the team has learned much about computers. After the results of processing the application which the project team has worked out are known, a specific system should be recommended. However, before the team report is finally written, key men of the organization should attend a seminar, the purpose of which would be to educate them in the use of electronic data processing as it is done by a specific computer. After the principles have been explained, the computer demonstration should be presented. The old adage, "seeing is believing," is especially applicable in this case. A familiar company application should be used in the demonstration to show that the computer can, and does, process data better than is the case with presently used processing methods. Theory alone is not sufficient to sell the product. It is sold more easily when the customer observes its operation. That is one reason why Ralph Bender drove demonstration models before he finally chose his particular automobile.

When the seminar and demonstration are over, a question-and-answer period should be conducted. Personnel should be encouraged to ask questions with regard to the installation. Normally questions are asked without any prompting from those demonstrating the equipment. Each key manager is likely to be interested in utilizing the computer, especially if his department is in need of help in the processing of its data. His suggestions as to how the computer can be used successfully to help him solve his problems could contribute greatly to the success of the system when installed.

The Decision-making Stage

Decision-making involves the formulation of an opinion and the arrival at a course of action for solving a given problem. After the project-team members have had an opportunity to survey the need for a computer, and have compared the results obtained by processing the same application on different computers, their next logical step is evaluation of their findings.

They must recommend a system which in their opinion, based on the facts available to them, will do the best job for their firm. Despite what the team has learned from the claims of various computer manufacturer(s), or from other companies' experience with a specific system, the final responsibility for the choice lies with the team members alone.

All pertinent facts are studied and weighed. The team's recommendation is the only step lacking before a final decision can be made by top management either to approve or to reject the computer installation.

In arriving at a recommendation, the team must consider: (1) the results desired from an electronic installation, (2) the size and type of system to be ordered, and (3) whether to purchase or rent.

Benefits desired from an electronic data-processing installation

Most firms, whether large or small, hope that, when a computer is installed, they will realize benefits abbreviated in a four-letter word, *PEAS,* which stands for *p*ublicity, *e*conomy, *a*ccuracy, and *s*peed. Like the Japanese specialty-shop owner, a forward-looking, progressive company wants to identify itself with the latest equipment, thus impressing both its customers and its competitors. The installation is usually, but not always, a sign of efficiency, progress, and prosperity. Often "computerized" organizations make their equipment available to others, for a price, and encourage local citizens to visit the installation. This is considered free advertisement for the firm. On the other hand, it can be costly, because one or more company representatives will have to be around to show and explain the system to the visiting group(s). Some companies hire guides whose sole job is to take groups on tours to explain the system and the applications it processes. Not only does this make a good impression on the local citizenry, but it is likely to have a favorable effect on the company's employees as well. If the company employees are aware of the uses of, and the benefits derived from, the system, they tend to take pride in it and consequently publicize it in their community to the best advantage of the firm.

When a project team reviews the reasons why a computer installation is being considered, economy in space and cost reduction are usually stressed. A business firm using manual methods of data processing may be using a large room or rooms, where many clerical employees, bookkeepers, and other aides work behind desks, using calculators, adding machines, typewriters, pencils, and paper. Such a system can be costly with regard to the amount of space allowed for this purpose, if a satisfactory amount of space is allowed for each employee. A fraction of this space might be satisfactory for an average-sized computer installation designed to do the same job. With regard to economy through cost reduction, a significant saving in time may occur, thus reducing the marginal cost of data processing, especially in the "bread-and-butter" type applications.

With a computer installation, *accuracy* mounts, owing to minimum human intervention during processing and, also, because of the self-checking features which are built into the equipment. The project team should consider the *speed* factor with relation to the saving in time, which can be of great importance to certain departments within the firm. For example, in a retail store, the credit department can use the computer to process customer accounts, keeping special track of delinquent accounts. The credit department can hope to collect more quickly, when statements are prepared and mailed promptly, than can be expected under slower manual methods.

Size and type of computer system to be used

The project team should choose either a *special-purpose* or a *general-purpose* computer, whichever more nearly fits its particular needs. Briefly, a special-purpose computer is less flexible in running different applications than a general-purpose computer. In ordering a special-purpose computer, the firm placing the order bears the total cost of design. This makes it quite costly. The team should be able to justify the need for its use in detail, considering the higher cost. A general-purpose computer is more widely advertised, more widely used, and much more flexible than a special-purpose computer. It can be used for several different kinds of applications. It is less costly, because it is a standard item and the cost of its design is spread among all of the firms which decide to use it.

Computers are classified under three general sizes: (1) small size, (2) medium size, and (3) large size. When considering size, the team should think in terms of the applications to be processed at present as well as those anticipated in the future. In other words, the computer system under consideration should be capable of handling the present problems of the firm as well as those anticipated from future expansion.

The price that a company pays for a computer is based on the size it orders and the number of auxiliary components that come with it. In purchasing an automobile, for example, a low-priced, fully equipped automobile can be as costly as a high-priced, luxury, stripped model. In considering ordering a computer, the project team should determine whether a small-sized computer with additional auxiliary components is more suitable than a medium-sized or a large-scale installation with the basic components only. Size has a bearing on cost. The larger the computer, the more primary storage capacity it is likely to contain, and its speed is usually greater than that of smaller computers. Speed and the amount of storage space are two chief factors that determine the cost of the basic computer. Also, the need for input and output equipment and the speed with which they operate help to determine the total cost of the system.

Another important consideration is the "compatibility" of the computer system. *Compatibility* means a system the components of which operate in harmony with one another. If the central processing unit has access time at the millisecond speed, for instance, the use of a punched paper tape for input is considered incompatible, because the speed with which data are read from punched paper tape is not great enough to use the central processing unit to its best capacity. Some companies put stress upon speed and accuracy with less emphasis upon economy. Others stress processing of data accurately and economically, with speed being a minor point. Still other firms stress accuracy only, with little consideration for speed or economy. A project team must weigh these factors in the light of what its firm needs and can afford.

Purchase versus rental

Should a given firm purchase or should it rent a computer? What factors determine the choice between these two alternatives? After the project team has decided upon the type and size of computer that will satisfy its data-processing needs, the next step would be a decision on whether the equipment should be purchased or leased. Many firms rent a computer chiefly because of the technological obsolescence factor. New computers are put on the market every year. Manufacturers improve and modify the equipment constantly and offer it in better form periodically. Renting permits flexibility in adapting a new system to the firm's particular problems, whereas the purchase of a computer may mean that revising the problems to be processable for the computer may be necessary.

Leasing usually includes maintenance and repair. The computer manufacturer prefers to provide his own personnel to service the equipment, in order to ascertain whether it is in good operating condition. This relieves the company which is using the computer of any responsibility in this regard. Rent usually includes the cost of servicing the equipment. If the system is purchased, however, the firm may need to train and provide its own maintenance personnel to service the machinery. If such personnel are not available, the manufacturer can be called upon to do so for a reasonable charge. In any event, maintenance can be expensive to a firm that is responsible for servicing its own equipment.

The decision to rent a computer is easier to make, because it puts less responsibility on the project team in deciding on the installation than might be the case in purchasing it. When a computer is rented and later proves unsatisfactory, it can be returned to the manufacturer without costly investment. This, however, depends largely upon the terms of the lease agreement. A company which is bound by a five-year lease policy, for example, may not find it as convenient to return a computer as would be the case under a one-year lease contract. Not only the terms of the lease, but also the cost of the computer rented, should be considered. A company with a good cash position, expecting to use a particular computer for a long time, might find purchasing more profitable than renting the equipment. Finally, the project team should consider this problem from the standpoint of the initial cost of acquisition as well as from that of the costs involved in operation after the acquisition has been made. As complete a cost picture as possible should be procured. Because many data-processing installations are on a lease basis, the rent paid each month must be considered as a capital investment over and above any operating costs incident to using the machines involved. The rent is a fixed cost which will have to be paid whether the system is in constant use or not. This, plus the daily operating costs, constitutes the firm's cost of processing data electronically. If this cost on a daily, weekly, or monthly basis amounts to more than that involved in the manual system in use, the firm's management probably should discontinue thinking about procuring any type of mechanized system. If, on the other hand, the cost of processing data electronically is lower, every argument exists for procurement on a cost basis. If the two equal each other, arguments other than that of cost will have to be presented to justify an installation. If possible, cost should be put on a per-unit basis rather than on the basis of total cost, because the former in many cases is more revealing than the latter.

Assuming that top management decides to approve the installation, a budget is approved and an order is placed with one particular computer manufacturer. Once a computer is placed on order, the company begins a preinstallation phase, during which time some employees go through training programs in how to operate the equipment to be installed. Usually there is a waiting period of six months to two years after the order is placed, depending upon the type and size of computer ordered and the demand-supply situation at that time. The waiting period should not present any particular problem to the firm, because normally approximately that much time is needed to get ready to use the system efficiently.

One of the questions often asked is: "How long does it normally take to conduct a feasibility study for the introduction of a computer installation?" The answer differs with the firm. Some of the factors that have an effect on the time limit are:

1. *The competency of the project-team members and the extent of their knowledge about the problems and policies of their firms, as well as their general understanding of the computers available on the market.*
2. *The speed with which the team collects cost and other needed data for the preparation of its final report and for the forming of an opinion as to whether a computer system should be installed.* If cost data, for example, are not available because of present inefficient methods, or because of a deliberate attempt on the part of employees to withhold such vital information, a great deal more time would be needed for the project team to form an opinion than would be the case if these conditions did not exist.
3. *The size of the firm doing the study.* The larger the firm, the more complex its operations are likely to be. These operations include sys-

tems, procedures, and people. In order for a project team to understand the systems and procedures that will be affected by a computer installation, detailed studies have to be made which would be time consuming. The people consulted during the procedure can reduce this time by cooperating in promptly producing the data sought by the team.

4. *The size of the computer installation under study.* Regardless of the size of a given computer, a firm needs time to become familiar with it and to learn about the techniques which cause it to produce results. However, less time is needed to select a desk-size computer, for instance, than a large-scale computer. In the first place, a desk-size computer is easier to operate than a large-scale one. A large-scale system can be very complex, and it is a challenge to learn its maze of peripheries and the ways it can be programmed. Determining the need for a computer of this size would involve lengthy surveys and an equal amount of time to evaluate its usefulness in the particular processing applications for which it is being considered.

In conclusion, generally, a large firm needing a large-scale computer would need more time than a small firm needing a smaller size to arrive at a satisfactory conclusion. The range is, roughly, between four months and five years. This generality is not meant to imply that any connection necessarily exists between size of the firm and the size of the computer needed. That depends solely on processing needs rather than firm size.

REVIEW QUESTIONS

1. What is meant by the term *computeritis?*
2. What alternatives can a business firm select from when confronted with the installation of data-processing equipment? Explain.
3. What problems must top management decide on before data processing is introduced?
4. What factors characterize the firm which is likely to purchase a computer? Explain.
5. What major objectives can be realized from an electronic data-processing installation?
6. What factors determine the success of a feasibility study? Explain.
7. Who stimulates interest for a feasibility study? Why?
8. Who is usually appointed as a project-team member? What is the project team's main function? Explain.
9. What qualifications (personal and technical) should a project director have? Explain.
10. What are the desired qualifications of each of the project-team members? Explain in detail.

11. Why are some team members reluctant to be on the team or unlikely to do a satisfactory job?

12. What is your opinion with respect to companies pirating personnel from other firms?

13. Explain fully the preliminary survey stage.

14. Discuss the advantages and the drawbacks of a project team's concentration on one manufacturer's equipment.

15. What types of firms are likely to hire a consultant? Why?

16. Present and describe some of the services which are offered by a consultant.

17. What two main areas are open for training a project team? Explain these areas in detail.

18. What application should be selected for the purpose of programming and testing a given computer? Why?

19. How should the company employees be informed about and educated on electronic data processing? Explain.

20. What factors are included in the preparation of an estimated annual savings statement?

21. List and explain briefly the incidental costs of a computer installation.

22. Who and what is involved in the decision-making stage? Explain.

23. Explain in detail the actual benefits desired from an electronic data-processing installation.

24. Discuss the advantages and disadvantages of a special-purpose computer and a general-purpose computer.

25. What determines the price of a computer? Explain.

26. Expound on a firm's purchasing versus renting a computer.

27. What factors determine the time it takes to conduct a feasibility study?

chapter

26

DATA
PROCESSING DEPARTMENT

445

CHAPTER 25 INTRODUCED THE PROBLEMS faced by management in the introduction of a data-processing system and the manner in which they may be solved. This chapter presents briefly the problems which are likely to occur when a data-processing department is added to the organization and discusses the services such a department renders.

Transition Problems

When a company is changing from a manual system to a punched-card or electronic data-processing system, problems are bound to occur. These problems stem mainly from the conversion stage and affect employees as well as data.

The Effect of the New System on Employees

Many firms feel morally obligated not to lay off (at least for a while) employees who are not likely to "fit in" with the new system, especially those who may be too old to learn but not ready to retire. Their replacement, or displacement, would seem to be a step in the right direction, because the goal of the new installation is to maximize efficiency and minimize costs. However, a company, regardless of its size, cannot lay off those employees, either gradually or abruptly, without suffering undesirable effects. These effects may also result in the reduction of morale of the remaining employees, poor community-company relations, or, in the case of a unionized firm, harassment, if not a costly legal battle. Mindful of these factors, many firms which choose to install a computer system conveniently neglect to take any action. In fact, the manager of the new data-processing department may choose "the lesser of two evils" by assigning trifling duties to "unfit" employees, thus retaining them on the company payroll. This move is sometimes taken to show the employee that the company is acting in good faith, although its real motive is to discourage him from remaining with the firm. The net effect in this case would be one of two alternatives: (1) The employee would eventually find his job so meaningless and himself so unwanted that he would resign and find a more suitable position elsewhere. (2) The employee would decide to stay on the job, a course which results in frustration for all concerned. If the first alternative is chosen, the company hopes that the assumed result will take place. The second alternative leaves much to be desired: Both the company and the employee are unhappy about the *status quo*.

The employee's morale suffers, as he expects the worst and hopes for the best continually. His presence in the department affects the morale of the other employees as well.

Can a company realize any significant savings if it is to retain many of its employees who do not contribute adequate service to their employer because of the new data-processing system? The answer depends on the circumstances resulting in the decision to retain or displace them. Generally speaking, the answer is *no*. No company can or should retain employees who were formerly engaged in the operation of the manual system and whose background now makes them no longer needed. The exceptions include:

(1) Those who are willing and qualified to be retrained for a new position. For example, a typist whose job previously was to type statements can be retrained to operate a key-punch machine and thus fill a useful position in a punched-card installation. The attitude and ability of the employee are very important. In one case, a forty-two-year-old production-scheduling clerk was asked by his supervisor to improve his academic background by taking courses in mathematics at night school to prepare himself for helping to program the new installation. He refused on the basis that he could no longer compete with younger students because he had not been to school for a number of years. Math was his weakest subject, and he felt that he could not possibly take the computer math course which his supervisor recommended.

(2) Those who can be transferred to another department where, with a brief orientation, they would be able to render service in that department. This is possible especially when the work of one department is similar to that of another department. When this is the case, the possibility of employee transfer is worth investigating.

The Effect of the New System on Data

A new installation, punched-card or electronic, requires standardization of input data and their preparation in a manner acceptable to the system for processing. Problems in this regard are bound to occur. When an error is not detected in the planning stage, it is bound to reappear at a later stage as the new system becomes more complete. Whenever errors occur, they should be corrected immediately. This is not meant to imply that the system itself is inadequate or ineffective. We should remember that a system can be no more effective than the accuracy of the input data allows it to be. To help achieve effectiveness from the new system, all errors should be debugged from the source documents and the latter presented in a standardized, clear manner. Such presentation relieves the key-punch operator and other personnel responsible for the preparation of data from the need for verifying the accuracy of the source documents or the sequence in which they are presented for key punching.

Many people feel that the fewer the people, the greater the department's accuracy. However, because it would be difficult for a data-processing department to be completely automated, people will always be needed to perform key tasks. This fact emphasizes the vital role of effective and clear communications. Communication is the act of transferring information either orally or in writing. Clear instructions should be communicated to those employees preparing the source documents as well as to those who convert the documents into input. In the case of the latter employees, they must know exactly what is to be done and how they are to proceed in converting the source documents into the specified form. Naturally, when anything goes wrong, poor communication may not always be the reason. The reason may be the incompetence of those doing a job which requires some degree of skill. The inadequate knowledge of an employee doing a given job can usually be easily detected. It should be solved immediately, either by further training or by replacement. Before any hurried replacement is made, however, the supervisor should analyze the situation thoroughly to find out whether the problem arises from poor presentation of the source documents, from the complex nature of the job, or from the incompetence of the person performing the work. In the first possibility, a contact should be made with the proper personnel, the purpose of which would be to call attention to the need for better presentation of the source document. If, however, the source document is presented properly but its contents are too involved, allowance should be made for its conversion into punched cards or any other medium. For instance, a key-punch operator would need more time to punch alphanumeric data in a given field such as product number 1AK27 than to punch either alphabetic (CABLE) or numeric (5604) data separately, especially when automatic shifting into alphabetic or numeric mode is not programmed into the key punch. Therefore, if input data are to be punched and processed successfully, the cooperation of the departments preparing the source documents is necessary.

The Data-processing Department

Location

The exact location of a data-processing center differs in different firms. Some firms believe that the computer facility should be under the "department of most use" or in the department where clerical costs are the highest and savings to be achieved are greatest. Others believe that it should be an independent department not tied directly to any other department. The "department-of-most-use" approach is likely to be a better choice when most of the applications processed belong to a given department. As far as the manager of the computer center is concerned, his responsibility ends in satisfying the head of that department. However, when the computer installation is made an independent center, the manager must have a broader knowledge about company procedures and systems, because he will be serving the company in general. The independent organizational status of a computer center is most likely to reflect management's view that the center is a tool to aid in controlling the organization. Consequently, it should have an independent position where its manager reports directly to a top key officer.

Organization

Generally, a data-processing center is manned by systems analysts, programmers, console operators, key-punch operators, and others who aid in the preparation of data. These personnel are headed by an experienced data-processing man referred to as the "manager" of the data-processing department or center (Fig. 26-1).

The data-processing manager

The highest position in the data-processing center is that of the manager. *Management* has been described as a social process. It is social because it deals with people. It is a process because it involves a specific way of doing things. The manager's job involves dealing with people in achieving an integrated data-processing system to accomplish certain goals. The manager is fully responsible to his superiors for the work of his employees and for the results of the processing. His position as a manager should command respect from without his department as well as from within. If used effectively, the manager's knowledge about data processing and his ability to sell to other department heads what his department has to offer them will have a great influence on his effectiveness within the organization. If the services received are satisfactory, very likely his status and recognition of him by top and middle management will become firmly established. Most people respect a man who can prove his worth by the knowledge he possesses and by the actions which he takes. If the result of what he offers is a sincere reflection of his personality and ability, the "old-timers" will accord him due respect. On the other hand, if a manager tries to "bluff his way through," he will find it equally as difficult to gain the respect and cooperation of his colleagues.

LEADERSHIP AND HUMAN RELATIONS. A manager can gain respect within his organization by the way he manages his subordinates. In the

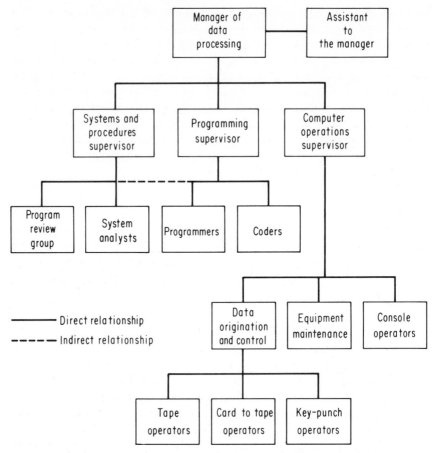

Fig. 26-1.   General organizational structure of a data-processing center

management and human relations areas, a manager must develop skills and qualities to lead people at all levels within his department, and especially those with whom he copes daily. Coping with people requires understanding of their needs and wants. Human needs are highly individualized and change constantly. That is, what an employee needs today may change tomorrow. These needs and wants can generally be satisfied by: (1) praising the employee for good work, (2) showing appreciation for work, (3) instilling in the employee's mind the fact of job security and the opportunity for promotion and advancement within the department, (4) payment of competitive wages and building hopes for regular salary increases, (5) offering work that sustains interest and motivation, and (6) providing good working conditions. In brief, an employee's main goal is the attainment of personal job satisfactions, recognition of his status, and the respect of his fellows. Once he is convinced of the possibility of attaining this goal, his morale and attitude will be such that the problem of motivating him solves itself.

The foregoing discussion suggests that a manager's real authority be granted and recognized by the group which he heads, because what they think of him as a leader is what makes him respected and effective. The authority which he receives from his superior is not sufficient in and of itself. In other words, the effectiveness of a manager comes from below upward, not from the top downward. When his employees report to work on time, are self-directed, self-motivated, and anxious to do their job assignments, he is considered a good "boss," because people work *with* him rather than *for* him. If the opposite occurs, the result usually leads to confusion in the department, which certainly does not promote maximum effectiveness in performance.

TYPES OF LEADERSHIP. This discussion brings us to the question of the type of leadership that a data-processing manager should possess. There are three main types of leaders, namely, democratic, authoritarian, and free-reign type.

Democratic leadership emphasizes informal group participation and the desire to satisfy its members. A data-processing manager will get much done if he allows his subordinate supervisors, and, indirectly, his systems analysts and programmers, to participate in evaluating a project and to suggest solutions to it. Naturally, the final decision rests with the manager. It is assumed that, for a democratic-type leadership to succeed, the employees must be competent and be briefed on the details of the project under discussion.

Authoritarian leadership implies that leadership is a right given and approved from above and one that should be exercised. In this approach, the manager assigns jobs to his subordinates, and only one-way communication takes place with regard to commands and the delegation of work assignments. This type of leadership can accomplish results fast, because it does not allow undue delays in consultations or group participation. On the other hand, if the individual employees do not feel as though they are a part of the group as a result of this approach, they can make the manager's job unpleasant.

The free-rein approach regards the employees as competent, well-qualified members of the department who are able to function on their own. They are asked to make independent decisions on problems which affect them, and as long as they accomplish results in a satisfactory manner, they are left largely unsupervised. This is advantageous in that it gives each employee a chance to think and to help arrive at decisions in problem solving. However, the lack of supervision may cause unnecessary confusion in the department if the employees involved abuse their freedom. In this approach, the manager must be willing to take the final responsibility for the actions of his subordinates.

In conclusion, an ideal manager is a person who has knowledge of his employees' needs and wants, who allows his subordinates to participate in discussing and evaluating a given project but reserves to himself final authority in the matter, and who is a leader who *earns* rather than *demands* support and respect.

TECHNICAL BACKGROUND. An elementary but significant qualification of a data-processing manager is the possession of a broad knowledge of data processing generally and an expert knowledge of the particular system with which he must deal. He is considered an expert in his field, and other department heads within the organization will rely on his judgment and technical knowledge to plan and process their data on the computer.

Being an expert in data processing means that the manager will need to evaluate the results achieved with the present installation and keep abreast of the technical developments in other systems available in the market. He should make sure that the company is not lagging behind because of either obsolescence in its equipment or his failure to suggest modifications or introduce new ideas which would help in improving the efficiency of the present installation.

A manager's technical knowledge is necessary for handling internal problems. Programmers, for instance, who are working on a problem where they are not sure of the proper procedure or who are uncertain about some phase of the procedure, should feel free to consult the manager for help in solving such technical problems. If he is unable to do so, his prestige as the top man of the department in the eyes of his subordinates suffers a blow. Although it would be desirable for him to be so, this does not mean to imply that a manager should be an expert in all phases of the technical work, nor that he should take over the completion of each job which cannot be completed by his subordinates. The manager is not necessarily a machine operator or a specialist in programming, although, with limited training in management, some men with a natural bent for it have risen from a position as a programmer or systems analyst to head of the department. In management, stress is more upon the synchronization of team efforts in such a way that all work harmoniously toward the accomplishment of the goal than on the specialized technical knowledge in any one of the areas delegated to other men.

Where can a business firm find a manager for its data-processing department who has both managerial and technical background? In the first place, a man of this caliber is not easy to find. Firms have a tendency to recruit from without the organization. This is done in the hope that an outsider may inject impetus and introduce new ideas to the department.

Another approach is to promote from within the organization. It may be that a qualified person is already available who can be replaced in his present position with greater ease than an "outsider" can be found to manage the data-processing department. A third approach is to select a well-trained technician from the ranks of the firm and train him in the fields of management and human relations before he is assigned to his new post.

Subordinate groups

Immediately under the data-processing manager there are three main groups (Fig. 25-1), each of which is often headed by a section head or a supervisor: (1) the systems and procedures group, (2) the programming group, and (3) the computer operations group.

SYSTEMS AND PROCEDURES. Systems and procedures discover what information must be provided to management and the ways in which it can be obtained. In other words, after an order has been received with regard to "what is required," the systems and procedures group devise a data-processing procedure which produces the results most efficiently. They are also concerned with designing a system which makes possible the use of manual, mechanical, and electronic machines sequenced in such a way that each application can be processed successfully. This requires thorough knowledge of the capabilities and limitations of the installation.

To qualify as a systems and procedures analyst, a college background in one of the business areas—that is, production, finance, accounting, management, or marketing—as well as a basic background in mathematics and statistics, is desirable. Some business firms find that experience in the operation of a computer, in addition to systems analysis, is desirable. People with the "ideal" background, however, are difficult to find. The average business graduate may have an excellent background in production, finance, marketing, accounting, or management but a poor one in mathematics and data processing. The demand for this background varies with the firm. Because mathematics is related intimately to the workings of a commercial electronic computer, it is highly desirable for a business student to take courses in numerical analysis or computer mathematics if he is interested in entering this field.

The program-review group consists of systems analysts and selected senior programmers whose jobs are evaluating and revising proposed data-processing procedures. In small installations, they may also be required to develop mechanized procedures in addition to their regular assignments. The combined background of the group helps to ascertain that all procedures and/or programs being evaluated are workable and efficient.

PROGRAMMING. Generally, programming involves determination of the results expected of the computer, block diagramming, preparation of a set of instructions for the computer, coding the program, and debugging. Programming in itself includes the first three steps. In large organizations, programmers concentrate on the construction of block diagrams and writing instructions in symbolic language. The coder carries out the rest by converting the symbolic instructions into machine language to be used directly by the computer.

Programmers are often expected to do coding as well as block diagramming and writing the program. Coders do not have to know how to program in order to retain their positions as coders. In fact, their duties, in some cases, are performed by the use of auto-coders or other devices that translate directly from symbolic into machine language.

COMPUTER OPERATIONS. Any duties involved in the preparation of the data for input, in maintenance, and in actual operation of the equipment are parts of the computer operations area. The bulk of the employees of the data-processing department are employed here. The group consists of console operators, tape operators (if any), maintenance employees, and key-punch operators. This is an area which requires close attention to details. The supervisor should check on the flow of data from the input stage to the processing stage to see that they are completed satisfactorily. This will minimize any machine "downtime" or "idle time." The supervisor should also make sure that employees are cooperating with one another. For instance, the console operator must rely on the key-punch operator for the initial punching of the source data in cards before he is able to process them on the computer. If any delay occurs, his job will be delayed also. The required training for operative employees differs with the position. The key-punch operator normally is expected to have had some experience in the use of the key punch, either from a former employer, through courses taken in a private educational institution, or on the job. However, in the event that a firm is interested in retraining its own employees, they are sent to a manufacturer's training center for the purpose of learning the concepts and operation of the key punch. When they return, an on-the-job-training program should supplement their formal training and give them practice in operating the key punch.

Console operators follow the same procedure as key-punch operators except for the time limit. More time is needed for a complete orientation in the operation of a computer than for orientation in key punching. A computer console consists of a number of buttons and switches which have to be manipulated and used in a given sequence if processing is to be done correctly. The depression of a button at the wrong time may foul up the loading of the program or the processing of data. Manual dexterity and alertness on the job are required of a console operator. Alertness on the job means being able to detect and correct any machine malfunctioning or to handle emergencies during processing. A console operator should have some programming background, so as to correct any minor errors on his own. Some programmers begin as console operators and then gradually advance to the job of a programmer.

The jobs of the employees who operate the equipment become monotonous. Because employees usually produce better results if the type of work they perform differs occasionally, it is desirable to rotate them on different jobs. For instance, the programmer can operate the console on one application and act as a coder on another application. A console operator with a programming background can develop a program in one application and code a program in another application. This will not only allow employees to gain broad experience, but will also act as a back-up system in the event of an emergency such as illness, vacation, or the like. Employees can substitute for one another temporarily or as needed. This gives flexibility to the operation of the data-processing department.

Key punching can become routine and boring, especially when a large volume of data is to be punched in the same location in each card. This monotony often results in high labor turnover. The author is familiar with an installation which employs eleven key-punch operators. Within one year, only two of the original eleven operators were left. The other nine were new and semiexperienced. Some of the reasons given by those leaving were: (1) little incentive, (2) no challenge, (3) monotony and boredom on the job, (4) too much like a factory job, (5) no opportunity for advancement, (6) low pay and heavy work load, (7) irregular and unsatisfactory raises, (8) limited social opportunity, and (9) little brainwork.

In order to avoid the drudgery of the job, the supervisor should assign to key-punch employees duties which involve some decision-making and a variety of tasks. For example, a key-punch operator could be asked to prepare a program card for the key punch or to make suggestions as to better ways of designing a data card. A key-punch operator can also operate the sorter or the collator in the routine of preparing punched data for processing by the computer. Many key-punch operators have been found to be excellent in operating such machines. Management can be instrumental in reducing labor turnover by developing a balance to cut monotony and by introducing creativity, thus improving morale.

Responsibilities of the Data-processing Center

The data-processing center should be regarded as a service department, the purpose of which is to make the job of the other departments easier through the preparation of reports based on data which they supply for processing. If this attitude prevails throughout the organizational structure, the job of data processing will be made easier. The issuance of accurate and meaningful reports is the primary responsibility of the data-processing center.

Accurate input data

Before the data-processing department can assume the responsibility of serving other departments and producing reports and statements for them, the source documents it receives must be accurate. Accurate input data depend, to a large extent, upon three factors:

(1) *Correct procedures.* Other departments must follow correct procedures. Managers at different levels in the organization must first know what information they want. To illustrate, the general manager of the production department is responsible to the president for the application of the overall broad policies adopted by the board of directors. The general manager would not be interested in the voluminous details which are generated in the departments of his subordinate supervisors. Unless exceptions occur, his way of managing is through the reports and other condensed statements which he receives concerning their activities and operations. Likewise, the department head is responsible to the general manager for efficient operation of his department within the budget appropriated for that purpose. The department head, too, would not generally be concerned with routine matters occurring at the lower level unless exceptions to the formulated policies and procedures occur. What each manager requires for managing his department determines the types of reports which must be prepared by the data-processing department. Unless the department managers are specific on this matter, the data-processing department is in no position to act on the data received.

(2) *Authority to request data processing.* The data to be processed must be forwarded by someone in each department who has the authority to request the work directly from the data-processing department. If a given department head, for instance, has complete autonomy over what goes on in his department, he should request the service of the data-processing center directly. If, on the other hand, his authority in this matter is limited, he should have the approval of his immediate superior, who would be in reality the one requesting the services. In the latter case, the data-processing manager should be so informed.

(3) *Standardized procedures.* Those departments that are authorized to use the service must follow standardized procedures. For instance, before a payroll application can begin, the exact regular and overtime pay for each class of employees must be determined and exceptions, such as sickness and vacations, with or without pay, systematized. Also, the time and frequency of payment of bonuses, commissions, and dividends should be determined. The data-processing department cannot process the payroll unless the amount and frequency of payments of the elements included in it are outlined by the particular department heads involved.

Once the type and number of reports are determined, the authority of each person requesting service clarified, and procedures with regard to basic input data systematized, the data-processing department is ready for effective operation. It can obtain accurate and timely results, however, only if its manager devises proper procedures to systematize the service. The procedure begins with a request form and ends in the presentation of the finished results.

The request form

Before any service is rendered, authorized personnel must first contact the data-processing manager, requesting service. This *can* be done on the phone. However, to eliminate any misunderstanding or misinterpretation of the facts, the request should be in writing. Employees in the data-processing department should not accept or authorize the rendering of service for any other department without the approval of their manager. When a request form is presented, the data-processing manager is the proper person to approve or disapprove it. The form should include spaces for information, such as: (1) the name of the department requesting service, (2) the names and titles of the persons filling out the form, (3) the type of data to be processed, (4) the form in which the results are to be presented, that is, summary form or detailed form, (5) the sequence of the results to be presented, (6) the number of copies needed, (7) the frequency of the processing of the reports, that is, whether the application needs to be processed daily, weekly, or monthly, (8) the party who should receive the results, and (9) the signature of the party authorized to request the service.

In requesting a new application, the department requesting the service should arrange a meeting with the data-processing manager to discuss the problem from the standpoints of economy and workability of the application on the computer system. Once a procedure is devised and the application prepared, further meetings are not necessary, as the application can be run at the regular intervals requested.

Some of the advantages of a request form are: The data provided on the form help the data-processing manager to estimate the time that the application would take, permitting him to promise delivery of the results on a certain date. The use of the data-processing equipment is limited to the number of hours in a given shift. Considering other jobs to be done, the manager must check as to whether the application can fit into the schedule without disrupting it. Without the request form, confusion in scheduling could result very easily.

Also, the request form serves as an historical record of the completed application or of the services rendered. The manager can tell how much time is spent on each machine, the frequency of usage, and, consequently, the cost of each application. This machine cost, plus the portion of the employees' salaries charged to the completion of the application, would constitute the cost of the application. This cost can be reported to the proper department so that it can absorb its share of the cost of operating the data-processing center. In a small firm, this procedure may not be necessary. If emergency requests for service are made, the data-processing department should have enough flexibility to handle them immediately. Effective communications in this regard are important. When they are verbal, the manager should "listen" and not just "hear." A story is told of a general manager who called the data-processing manager and inquired about the time when the regular trial balance would be ready. The processing manager answered, "Immediately," thinking that the general manager telephoned because the trial balance had priority. This resulted in running the trial balance ahead of other equally important applications and causing complaints from other departments.

Scheduling

Once the request form is evaluated, a schedule should be set up for running the application. The manager or his subordinate in charge of scheduling should promise a realistic delivery date, making proper allowance for the processing of other applications, machine breakdown, and unforeseeable problems. It is commendable of the manager to promise a deadline earlier than usual if he is sure it can be met. However, it would not be fair for him to do all or part of the work just to please the department requesting the service, although at times it is considered a good gesture for him to participate in operating the machines as a last resort and when no other help is available. In the event of emergencies, an overtime shift should be arranged. In this case cost is a factor which should be weighed to see whether the emergency processing of the application is justified.

In small installations, a manager often spends approximately 40 per cent of his time operating the equipment and the remainder of his time managing the department. He performs the functions which should be assigned to a machine operator. Some managers have limited authority, are overworked, and are underpaid as well as understaffed. Their authority is so limited in some cases that even the purchase of a professional book would require a superior's approval. This limited authority appears to be unfortunate in that ideally a manager should spend his time planning the work of those in his department so as to get things done through them. Final responsibility for the accuracy of the results and for their delivery to the proper party rests in the manager of the data-processing department.

REVIEW QUESTIONS

1. Discuss the effect of the new system on the firm's employees.
2. Discuss the effect of the new system on data.
3. "The fewer the people, the greater the department's accuracy." Do you agree with this statement? Defend your answer.
4. Where should the computer be located? Under whose direction should it be? Why?
5. What are the qualifications of a data-processing manager? What are his duties and responsibilities?
6. What can a manager do in order to satisfy the needs and wants of his subordinates?
7. List and explain the three types of leaders. Which type do you prefer? Why?
8. What three main groups are under the manager's direct supervision?
9. What technical background should a manager possess? Explain.
10. What is the main function of a systems and procedures analyst? What qualifications should he have?
11. What steps are involved in programming? Which of these steps are considered the most pertinent to programming?
12. What types of positions are available in the area of computer operations? Explain each position briefly.
13. Name seven reasons why key-punch operators leave their jobs.
14. Discuss the responsibilities of the data-processing center.
15. What purpose does a request form serve? What type of information does it contain?
16. Do you believe that a manager should spend a reasonable amount of his time operating equipment? Explain.

BIBLIOGRAPHY

Basic Books in Business Data Processing

Ackoff, Russell L. and Patrick Rivett, *A Manager's Guide to Operations Research*. New York: John Wiley & Sons, Inc., 1963.

Arnold, Robert R., Harold C. Hill, and Aylmer V. Nichols, *Introduction to Data Processing*. New York: John Wiley & Sons, Inc., 1966.

Awad, Elias M. and Data Processing Management Association, *Automatic Data Processing, Principles and Procedures*. Englewood Cliffs, N.J.: Prentice-Hall, Inc., 1966.

Becker, Joseph and Robert M. Hayes, *Information Storage and Retrieval*. New York: John Wiley & Sons, Inc., 1963.

Bergamini, David, and the editors of *Life, Mathematics*. New York: Time Incorporated, 1963.

Bibby, Dause L., *Your Future in the Electronic Computer Field*. New York: Richards Rosen Associates, Inc., 1962.

Bowden, B. V., *Faster than Thought*. Middlesex, England: Penguin Books, 1954.

Brandon, Dick H., *Management Standards for Data Processing*. Princeton, N.J.: D. Van Nostrand Co., Inc., 1963.

Brooks, Frederick P. and Kenneth E. Iverson, *Automatic Data Processing*. New York: John Wiley & Sons, Inc., 1963.

Brown, R. Gene and Kenneth S. Johnston, *Paciolo on Accounting*. New York: McGraw-Hill Book Company, 1963.

Buchholz, Werner, ed., *Planning a Computer System*. New York: McGraw-Hill Book Company, 1962.

Burck, Gilbert, and the editors of *Fortune, The Computer Age*. New York: Harper & Row, Publishers, 1965.

Business Systems, Vols. I, II. Cleveland, Ohio: Systems and Procedures Association, 1963.

Calingaert, P., *Principles of Computation*. Reading, Mass.: Addison-Wesley Publishing Co., 1965.

Chapin, Ned, *An Introduction to Automatic Computers*. Princeton, N.J.: D. Van Nostrand Co., Inc., 1963.

Churchman, C. West, Russell L. Ackoff, and E. Leonard Arnoff, *Introduction to Operations Research*. New York: John Wiley & Sons, Inc., 1957.

Computer and Thought, eds., Edward A. Feigenbaum and Julian Feldman. New York: McGraw-Hill Book Company, 1963.

Computer-Oriented Mathematics. Washington, D.C.: National Council of Teachers of Mathematics, 1963.

Crowder, Norman A., *The Arithmetic of Computers*. Garden City, New York: Doubleday & Company, Inc., 1960.

Cutler, Donald, *Introduction to Computer Programming*. Englewood Cliffs, N.J.: Prentice-Hall, Inc., 1964.

Decision Table Tutorial Using Detab-X. Instruction Task Force CODASYL Systems Development Group. ACM Headquarters, 211 East 43rd St., New York, N.Y.

Decision Tables—A System Analysis and Documentation Technique. Form F20-8102. International Business Corp., 112 East Post Road, White Plains, New York.

Department of Defense, *COBOL-65*. Washington, D.C.: U.S. Government Printing Office, 1965.

Desmonde, William H., *Real-Time Processing Systems: Introductory Concepts*. Englewood Cliffs, N.J.: Prentice-Hall, Inc., 1964.

Elliott, C. Orville and Robert S. Wasley, *Business Information Processing Systems*. Homewood, Ill.: Richard D. Irwin, Inc., 1965.

Farina, Mario V., *Fortran IV Self Taught* (General Electric Co.). Englewood Cliffs, N.J.: Prentice-Hall, Inc., 1966.

Favrett, Andrew G., *Introduction to Digital Computer Applications*. New York: Reinhold Publishing Corp., 1965.

Fisher, F. P. and G. F. Swindle, *Computer Programming Systems*. New York: Holt, Rinehart & Winston, Inc., 1964.

Flores, Ivan, *Computer Logic: The Functional Design of Digital Computors*. Englewood Cliffs, N.J.: Prentice-Hall, Inc., 1960.

———, *Computer Design*. Englewood Cliffs, N.J.: Prentice-Hall, Inc., 1967.

Gallagher, *Management Information Systems and the Computer*, AMA, 1961.

Galler, Bernard, *The Language of Computers*. New York: McGraw-Hill Book Company, 1962.

Gibson, E. Dana, *International Data Processing*. Elmhurst, Ill.: The Business Press, 1965.

Golden, James T. and Richard M. Leichus, *IBM 360 Programming and Computing*. Englewood Cliffs, N.J.: Prentice-Hall, Inc., 1967.

Grabbe, Eugene M., Simon Ramo, and Dean E. Wooldridge, ed., *Handbook of Automation, Computation, and Control*, Volume 2. New York: John Wiley & Sons, Inc., 1959.

Gregory, Robert H. and Richard L. Van Horn, *Business Data Processing and Programming*. Belmont, Calif.: Wadsworth Publishing Co., Inc., 1963.

Grossman, Alvin and Robert L. Howe, *Data Processing for Educators*. Chicago: Educational Methods, Inc., 1965.

Haga, Enoch, *Understanding Automation*. Elmhurst, Ill.: The Business Press, 1965.

Halacy, D., *Computers, the Machines We Think with,* 1st ed. New York: Harper & Row, Publishers, 1962.

Head, R. V., *Real-Time Business Systems.* New York: Holt, Rinehart & Winston, Inc., 1964.

Hearle, Edward F. R. and Raymond J. Mason (The RAND Corp.), *A Data Processing System for State and Local Governments.* Englewood Cliffs, N.J.: Prentice-Hall, Inc., 1963.

Hein, Leonard W., *An Introduction to Electronic Data Processing for Business.* Princeton, N.J.: D. Van Nostrand Co., Inc., 1961.

Hull, T. E., *Introduction to Computing.* Englewood Cliffs, N.J.: Prentice-Hall, Inc., 1966.

Inman, Kenneth L., *Fundamentals of Electronic Data Processing.* Englewood Cliffs, N.J.: Prentice-Hall, Inc., 1965.

IBM, *Programming System Concepts.* Form F20-8102, 1963.

Iverson, Kenneth E., *A Programming Language.* New York: John Wiley & Sons, Inc., 1962.

Johnson, R. A., *et al., Theory and Management of Systems.* New York: McGraw-Hill Book Company, 1963.

Kaufman, Felix, *Electronic Data Processing and Auditing.* New York: The Ronald Press Company, 1961.

Kemeny, John G., Arthur Schleifer, Jr., J. Laurie Snell, and Gerald L. Thompson, *Finite Mathematics with Business Applications.* Englewood Cliffs, N.J.: Prentice-Hall, Inc., 1962.

Laden, H. N. and T. R. Gildersleeve, *Systems Design for Computer Applications.* New York: John Wiley & Sons, Inc., 1963.

Laurie, Edward J., *Computers and How They Work.* Cincinnati, Ohio: South-Western Publishing Co., 1963.

Lazzaro, Victor, ed., *Systems and Procedures: A Handbook for Business and Industry,* 2nd ed. Englewood Cliffs, N.J.: Prentice-Hall, Inc., 1968.

Leeds, H. and G. Weinberg, *Computer Programming Fundamentals.* New York: McGraw-Hill Book Company, 1961.

Leeson, D. N. and D. L. Dimitry, *Basic Programming Concepts.* New York: Holt, Rinehart & Winston, Inc., 1963.

Lott, Richard W., *Basic Data Processing.* Englewood Cliffs, N.J.: Prentice-Hall, Inc., 1967.

Maley, G., A. and Edward J. Gerald, and E. Skiko, *Modern Digital Computers.* Englewood Cliffs, N.J.: Prentice-Hall, Inc., 1964.

Martin, E. W., Jr., *Electronic Data Processing.* Revised edition. Homewood, Ill.: Richard D. Irwin, Inc., 1965.

McCameron, Fritz A., *COBOL—Logic and Programming.* Homewood, Ill.: Richard D. Irwin, Inc., 1966.

McCracken, Daniel D., *A Guide to COBOL Programming.* New York: John Wiley & Sons, Inc., 1963.

———, *A Guide to FORTRAN Programming.* New York: John Wiley & Sons, Inc., 1961.

——— and William S. Dorn, *Numerical Methods and FORTRAN Programming.* New York: John Wiley & Sons, Inc., 1964.

———, Harold Weiss, and Trai-Hwa Lee, *Programming Business Computers*. New York: John Wiley & Sons, Inc., 1959.

McGill, Donald A. C., *Punched Cards: Data Processing for Profit Improvement*. New York: McGraw-Hill Book Company, 1962.

McMillan, Claude and R. F. Gonzales, *Systems Analysis: A Computer Approach to Decision Models*. Homewood, Ill.: Richard D. Irwin, Inc., 1965.

McNerney, John P., *Installing and Using Automatic Data Processing Systems*. Boston: Harvard University Press, 1961.

Moder, Joseph J. and Cecil R. Phillips, *Project Management with CPM and PERT*. New York: Reinhold Publishing Corp., 1964.

Morrison, Richard J., Robert E. Nolan, and James S. Devlin, *Work Measurement in Machine Accounting*. New York: The Ronald Press Company, 1963.

Nelson, Oscar S. and Richard S. Woods, *Accounting Systems and Data Processing*. Cincinnati, Ohio: South-Western Publishing Co., 1961.

Neuschel, Richard F., *Management by System*. New York: McGraw-Hill Book Company, 1960.

O'Neal, Leeland R., *Electronic Data Processing Systems: A Self-Instructional Programmed Manual*. Englewood Cliffs, N.J.: Prentice-Hall, Inc., 1964.

Optner, Stanford L., *Systems Analysis for Business Management*, 2nd ed. Englewood Cliffs, N.J.: Prentice-Hall, Inc., 1968.

Organick, E. I., *A FORTRAN Primer*. Reading, Mass.: Addison-Wesley Publishing Co., 1963.

Postley, John A., *Computers and People*. New York: McGraw-Hill Book Company, 1960.

Randall, Clarence B., Sally W. Weimer, and Maynard S. Greenfield, *Systems and Procedures for Automated Accounting*. Cincinnati, Ohio: South-Western Publishing Co., 1962.

Saxon, J. A., *COBOL—A Self-Instructional Programmed Manual*. Englewood Cliffs, N.J.: Prentice-Hall, Inc., 1963.

——— and P. William, *Programming the IBM 1401, A Self-Instructional Programmed Manual*. Englewood Cliffs, N.J.: Prentice-Hall, Inc., 1962.

——— and Richard W. Senseman, *Programming and Wiring in UNIVAC 1004 Card Processor: A Self-Instructional Programmed Manual*. Englewood Cliffs, N.J.: Prentice-Hall, Inc., 1964.

——— and W. Steyer, *Basic Principles of Data Processing*. Englewood Cliffs, N.J.: Prentice-Hall, Inc., 1967.

Schmidt, Richard N. and William E. Meyers, *Electronic Business Data Processing*. New York: Holt, Rinehart & Winston, Inc., 1963.

———, *Introduction to Computer Science and Data Processing*. New York: Holt, Rinehart & Winston, Inc., 1965.

Schultz, L., *Digital Processing: A Systems Orientation*. Englewood Cliffs, N.J.: Prentice-Hall, Inc., 1963.

Schweyer, Herbert E., *Analytical Models for Managerial and Engineering Economics*. New York: Reinhold Publishing Corp., 1964.

Simon, H. A., *The New Science of Management Decision.* New York: Harper & Row, Publishers, 1960.

Sprague, R. E., *Electronic Business Systems.* New York: The Ronald Press Company, 1963.

Sprowls, R. Clay, *Computers, A Programming Problem Approach.* New York: Harper & Row, Publishers, 1966.

Swallow, Kenneth P. and Wilson T. Price, *Elements of Computer Programming.* New York: Holt, Rinehart & Winston, Inc., 1965.

Taube, Mortimer, *Computers and Common Sense.* New York: McGraw-Hill Book Company, 1961.

Van Ness, Robert G., *Principles of Punched Card Data Processing.* Elmhurst, Ill.: The Business Press, 1964.

———, *Principles of Data Processing with Computers.* Elmhurst, Ill.: The Business Press, 1966.

Weinstein, Seymour M. and Armand Keim, *Fundamentals of Digital Computers.* New York: Holt, Rinehart & Winston, Inc., 1965.

Young, Frederick H., *Digital Computers and Related Mathematics.* New York: Ginn & Company, 1961.

Periodicals

Business Automation, 288 Park Avenue, West, Elmhurst, Illinois.

Communications of the ACM, 211 E. 43rd Street, New York, New York 10017.

Computers and Automation, 815 Washington Street, Newtonville, Mass.

Computers and Data Processing, 217 Broadway, New York, N.Y.

Computing Review, ACM, 211 E. 43rd Street, New York, N.Y. 10017.

Data Processing for Management, 22nd floor, Book Tower, Detroit 26, Mich.

Data Processing Digest, 1140 S. Robertson Blvd., Los Angeles, Calif.

Datamation, 1830 W. Olympic Blvd., Los Angeles, Calif.

Journal of the ACM, 211 E. 43rd Street, New York, N.Y. 10017.

Journal of Data Management, Data Processing Management Association, 525 Busse Highway, Park Ridge, Illinois.

Operations Research, Mt. Royal & Guilford Avenue, Baltimore, Maryland.

Systems and Procedures Journal, 7890 Brookside Drive, Cleveland, Ohio.

INDEX